No Fixed Add.
Life in the Foreign Service
Christine Hantel-Fraser

'Foreign service' – the phrase conjures up images of white villas under softly swaying palms, of distinguished-looking gentlemen and elegant ladies drinking cocktails and conducting light-hearted conversation before dinner is announced.

Daily reality lies worlds apart from such tempting imagery. In *No Fixed Address,* Christine Hantel-Fraser draws on twenty-five years of personal experience and on hundreds of interviews with foreign-service employees and their families to present the facts of foreign-service life. She relates the turbulent cycle of transitions undergone by foreign service members, from arrival at Headquarters to first posting abroad. Bewildering new environments, different cultural norms, and endless language lessons are all part of an international roller-coaster ride.

Hantel-Fraser also presents some of the most desirable features of life in the foreign services of nineteen other countries, and sums up the circumstances in which foreign service members flourish, merely survive, or fail. She describes measures taken by some of the world's most successful private companies to improve living conditions for their rapidly growing international teams. *No Fixed Address* is for everyone who wants to know more about the people who represent them abroad.

CHRISTINE HANTEL-FRASER, the wife of the Canadian ambassador to Hungary and the mother of four children, has lived in Bonn, Moscow, and Brussels. With a PhD in political science, she is a consultant on personnel management and a guest professor for organizational psychology at the University of Budapest.

No Fixed Address

Life in the Foreign Service

Christine Hantel-Fraser

UNIVERSITY OF TORONTO PRESS
Toronto Buffalo London

© University of Toronto Press Incorporated 1993
Toronto Buffalo London
Printed in Canada

ISBN 0-8020-2754-7 (cloth)
ISBN 0-8020-6799-9 (paper)

Printed on acid-free paper

Canadian Cataloguing in Publication Data

Hantel-Fraser, Christine.
  No fixed address : life in the foreign service.

  Includes bibliographical references.
  ISBN 0-8020-2754-7 (bound). – ISBN 0-8020-6799-9 (pbk.)

  1. Canada – Diplomatic and consular service.
  I. Title.

JX1729.H36 1993   327.71   C93-093122-X

This book has been published with assistance from the
Canada Council under its block grant program.

To Derek, Alexandra and Julia,
Jeremy and Robin, family and friends,
and to my fellow transients

Contents

Preface

On 1 July 1966, I attended a garden party held in celebration of 'Canada Day' at the Cologne residence of the Canadian ambassador in Bonn. At that time, I was studying political science, history, and German literature at the University of Bonn, and was working on a doctoral thesis about the League of Nations, with the intention of joining the German diplomatic service.

I still remember today the enchanting beauty of that particular evening. It was one of those rare days on which the entire Rhine valley between Bonn and Cologne seemed bathed in the warm and golden glow of the slowly setting sun. The ambassador's residence seemed also to be under the spell of this luminous summer evening.

As soon as I had descended the stairs from the house to the lawn, a strikingly tall, slender, bespectacled stranger with a slightly yellow complection approached me and was introduced as one of the junior officers of the Canadian embassy. The conversation quickly moved to the subject of life abroad. He had spent the previous year in Saigon on his first assignment with the Canadian foreign service. The yellow tinge to his skin turned out to be the result of a year's dose of anti-malaria pills. I had spent a year as a student in the United States, but, to my regret, my skin had not turned any exotic shade to confirm my overseas experience.

We compared notes, sharing our interest in foreign countries, cultures, and languages. I was quietly assuming – in the best European tradition – that the knowledge I had recently acquired about society and politics in the United States had prepared me well for an in-depth dis-

cussion of society and politics in Canada; however, I was given ample
opportunity to revise my views.

I realized only later that, on this evening, I had begun not merely a
lasting human relationship, but a permanent association with the Canadian foreign service.

The following year, 1967, we got engaged, and because Canada was
celebrating its hundredth anniversary at that time, we called this personal contribution we were making to the country-wide festivities back
in Canada 'our centennial project.' In 1968, we got married. Thus, I was
awarded the status of Canadian foreign-service wife.

This new distinction did not prevent me from finishing my thesis on
the League of Nations. In 1969, I graduated from the University of
Bonn with a doctorate in political science. But my career in the German
diplomatic service had come to an end before it had been given a
chance to begin. Much to my regret, I will never know whether my
decision in favour of the Canadian foreign service ultimately meant a
loss or a gain for the German foreign service.

The idea of this book has been with me ever since I plunged into
marriage with a nomad. Twenty years later, I felt the time had finally
come to take a close and critical look at the type of life I had come to
share.

The primary source for the tale of my own family's foreign-service
experience has been my memory, which enjoys an excellent reputation
among family and friends. I have also relied on the diaries I have been
keeping for more than twenty years.

I did not, however, want to limit myself to a personal account. Thousands of individuals and families have led and continue to lead a similar
type of life in the Canadian foreign service, in the foreign services of
other countries, and in the rapidly growing number of services of internationally oriented private corporations. The experience of all those colleagues was equally important to me.

In order to explore and record the stories of such a vast and varied
group of people, I had to go beyond my memory and diaries. I conducted approximately two hundred interviews with members of the
Canadian foreign service in Ottawa between January and May 1988.
This group comprised representatives of all conceivable ethnic, social,
and educational backgrounds, and of a great variety of positions in the

hierarchy of the foreign service. I tried to find out from them how their profession had affected and was still affecting their lives and those of their family members. Using the semi-structured style of interview, I asked everyone the same kinds of open-ended questions, with individual modifications. This interview format allowed for a free flow of memories and reflections within a given framework. At that stage, it was my aim to identify the principal issues bearing upon the hearts and minds of foreign-service personnel.

In the course of the next phase I intended to pursue those issues farther, with the help of three sets of questionnaires: for the foreign-service employee; for his or her spouse; and for the employee's children aged sixteen and older. I designed the questionnaires in such a way that they would provide as detailed and as accurate a picture as possible of the impact international rotationality had on the lives of employees and their families. To my mind, a satisfactory number of these documents would probably be returned, given the enthusiastic 98 per cent turnout I had had from employees and their dependents whom I had called for interviews.

As the photocopier was churning out the final copies of my questionnaires – all of them tested and approved by colleagues – my foreign-service fate caught up with me: my husband was appointed ambassador to Hungary.

This otherwise welcome assignment did not look like a promotion of my own project. I discovered that the completed questionnaires could not be evaluated and analysed in a country that, at that time, was behind the Iron Curtain unless I situated my office in the secure zone of the embassy. However, I was not entitled to an office there, since I was a foreign-service wife, not a foreign-service employee.

Rather than give up my cherished plan or wait for three years until our return from Hungary before sending out the questionnaires on which to base the book, I decided to demonstrate to myself and to anyone interested in the project that I possessed a quality that seasoned foreign-service personnel consider essential for survival in this life: flexibility. If there could be no completed questionnaires, I would go ahead without them.

The interviews, during which I had taken detailed notes, and my own posting history provided a wealth of material. I also expected that my renewed exposure to the fieldwork at an embassy – this time in the unaccustomed role of ambassador's wife – would enable me to study at close range the effect this profession has on all aspects of family life. I knew that I could count on having a heightened degree of sensitivity to a number of issues. Much of what I had never personally encountered during our earlier postings had been brought to my attention by fellow foreign-service members in the course of our interviews in Ottawa. I had the feeling I would be able to examine the decisive aspects of this kind of life better during an assignment abroad than in the familiar environment and privacy of a home posting.

All this would undoubtedly make up for the loss of the important data I had hoped to obtain from the questionnaires. Nevertheless, I mourned the premature passing of the precious information the completed forms would have provided. As I bundled the questionnaires for storage instead of dispatching them all over the world, I made up my mind to regard the forthcoming assignment as a promising opportunity for the book.

Budapest turned out to be exactly that. The experience of having to leave Canada once again; of separating for the first time from our eldest son, Robin, who moved to Toronto for his first year at university, and from our second son, Jeremy, who had to stay behind in boarding-school since Budapest offered no schooling for him at the Grade 11 level; of putting our little daughters, Julia and Alexandra, into a new, international school; of sharing our daughters' painful longing for brothers, friends, home, country, and a familiar world; of once again embarking on an entirely different life in a foreign country with an unusually complicated language; of struggling with a host of new and difficult tasks – all of this seemed to me a refresher course in foreign-service living.

Beyond my own immediate horizon lay a rich harvest waiting to be brought in. I was surrounded by Canadian families, whom I got to know quickly. They offered authentic and immediate examples of foreign-service life abroad, and their stories balanced the accounts their colleagues in Ottawa had given me of their experiences abroad, but from the perspective of a home posting.

While the book remains essentially a description of life in the Canadian foreign service, it is intended to open up a broader view: that of the impact of international rotationality on individuals, marriages, and families. The Canadian example represents – to borrow a concept from the realm of music – variations on the theme of 'people permanently on the move.'

Few professions and lifestyles attract quite as much attention as do those of foreign-service members. As representatives of any foreign service will confirm, the mere mention of their occupation to a stranger will release a flood of questions that tend to reveal either a rich imagination on the part of the uninitiated or earlier exposure to distorted accounts of diplomatic life presented by novels of questionable quality or by Hollywood movies. Images are conjured up of white villas under softly swaying palms, where a host of humble, but efficient servants offer exotic food and drink on burnished silver trays to distinguished-looking gentlemen in dinner jackets and exquisitely gowned ladies, all of them conducting sometimes witty, sometimes weighty conversations in a multitude of languages learned and spoken effortlessly. Occasionally, well-mannered children make their appearance, led by their nannies, and charm the guests before being returned to immaculate nurseries for tea and bedtime stories under a froth of mosquito netting. For diplomats, work consists of a few short hours each day of writing dispatches and receiving dignitaries, all without wrinkling their dark-blue, pinstripe, three-piece suits. By sunset, at the latest, they have turned their attention once again to their principal activities: cocktails, dinner, and light-hearted conversation.

For some reason, the life of the upper classes in nineteenth-century colonial Africa and Asia seems to be the model of foreign-service life as it exists in the minds of strangers to the profession. The daily reality of that life is worlds apart from this tempting fantasy.

The purpose of this book is to offer the facts about foreign-service life. I have five groups of readers in mind. First, present and former members of the Canadian foreign service: I hope they will recognize the experiences described here and will find reason for reflection, and for celebration. Second, present and former members of other foreign services from the public as well as the private sector: I hope that the recognition of common problems will ultimately promote cooperation among various services to improve living conditions for personnel. Third, the more than five thousand young Canadians who write the entrance examination for their country's foreign service every year, and every Canadian who is thinking of joining External Affairs: I hope this book will provide them and their families with an accurate picture of the kind of life that awaits them. Fourth, members of Parliament, government officials, and senior managers of private corporations responsible for the management of their international team: I hope that insight into the details of foreign-service life will assist them in their decision-making process. Finally, the general public, who might be interested to know how the people live who represent them abroad: I hope this book will enlighten and entertain.

The book is divided into three parts. Part I can be compared to a modern theatre production in which the main components of the piece – setting, cast, costumes, and plot – are introduced sequentially. By the time the curtain closes on Part I, the reader will have met the principal members of the cast and observed the individual, and yet somewhat typical, personality traits that eventually influence their performance in the play, and become familiar with the most important elements that constitute life in the Canadian foreign service. The organization and its mandate, the large variety of people employed by it and their innumerable tasks – all will have been positioned against the background of the world stage, in this case the 117 Canadian missions abroad.

Part II sets all components of foreign-service life into motion. Biographies of hundreds of foreign-service employees, their spouses, and their children are woven together into a narrative to reveal complex individual and family histories. The reader will be able to follow members of the service in their personal life cycles: share in their arrival in Ottawa and first years as brand-new recruits at headquarters, accompany them on their first posting abroad to life in a bewildering new environment, experience with them the confusion of adapting to different cultural norms and the uncertainties of daily life, sit with them through seemingly endless language lessons, return with them to Ottawa as life has begun to stabilize in the foreign posting, and continue to watch them dig up and transplant their roots every few years until the roller-coaster of their lives comes to a breathless halt upon retirement.

Part III describes the most desirable features of nineteen other countries' foreign services and sums up the circumstances under which foreign-service members flourish, survive, or fail. It includes ideas on what employees and their organizations might want to do and want to avoid in order to reduce the number of victims and increase the number of individuals and families who blossom. It describes specific measures taken by some of the best organizations to improve living conditions for their internationally rotational team.

All the stories recounted in this book are based on foreign-service tales. To protect my sources' privacy, I have not only changed names, places, and other details, but seen to it that almost every case-study is an amalgam of individual situations and not the circumstances of one particular person or family. However, all quotations are authentic and are reproduced verbatim, except for place-names or other revealing details.

The views expressed in this book are, of course, entirely my own, and are by no means endorsed by or a reflection of the views of the Department of External Affairs.

In order to thank the hundreds of fellow migrants who so generously volunteered their experiences, I have used a strand of everyone's personal story in my attempt to weave a tapestry depicting lives permanently in transition.

PART I

The Canadian Foreign Service

1

The Organization
The Department of External Affairs

Headquarters in Ottawa

Bronze doors don't swing open lightly. They move slowly and heavily, as if reluctant to give way. The four pairs of richly sculptured bronze panels leading into the Department of External Affairs in Ottawa are no exception. Young men and women arriving at the main entrance of the Lester B. Pearson Building to begin a career in the Canadian foreign service express surprise at the body weight and determination necessary to pull open one of these doors. According to a rumour among established foreign-service members for whom setting nine hundred pounds of bronze into motion is routine, physically gaining entrance is part of the foreign-service selection process. Only the gifted few who manage in one attempt to pry open one of the doors can be considered qualified to enter the world of the Canadian foreign service.

Architects of the building assigned a rather different role to the doors. One of them, Boris Zerafa, explained to me that the panels are works of art intended to accentuate the main entrance and to create a sphere of transition from exterior to interior. The electronic devices installed in recent years to open the doors automatically don't seem to have interfered with the original artistic intention. Yet they have deprived the doors of their symbolic significance, relegating all tales surrounding them to the world of foreign-service mythology.

On the threshold of a life in the Canadian foreign service, newcomers usually approach the building with a high degree of curiosity, even before they reach the gates. What catches the eye first is the three-dimensional geometrical form of the complex. It consists of a group of five interconnected buildings and towers of various heights, stretching three hundred metres along Sussex Drive. The entire structure is raised above street level on a four-metre-high podium from which it appears to hold a commanding position over all neighbouring buildings. The single ten-storey tower notwithstanding, the building complex conveys a strongly horizontal impression, its panels of concrete alternating with bands of deep-set windows.

Depending on the season and the time of day, the pink Quebec granite and black sand filler that form the precast-concrete panels appear in a shade of dark pink, bronze, or deep brown. Windows of bronze-coloured solar glass complement the pink-brown hue.

Young foreign-service recruits about to settle down for a career behind these walls rarely remain neutral on the subject of the building as a work of architecture. Some share the view of colleagues for whom it represents a gloomy cluster of heavy office towers. Others consider it to be, together with the National Arts Centre and the National Gallery, a great architectural achievement in the national capital.

Whether foreign-service novices look favourably or not on the structure that houses their future offices, the Lester B. Pearson Building was designed to perform a large number of functions of the Department of External Affairs. Newcomers will be exposed to some of these once the bronze doors ponderously close behind them, as slowly and reluctantly as they had opened.

Immediately inside is a small vestibule, a form of no-man's-land between the bronze barriers to the outside and a band of four glass doors to the inside. In this momentary vacuum between the world left behind, and the world not yet entered, future employees find themselves in a musical zone. Columns of air vibrating in the thin vertical spaces between the panels of glass, set in motion by the powerful air pressure from the closing bronze doors, produce a high-pitched siren-like sound that fills the vestibule for a few moments before falling into a mournful hum, then slowly fading away.

The glass doors can be managed easily with one hand, and the way is free to the huge, two-storey foyer. Designed as the equivalent of a central town square and bordered by a group of buildings, the foyer is connected with the office towers by a series of corridors. At all times of the day –

and often at night – the foyer becomes a sea, ebbing and flowing with people pouring out of hallways and dispersing in all directions, churning around the Conference Centre, streaming out of one set of elevators and being sucked up by another.

The young recruits will ply through the human currents, taking a place in the queue at the reception desk. Eventually they will ask to be announced to a designated personnel officer. A uniformed guard will steer the recruits through the corridors of Tower D and deliver them to a brightly lit office. It is not unheard of for an officer who is expecting the visitors to offer a welcoming slap on the back, and for new arrivals to wonder whether they have just witnessed their own ritual rebirth.

Whether a case of reincarnation or not, a life in the Canadian foreign service has begun.

Historical Background

The Lester B. Pearson Building was completed in 1973. The foreign service itself is of a more venerable age.

On 19 May 1909, a parliamentary act established the 'Department of External Affairs,' with responsibility for the 'conduct of all official communications between the Government of Canada and the government of any other country in connection with the external affairs of Canada.' The term 'External Affairs' had been carefully chosen: 'Foreign Affairs' would have been incompatible, in 1909, with the diplomatic unity of the British Empire. According to this concept, all of Canada's external activities had to be coordinated with the foreign policy of the Empire and to be carried out under the overriding authority of the Imperial government in London.

In so far as the External Affairs Act of 1909 signalled the birth of the Department of External Affairs, it also brought to an end a long period of gestation, in which the need for an organized Canadian foreign service had become apparent.

Unlike most countries whose earlier diplomatic relations with neighbouring countries sowed the seeds of an eventual foreign service, Canada's foreign service began with a quest for immigrants. In 1868, the one-year-old Dominion of Canada, in the hope of filling its underpopulated territory with English-speaking settlers, opened the Dominion

Emigration Agency in London. This was the first Canadian government bureau abroad.

Soon a much wider range of Canadian interests demanded a representative in London. In 1880, Sir Alexander Galt was appointed Canada's first high commissioner in London. His responsibilities included the general representation of Canada and the protection and promotion of Canadian interests in the areas of immigration, trade and commerce, and financial matters.

When, in 1882, the provincial government of Quebec, following the example of the federal government's appointment of Sir Alexander Galt in London, named Sir Hector Fabre as the first Quebec representative in Paris, the federal government decided to appoint him commissioner general for all of Canada in France, with the same responsibilities as those held by his colleague in London. Thus the foundations for a foreign service had been laid. The parliamentary act of 1909 not only established the Department of External Affairs, but also formally recognized a foreign service, which was, with more than thirty immigration agents and close to twenty trade offices abroad, a modest reality.

One important element, however, was still missing from the catalogue of responsibilities held by the Canadian representatives in London and Paris, even after the External Affairs Act had been introduced. They were not the official channel of communication between the Government of Canada and the British and French governments. This function had remained with the governor general.

The Imperial Conference of 1926 in London turned out to be a milestone on the road to independent Canadian diplomatic representation. Delegates agreed that the official channel of communication should be handed over from the governor general to the official representatives of the Dominion. In 1927 the Canadian high commissioner in London became the first fully diplomatic Canadian representative abroad.

As the number of representations grew from year to year, with offices opening in Geneva at the League of Nations, in Brussels, and in The Hague, separate trade and immigration offices sprang up around the world. The Second World War saw an even greater demand for diplomatic missions. In 1945, the Department of External Affairs maintained 38; by the time the department marked its eightieth anniversary in May 1989, Canada was represented in 117 missions throughout the world.

The originally unified management of Canadian interests in the areas of immigration, trade and commerce, and external relations – as practised by high commissioners around 1880 – had soon become more diversified. Although from 1909 to 1980 the Department of External Affairs retained responsibility for the coordination of all policies and programs abroad, it shared that for the actual development of government policies and the delivery of programs with the Department of Industry, Trade and Commerce; the Canada Employment and Immigration Commission; and the Canadian International Development Agency.

As a result of this division of labour, the Canadian public service maintained four separate foreign services, one for each department operating abroad: the Trade Commissioner Service, the Immigration Foreign Service, the Foreign Aid Service, and the Foreign Service under the Department of External Affairs. Canadian missions abroad were staffed by and received orders from four different government departments. Government officials who looked kindly on such an arrangement perceived it as an administrative mosaic. Others, less favourably disposed, called it an administrative nightmare.

Sometime in the 1970s, the government, under Prime Minister Trudeau, became convinced that Canada's interests would be best served if all of the country's activities abroad were managed by a unified foreign service, in a single superministry. The process of integrating all four foreign services into the consolidated Department of External Affairs and International Trade Canada, as it is now called, began in 1980 and was completed in 1984.

The subject of 'integration' divided the foreign-service population into two camps: those who mourned the end of a small service 'with a human face' and those who hailed the beginning of a more efficient service. As the chaos created by the change subsided, support for the integrated service seemed to be growing, aided by every newcomer to the department after 1984, who had known nothing but the integrated service. For many of the older employees, who had cherished the family atmosphere in the earlier period, some reasons for mourning remain.

Although the External Affairs Act has been amended several times since 1909, notably in 1912 and 1983, it qualifies to this day, in spite of profound changes to foreign-service structure and operations, as the legal basis for the existence of the Department of External Affairs and for all activities of members of the Canadian foreign service.

The Mandate

Two main tasks were originally assigned to External Affairs and continue to be the pillars on which all foreign-service operations rest: to determine the nature of communications and operations between the Canadian government and foreign governments and to formulate a specific policy governing them, and to manage those communications and operations in keeping with that policy.

This basic mandate determines three different roles the foreign service has to play: to provide and integrate policy advice; to coordinate and integrate Canada's relations with foreign governments; and to carry out operations with foreign governments, based on the formulated policy.

The number and variety of concrete tasks deriving from this abstract mandate strike not only strangers to the foreign service as overwhelming at times. Hercules, one of the great heroes of Greek mythology, acquired immortality, and divine status, for achieving his fabled twelve tasks. Yet even he would have been hard-put to accomplish what is expected of the Canadian foreign service.

The Department of External Affairs, in a pamphlet published by the Public Service Commission in 1987 for the purpose of recruitment of foreign-service officers, lists thirteen principal areas of responsibility for the foreign service, altogether one task more than assigned to Hercules and every one of them of Herculean proportions.

1 The coordination of Canada's foreign relations in conjunction with other government departments
2 The supervision of relations between Canada and other countries, and of Canadian participation in international organizations
3 The negotiation and conclusion of treaties and international agreements
4 The protection of Canadian interests abroad
5 The recognition and evaluation of economic, political, and social trends of importance to Canada
6 The representation of Canada in foreign capitals and cities and at international conferences

7 The development and management of cultural and information programs abroad
8 The application of Canadian immigration policy abroad
9 The promotion of tourism to Canada
10 The promotion of industrial development
11 The promotion of exports for resources, manufactured goods, and services that are produced in every region of the country
12 The identification of export markets and assistance to businessmen who wish to develop those markets
13 The negotiation, implementation, and supervision of aid programs in developing countries, in collaboration with the Canadian International Development Agency.

Evidence of the foreign service's engagement in these tasks can be gleaned from newspapers every day. Any one of such projects requires the participation of many foreign-service employees in innumerable activities undertaken simultaneously at headquarters in Ottawa and at missions throughout the world.

Rotationality

In the face of Canadian foreign-service duties Hercules most likely would have shuddered, in spite of the cooperation immortal Athena usually accorded him. Wherever he tamed, captured, and slew, he could count on the omnipresence of the goddess. The Department of External Affairs has to rely on the help of mortal men and women, who can be in only one place at a time. Under such circumstances, the system of rotationality is a necessity.

Rotationality is best described as a system of moving personnel from job to job. For members of all foreign services, the concept translates into the fact of frequent international moves. For Canadian members, it means that jobs at headquarters and in foreign countries require rotation of employees and their families between Ottawa and missions abroad, or between one foreign assignment and the next without a posting to Canada in-between. The latter are known as cross-postings.

'Why are you always moving about?' is a question typically posed by outsiders. The answer can be found in a set of four basic assumptions underlying the rule of rotationality: 1 / Internationally, social, political, and economic forces are constantly in motion, placing Canadian interests permanently at stake; 2 / Embassies abroad have to be kept staffed at all times; 3 / The degree of desirability of foreign postings and assignments at headquarters varies considerably; and 4 / People who live within a foreign country for many years tend to identify with the local culture after a certain length of time.

A combination of these assumptions acts as the motor that turns what is often perceived by foreign-service members as the perpetually revolving posting carousel.

Some foreign-service employees still remember from childhood days the carousels of country fairs, each offering a promising array of rides: horses, elephants, unicorns, dragons, and fabled creatures of every colour and size, mingled with more modern mounts, such as racing cars, fire engines, planes, helicopters, and rockets. Galloping on a ferocious beast, speeding around in a flashy vehicle, and changing rides to explore other possibilities meant excitement and joy. But giving up a favourite ride for a less desirable one, or sitting out a turn to let someone else have a chance, could spoil all delight in the magic round.

Assignment officers in the Personnel Branch of External Affairs are saddled with the unenviable task of having to distribute their charges over the merry-go-round, without losing sight of employees' and families' personal needs and without neglecting the rule of fairness among members of the rotational team. In all their decisions, personnel officers must bear in mind that approximately half of the 117 missions are classified as hardship posts, that nobody can be expected to look after Canada's interests in a dangerous hardship post forever, that attractive assignments should be made available to as many employees as possible, and that tours of duty at headquarters and postings abroad should be well balanced in each career. Such considerations keep the foreign service roundabout in constant motion.

The length of time spent in a country varies by occupational group. Hardship levels have always played an important role in determining the duration of an assignment and continue to influence the length of a posting for almost every occupational group.

A hardship level has been carefully assigned to each foreign capital, depending on general living conditions in the country, security, social and political climate, degree of isolation, distance from Canada, and a large number of other factors. Members of the officer group spend two years in the most difficult postings; three years in a posting of the next-easier hardship category; and four years in capitals not considered a hardship assignment, such as London, Paris, Washington, Bonn, and Bern.

If three years is taken as the average length of time spent in a foreign country, theoretically one-third of the entire rotational foreign-service population changes place each summer. In practice, personnel move more frequently than that, often in order to accommodate unexpected personal or departmental needs.

Posting patterns vary greatly from case to case, depending on organizational requirements and on the needs and wishes of individual employees. Some foreign-service members favour a regular rhythm between home postings and postings abroad. Others enjoy the experience of cross-postings. There are no strict rules about posting patterns. Flexibility is necessary since the length of time spent in Ottawa is not firmly regulated. Within the upper limit of six uninterrupted years at headquarters, any length of time between one and five years is possible. Each employee has his or her own personal posting cycle and favourite rhythm, which tends to be tempered by the requirements of personnel managers. All employees, though, share the high frequency of moves.

In some professions, the concept of rotationality suggests mobility only within the organization; in others, it means geographic mobility. In the foreign service, rotationality implies, in addition to geographic mobility, exposure to foreign countries and cultures. Any foreign-service member who takes down his or her tents in one culture can be certain of having to set them up in a different culture before long, and that, within a few years, he or she will be repeating the process in yet other cultural surroundings. Swinging back and forth between continents, countries, and cultures is a hallmark of foreign-service rotationality.

Long periods of time spent in a foreign culture can lead to a phenomenon, dreaded in External Affairs, that is known as 'localitis,' or, in less scientific-sounding terms, 'going native.' An employee is diagnosed as having a case of 'localitis' if he or she shows symptoms of considering the host country the navel of the world and begins to adopt the worldview of the local population – or worse, that of local politicians. The messages sent by an officer who is afflicted with the disease indicate that the thought processes and patterns of the host culture, together with the philosophical assumptions underlying them, have been adopted. This can happen easily when the employee has learned to speak the local language fluently and has become well integrated into the social environment. Such a development, however, runs contrary to the purpose of an employee's mission and is considered particularly undesirable in cases of officers responsible for political, economic, and immigration affairs, on whose detached judgment the successful representation of Canadian interests depends. In order to prevent outbreaks of 'localitis,' External Affairs has put a limit on the time allotted for a stay in each country.

Exceptions confirm the rule. In some cases, where the border between being thoroughly familiar with a culture and identifying with it is consciously and carefully guarded, a foreign-service member may remain in the same country for an extended period of time. The acquired expertise is then seen as more useful than harmful. Robert Ford, Canada's long-time ambassador in Moscow, serves as the most often quoted example. His fluency in the Russian language, his familiarity with Russian poets and Soviet politicians, his thorough knowledge and understanding of the Russian and Soviet world were deemed too precious to sacrifice to the principle of rotationality. He served as ambassador in Moscow for sixteen consecutive years, from 1964 until 1980, following a long and distinguished career in other postings.

For most foreign-service members, however, the carousel makes no such stops. Some riders are more content than others, and the rule of rotationality sees to it that there is always a next round.

2

The People
Profiles, Duties, Transitory Lives

The Team

A few weeks after marriage had converted me into a Canadian foreign-service wife, my husband, following a well-established daily routine, called me around lunchtime to announce his departure from the embassy and his arrival at home within fifteen minutes, in cheerfully admitted pursuit of the culinary delights I had promised. I put finishing touches to soup and salad, and then began to listen for the sound of his car and his steps on the stairs. After half an hour of such vigilance, I had gone from concern to worry. By the time an hour had passed, I had come to the conclusion that I had better brace myself for a future as a lamentably young widow. What was responsible for the sad turn my marriage seemed to have taken so soon after the wedding, I was certain, must be the 'Diplomatic Race Course,' as the road between Bonn and Bad Godesberg was unofficially called. There, I feared, somewhere between the embassy and our apartment, disaster had struck. And what an unheroic end at that for a young diplomat, considering alternatives for earthly departure that had already been introduced to members of his profession in more remote parts of the world. In Western Europe, however, kidnapping and holding diplomats hostage before disposing of them in some dramatic fashion apparently had not quite got beyond the planning stage – unless, of course, he had been singled out to become the first such case. This was unlikely, given the humble position he occupied in the diplomatic hierarchy as first secretary and consul.

Disaster actually had struck – a milder version, though, than suspected.

My husband had not been the target, nor was the 'Diplomatic Race Course' in any way implicated in a robbery to which a young Canadian student had fallen victim earlier in the day. Having lost his money, travellers' cheques, airline tickets, and passport, the hapless backpacker had walked for about five miles, in a state of desperation, only to reach the haven of his embassy at exactly the moment when the consul, his mind on a tenderly prepared lunch, was locking his office door. The student's plight made the consul forget his luncheon plans, unlock his office, and set in motion the complicated and time-consuming administrative mechanism linking the embassy in Bonn and External Affairs in Ottawa that would, within twenty-four hours, provide the student with a temporary passport and a government loan to pay for his return trip to Canada and for accommodation and food in the meantime.

Two hours later, the consul explained to his wife over cold soup and warm salad that 'a Canadian in distress' represents an emergency that demands instant and undivided attention. In such cases, even phone calls to waiting wives tended to slip consuls' minds. A small army of distressed Canadians at our doorstep would be more of an occupational probability than premature widowhood.

His prediction proved to be correct. Our first consular case was not our last. Many were to follow in the next twenty years, not all of them ending quite as happily.

Consular assistance constitutes one of the most important and most frequently performed tasks at missions abroad. It consists of any form of help to Canadians who are travelling or living abroad and requires close cooperation between the embassy and headquarters.

In 1984, according to Statistics Canada, foreign-service personnel at External Affairs and in Canadian missions throughout the world, in addition to issuing about 700,000 passports, dealt with 400 cases of death abroad, 600 cases of hospitalization, approximately 2,500 cases of financial difficulties, and 800 cases of imprisonment resulting from drug-related or other offences.

Consular emergencies, as well as every single one of the host of other tasks assigned to the foreign service, require the carefully coordinated efforts of a large number of employees of all occupational groups in the hierarchy of the Department of External Affairs.

A team of 9,074 foreign-service employees (as of November 1992) looks after the interests of Canadian citizens at home and abroad. More than half of them, a group of 4,889 employees, belong to the category 'locally engaged staff.' These employees are, in most cases, non-Canadian, foreign nationals, hired from among members of the local work force by Canadian embassies anywhere in the world. Their command of the local language and familiarity with the surrounding culture, together with a required knowledge of at least one of the two official languages of Canada, build the bridge over which any form of official or unofficial communication and cooperation between two countries and cultures can flow.

A Turkish receptionist at the embassy in Ankara, a Peruvian interpreter in Lima, a Korean secretary in Seoul, or an Egyptian visa clerk in Cairo will link Canadian citizens who travel, work, or live abroad with the local culture.

Locally engaged staff play an important role in every embassy, especially in countries with exceptionally difficult languages. The Hungarian language, for example, is considered by experts to be one of the ten most complicated tongues in the world. It constitutes an enormous obstacle to every foreigner who wants to live and work in that country. A locally engaged Hungarian, therefore, who speaks English or French fluently, in addition to his or her native language, is an indispensable member of the Canadian embassy in Budapest.

As every ambassador and his or her spouse will confirm, locally engaged staff working in official residences occupy a particularly important position. Our five Hungarian servants, with their fluency in the Hungarian language; their familiarity with local customs, food and drink, and all the shops in town; and their ability to locate and obtain goods and services – meat and cooking oil during weeks of scarcity, candles that give light without dissolving into puddles of wax on the table cloth, kosher food and utensils for Jewish guests, smoke-detector batteries in a country without smoke detectors, a constant supply of high-quality flowers at a reasonable price, a dry cleaner, a tailor, a picture framer, or a crew of professional waiters to help out at cocktail parties in the residence – provide invaluable expertise. They plug us into the local economy and allow for the smooth running of a Canadian household in a Hungarian environment, which, because of the constant flood of official visitors, has to operate like a restaurant most of the time. Without our Hungarian staff, we would have to put up an 'Out of Order' sign right next to the brass plate at our front gate that bears the solemn inscription 'Canadian Embassy – Ambassade du Canada – Residence – Kanadai Nagykövetség – Rezidencia.'

Most locally engaged employees work for the Canadian government for years, many for decades, without every having seen Canada and without the slightest chance of ever seeing it. For many, a visit to Canada, which is perceived to be their second home, remains their most ardent wish. They proudly display pins depicting the maple leaf on sometimes rather exotic garments, sip adventuresome drinks out of mugs decorated with images of Mounties in full regalia and the Parliament Buildings in Ottawa, wear ties bearing the coat-of-arms of any Canadian province and scarves decorated with Inuit motifs or the CN Tower in Toronto. All these items are treasures they have received from Canadians on an official visit or their Canadian colleagues in the mission.

The teenage son of one of our maids festooned an entire wall of his bedroom with a huge Canadian flag. It was a hand-me-down. We had decided to replace the badly frayed and faded flag that had been exposed to wind and weather in front of the official residence. When the new flag was going up on the mast, our maid – casting a longing eye on the grey and worn-out Maple Leaf we had just pulled down – wondered aloud what kind of retirement lay in store for the old flag. She indicated that she would dearly love to have it, and we gave it to her. She lovingly washed, mended, and ironed it before making it the centre-piece of her son's room.

Locally engaged staff, regardless what nationality they are, in which Canadian embassy they work, and what position they occupy in the mission, are employees of the Canadian foreign service, and therefore of the Government of Canada. They constitute an important part of the foreign-service team. Without their competence, devotion, and loyalty, the foreign service would function only half as well.

The smaller part of the team, 4,185, are known as 'Canada-based' personnel. These employees, Canadian citizens and civil servants, are divided into two distinct groups: 1,846 non-rotational and 2,339 rotational.

Members of the non-rotational group work at headquarters in

Ottawa, without ever being posted abroad, in administrative services, commerce, computer systems, data processing, engineering, electronics, economics, finance, information, law, personnel, purchasing, and secretarial and stenographic services.

At times, members of the non-rotational group feel their role in the foreign service is comparable to those of stage designers, costume and make-up artists, lighting technicians, and stage-hands in the world of theatre, opera, and ballet. Struggling behind the scenes in unglamorous jobs, some of them resent having to disappear into obscurity as soon as the curtain rises, leaving the stage, limelight, applause, and fame to the actors – the rotational members of the crew.

Rotational employees know very well, as they move about on the world stage, the extent to which their performance depends on the contribution of those behind the scenes. Just as, in the theatre, the invisible experts in the wings form an indivisible unit with the actors, non-rotational, rotational, and locally engaged staff are the equally indispensable components of the foreign-service team.

The foreign-service merry-go-round, however, turns only for the rotational crew, composed of eight different occupational groups. One representative of each of these groups is introduced below. His or her personality, talents, and skills are revealed, together with the tasks assigned to each position in the foreign-service hierarchy. Enter the first of a series of eight families permanently in transition.

Administrative Officer

Jean-Claude Lamarche has been working for the Department of External Affairs as rotational employee for twenty-three years and has now reached the position of 'Administrative Officer 3.' Forty-five years old at the time of this interview, he was born in Trois-Rivières of a French-Canadian father and an English-Canadian mother, and grew up in Montreal, where he finished high school and briefly, and without any particular profession in mind, attended the Université de Montréal. His parents wanted him to follow in his father's footsteps, but, during two unhappy years as bank teller in a caisse populaire in suburban Montreal, Jean-Claude knew that was not the career he wanted for himself. Ever since childhood he had dreamed of seeing the world.

This dream was well on its way to becoming reality when he came across an advertisement for foreign-service clerks on the bulletin-board of a community college where he was trying to finish a course in public administration. The successfully completed course and his fluency in French and English soon resulted in an interview and a job offer from External Affairs.

Leaving behind a dreary, slushy Ottawa day in late March, eight months after his arrival at headquarters, Jean-Claude was sitting, for the first time in his life, in a plane. He was heading for the Canadian embassy in Madrid, although he had to admit that the prospect of a Mediterranean version of spring was more on his mind than his new office in the Spanish capital. The world was opening up for him, as the view through the window attested, and he settled comfortably in his seat for a pre-dinner drink.

The first few months in Madrid did not turn out to be his idea of happiness, he confessed. His work in the embassy evoked memories of his most miserable days at the bank. As a junior clerk, he had to register the arrival of piles of newspapers and magazines and keep track of mountains of incoming and outgoing mail. He was also responsible for maintaining innumerable files. The job was not half as interesting as he had expected, and the problems of having to cope with a foreign language and culture outside the walls of the mission only added to his troubles. So much for Mediterranean spring. It had soon become too hot anyway.

Jean-Claude would have seriously considered asking headquarters for a transfer back to Canada at the earliest possible moment if it had not been for a Spanish visa clerk hired by the embassy a few months after his own arrival. Ana, he told his parents in a letter, was unlike any of the girls he had ever dated in Canada. This blossoming relationship with her, and with her family, and his growing ease with the local language, customs, and people, gradually converted Madrid into the most magical spot on earth, and cast Jean-Claude's clerical duties in a more favourable light.

Two and a half years after he had landed in Europe for the first time, Jean-Claude found himself – together with Ana, his wife, and their five-month-old son, Jean-Pablo – Africa bound, on a plane to Nigeria. They lived in Lagos for three years. During that time, their daughter, Ana-

Chantal, was born. Ten months in Ottawa followed, a time intended to allow Ana and the children to get to know their new home and to meet Jean-Claude's family. It turned out to be the most difficult period in their married life. Jean-Claude discovered that he had lost his taste for Canadian winters; Ana was convinced she would never acquire such a taste. At the first opportunity, they requested a foreign posting.

Two years in Dar es Salaam followed, two years in Vienna, two years in Tunis, one year in Ottawa, three years in Paris, two years in Nairobi. By the time he was leaving Kenya with his family, Jean-Claude had reached the highest rung on the career ladder for clerks. He decided to try to move up to the rank of administrative officer.

After having been recommended by his superiors and passing an aptitude test, he was assigned to a training program designed for future administrative officers. Several months of lectures and courses followed, with written and oral exams, before Jean-Claude became an administrative officer. It amounted to a considerable rise in the hierarchy and allowed him to become head of administration at the embassy in Brasilia. Three years in Latin America led to his appointment to a senior administrative position at headquarters in Ottawa, where winters, he stated with a frown, had not changed during their absence. But the family's attitude towards snow and local temperatures had undergone a change after they had invested in ski equipment for all four of them. They had also bought a house in Kanata, he added. It gave them the feeling of having a home in Canada. They were thinking of staying in the country for a while, now that Ana and the children had made friends in their new neighbourhood.

Many of the 141 administrative officers currently employed by External Affairs followed career paths similar to Jean-Claude's. After high school graduation, they took courses in business or public administration at a community college before entering the foreign service, pursued long careers as clerks, and then completed the requisite training to become administrative officers.

Others began their foreign-service careers as communicators, having originally received their training in the Armed Forces. After working their way through the communicator hierarchy, they eventually moved up to the position of administrative officer in the same way as had their colleagues from the clerical side.

Still others started out as foreign-service stenotypists and secretaries. When they had reached the highest level in that field, and after the prescribed training and testing, they moved on to join administrative ranks as well.

By no means is a promotion from clerk, communicator, or secretary to administrative officer an automatic procedure. Candidates are carefully selected on the basis of qualifications established through annual ratings, and the final written and oral examinations for the training program are administered by the Public Service Commission in Ottawa. In the course of these exams, candidates have to demonstrate knowledge in the areas of personnel management, finance, budgeting, passport regulations, registry procedures, and consular affairs. 'How do you deal abroad with a Canadian in distress?' is one of the standard questions. Each candidate has to show that he or she is thoroughly familiar with a sequence of clearly defined procedures. It is permissible to repeat an exam once. A second failure, however, means a return to the position held before entry into the training program for administrative officers.

Such a career pattern persisted until the late 1970s. In 1978/9 External Affairs began to hire as administrative officers university graduates and, in some cases, MAs in public or business administration.

At present the department recruits administrative officers from two sources: from within the organization and from outside, directly from among university graduates. Those who have worked their way up through the hierarchy are considered valuable because they are 'familiar with the system'; their colleagues who have arrived just after graduation from university are considered precious because they represent 'new blood' and are therefore expected to be 'refreshing.'

Jean-Claude's posting cycle is not uncommon among members of his group. Of his twenty-three years with External Affairs, he spent four years in Ottawa and the remainder in eight different countries on three continents, averaging a little more than two years in each posting, with three overseas assignments separating tours of duty at headquarters.

During a foreign posting, the administrative officer's role in the foreign-service team consists of a confusing array of duties that can be grouped together into four essential areas of responsibility.

First, an administrative officer is responsible for management of all

Canadian property in the posting, which includes the embassy building, known as the 'chancery'; the home of the ambassador, known as the 'official residence'; all staff quarters, that is, Crown-leased apartments or houses for Canadian staff; and all official vehicles, such as the ambassador's and other cars, trucks, and school buses for the Canadian children in the posting. In practical terms this means managing leases with local landlords and contracts with local contractors; and planning and managing the purchase, maintenance, and repair of furniture, appliances, curtains, carpets, and any property necessary to run the households of Canadian staff in the post.

Second, as financial officer, he or she draws up the embassy's budget, after having collected from all sections of the mission estimates of their financial needs. Out of each embassy's budget come the salaries for locally engaged staff, capital expenditures such as those for furnishings and appliances, and operational expenditures such as those for telephone service, newspaper subscriptions, and repairs and gasoline for official cars. An administrative officer in a medium-sized mission may have to manage an annual budget of about $9 million.

Third, an administrative officer coordinates and directs the personnel administration and services for both the Canadian members and the local staff. In practical terms, he or she deals with all personnel issues, such as holiday schedules, sick leave, and advertising for local staff, and interprets the foreign-service directives, the rules and regulations set out by the government that define the rights and duties of Canadian foreign-service employees.

Finally, he or she directs administrative support services, for example, the registration of all incoming and outgoing mail, including the special diplomatic mail, magazines, and newspapers; the translation, health, reception, and messenger services; and the local transport of embassy members and general supervision of local staff. In short, an administrative officer performs all the duties that ensure the coordinated management of the mission's administration.

During an assignment to headquarters, an administrative officer performs duties that are generally considered to be less varied than those undertaken during a posting abroad. He or she may work in a financial operations division, in the area of material procurement; deal with the administrative details of employees who return to Ottawa or who go out on an overseas assignment; or serve as personnel officer for employees of his or her own occupational group.

Jean-Claude Lamarche sums up his years in the foreign service as an experience 'with a lot of ups and downs' that he would not have wanted to miss for anything.

Clerk

Lyn Tina Tervost is thirty-seven years old and classified in the foreign-service hierarchy as a 'Clerk 5.' She shakes her head and laughs as she recalls the day, fourteen years earlier, when she started to work for External Affairs. She says she did not have the slightest idea what she had got herself into, and adds: 'Boy, did I ever learn fast!'

Learning fast to adjust to new circumstances had been one of Lyn's specialties ever since she had arrived in Canada from her native Nijmegen in The Netherlands at the age of five. Settling with her parents, both of them from Amsterdam, in the small town of Courtney on Vancouver Island, British Columbia, Lyn quickly shed her Dutch accent together with her braids and her homesickness. She might have flourished in her new life even sooner if it had not been for her father's inability to put down roots in Canada. As her parents' marriage disintegrated, she struggled to understand her father's and her mother's opposite reactions to their new environment. By the time her father packed his trunk to return to his home town, Lyn had no doubts that her own home was in Canada.

She stayed with her mother, who was about to marry a second-generation immigrant from Finland, the owner of a small grocery store. The new domestic situation called for some adjustment, but her stepfather soon rewarded her conscientious way of keeping the store's accounts with the offer eventually to pass the business on to her. With a high school diploma in business and commerce and a completed two-year course in accounting, Lyn felt the time had come to do what most of her female friends were busy doing: get married.

The most obvious choice was her driving instructor, whom she had been dating for two years. But, as soon as she had put away all the wedding gifts, and wedding day and honeymoon in California had been exhausted as a topic of conversation with her husband, life did not seem as blissful as her friends had described it. Her husband went off each morning to teach defensive driving to high school kids, while she installed herself between the bills and the receipts in the gloomy back room of her stepfather's corner store. The permanent smell of cheese around her desk only added to her growing dissatisfaction.

Two years into a rapidly growing feeling of having manoeuvred herself into a dead-end life, Lyn was stirred into action by a letter from her father in Amsterdam, inviting her to visit him.

That summer she criss-crossed Europe, hitch-hiking with one of her Nijmegen cousins, and feeling an increasing attraction to the variety of cultures in Europe, fuelled by her own ability somehow to find accommodation, food, drink, and a hundred other necessities by using the local language. She had not known she had a facility for languages. Europe, she said, seemed both delightfully strange and delightfully familiar. She had no idea what to make of this paradox. One thing, however, was certain: returning to Courtney held no delight for her.

The turning-point in her life came on the outskirts of Marseille. The driver who had offered her and her cousin a ride invited them to load their backpacks in the trunk and, before they knew what had happened, drove off with their belongings. Travelling lightly in the absence of any luggage, but heavy with a feeling of absolute helplessness, the cousins managed to reach what Lyn perceived to be the gates of paradise: the Consulate General of Canada, in Marseille.

She was almost overwhelmed by a mixture of feelings: gratitude for the help she received, pride in being a Canadian citizen with privileges she had never known she had, and a burning desire to sit behind one of the desks in the consulate and help others in similar situations. For some time she had been aware of having outgrown her previous life, but had been unable to see an alternative. The hours spent in the consulate had revealed to her the possibility of a new kind of existence and given rise to the ardent wish to work for the Canadian government – for External Affairs. Lyn inquired right there about how to apply.

As soon as she had returned to Courtney, she submitted her formal application. Tests, interviews, and job offer followed within half a year. To her relief, her husband entertained the same desire to dissolve their marriage as she did. Her parents proved to be the main hurdle and refused to make peace with her decision to join the foreign service.

After an acrimonious separation from her mother and stepfather, Lyn got on a plane to Ottawa and crossed the threshold of the Lester B. Pearson Building, eight months to the day after her visit to the consulate in Marseille.

She spent her first year in Ottawa, then was posted to Copenhagen for two years. She went back to Canada, was sent to Caracas for two years, then to Belgrade for two years; returned to Ottawa for two years; and finally got the assignment she had been dreaming of throughout her career in the service: the consulate general in Marseille. For two years she sat behind the desk in the consular section she had first seen when she had been in trouble and marvelled at how many consular cases gave her a chance to practise her skills with Canadians in distress. Lyn is now back in Ottawa and works in one of the administrative divisions, but has her eye on an African post that she had visited while living in southern France.

Lyn's educational background and her career correspond to those of a large number of the 193 clerks at present employed in External Affairs. Most of them have finished high school; many of them have taken extension courses in subjects ranging from financing and accounting to public or business administration; several have previously held clerical positions with other agencies of the federal government.

Her posting history resembles that of many of her colleagues. Of the fourteen years she has been in the service, four years were spent in Ottawa and ten years abroad in five different countries on three continents. Two postings abroad have alternated with one posting at home.

Over the years the range of her activities and responsibilities has increased considerably. She has risen from the position of 'Clerk 1' to 'Clerk 5.'

A 'Clerk 5' has three major functions. First, in the consular area, he or she issues passports and notarizes documents; provides assistance to Canadians hospitalized or detained in the host country; answers customs, citizenship, and pension questions and offers assistance to families of Canadians who have died in the host country; examines requests for financial help; prepares routine consular and passport statistics; and assists in the training of local employees for consular activities.

Second, during the absence of the immigration officer, the clerk examines visa applications, interviews candidates, and supervises the locally engaged staff.

Third, in the administrative area, the clerk is responsible for all registry functions, including the preparation and sealing of the diplomatic bag for shipment and the receiving and opening of the diplomatic bag, plus the distribution of its contents. The clerk manages the filing system and office stationery supplies.

On assignment at headquarters, clerks tend to have more specialized and less varied responsibilities. Many members of this group consider their work in Ottawa to be monotonous and routine and long for the close contact they enjoy in the consular and visa sections of embassies abroad with Canadians and foreigners alike.

Asked how she would sum up her foreign-service experience, Lyn replies that she is glad not to have known in advance how difficult many aspects of life in this profession are. She certainly no longer sees a Canadian mission abroad as paradise. But she gladly lists several highly attractive features of her career.

According to Lyn, foreign-service life is sometimes heaven, sometimes hell, but it is mostly down-to-earth and rather grey. She regrets that it is all-consuming and leaves little time and energy for much of a private life. She would have loved to remarry, but remarks with a grin that it would have been a clear case of bigamy: 'I am already married to the foreign service!'

Communicator

Richard Frank O'Donnell is eager to point out that he has – at the young age of forty-two – served Canada as communicator for a quarter of a century. The first ten years of his career he spent with the Royal Canadian Air Force, the next fifteen with the Department of External Affairs, where he has reached the level of 'Communicator 5.'

He adds that he is also a proud member of the amazingly small group of federal public servants who were actually born and raised in the national capital. In spite of his Irish family name, he counts himself as a French Canadian, and uses the French pronunciation of his given name. His mother, a French Canadian from Rimouski, was the dominant force in his childhood. His father, an English Canadian from the

Ottawa valley, was a quiet man, too absorbed with his books and documents in the National Archives to say much to anyone, let alone to pass a cultural identity on to his son.

With French the language of the home and English the language spoken at school and in his Sandy Hill neighbourhood, Richard grew up bilingual, an asset he says came in handy when he decided to follow family tradition and became a fourth-generation federal public servant. The path he took to this end was unusual in his family. The Air Force had captured his imagination and, since he had spent much of his teenage years operating a ham radio in the basement of his parents' house, telecommunications in the Armed Forces was a natural career choice for him.

His frequent moves from one military base to the next suited his need for change and excitement. He never doubted that he would spend the rest of his career in the military; then he met Susan, a dietitian working in a hospital in Smiths Falls. Soon after Richard and Susan had got married, Richard found himself under intense pressure from his parents-in-law to abandon his military life so that Susan could pursue her career and she and Richard could have the stability necessary to raise a family.

Richard gave in, and immediately began to regret it. None of the jobs he applied for in Ottawa could match the attraction the Air Force held for him. He did not relish the prospect of a nine-to-five job in a high-rise office building in downtown Ottawa for the remaining thirty-odd years until retirement. He did not feel quite ready, either, to settle down to the life of husband and father in the semi-detached two-bedroom townhouse under construction in a development in Nepean Township, for which his parents-in-law had supplied an interest-free loan for the mortgage.

External Affairs, in search of military-trained communicators and eager to find bilingual employees five years after the Official Languages Act had been passed, provided what looked to Richard and Susan like the perfect opportunity to combine career and family. Susan was enthusiastic about looking beyond the boundaries of Smiths Falls and told her reluctant parents that she would gladly mothball her dietitian's lab coat in order to breathe some fresh air overseas.

Ironically, a two-bedroom house in a small housing development similar to the one Richard and Susan had escaped in Nepean Township was awaiting them on the outskirts of Algiers a year after Richard had been accepted in External Affairs. Five months before arriving in their first home abroad, Susan had given birth to twin boys, Roger and Ray – healthy little fellows, and clearly Air Force material, the proud father had announced to his fellow communicators in Ottawa, while passing around cigars.

But the babies did not thrive in their new home. Whether it was the water, the diet, or the climate, they were listless, looked pale, and did not gain the weight Susan knew they ought to. Susan herself did not seem able to recover from an intestinal ailment she had come down with soon after settling in Africa. Every few weeks the symptoms of a sickness that had never been diagnosed or treated flared up, leaving her increasingly weaker.

Susan found the isolation and the resulting loneliness every bit as painful as her physical ailment. Every morning, when Richard set out on his long drive to the embassy, Susan felt abandoned. The house was still unfinished and half-empty, with only the rudiments of furnishings and appliances. The embassy had ordered furniture, curtains, and carpets long ago, but nothing had arrived. She longed for her family and the friends she had made at the hospital in Smiths Falls. Her few neighbours in the half-finished houses around her spoke only Arabic. As she had no car, she was unable to visit the few Canadians she knew from the embassy.

Worst of all, no telephone had been installed in the house. Susan had nightmares about an emergency with her little boys. The embassy tried to pressure the local authorities to speed up the installation of a phone, only to learn that none of the other newly constructed houses in the area had telephones either. There was little comfort in this knowledge for Susan, trapped in the hollow-sounding, sizzling-hot house.

Whether it was a renewed intestinal attack or a combination of emotional and physical distress, after five months of lingering sickness Susan had to be emergency evacuated to Canada on medical grounds. There was no one to look after the children, and she would not have left without them in any case. There was also no one to help her with the little boys during the twenty-hour return trip to Ottawa, with a change of planes in Paris and in Montreal. Richard had to stay behind. The embassy could not get a replacement for him on short notice, and his departure without a substitute would have shut down telecommunications between Ottawa and Algiers. As the plane was lifting off, Susan looked down on the white city disappearing in yellow sand and swore never to set foot in it again.

She never did come back. After the cause of her illness had been diagnosed and treated at the Civic Hospital in Ottawa, Susan refused to return to the posting. During the faint and frequently interrupted telephone calls from Africa, Richard pleaded with her to come home. Carpets and curtains, he said, had arrived, and there was renewed hope for a phone in the house. Susan remained firm. Nothing and no one, she told her husband, could force her to return to that part of the world.

When Richard arrived in Ottawa several months later, their relationship seemed unable to recover from the 'Algiers blues,' as they called the source of their frequent arguments. Since they had no home of their own, they had moved in with Susan's parents, and to escape the crowded conditions, and the tension with his wife, Richard, with Susan's approval, applied for temporary-duty assignments to fill in for fellow communicators on holiday or sick leave. Although he was officially posted to Ottawa, temporary duties took him to Latin America and Asia for four to six weeks at a time, five times within one year.

In the hope that a more congenial environment would give his marriage and family life a new chance, Richard asked for an overseas posting, and was thrilled to be assigned to the Philippines, a country that had captured both his and Susan's imagination. But less than one year after they had landed in Manila, Richard and Susan agreed to separate. Richard said the months before and after the separation were the worst time of his life. 'When a marriage is under strain, it is dreadful abroad. You can't talk to colleagues; you are totally isolated. I have never felt so isolated in my life!'

Richard saw Susan and their little boys off at the airport in Manila. Until the last moment, he had hoped Susan would change her mind, as he had expressed a willingness to do. But Susan, a child at each hand, did not even turn around for a last glance before boarding the plane. Richard returned to an empty, silent apartment in the heart of the deafening noise and steamy pollution of the city, surrounded by thirteen million strangers. He still shudders at the memory of that day and the following weeks.

In order to recover his bearings, Richard put in a request for an assignment to Paris. After three years in the French capital, he was posted to Chile for two years. Three years in Malaysia followed, where he married Flora, a young Philippine woman who was working as secretary at the Philippine embassy in Kuala Lumpur. Richard is now back in Ottawa with his wife and baby daughter. Although she still misses her family and country, Flora enjoys living in Canada. She has made friends among members of the large Philippine community in Ottawa, and both she and Richard like the idea of spending another year or two in this home posting before heading out again.

Richard's story is unique, as is the personal story of any foreign-service employee. But the forces that have shaped his life, his training and military past, the nature of his work, and the demands and delights of international mobility are a common thread in the lives of most communicators and their families.

Approximately 90 per cent of the 194 communicators employed by External Affairs began their careers with the Canadian Armed Forces, the only source for the kind of training External Affairs requires of foreign-service communicators. The transition from military to foreign-service life demands a high degree of adaptability from communicators and their families. Switching from a familiar culture and the protective environment and close-knit community of the armed services to a succession of strange, sometimes hostile, foreign cultures, and a work life of solitude – or, as some communicators refer to it, 'solitary confinement' – is not easy. The secure zone in the Communication Centre is off bounds for members of the embassy, except for the ambassador, and certainly for spouses and children, which forces communicators into physical and psychological isolation. Because they are handling classified information much of the time, communicators cannot freely talk about their work. Their families remain excluded from the world in which they spend their days. They can open up completely only with their fellow communicators. With them they share not merely knowledge of the same classified material, but also the easy camaraderie that characterized life in the Armed Forces. With their spouses and families, however, they tend to be taciturn and withdrawn. Many of them find it difficult to forge a link between the professional and the domestic parts of their lives. As a result, the toll on marriage is heavy. According to their own estimates, the divorce rate in their occupational group, between 60 and 80 per cent, is considerably higher than that in any of the others.

A posting history of five years spent at headquarters and ten years abroad in five different countries on three continents is considered normal. It is equally normal for a communicator to interrupt a foreign assignment or a home posting for a few weeks of temporary duty anywhere in the world.

While a communicator is serving abroad, his or her responsibilities include transmission and reception of messages, enciphering and deciphering of messages between headquarters and foreign postings, ensuring that messages receive proper routing and the appropriate classification – unclassified, confidential, secret, or top secret. A communicator also acts as crypto-custodian, being responsible for the safety of cipher material and for general security of the Communications Centre. A certain amount of technical knowledge is required as he or she is also expected to correct small faults in the communication equipment.

During a posting to Ottawa, a communicator trades the isolation of an office in a mission abroad for the lively community of the Communication Centre in the basement of the Lester B. Pearson Building, where, in a maze of huge, windowless rooms, 80 communicators maintain contact between Canada and its 117 missions around the world.

Asked whether he feels that his work in the foreign service was worth the family problems it caused, Richard points to a room filled with communicators, all of them bent over humming, ticking, and beeping machines, and replies: 'For my first wife the foreign service was a stone around her neck. But I love the variety of my work!'

Courier

An ornithologist in quest of a rare bird in its natural habitat would hardly have needed more devotion and patience than I did in my efforts to sight one particular member of the foreign-service species known as 'Diplomatic Courier.' 'You must see Neill Lancaster,' I had been told in External Affairs whenever my conversations with insiders turned to the subject of couriers. I was determined to do everything in order to meet him and to discuss his work and life, but I also wanted to watch him in operation. The latter turned out to be as challenging as catching an eagle.

During one of my visits to Canada from Hungary, Neill's boss at headquarters assured me that Neill would greatly welcome such a get-together and would live up to his reputation as an eloquent spokesperson for his fellow couriers. Not only would he encourage Neill to come forward, but he would also reveal to me places where Neill could be observed as he was going about his singular business. Consulting a chart filled with names of capitals around the world, and with arrival and departure times of international flights, he tracked Neill down on that day somewhere between Singapore and Hong Kong. After a subsequent foray into Latin America, he would be taking on the Eastern Europe route, and was scheduled to alight in Budapest with the diplomatic bags on a particular day in June. I would be able to watch him in action in what had become the equivalent of his natural habitat.

There was a problem, though, he added. Because Neill could stay on the tarmack in Budapest for only a few minutes before taking the plane in which he had arrived back to Vienna, I would be best advised to go to Vienna myself if I wanted to have a long talk with him. Neill would be using the Austrian capital as temporary home base for his flights to various Eastern European capitals. I could pick any one of four evenings to speak to him – Monday, after his day-trip to Prague; Tuesday, after his return from Warsaw; Wednesday, after his foray into Belgrade; or Thursday, after his trip to Moscow.

Since my own schedule in Budapest could not accommodate a trip to Vienna that week, I asked Neill's boss to pass on to him the message that I would call him in Vienna instead. I would interview him long distance from Hungary. The Canadian embassy in Vienna, I was promised, would disclose the name and telephone number of Neill's hotel a few days before his arrival.

In spite of this promising-sounding arrangement, I remained sceptical. Encounters with rare birds should not be taken for granted. Just in case, I asked Neill's boss in Ottawa for an introductory course in the mysteries of diplomatic couriers' duties. He was happy to oblige.

Responsible for the entire mail service in two directions between headquarters and embassies, couriers must also guarantee that the contents of any bag entrusted to them are not touched by anyone between point of departure and point of arrival. The confidential nature of much of the correspondence demands such vigilance.

Extraordinary measures are necessary to keep the enormous volume of mail flowing steadily back and forth between Ottawa and 117 missions and to maintain the most stringent security regulations; only eighteen couriers are available for such a task.

The safety of the diplomatic bag is the centre of every courier's thoughts. A large-size fire-red sack, imprinted in huge black letters with the words 'Diplomatic, Diplomatique, Diplomatico,' must be carefully sealed by the person specifically authorized for the task in the presence of a witness. Each seal bears a registered serial number, and a list of these numbers, together with the sealed bags, is passed on to the person authorized to turn the bags and written record identifying them over to the courier. The large number of bags dispatched from headquarters, usually more than a hundred at any one time, are sent to the airport in Montreal by special truck and are accompanied by authorized personnel. There, they are handed over to the couriers who will escort the bags to their destination, without ever losing sight of them. At missions abroad, an authorized Canadian member of the embassy drives the embassy's bags to the airport in time to pass them to the incoming courier.

A courier who arrives with a load of bags, whether in Montreal, Santiago de Chile, or anywhere else in the world, is always met at the airport by a fellow Canadian with whom he trades bags. Receipts have to be signed for each bag that changes hands. The series of signatures and the registered time of transfer on the accompanying documents record the transport history of each bag, together with a report each courier has to write about the details of the transfer. Difficulties with airport authorities, for example, must be brought to the attention of External Affairs and of the courier whose turn it will be next to deliver bags to the same spot.

Problems at airports occur frequently. Conscientious reporting alerts couriers to upcoming trouble with local authorities. Neill's boss mentioned the case of a Middle Eastern country where airport officials insisted on X-raying the bags before allowing them into the country. As no country is permitted to examine the contents of another country's diplomatic bag, X-raying would have amounted to a breach of an international agreement. The courier refused to have the bags examined and returned with them to the point of departure. A subsequent stiff diplomatic note from External Affairs to the government in question led to a change of airport policy. The next courier to arrive at that airport received the red-carpet treatment. The welcoming ceremony for the bags in his care did not include an invitation to the X-ray machine.

In the course of their trip around the world, bags are passed from hand to hand through an uninterrupted chain of couriers who guarantee the safety and uncompromised integrity of the contents of bags entrusted to them.

'How can a group of no more than 18 couriers form an uninterrupted chain from headquarters to 117 missions around the world?' In reply to my question, Neill's boss thumbed through a file, then took out a page and handed it to me. One glance told me that the world had been divided into regions, designated purple, orange, brown, blue, red, sand, jade, silver, and gold, each representing a courier route. 'All our routes are colour-coded,' he explained, and then began to recite the list of regions. From Ottawa to all missions in Central America, couriers take the Purple Route. The Gold Route takes them to all Caribbean postings. The Red Route is the New York–Washington run. The Sand Route appropriately leads to Cairo and other cities in the Middle East. The Jade Route includes all capitals in Asia.

From a support base in Paris, to which all bags from Ottawa destined for Europe and Africa used to be sent before being distributed for onward destinations, all bags from Europe and Africa that were Ottawa-bound were collected and shipped home once a week. For economic reasons this base was shut down in January 1991.

Neill's boss, himself a former courier, told me that a mystique had surrounded the work and life of a diplomatic courier when he had joined the group. He recalled movies showing elegantly dressed gentlemen carrying leather briefcases chained to their wrists, the hardware discreetly covered by immaculate starched and ironed cuffs. Couriers, he said, do not travel quite that way, and actually never did.

In fact, nowadays couriers hardly ever move about in the comfortable company of a single bag. The volume of diplomatic mail has been increasing dramatically over the past several decades. Each courier is usually loaded down with dozens of huge, heavy sacks over most parts of his route. A single shipment may consist of as many as a hundred bags.

The image of an exquisitely dressed courier lounging elegantly in the first-class cabin of an international jet-liner, sipping champagne and eating both his complimentary caviare and smoked salmon and that allotted to the mysterious bag occupying the next seat, is romance rather than reality. Canadian couriers do travel first class, wherever the airline they use offers it; however, not every obscure carrier in central Africa or Latin America, for example, has a first-class section. The Canadian government does not pay first-class air fares to pamper its couriers with gourmet food and ample leg-room. As it turns out, a first-class ticket is a more economical form of transportation for a courier than is an economy-class ticket. Couriers normally travel with mountains of baggage. Airline weight allowances cover at most two or three diplomatic pouches, but certainly not the usual range of ten to one hundred bags. A first-class ticket includes a generous allowance for excess weight, and some airlines grant their first-class passengers the privilege of paying cargo rates for those pieces of extra luggage that exceed even the most generous of excess-weight allowances. On an economy-class ticket, the entire diplomatic shipment would have to travel at ordinary excess-baggage rates, adding enormous sums to the transportation costs.

A second important advantage included in the first-class ticket is the passenger's right to board last and to disembark first – essential privileges for a courier. Because a courier must remain with the bags at all times, except during flight, when frequently the bags are entirely out of reach in the luggage compartment, he has to supervise their loading into the luggage compartment after all the passengers' suitcases have been stored away. He remains with the bags until the luggage compartment is closed shortly before take-off. Only then does the courier board the plane. Similarly, a courier must be present when the luggage compartment is opened and the bags are taken out. In some remote parts of the world, airlines are not able to arrange for the courier to monitor the bags in this way. In such cases, the courier buys two tickets and piles the bags on the next seat. 'At times they are back-breaking loads,' Neill's boss pointed out.

It is altogether a very strenuous job. Couriers are either in the air or lugging tons of weight around. They hardly ever see anything of the cities in which they deliver and pick up mail. They are always on the run, and suffer permanently from jet-lag. Neill's boss said he left the job after a year: 'All I wanted was to sleep!'

I could, however, expect a rather different assessment of a courier's life from Neill, he added, who, like many, found it a very attractive job.

After my crash course in the courier's duties I was eager to talk to the most experienced courier of them all. What had attracted him to the job, what maintained his enthusiasm, what was life like for a courier, how did he combine with marriage and family a lifestyle that was more transient than any in External Affairs? Did he still enjoy the work and would he recommend it to others, for example, to his own children? All these questions and more I wanted to ask Neill during the planned Budapest-Vienna long-distance interview.

A few days before he was to descend on Vienna with his cargo for Eastern Europe, the eagle, himself, announced his imminent arrival. Neill phoned me from Paris to confirm that he would, indeed, be the one to travel the Brown Route the following week and to say that he would be happy to answer all my questions and was looking forward to my call at his hotel in Vienna. We settled on Thursday night, at six o'clock. He did not yet know which hotel he would be staying at, but the embassy in Vienna would.

I obtained the number from the embassy and phoned the hotel at the appointed time, but the receptionist informed me that the Canadian embassy had made different arrangements at the last moment and had put Mr Lancaster up in another hotel. The receptionist did not know which one, and the embassy in Vienna was closed for the evening.

While I was desperately trying to find a way to locate him, Neill was sitting in his hotel room, by the phone, waiting for my call. Hours later, he concluded that I had had a last-minute change of plans. He had no idea that the embassy had not informed me of the new hotel reservation.

The next day was Friday, celebrated as 'bag day' among foreign-service personnel, a biweekly event at the Canadian embassy in Budapest when a courier brings mail from Canada. Upon my request, the mission had officially informed the Budapest airport authorities several days in advance that, in addition to the authorized personnel accompanying the diplomatic bag onto the tarmack, the ambassador's wife would be present. Permission had come through in time.

When the embassy van, filled with bags for shipment to Ottawa, arrived at the heavily guarded gate to the tarmack, we were told that no application for an additional person to pass had been received. Permission for me to proceed with the others could not be granted. Our Hungarian driver set to work, using all the eloquence and reasoning power at his disposal – but without success. Phone calls followed. We sat in the van behind the closed gate and waited. The plane from Vienna would be landing any minute and was scheduled to take off again within the half-hour. One of the guards at the gate was eating a sandwich. More phone calls were made. Another sandwich disappeared. When the time of the plane's scheduled landing arrived, I decided to get out of the van so that I would not prevent our team from delivering the bags and picking up our shipment. Just then, permission for all of us to pass arrived by phone. The gate opened.

No sooner had our driver, unleashing all his Magyar temperament, raced the van to the appointed place on the tarmack than the Austrian Airlines plane slowly taxied into position. The eagle had landed. Like a magnet, the plane drew innumerable vehicles. From all directions, passenger buses, gasoline and service trucks, catering vans, and baggage trolleys converged on the aircraft. Doors opened, and passengers and luggage emerged. A few minutes later, an open trolley loaded with bright red cargo disengaged itself from the cluster of vehicles surrounding the plane and headed towards our van. I could make out a tall figure towering above the cargo. As soon as the trolley jerked to a halt in front of us, the bearded passenger, dressed in grey flannels and dark blue blazer, jumped off. I recognized on his lapel a large identity tag, prominently displaying the Canadian coat-of-arms.

Handing me a box of 'Mozart Kugeln,' chocolate truffles of Viennese sweetness offered by Austrian Airlines to its passengers, Neill asked me, 'Why did you not phone me last night?' 'Why on earth did you change hotels?' I countered. There were only a few minutes to untangle the mix-up and to laugh about it. Seven or eight huge bags had to be transferred from Neill's buggy into the embassy van, bags and seals checked, receipts signed, the pile of bags from our embassy transferred into Neill's care, seals checked, receipts signed, the names of those present registered in Neill's report – altogether a long and complicated process demanding undivided attention.

I had brought my camera and, while I watched with fascination, recorded on film every step of the transaction.

Five minutes remained between the end of the official business and the loading of our embassy bags onto the plane. Neill regretted as much as I did that we had missed out on the interview the previous evening. The opportunity had now passed. That night he was flying back to Paris, and then on to Ottawa. Would I join him on the trolley to the aircraft? We could use the brief moments to talk. Presiding together over the safety of the bags and the integrity of their seals, we discussed how we could arrange another meeting. According to the couriers' schedule, Neill would not be back in this part of the world for at least another six months. Should we wait until then, should we write, or should we abandon the project to the adversity that surrounded it?

Although I did not know exactly what my next move should be, I was certain of one thing: I would not give up quite that easily. Adversity would have to put on a more impressive show before I would lose heart. After all, if I wanted to describe the professional activities and the lifestyle of a diplomatic courier, a vivid report of our ill-fated attempts to get together, blocked by just those professional activities, might serve as the most realistic and entertaining description.

I photographed the final stage of the transfer of our embassy bags – Neill's loading of them into the baggage compartment of the plane – and took a picture of Neill to record the thirty-fifth anniversary of the day on which he had entered government service. We said goodbye, agreeing to pursue the possibility of a long interview.

The Canadian team, following a routine procedure established for couriers' departures, remained on the tarmack, in case the take-off was aborted. But the plane left without incident and was soon out of sight against the clear summer sky. We headed back into town with our precious cargo. All Canadian members of the embassy were assembled, eagerly waiting for letters from home. My favourite booty of the day were the photos I had taken of the official courier on duty. They turned out well. Bright red diplomatic bags proved to be highly photogenic objects.

Five months later, I was in Ottawa. Neill's son told me on the phone that his father was currently in Asia, but was expected back home the day before my own departure for Hungary. I could not believe my good fortune. The interview would finally take place. The next day I learned from Neill's boss that Neill would, in fact, be returning the day of my departure for Budapest. We would miss each other by three or four hours at the airport in Montreal. Then came the good news: Neill was once again due for the Brown Route. In four weeks he would be back in Vienna for five days and, of course, for a bag delivery in Budapest at the end of the same week.

A few days before he was to embark on his trip to the Austrian capital, Neill phoned me from Paris. I told him that, this time, I would not rely on a long-distance interview. I had a made a train reservation to be in Vienna on 11 December, the only free evening I had during this particular week. He would, of course, be there, he said, but it was not the very best of his five evenings. He had to go to Moscow that day and would be back later than on any of the other nights. To make matters worse, the plane from Moscow had a tendency to arrive late. I should phone the airline to confirm the arrival time. If all worked out well, we would meet in the lobby of his hotel. This time, there would be no last-minute change of reservation.

On the evening of my arrival in Vienna, a phone call to the airline, one hour before his plane was due, produced the information that the flight from Moscow had been delayed. My heart sank. If 'Otyets Moroz,' Father Frost, the personification of Russian winter, had grounded the plane at Sheremetyevo Airport, I would have no choice but to abandon the entire cherished project. I had to be back in Budapest the next day, Neill had to fly to Warsaw the following morning, and to a number of other East European capitals before going back to Canada. Except for a few minutes at the airport in Budapest three days later, we would probably not be on the same continent for another six or twelve months. The fate of the interview and my story about foreign-service couriers rested now with the weather in the Soviet capital. Bracing myself for the worst possible news, that a snow storm was raging over Moscow and had prevented the plane from taking off, I asked the airline by how many hours the plane had been delayed. I held my breath. 'It is forty-five minutes late' was the reply.

The final obstacle to our meeting was a detachment of Austrian soldiers in battledress guarding all entrances to Neill's hotel, armed with sub-machine-guns. The day we had set aside for our conversation happened to be the day OPEC members had chosen for a conference to discuss the price of crude oil in the wake of the pending Gulf War. It appeared that Neill was as inaccessible as the OPEC delegations.

The Austrian Army, albeit in battle gear, seemed a less formidable impediment than the kind of couriers' schedules Neill and I had had to contend with over a period of eight months. Somehow I got past the soldiers. As soon as I had entered the hotel lobby – a huge hall, crowded with people, suitcases, and Christmas trees, and thick with cigarette smoke and the scent of alcohol and perfume – a tall figure rose from an armchair and ploughed his way through a tangle of Arabic, German, French, and English conversation, and suddenly stood in front of me. I recognized a familiar face, and a maple leaf somewhere on a lapel. Old friends could not have expressed joy in their reunion more cordially.

A brisk walk through the winding streets of the old city took us to Neill's favourite pub, 'Zum Weissen Rauchfangkehrer' ('The White Chimney-Sweep'). We settled in a wood-panelled corner and, following the foreign-service rule for any foreign city, did in Vienna as the Viennese do: we ordered the most authentic dish. We did not need to consult the menu. Our choice would be Wiener schnitzel with roast potatoes and red cabbage. Next to us, sitting at a grand piano, a melancholic-looking lady offered musical fare, masterly rendered, of Bach sonatas, Christmas carols, popular tunes from musicals, Johann Strauss waltzes, and other classics composed by equally popular local immortals such as Schubert, Mozart, and Beethoven.

The feeling that I was listening to familiar stories told by an old friend never left me that evening. Perhaps the obstacle course we had run to reach this meeting had revealed more about the work and life of a diplomatic courier than we had realized. Whatever the reason, I certainly felt I was no stranger to the courier's world. I had the basics of their tasks and work habits. Now I was looking for answers to other questions, among them the most obvious one: Who are the couriers?

'There are seventeen of us,' Neill replied. 'The eighteenth is coming.' He sounded as if he was talking about his brothers. 'We are all ex-military. Only one came from the railway. Ten of us are from the Navy.' Neill then went on to describe the training as communicators most couriers had received in the Armed Forces long before deciding to join External Affairs. Their careers, he explained, and even their private lives, show so many similarities that they see themselves as a homogeneous group. Yet, the life story of each courier is unique.

'Family research is my hobby,' Neill told me, when I asked him about his family background. This preoccupation allowed him to trace the family roots on his father's side back to the tiny village of St Clears in Wales, where his family name, although English in origin, cropped up in the archives he combed during summer holidays in Europe. 'On my mother's side, I am of German origin,' he added, savouring the listener's delight in the disclosure that his great-great-grandfather had held the position of gamekeeper for the Duke of Weimar. Had the same ancestor ever encountered Johann Wolfgang von Goethe, another employee of the Duke of Weimar? Neill replied that the newly reunited Germany will permit him to travel for the first time to the family's old hunting-grounds in former East Germany to look in the archives of Weimar for an answer to that question.

The families of both parents emigrated to the United States in the nineteenth century and eventually settled in Regina, where Neill was born in 1938. 'We read a lot at home. We read for pleasure,' Neill said, summing up family life. Books brought the world to his parents' home in the Prairies.

The Navy entered Neill's life when he was twelve. A school chum's sea cadet uniform caught his attention. Soon Neill wore the Navy uniform himself at weekly meetings of the cadets in his home town, at summer camps at Lake naval barracks near Regina, and eventually at training camp in Vancouver. At age sixteen, he joined the reserve, and since he enjoyed the comradeship and the outdoor action-oriented life in the reserve, he left school after Grade 10 and joined the Navy in 1955.

'Learn to Serve' – the motto was instilled in him during twenty-six weeks of basic military training and a one-year course in communications at the naval base in Cornwallis, Nova Scotia.

Not quite eighteen years of age, Neill got his first assignment as communicator on an aircraft-carrier, HMCS *Magnificent*. The assignment coincided with the Suez Crisis, and that political event had a direct impact on his life. He never set foot on the vessel. The aircraft-carrier was needed to ship troops on its peacekeeping mission to the Suez.

Victoria, BC, home port to HMCS *Jonquière*, became Neill's new home, as much as the training-ship itself that took Neill on a five-month cruise of the Far East. 'It was wonderful!' Neill seems excited still when he describes seeing for the first time Pearl Harbor Naval Base, Guam, Manila, Singapore, Hong Kong, and Japan, all familiar and thrilling sites for an eighteen-year-old who had read his way through the history of the Pacific battles of the Second World War.

He loved all the cruises that followed, life on board ship, the sense of adventure, and the camaraderie. He missed only his privacy for reading. 'Mind you,' he added, 'as communicator, I had more privacy than others.' In his free time he took correspondence courses to earn a high school diploma.

The dental treatment he required prior to an assignment in the Arctic took him to Ottawa. 'That's where I met my wife,' he said, and still seemed to marvel at his good fortune and the sheer coincidence of the meeting. The young couple moved to Victoria and, during his first year of marriage, Neill spent two hundred days on board ship, away from home. The second year he was away even longer. He was sent across the country from coast to coast in training as an electronic technician. His wife, Nancy, did not allow herself to complain about her absent husband. She became a full-time student, working towards a nursing degree.

Fully qualified not only as a communicator but also as an electronic technician, Neill decided that he would continue his travels around the world, but in the company of his wife. Nancy, by that time a newly registered nurse, wanted to travel as much as he did.

External Affairs was the obvious choice. Neill resigned from the Navy and applied to join the foreign service. He had to wait eighteen months for his application to be processed, a period he used to work for other government departments. Eventually External Affairs offered him a job as communicator. 'I transfered my Navy time for pension to External Affairs,' he told me, a transfer symbolizing continuity in his career.

Seven months after he had started his new job, Neill and Nancy were posted to India. 'My wife found it tremendous,' he said. 'We had five servants in India, straight from scrubbing the deck in the Navy.' He laughed at the memory and then went on to describe backpacking holidays 'all over northern India' and a Christmas spent at a camp for Tibetan refugees in the northern part of the country. 'India needed some getting used to,' he conceded. 'I got hepatitis.' But, altogether, it was 'a great, wonderful adventure' for both of them.

After sixteen months in Asia, Neill and Nancy were posted directly to Moscow. 'We had no winter clothes, so we ordered them from the Eaton's catalogue,' he said. They found the former Soviet Union as exciting and fascinating as the previous assignment, and as the posting to Ceylon that followed. By that time, they had their first son. The little boy felt completely at home in Colombo. He had many children to play with, spoke English with the local accent, and quickly and naturally adopted local customs and mannerisms.

Neill still relishes the story of the young family's home leave from Ceylon to Edmonton, an occasion for the four-year-old boy to demonstrate to his Canadian grandparents traces of a culture that was more familiar to him than to them. Holding a slice of raisin bread, which his grandmother had toasted for him, against the light, he announced with a perfect Ceylonese accent and with authentic head movements: 'We can't eat that, Grandma; it has cooties in it!' Neill and Nancy had to explain to the mystified grandmother that, in Ceylon, bread had to be held against the light and checked for 'cooties,' the dark-coloured local bugs, before it could be eaten. The raisins had obviously struck the little fellow as a particularly large, Canadian version of their Ceylonese cousins.

Upon returning to Canada after more than five years as communicator in three different missions, Neill was asked to take the job of courier for one year. At the end of the term he would have the choice of a posting abroad for himself and his family. While Nancy settled down with their two little sons in Ottawa, Neill set out on his trips around the world.

The year 1970 saw not only the budding of Neill's career as a courier, but also the unfolding of terrorism in Latin America. Tupamaros, Marxist urban guerrillas in Uruguay, had already held several diplomats hostage, killing some of them, and had introduced the hijacking of planes. On 1 July 1970, their Brazilian counterparts' path crossed Neill's courier route.

As Neill was boarding a São Paolo–bound aircraft in Rio de Janeiro, he noticed a young woman in an advanced state of pregnancy accompanied by a young man with one arm in a cast. The couple took the seats across the aisle from his. His hand on the diplomatic bag in the seat next to him, Neill dozed off. A few minutes later, he awoke to the sound of running and shouting in the aisle behind him. When Neill opened his eyes, the young man was pointing a gun at him. The cast was gone. Behind him stood his female companion. Her pregnancy had vanished as mysteriously as his broken arm. The weapons they and two other hijackers were brandishing indicated that the woman had been delivered of a litter of pistols and hand-grenades, while her companion seemed to have brought forth a small arsenal of explosives in his own way.

Neill told me that his thoughts at that moment were quite simple: 'This is an interesting development. I better look up the telephone number of the embassy in Havana.' Because Brazilian hijackers had previously commandeered planes to Cuba, Neill reached for his briefcase to get the information he was convinced he might need soon. 'São Paolo seemed to be out,' he added casually.

As soon as Neill opened his briefcase, the male hijacker pointed his gun at the red bag next to Neill and demanded to know what was in it. Neill spoke no Portuguese; the hijacker, no English. The woman offered her services as translator. Her fellow hijacker, upon learning that this was a diplomatic bag, jumped to the conclusion that he had netted an American diplomat. Judging by the expression on his face, Neill said, this development looked to be highly rewarding. But when he learned via the interpreter of the bag's and Neill's Canadian origin, he looked defeated. According to Neill, 'boring' was written all over his face.

In the meantime, the guerrillas on duty in the cockpit had directed the plane back to Rio and were demanding that the Brazilian government negotiate for the release of prisoners who had recently hijacked a plane. As soon as the aircraft had come to a stop on the runway in Rio, the Brazilian army shot out the plane's tires.

For the next few hours, the hijackers repeated their demands over the pilot's radio and announced that, if the government did not comply by the deadline, they would shoot one hostage after another until their demands were met. They would start with the pilot and work their way down the cockpit hierarchy first. Stewardesses would follow. The Canadian courier was chosen as the first of the passengers to be shot. Neill had already been singled out and awarded celebrity status. The Canadian embassy in Brazil had demanded immediate release of its courier. Neill had overheard the message broadcast on the pilot's radio. He still remembers the hijackers' roaring laughter and their reply that the courier would be dropped on the tarmack soon.

Negotiations dragged on for almost five hours without any signs of a peaceful solution. The crew served a sumptuous meal. Forty passengers gorged themselves on food and wine. Neill said they even sang. The first symptoms of what would later be known as the 'Stockholm Syndrome' began to appear as the passengers' acted out their need to identify with the hijackers. Neill could neither eat nor sing.

Throughout this seemingly endless period, the ventilation system had been shut off. The cabin was suffocating. Minutes before the deadline, the ventilation system suddenly came on. One deep breath told Neill that he was not inhaling fresh air, but tear gas. Within seconds, the cabin was filled with a sour, stinging smell, thick fog, and the sound of coughing and yelling from the passengers. Moments later he heard a deafening explosion and saw a door blown open and Brazilian soldiers storming the plane. The first shots were fired. Pandemonium broke out.

'This place is not for me,' Neill said, summing up his feelings. During those critical minutes his military training was of enormous help to him, he pointed out. While shots were being fired, he hid under his seat. When they stopped, he darted to the open emergency exit, flung himself onto a wing of the Caravelle, and from there leaped down to the tarmack. He was grabbed by the soldiers and dragged into a passenger bus. There, on the floor, bleeding heavily but still alive, lay one of the hijackers.

Recounting the incident, Neill was still wondering whether the soldiers knew at that stage in the drama how to distinguish hijackers from their victims. He was held for several hours in the military barracks, until an emissary from the embassy who spoke Portuguese identified Neill as the Canadian courier.

Neill refused to leave the scene without his bag. The Brazilian army finally retrieved it from the plane, where it had peacefully remained in place during the shooting and killing. The seal was still intact.

The Canadian envoy took Neill to the ambassador's residence, where the first guests were arriving to celebrate Canada Day. Neill turned down a journalist's request for an interview. He phoned his wife in Ottawa and learned that word of the hijacking had travelled around the world as soon as the drama had begun. The head of the couriers in External Affairs had instantly informed her of Neill's situation and had remained in touch with her throughout the crisis. Less appreciated was a phone call she had received from an anonymous journalist who conveyed the message: 'Your husband has been shot.'

Neill spent the night with the embassy's communicator. The next morning, a dispatch arrived from External Affairs headquarters: 'Proceed at your discretion.' He proceeded, taking an uneventful flight to São Paolo, and delivered the bag twenty-four hours later than originally scheduled.

He said he can now laugh about the aftermath of the incident. The suit he had worn during the hijacking was in rags. He sent a claim to the government for replacement of a garment worth about a hundred dollars and received a reply stating that 'the Crown had no provisions to pay for this suit.' He did succeed with the airline though. After four months of waiting for a response, he received a cheque for $125 and converted it into a new suit.

'No,' Neill said, emphatically, the hijacking did not diminish his enjoyment of his work. He would have stayed with it, but, at that time, External Affairs did not maintain a permanent team of couriers. It had been a profession earlier, but prior to 1970 had been changed to a one-year special assignment for communicators.

When Neill's year was up, External Affairs offered him the posting he had asked for: Hong Kong. The family moved to Asia. Neill took eight weeks of intensive, eight-hour-a-day language training in Mandarin before he began his three-year service as both communicator in Hong Kong and regional courier. During that period, the Canadian embassy was opened in Beijing, and Neill transported diplomatic bags back and forth between Hong Kong and China. 'I took the train from Hong Kong to the border, then pushed the bags on a little cart to the Chinese side and took a train to Canton, eighty miles away.' From there he continued his journey by plane.

In 1974, Neill returned with his family to Ottawa and was assigned once again to courier duty. In 1978, a permanent, full-time courier team was put together, and Neill joined the group.

Although by 1979, after five years as courier, he needed a break from constant travelling around the world, two years of special duty at headquarters and a subsequent posting to the high commission in Singapore convinced him that his life as courier had, once and for all, spoiled his appetite for work as a communicator. In 1982, he rejoined the team of couriers. 'And there,' he remarked with a big smile, 'I have been ever since.'

'Sure it is stressful,' he added. 'The stress is constant.' But, the negative aspects of this life are not limited to stress. Some diseases are so wide-spread among his fellow couriers they seem to be occupational hazards. Like several of his colleagues, Neill has a chronic sinus problem and strep throat. His physician sees a link between the strep throat and Neill's kidney condition. Neill wonders about the connection between jet-lag and the high blood pressure from which many of his colleagues suffer. The radiation exposure during endless hours in the air worries him. One of the main causes of death among airline pilots is cancer caused by radiation. Neill and his colleagues are particularly concerned about this source of danger in their job.

But all these problems, he said, are outweighed by the positive aspects of his work. Towering above all advantages, as far as he is concerned, is 'a high degree of freedom. You don't have to go to that office every day.' He loathes the idea of being caged from morning until night. 'I am an independent operator,' he pointed out. No other job could match the sense of independence his career offers.

'How does my wife take it?' Neill laughed heartily. 'She doesn't know how to cope when I am home all the time!' His wife has had her own career ever since they got married, and she loves her work as much as Neill loves his. At present she is a full-time university student and hopes to graduate soon. Neill spoke with love and admiration of the role she has played in his and their children's lives. She was fascinated by their foreign postings. Hardships never got her down. Now she cherishes the things she can learn and do while living in Canada.

'All the couriers' wives are independent. They hold responsible jobs as entrepreneurs, as civil servants, and in other fields.' One wife worked for the United Nations. As a courier's wife, 'you must get involved in your own thing,' Neill emphasized. The divorce rate in his group lies well below the national average. Fewer than 25 per cent of couriers have been married more than once.

'How do the children like it?' Neill thinks a courier-dad has a lot to offer to younger and older children alike. 'When I come back from an assignment I am home for ten days with the kids.' He explained the three-month cycle in which a courier operates. Usually a courier manages to compress the 520-5 hours of work required of him every three months into ten weeks by working 12- or 13-hour shifts most of the time. Such an arrangement amounts to ten full days at home every three months, in addition to regular holidays. He wonders how many husbands and fathers enjoy such a luxury. His career has left ample time for his wife and two sons. 'Our kids,' he added, 'have the ordinary school problems, due to our moves.' He knows the wives and children of all members of his team. He mentioned one problem child among them. 'But it was all sorted out. There are no enduring problems in this group.'

Neill will be retiring within a year. He is enthusiastic about the prospect of devoting himself to all the things he has never had enough time to do. He will be selling the house near Ottawa and will settle with his wife where they started their life together, in their original 'home port' of Victoria. Neill will be joining his wife at university and plans to take courses in geography, history, and anthropology – all familiar territory for him after thirty-five years of travel around the world.

Asked about courier lore, Neill relates incidents that have become part of the courier epic. In the winter of 1966, the courier on duty on the Ottawa–New York–Washingon run found himself grounded at John F. Kennedy Airport by a major snowstorm. No one from the Canadian mission at the United Nations had been able to reach the airport to meet him and his cargo. He was not the only passenger in this type of predicament. But he was, as far as he could see, the only one left in charge of approximately forty diplomatic bags and unable to move with such a load. Only an authorized Canadian would be able to relieve him of his responsibility, and no such person could be expected for the remaining eight hours of the night. After he had neatly arranged the bags into a bed just big enough to accommodate a person of his size, he stretched out on top of it and slept through the rest of the snowstorm. No one could have got at any portion of the bed without first removing the human blanket.

A special place in the heart of couriers is reserved for Eastern Airlines because of the exceptionally warm treatment their crews accorded couriers on their Ottawa–Washington–New York route. On one occasion an aircraft ready for take-off did not leave because the crew was waiting patiently for the regular Canadian courier, who was easily recognized by his shock of white hair. On that day, he had been replaced by a young colleague. The crew did not discover that the Canadian courier was on board until they announced to the passengers the reason for the delay and the substitute disclosed his identity. The same airline gave the white-haired courier who had flown with them for years a first-class seat converted into a living-room armchair as a retirement present.

The pianist in 'Zum Weissen Rauchfangkehrer' had ended her concert an hour earlier with 'Midnight...,' the appropriate tune from the musical *Cats*, when we left the pub for a walk back to the hotel. The Austrian Army was still guarding the doors. Saying goodbye, we marvelled at the evening. That our meeting had actually taken place bordered on the miraculous, after the nearly insurmountable obstacles we had encountered. Before shutting the door to my taxi, Neill cheerfully offered to answer any further questions that came up.

The next morning, on the Orient Express back to Budapest, I realized that a few issues remained to be discussed. Fatigue and my inability to take an eleventh page of notes had slowed down the flow of questions towards the end of the evening. In two days, Neill was due to deliver the Christmas mail to Budapest, an occasion for the final questions and answers.

I decided to join one of our embassy's military guards who was to take the bags and pick up the mail from Neill. On the way to the airport, we talked about his forthcoming tour of duty in Saudi Arabia, where the Gulf War was about to begin.

Neill, emerging from the darkness that cloaked the tarmack, with a huge load of bags, turned over to me the latest package of 'Mozart Kugeln.' When all the sacks had been safely exchanged and all formalities completed, a few minutes remained. He answered my questions quickly and succinctly, and then volunteered several pieces of information he felt he had negleced in the course of our evening in Vienna. Eventually I turned to the last couple of questions: 'Tell me honestly, would you recommend this job to your kids?' He did not need to recommend it to his kids, he replied. 'My son, the one who is at university now, would love to do it.' 'Would you choose this career again?' Neill burst into laughter. At that moment the call came for him to return to the plane. Pushing the door of the transit lounge open with the heavily loaded airport buggy, he turned back to me and called, still laughing: 'I certainly would. This is the best job in the government, including the prime minister's!'

Neill and his red bags were instantly swallowed up by the winter darkness of the tarmack. Minutes later, his plane took off. Like a huge silvery bird in quest of freedom, it soared high and soon merged with the snow-laden sky. We picked up the bags he had brought and delivered them safely to the embassy.

Electronic Technician

Jozef Zygmunt Piatkowski pulls out his passport. It contains more entry stamps than any other passport he has ever examined. He has just celebrated his fiftieth birthday and his thirtieth year in the public service. He has been working for External Affairs for twenty years and is classified as 'Electronic Technician 7.'

Born in Toronto of a Scottish mother, and a Polish father who had left Warsaw only two years before the war broke out, Joe had grown up in Scarborough, where his father was employed as an engineer and his mother as a librarian in the high school from which Joe eventually graduated. From early childhood on, his passion had been the piano. He had started to take lessons at age five and by age sixteen had reached the Grade 10 level at the Toronto Conservatory of Music. At his graduation ceremony, he entertained the audience with a complete Beethoven sonata and with Chopin nocturnes. He would have studied music if his parents had not convinced him that his interest in electronics could more easily be converted into a promising and well-paid career.

His father, having served in the Royal Canadian Air Force throughout the war, out of a sense of gratitude and loyalty to the country that had offered him a home during one of the darkest hours in Poland's history recommended the Air Force, where he knew Joe could pursue a career as electronic technician.

Joe thrived on the challenge of frequent new assignments and in the company of the cheerful community he encountered at the succession of military bases he was posted to. He moved, on average, every eighteen months, travelling lightly as a bachelor, except for his permanent companion, the piano, which was not included in his weight allowance.

On the Air Force Base at Cold Lake, Alberta, he met Janet, a kindergarten teacher and a recent arrival from Lloydminster. Janet played the flute, had an inquiring mind, and thrived on Joe's moving cycle within Canada, to which she was exposed as soon as they married. She taught school until their first child, Cathy, was born and then switched to substitute teaching. A second child, Peter, followed two years later.

The beginning of a certain weariness with military life after ten years coincided with Joe's reassignment to Cold Lake – the second time in a somewhat similar job on the same base – and the welcome news that External Affairs was looking for electronic technicians who had Joe's military training. Six months after he had applied, Joe was accepted, a particularly smooth process in his case, since he did not require additional security clearance. Within another six months, Joe and Janet found themselves posted to London – 'not in Ontario,' as they happily announced to their friends on the base, 'the one in Britain.'

In this new environment Joe enjoyed his work whole-heartedly. It was the variety, he said, the high degree of responsibility, and the jolly camaraderie with his British and Commonwealth colleagues. An additional bonus proved to be his business trips to Europe. He criss-crossed the continent, from Oslo to Ankara and from Lisbon to Warsaw. It was an education for him, and he was looking forward to every new trip, until he discovered that he was paying a high price for each one of the excursions. Domestic harmony was suffering gravely. His life story, he pointed out, is that of a foreign-service marriage, with all its ups and downs, and a prolonged and heavy emphasis on the latter.

To begin with, Janet and the children had found it difficult to settle in their new surroundings. The house in London was small and confining. They tried to get out as much as possible, but weekend visits to the British Museum quickly lost their appeal for the children. They missed their old friends as they were not making friends at school easily. No one came to see them, and there was no one whom they could visit. In spite of a few shy overtures with neighbours and other schoolchildren, Janet, Cathy, and Peter received no return invitations. Everyone around them remained aloof. In Canada, wherever they had been posted, friendships with Air Force families and with neighbours had come easily.

The large city did not seem to favour close human relationships, for which she and the children longed more than ever before now that Joe was absent so much. His monthly trips, lasting three to fourteen days, were decidedly too frequent and too long as far as the family was concerned. For the first time in her married life, Janet had no classes to teach and, with her husband away and the children at school until late in the afternoon, Janet's human contact was restricted to a morning walk down the street for milk and bread and her weekly shopping trip. What started as a bad day here and there rapidly turned into longer and longer periods of depression.

To make matters worse, she did not feel much better when Joe came home from his trips and remained with the family for a few weeks. He was usually travel weary and reacted irritably to Janet's complaints. Why, he asked her, could she not enjoy herself as much as he was? After all, did she not have more free time to do things than he did? Wondering why she did not make use of the many possibilities this city offered her, he went back to his office to prepare for his next trip.

During the second gloomy, rainy November spent in London, with Joe away for ten days in southern Europe, Janet experienced a feeling of abandonment so powerful that it frightened her. She had only one desperate desire: to go home. It came as a shock to her to discover that she did not know where 'home' was. It certainly was not Lloydminster, her birthplace, a town she had been more than eager to leave after high school graduation, and where nothing drew her, now that both her parents were dead. Nor was it Cold Lake or any of the military bases where she had lived temporarily. 'Home,' it seemed to her, was nowhere.

But Janet's feeling of dislocation was not merely one of place. Even the sense of belonging, being part of a family, a school, a close-knit military community, seemed to have been an illusion, now vanished forever. Had too many of her friendships been superficial? Where was everyone now that she needed help? Her friends did not write, except for newsy Christmas cards that listed their family's accomplishments in the course of the past year, but never bothered to ask how the exiled friends were holding up. There was nothing and no one for her to hold on to. Even her husband was beyond reach, too content with his work and travels to allow her to drag him down into her misery. Janet had an acute feeling of being adrift at high sea, about to drown in the waves.

When Joe returned from Italy, tired as expected, but delighted with the people he had met and full of stories of Roman ruins and Trastevere restaurants, one look at Janet told him that matters were not as rosy at home as they were in his career. Janet, pale and haggard, announced that she was going back to Canada to build a life for herself and the children. The aimless drifting had to come to an end.

Janet seemed as badly shaken by her decision as Joe was. In desperate search of certainties, both established one point, that neither of them wanted a separation, let alone a divorce. To Joe's indescribable relief, Janet assured him that she did not want to leave him at all, not even temporarily, but simply had to get away from what she called the 'disastrous fall-out' of his rotationality.

Joe offered to leave the foreign service, saying that Janet and the children were more important to him than his career, regardless of how much he enjoyed it. He could always find another job, in an environment that would be stable. But, in spite of her yearning for a different kind of life, the prospect of a completely new beginning in uncertain circumstances caused more anxiety for Janet than consolation. Both were at their wit's end not knowing where they should go, or what they should do.

In the course of a long weekend Joe and Janet talked more than they had for months, and agreed on a three-stage rescue operation. Joe would apply for an assignment in Canada at headquarters, they would use their small savings as a down-payment for a house in Ottawa, and Janet would look for a job. In the meantime, Joe would try to cut down on business trips as much as possible and they would use their remaining time in Britain to explore London and the surrounding areas. Janet and Joe still think of that weekend as a turning-point in their marriage.

In spite off this promising-sounding future, Janet did not recover. Her turmoil had lasted too long and had been too intense. She knew the children had suffered as a result of their mother's depressive episodes. The crisis had opened Joe's and Janet's eyes to the damage they had done, not only to their marriage, but to their children as well. While Joe held himself responsible for Janet's misery, Janet felt guilty about Cathy and Peter. These heavy burdens both of them carried for a long time.

But Janet knew that they had started an uphill climb, however difficult, once Joe had recognized the seriousness of their situation and had given his marriage and family clear priority over his career. He was now turning his full attention to the task of healing wounds. Being able to talk things over with him and to have his attention and goodwill, she said, was therapy for her. But Joe, whether consciously or unconsciously, turned to a particular type of therapy: the piano. Music helped him as much as it did Janet and the children to regain equilibrium. Janet, who had not touched her flute for years, accompanied Joe, bringing back memories of their courtship and early, happy years together.

But, at that stage in their life, they could not build their new relationship on music alone. Some concrete steps had to be taken. Joe regretted deeply having to make a request in Ottawa to cut short his London posting. It had been a plum assignment, the best job he had ever had. But he had taken his family for granted while blindly pursuing his career. Only during the moment of crisis had he realized that wife and children provided him with stability and a sense of purpose that he could not do without. When Janet had briefly opened up the prospect of this career minus the family to him, it had immediately struck him as a nightmare.

Confirmation of the requested Ottawa assignment arrived a little too early, not only for Joe's liking, but ironically also for Janet's. Their daily life in London had become rather appealing. Joe had been able to cut down on the number and lengths of his trips, and the family spent weekday evenings planning outings to visit the sights in and around London, on which they then embarked on Saturday mornings, complete with picnic basket. Once a month, husband and wife met in town for a romantic lunch in an inexpensive pub. Janet had invited the wives of some of Joe's colleagues for tea, and had received a series of return invitations. The children had begun to make friends. London had started to look attractive to Janet and the children when the movers arrived to pack their goods for shipment to Canada. But Janet had regained enough of a sense of humour to joke with Joe at the untimely onset of her fondness for the city.

After a cheerful farewell party thrown for them by Joe's fellow technicians, the family arrived in Ottawa. Stages two and three of the rescue plan turned out to be quite a bit more enervating and time-consuming than the return home. After weeks of searching, they found an older house with a large garden in Britannia Bay. House and garden needed a lot of work, a project the entire family attacked with enthusiasm and vigour.

Because the only job Janet was offered did not amount to more than infrequent substitute teaching, without much of a chance for full-time employment, she took university courses towards certification as a teacher of English as a second language. An ESL certificate, she was assured by members of the Foreign Service Community Association at headquarters, qualified as a portable career and was bound to be useful in any future overseas posting.

During the next five years in Ottawa, the family thrived. The children were quickly integrated at school, made friends in the neighbourhood, and joined the most Canadian clubs they could think of: the hockey and figure-skating clubs. As soon as Janet had earned her ESL diploma, she found a job teaching English to newly arrived immigrants from Asia. She said she loved her work more than anything she had done before because she got to know her students well and could sympathize with their daily struggle to come to terms with a new and strange environment. However, Joe found his duties only half as stimulating and rewarding as his tasks in London. But he had no regrets about their decision to return home. Whenever he found time to play the piano and Janet joined him with her flute, they knew beyond doubt that they had more than overcome the crisis and had come out of it stronger individually and as a family. When they put a 'For Rent' sign on their front lawn in preparation for their posting to Moscow, neither of them had any doubt about where the family home was. The house they had renovated and the garden all of them together had brought to full bloom represented their roots in a community from which all of them drew strength and to which they would always return after completing a foreign posting.

Although Moscow turned out to be objectively much more difficult an assignment than London, Janet found her life in the Soviet capital a lot easier. She still did not appreciate Joe's trips, especially since she was left behind with the children in a tiny, run-down apartment on a main boulevard in the centre of the noisy and severely polluted city. Painful memories of London did creep up once in a while during the first few months. But all shadows of the past vanished as soon as she had accepted a full-time teaching position at the Anglo-American-Canadian School. She recovered her lively curiosity and, with the new degree of independence she had acquired during the five years in Ottawa, she took the considerable hardships of Moscow in stride. Every time Joe returned from one of his trips, Janet seemed to him to be bubbling with vitality and good humour. She also had visited more museums and bookstores than any of their friends and still found time to enlarge her Russian vocabulary and her repertory of local dishes.

After two years in the Soviet Union, Joe was asked to go to Beijing on a cross-posting. Joe and Janet agreed that two hardship postings might be too strenuous for all of them. In order to allow the family batteries to be recharged at home, they turned the offer down and went back to Ottawa, to their house and their roots in the community. During the following four years, they saw their children graduate from high school. Once Cathy was well settled at Carleton University in Ottawa, and Peter at Queen's in Kingston, Janet and Joe headed out to their next foreign posting, this time in Africa.

From Harare in Zimbabwe, centre of an administrative region, Joe's responsibilities often took him to the Canadian missions in Pretoria, Cape Town, Lusaka, and Dar es Salaam. He made forty-one trips in three years. Janet accompanied him on his journeys whenever holidays in the International School, where she taught, allowed her to get away for a few days. Janet was now looking forward to each of their travel adventures in Africa as much as Joe had been looking forward to his trips in Europe thirteen years earlier.

Joe's education, training, career, and posting history resemble those of many of his 108 fellow technicians in the foreign service. The areas of responsibility have increased and broadened in the course of his career, but basic activities have not changed much. On postings abroad he spends most of his time on technical security duties; the rest he divides among installation, maintenance, and repair of telecommunications and telephone equipment and of personal safety and security equipment for embassy personnel. At headquarters he has to look after the same type of installations.

Of his twenty years in the foreign service, Joe has spent twelve in Ottawa and eight abroad, in London, Moscow, and Harare, He pointed out that he probably had longer home postings than did most of his fellow technicians. This situation was a matter of his and his wife's choice, and was not necessarily to everyone else's taste within their occupational group.

Janet and Joe have now returned to Ottawa. Their house is filled with souvenirs from around the world. For the moment they feel happily saturated with travel. But they don't exclude the possibility of another assignment within a few years. Even when Joe retires, the world will remain close by. Their daughter, Cathy, who had started to learn Russian while at school in Moscow and who recently finished university with a graduate degree in political science and Russian, has just passed the foreign-service exam. Her enthusiasm for the rotational life has convinced Janet and Joe that Janet's depressions in London have left no lasting scars on the children. Peter is about to graduate with a law degree. He probably won't write the exam, he has announced, adding that he may change his mind if life in Canada should become too predictable and monotonous.

Foreign-service life has many pitfalls, Janet said. She is still horrified at her own naïvety about possible problems when she and Joe decided to become internationally rotational. No one had given her directions through the maze, and she had not even imagined she might become disoriented. Unprepared to adapt to unexpected difficulties and unable to identify the conflicts she was struggling with, she almost destroyed her marriage and nearly ruined her husband's and her children's lives in order to escape from the turmoil of foreign-service life. But she scrambled out of the pit, she said, with her husband's help. Together they worked out solutions, allowing her and her family to benefit from the many positive aspects of Joe's career and to lead a life more stimulating and enriching than any other they can think of.

Joe settled back in his armchair and lit a pipe. 'This type of life is extremely hard on wives and children,' he said. Perhaps the most demanding duty and greatest challenge for anyone in his situation is the maintenance and repair not of telecommunications equipment, but of personal communications within a marriage and family. Ever since that critical November weekend in London, he had devoted his private life to reconciling his unusually demanding profession with a marriage and family threatened by exactly those demands. He had succeeded, he remarked, but only after having come dangerously close to the abyss.

He could not have continued his career in the foreign service if his marriage had broken up. He would never have forgiven himself for putting his profession ahead of wife and children. He quickly added that this issue was not only a moral one. In such a transitory life a happy marriage and family represent a portable and permanent home, an essential for the foreign-service employee. 'But a house and garden somewhere are pretty essential, too,' he added, looking to Janet for confirmation. She nodded, adding: 'And a piano!'

Foreign-Service Officer

Nicolas C.V. Broadwood remembers vividly his desire as a young boy to see all the countries identified on the world map his mother had fastened with blue thumbtacks to the wall above his desk. Now, at age forty-nine and twenty-four years into a career as foreign-service officer, he has seen many, but by no means all of them. He is not sure whether the map on the wall together with the subscription to *National Geographic* he received on his sixth birthday actually initiated his intense curiosity about foreign countries and cultures, or only strengthened what had been there. A certain amount of wanderlust was undoubtedly in his blood.

Born in Windsor, Ontario, shortly before his father, a chartered accountant, left for the war in Europe, he spent his first years with his mother, who had gladly interrupted her career as a home economics teacher in a Windsor high school to devote herself entirely to the upbringing of her son.

A second-generation Canadian of French origin on her father's side, she had, as a teenager, accompanied her parents on a voyage to Europe to see Britain and France, including the town of Granville in Normandy, where her father had been born. The two months in Europe, which had captured her imagination for years before the event and her memory for years after, remained the most exciting adventure of her life – and, to her regret, the only one of its kind.

Her husband opened another part of the world to her. Having been born around the turn of the century in China of Scottish missionaries he had spent his early childhood near Shenyang, chattering cheerfully in the local Chinese dialect, until his mother's serious illness convinced his father to take his family back to Canada for the somewhat less trying life in a Canadian church.

When Canada had entered the Second World War, the former missionary encouraged his son to do his duty for his country and sign up as a volunteer for the army, as he himself had done early on in the First World War. As soon as his son was called up, the Reverend Thurlow Broadwood promised to assume the duties of a father for the infant Nicolas.

Between the carefully nurtured Scottish connection, coupled with the family's life experience in China, on his father's side and the consciously preserved French element in his mother's background, young Nicolas grew up in a culturally diverse family. He marvelled at his beloved maternal grandfather's heavily French-accented English, and at his much-admired paternal grandfather's ease in writing Chinese characters. He felt utterly at home in both his parents' backgrounds, as long as he did not have to reveal it to his mocking classmates. Inevitably, laughter and jeering would break out at school whenever he was asked to explain once more the significance of his initials. Nicolas was generally considered an acceptable first name, but the initials C.V. remained a delicate issue. In a weak moment, Nicolas had confided to a school buddy that the the 'C' stood for Charles – not just any Charles, but Bonnie Prince Charlie – a permanent reminder of Nicolas's ancestors' gallant support of the Stuart Prince during his ill-fated battle at Culloden in Scotland 250 years earlier, an event that had precipitated Nicolas's family's hurried exodus from Scotland. Even harder to rescue from ridicule in the small English-Canadian community was his initial 'V.,' for Vinson, his mother's maiden name, which was to be pronounced in the French manner, with nasal sounds in both syllables and an emphasis on the second.

By the time his father returned from the war with books, maps, souvenirs, and a limitless supply of stories about foreign countries, Nicolas had already been listening for years to his paternal grandparents' tales of the Far East and to his maternal grandfather's memories of Europe. All their recollections had been illustrated in some form or another by back issues of the *National Geographic,* which had doubled as Nicolas's primer, and later by his precious copies, the arrival of each shiny new issue being the impatiently awaited event of the month.

Nicolas cannot recall when he began to dream of the foreign service as a career. It seems to have been at the back of his mind for as long as he can remember.

After four years of studies in history and international relations, earning him a BA from the University of Toronto, Nicolas felt he needed a change and enrolled for a year at the University of Grenoble to expand the knowledge of French he had acquired at high school in Windsor. Side-trips took him to Normandy and to Inverness, Scotland, 'for a certain amount of ancestor worship,' as he wrote to his parents. At the end of his course in France, he was granted a diploma certifying his fluency in reading, writing, and speaking French. He then toured Spain, Italy, Austria, Switzerland, and Germany in the company of a group of Canadian students who had all devoted a year to learning French.

As he boarded a ship of the Holland-America Line in Rotterdam to return to Canada and to university for law studies, he decided to be back in Europe at the earliest possible occasion, although he had to admit to himself that the plan was as shrouded in fog as the slowly receding shoreline of the continent.

Four years later, armed with a Bachelor of Law degree and in search of new horizons, he was notified that he had passed the foreign-service entrance examination. Not only Europe, but the entire world seemed to have moved within reach.

For the time being, however, his world consisted of a tiny room in the turn-of-the-century Daly Building, one of the twenty-odd structures in the heart of downtown Ottawa in which External Affairs maintained its offices, prior to the construction of the Lester B. Pearson Building. These initial ten months in the Legal Bureau, during which he felt he was mainly shifting drab files about, could have been disillusioning if it had not been for the friendship he struck up with six of his fellow probationary officers and their decision to rent jointly a rather run-down, but nevertheless comfortable house in Sandy Hill. Each of them had his own room and the run of the house. Half of the group were French Canadians with whom Nicolas kept up his French and whose parents invited the house-mates for long weekends in Montreal and Quebec City, where a growing number of girlfriends joined them for dinners in restaurants specializing in French cuisine.

Their domestic arrangements had to be dissolved a year later. Two of the occupants were about to get married, the result of successful weekend excursions to Montreal, and the remaining four officers were being sent abroad on their first assignments.

Nicolas found himself on the way to Cambodia, where the Canadian delegation to the International Truce Commission for Indo-China needed a French-speaking legal adviser, preferably a bachelor, since the war zone was close by. Nicolas set out with two young colleagues who had joined External Affairs when he had. One of them was going to Saigon, the other to Vientiane. As the clouds of war continued to mass around him, Nicolas sat in Phnom Penh, once again doing legal work. When he left Cambodia after fourteen months there, the two colleagues with whom he had gone to Indo-China were dead. One of them had perished on a plane that had disappeared between Saigon and Hanoi; the other one had died of a tropical disease. Nicolas had had a close call himself. During one of his visits to Vietnam a friend had invited him to dinner in a small restaurant known for its cuisine and frequented by Americans. An upset stomach kept Nicolas in his hotel, and the friend had cancelled the table reservation. That night, the floating restaurant on the Mekong River was blown up, killing everyone in it.

Having taken the Pacific route on his way to Cambodia, Nicolas returned to Canada by the Atlantic route, on the way stopping for a few days in Bangkok; Nepal, where he cycled through the streets of Kathmandu and gazed at the Himalayas; New Delhi; Tehran; Istanbul; and Milan, before climbing on a plane in Paris for the last leg of a journey that had taken him around the world.

Even before he had completed his few months in a Montreal hospital for 'medical debriefing' – his phrase for treatment of an intestinal tropical disease he had picked up in Phnom Penh – his personnel officer informed him that his request to be posted to Sweden had been granted. Nicolas had delightful memories of some of the female Swedish students with whom he had studied French in Grenoble, of their blue eyes, blonde hair, and marvellous good looks. His memory of his grandmother's advice, offered before he had set out for Grenoble, not to associate too closely with Swedish girls – or German girls, for that matter – as they tended to have a reputation as libertarians, was less vivid.

Stockholm seemed like a haven of sanity after Phnom Penh, except for the workload, which kept Nicolas running. As if his duties as second secretary were not quite enough, he was also the consul, a job that required travel outside the capital, often on weekends. During one of these consular trips, to Uppsala, where a Canadian medical student had been hospitalized following a car accident, he met Astrid Söderlund, the lawyer representing the Swede who had been involved in the accident that had left the young Canadian injured. The consular case dragged on, making several meetings necessary between Swedish lawyer and Canadian consul.

Astrid and Nicolas celebrated the student's release from hospital and the satisfactory conclusion of the Swedish-Canadian collision with their engagement. Seven months later, the time required to obtain Canadian security clearance for Astrid, a romantic midsummer wedding took place.

After having completed his four-year assignment in Stockholm, Nicolas returned to Ottawa, bringing home with him his blonde, blue-eyed wife, who was happily pregnant with their first child. The question of how to coordinate her own profession with her husband's had, at least for the time being, been superseded by the issues concerning imminent motherhood.

The initial months in a country and city where she knew not a soul other than her husband turned out to be very difficult. Astrid had not realized how much a person's sense of self depended on the affirmation of that self by other people – family, friends, and acquaintances. When she had left Stockholm, she had left behind everyone who had helped shape and confirm who she was. From being the centre of her parents' life, an important part of a group of old friends, and her own boss in her own legal practice, she had been thrown into a new environment where even a claim to a position on the periphery was tenuous. The new environment was simply unaware of her existence. In a way, her self had ceased to exist.

For Nicolas, however, Astrid's identity had not mysteriously dissolved in the course of their plane trip to Canada. Familiar with the people and the culture that had moulded her, and even more familiar with the culture he had brought her in contact with, he gently began to build a bridge between them. He bought books for her in great numbers, works of Canadian literature and history, and music, newspapers, and magazines. Astrid devoured it all. To balance the home seminar on Canadian studies, Nicolas insisted on making Swedish the family's second official language and ordered a small tide of books and magazines from Sweden to nurture Astrid's bond with her home and to strengthen his own link with her world. Without being conscious of doing so, Nicolas and Astrid had started to lay the foundation for a bicultural marriage.

After the birth of their first daughter, Astrid turned her full attention to the baby. She loved her new role as mother. Not even the most glamorous legal case could have lured her away from Annika, nor from Brigitta, their second daughter, born two years later. She slowly began to establish what she called the sandbox network: a group of mothers who dropped by with their toddlers for chats and cups of tea. Astrid enjoyed these light-hearted gatherings and was thrilled to discover that her little girls were gradually switching from their mother tongue, Swedish, to English when negotiating the ownership of building-blocks and stuffed animals with their English-speaking contemporaries.

Eventually Astrid's network of contacts began to expand beyond sandbox mothers. Nicolas's colleagues invited them over for cocktails and dinners. Astrid met more and more of his fellow officers and their wives, the younger ones among them as occupied with babies and toddlers as she was. Friendships began to blossom.

By the time Nicolas and Astrid put the small house they had bought three years earlier, upon their return from Stockholm, up for rent in preparation for a two-year posting to Beijing, Astrid felt comfortably at home in Canada and familiar with the country, its history, and – most of all – the people. In her luggage to China travelled the account of daily life in a hardship post, written by one of her favourite Canadian authors, Susannah Moodie. Although the hardship post described in *Roughing It in the Bush* had been Canada itself, Astrid considered the admirable attitude adopted by the author in extreme situations an asset that might be as valuable in China in the 1970s as it had been in Upper Canada in the 1830s.

Beijing was decidedly a hardship assignment. Housing conditions, food supply, health care, social and political climate, travel restrictions, and prolonged illnesses of every member of the family tested Nicolas's and Astrid's strength, as individuals and as a couple, and forced Nicolas repeatedly to evaluate his devotion to his career. During their darkest moments, Nicolas and Astrid tried to keep their spirits up by telling each other that they had plenty to compensate for their hardship: a chance to experience a different culture, to learn to speak a modest amount of Mandarin, to travel within Asia, and to establish friendships, with fellow Canadians and with members of other foreign services, that were bound to last since they had been forged in difficult circumstances. When they left China, they came to the conclusion that the decision to ask to be posted to that part of the world had been the right one. Even in the full knowledge of the enormous problems the posting would force them to face, they would choose it again.

Five years in Ottawa followed. Deputy director of a geographic division, Nicolas looked after relations with a group of African countries, a job that took him on long trips to his 'parish,' his area of responsibility.

Astrid began to feel a growing desire to return to her profession or to work in a comparable field. Enquiries sent to potential employers led inevitably to the answer that the wife of a rotational foreign-service officer was basically unemployable on a long-term basis. She got occasional contracts from the secretary of state's office for translations of legal documents from English into Swedish, and taught a few courses in introductory Swedish to foreign-service members on their way to postings in Stockholm, but remained without a career. She also missed being able to rely on two salaries to help meet the growing family expenses.

Nicolas offered to change his status in the service from rotational to non-rotational, as several of his colleagues had done in order to accommodate their wives' professional interests. He also volunteered to leave the foreign service altogether and to switch to another government department if doing so would give Astrid a better chance at finding employment.

While they pondered the question of how best to combine Nicolas's and Astrid's desire for a fulfilling occupation, an assignment to Abidjan caught them by surprise, and in the right mood to go abroad. The complicated task of coordinating two somewhat irreconcilable trades in one marriage could thus be mercifully postponed until after their return from the Ivory Coast.

As Nicolas was holding the posting confirmation in his hand, it dawned on him that this transfer to a French African country presented his children with a unique opportunity to learn French systematically. Having missed out on the early French-immersion program in Canada and most likely fated to miss out on the late immersion program as well because of further moves, Annika and Brigitta entered the French *lycée* in Abidjan equipped with no more than the daily hour of French instruction they had had during the first few years at English-Canadian elementary school.

Realizing that the girls would be in for a difficult period at school, Nicolas and Astrid had tried to prepare their daughters well for what awaited them at the *lycée*. In spite of their parents' predictions, both girls had eagerly agreed to change to the French system. But neither parents nor children had foreseen what was to come.

The need to live up to the rigorous demands and discipline of the French school system made Annika and Brigitta completely dependent on three to five hours of daily coaching. Overwhelming amounts of homework, day in and day out, with no breaks for weekends put enormous strain not only on the young pupils, but on their mother as well. Nicolas, tied up at the office from morning until night, joined Astrid as coach for their little girls as soon as he returned from the embassy. The entire foundation of the language had to be built while the children coped with the expectation that they perform at the same level as their classmates, whose mother tongue was French. Astrid likened Nicolas's and her own three-year labour in Abidjan to slipping a basement and a main floor under a house whose construction had started on the second storey.

Without Astrid's seven years of thorough French studies at her high school in Sweden and Nicolas's year in Grenoble, they could never have succeeded. The tireless dedication of their parental coaches enabled Annika and Brigitta to not only survive the French system (although they felt close to suffocation under the workload more than once) but earn high marks for their impeccable written and spoken French.

But the family had paid a price. Astrid called their three years in Africa a never-ending deluge of homework. Their entire life had been subordinated to school requirements. They had not seen half as much of the Ivory Coast and of neighbouring countries as they had intended to. Instead of exploring the fascinating world around them, they had all been staring intently at French grammar books. They deeply regretted having missed out on so much.

The family is back in Ottawa now. Nicolas has been assigned to a division in charge of policy analysis. He remains caught between his pleasure in the prospect of a Latin American posting and his desire to give up his rotational status so that Astrid can establish herself professionally.

Nicolas's interests, education, job history, and posting rhythm correspond to those of many of his 1,275 colleagues. He spent half of his
career in Ottawa, half in postings in Asia, Europe, and Africa, regularly
alternating between foreign and home postings. His duties and responsibilities have, of course, increased considerably with his rise in the
hierarchy. But the basic tasks, essential activities of a foreign-service officer, have remained the same.

While in Beijing, Nicolas had to observe, analyse, and report on
political, economic, and social developments in China and on trends in
China's foreign policy. He had to contribute to the implementation of
Canadian foreign-policy objectives. Through direct personal contacts
and invitations to luncheons and for cocktails and dinners, he was to
influence decision makers in the host country as well as foreign representatives, such as diplomats and journalists, to generate and maintain a
favourable attitude towards Canada in order to further Canadian interests. He had to assist Canadian official visitors to China by coordinating programs. Beyond these activities in the bilateral-relations program,
he had to exploit opportunities for promoting Canadian cultural products; influence local newspapers and broadcast media in their coverage
of Canada; promote meetings between Canadian artists, writers, journalists, and academics and their Chinese counterparts; act as bridge
between Canadian and Chinese authorities on exchange programs in
the areas of culture, education, and sport; and support a large number
of other programs promoted by the embassy.

The aim of headquarters and posts abroad is to promote Canadian
interests. Officers on home postings are expected to formulate policies
within the general framework of Canadian interests, while taking into
account the international environment in which they have to be pursued. Officers working abroad are expected to apply this policy in
accordance with instructions from home, while reporting on conditions
that influence their effectiveness.

Nicolas does not doubt that the foreign service is the ideal career for
him. But he points out that this is only part of his story. He pulls out of
his drawer a cartoon showing a receiving line at a diplomatic cocktail
party: in the foreground, an elegantly attired gentleman of remarkable
girth stands next to a shabbily dressed, haggard, and miserable-looking
woman and a scrofulous child, barefoot and in rags, and announces to

his guests, a glass of champagne in his hand: 'I have been in the public service thirty years at great personal sacrifice to my family!'

Military Guard

Master Corporal Jean-François Tremblay, dressed in the dark green pants and light green shirt of the Army, is keeping a close eye on the six monitors in front of him in a tiny, glassed-in cubicle at the entrance to the Canadian embassy in Prague, while talking through a window to a visitor who claims to have an appointment with the ambassador. The ambassador's secretary had just assured Jean-François over the phone that she has never heard of the person and that such an appointment does not exist. The visitor, obviously embarrassed, shrugs his shoulders, mutters something about mixed-up dates, and retreats. Leaning back in his swivel chair, Jean-François pushes it all the way against the wall to get a better view of the array of screens on the desk.

Jean-François Tremblay is not watching six soap operas at the same time, as he laughingly points out to me. He is not even watching six separate programs. Although each screen displays a different picture, all of them are part of the same program, closed-circuit television coverage of the entire embassy compound.

The job he is doing here, he says, is quite different from the work he did in Canada as a military policeman and represents a good change from previous routine. Military guards for the chancery of Canadian embassies are responsible for the security of personnel and property on the grounds. A threat to the safety of embassy personnel and property exists in every country and may originate with a variety of sources, from hostile governments and international terrorists to violent deranged individuals acting alone. The threat is not imagined; it is real, he adds. Ever since military policemen were assigned to the job of guarding embassies, ten members of the military police security guards have been officially honoured for acts of bravery on the job. Also those without medals will confirm that hardly a month goes by without an incident that has the potential for trouble.

The tasks required of a military policeman on duty abroad demand constant vigilance and alertness. 'To walk the embassy grounds alone at three o'clock at night takes a special kind of individual,' Jean-François explains. 'Remember the dark alleys city policemen have to patrol? It's the same thing. You never know what is lurking in the dark.'

Military policemen protect the Canadian embassies in the former Communist-bloc nations, where special vigilance was imperative – in Moscow, Warsaw, Prague, Budapest, Bucharest, and Belgrade. They also look after security at the missions in Beijing, Washington, London, and Paris.

Jean-François had always wanted to see the world. When the opportunity to become a military policeman opened up in Prague, he thought this was a good place to start his travels.

His family, originally from France, had settled in the Lac St Jean region of Quebec towards the end of the seventeenth century and had never left the province, let alone the continent, until Jean-François's elder brother was sent with the Air Force to the Canadian Forces Base in Lahr, West Germany. There he promptly got engaged to a German girl. Jean-François's father flew to the Black Forest to attend the wedding. Jean-François's mother claimed she could not leave the family bakery for so long, but admitted quietly to her husband that she would never entrust her life to an aeroplane. Jean-François, then sixteen and about to leave school in search of an interesting job, would have entrusted his life to any flying machine if it meant being able to look beyond the Lac St Jean region.

As soon as he had made up his mind to join the Army and to don the same smart-looking uniform his brother wore in the photos the family received from Lahr, the world of his quiet, uneventful childhood slowly began to fade behind what promised to become a more exciting life than any of his ancestors had led.

His brother, a military policeman, had spoken enthusiastically, first, about his training and, later, about his work. Jean-François decided to sign up for the same career as soon as he started his fourteen-week basic-training course outside of Montreal. He would have preferred to take the same course in Cornwallis, Nova Scotia, and thus see another part of the country. But there all courses were taught in English, and his was not quite up to that level. But he vowed to himself that he would switch to English at the earliest possible opportunity.

Training in his chosen trade followed at Camp Borden, Ontario. He requested to be assigned to the course for English Canadians and was accepted, thereby launching his bilingual career. In a three-week course he learned how to drive military vehicles, jeeps, patrol cars, and trucks. During the subsequent fourteen-week police training course, he moved on to lectures in military and criminal law, investigation techniques, and typing, report writing, first aid, and resuscitation methods. Ranking among the top three graduates of his class, Jean-François was entitled to the choice of his first assignment. He asked for Petawawa Base, where he eventually spent four years in training as a private and also began to practise his trade.

In the regular military force of 85,000, approximately 2,000 work as military policemen. Their job is to protect personnel and property and to maintain order and discipline in their military unit. Jean-François spoke about his work and the disciplinary problems a military policeman faces. 'Drugs in the military, that is handled well,' he said and pointed out how much more efficiently the military police can deal with any form of delinquency than the civil police can. 'My delinquents are familiar to me.' He knows almost everyone in his regiment. Regardless how grave the misconduct, the offender remains subject to military discipline. 'The guy fears his base commander and boss' and is more likely 'to smarten up' under the strict rule of military discipline than is a civilian delinquent. For the same reason, the life of a military policeman is considered less dangerous than that of a city policeman. Jean-François said he enjoyed his work and felt secure and comfortable in the small community.

His training completed, his career well on its way, and having been classified a bilingual military policeman following a six-month intensive English course, Jean-François married Sharon, a nurse from the Ottawa valley. Soon after their wedding, the couple moved to Kingston. A year later, Jean-François was sent to Cyprus.

This first foreign assignment, Sharon and Jean-François explained, whetted their appetite for overseas adventures. Jean-François had to leave Sharon and their baby daughter, Victoria, behind for six months. No soldier on a U.N. peacekeeping mission is allowed to bring his family along. But wives are entitled to one visit in Nicosia during their husbands' tour of duty in Cyprus. When Sharon returned to Kingston after two weeks in Cyprus, she told her parents, who had been looking after the baby during her absence, that she had 'caught the bug.' She was not referring to a particularly vicious Cypriot virus, but to a condition known among foreign-service members also as 'Itchy Feet Syndrome.' The afflicted crave life in foreign countries. Advanced cases require as treatment a quick succession of exotic assignments. Sharon's seemed to be a mild case, and in its early stages, but the symptoms could not be ignored.

In the autumn, after Jean-François's return to Kingston, when the Defence Department sent around the annual request for volunteers to serve as guards at embassies overseas, he put his name down. The initial part of the screening process was short and swift. As a young married couple with two small children – a new baby, Brian, had arrived in the meantime – and with no marital or drinking problems, they satisfied basic requirements for a posting abroad. After the Base Security Officer, in the course of an interview, had assured himself that he could recommend them as candidates, he forwarded their application to Defence Headquarters in Ottawa.

At the next stage of the selection process, headquarters asked for a new set of interviews, this time with a military social worker and a psychiatrist for Sharon. A thorough medical check-up was necessary for the entire family. Six months after Jean-François had signed the application papers, he arrived with Sharon in Ottawa for a two-week introduction to the job that was awaiting him in Prague and for briefing sessions for Sharon. Three months later, the entire family settled in an apartment hotel in the national capital for four weeks of intensive language training and further briefings. While a babysitter took care of their children, Jean-François and Sharon spent five hours each day with a language teacher, learning the intricacies of Czech vocabulary, grammar, and pronunciation.

When they finally landed in Prague, the young military policeman and his wife who had shared the first weeks of their language course were waiting for them at the airport. The drive into town showed them, beyond a doubt, that Czechoslovakia was not Cyprus.

Sharon admitted that the first six months in Prague were a miserable time for her. She found life so difficult she would have dearly loved to pack up and return to her comfortable staff quarters and life in Kingston. In Prague, she was living in staff quarters too, but it all felt as strange as did the language pouring out of radio and television set.

Venturing out into the streets or into the shops generated a feeling of having been displaced and being lost. The crowds, noisy streets, the grey shop windows, and the pollution hanging permanently over the city added to her misery.

Because there was nothing much to buy in the stores apart from canned goods, Sharon ordered most of their food from the Canadian Forces Base in Lahr. The most ordinary items in the food-order catalogue from Lahr began to seem like trade goods from paradise.

To entertain herself and the children, Sharon used to wander aimlessly in the centre of Prague, ride the streetcars, and travel to the outskirts of the city and back by bus. The highlight of the week arrived on Friday nights, when four of the five military guards and their wives got together for a pot-luck supper. Sharon spoke affectionately of all members of their group. 'We are a family,' she said, and added that they had all promised to stay in touch beyond this joint posting.

Jean-François confirmed that a strong community spirit does exist among the military guards and their families. He was quick to point out the reasons. Unlike the thousands of permanent foreign-service members, who hold a variety of jobs, military guards all share the same trade. They can look back on identical training and the same types of previous jobs, and similar careers lie in store for them in the future. Their shifts, which run from six o'clock to six o'clock, either for three days and two nights or for two nights and three days in a row, followed by five days off, make each of them aware that he is a link in a chain. This consciousness forges a powerful psychological bond between them.

A large majority of them are in their late twenties or early thirties, and all are married. Most have one or more young children. Each guard's account of his two or three years on overseas duty with the foreign service amounts to a family story, with all its ups and downs.

Under the fatherly guidance of Jean-François's head guard, who is the oldest member of the group, the young crew works and lives abroad under conditions so similar that even their reactions to the posting are consistent across the group. Jean-François's and Sharon's emotional responses to their new environment and gradual changes in their feelings resemble developments that most of their fellow guards and their wives underwent during their postings in the same country.

While the first year in a hardship post starts with a brief period of euphoria about the newness of everything, it tends to draw more negative reactions because predictability and comfort have been replaced by uncertainty and destabilizing strangeness all around. The second year is generally experienced as a much more enjoyable period, mostly because a certain amount of adjustment to new circumstances has taken place and partially because a genuine pleasure has been found in new friendships and an interest in local or neighbouring cultures, developed through travel and sight-seeing.

For families whose negative response during the first year does not shift to a more positive one in the course of the second year, the foreseeable end to the foreign assignment after two years often has a salutary effect on their mood.

The most important common denominator, however, under which military guards operate abroad and which sets them apart from all other members of the foreign service, is the fact that their overseas appointment will remain the only one of its kind in their military career. Whenever something goes wrong during the two years – and a lot of things do go wrong – they know they will soon be sailing back into the safe haven of Canada, their extended family, and the close-knit military community. The bitter experience, whatever its origin, may never be repeated. If a family has started the two years on the right foot, they will usually enjoy this precious single opportunity.

Jean-François sees this once-in-a-lifetime experience as an advantage guards have over the rotational members of the service. Most other guards agree with him. Such an assignment was considered a treat with few risks, even if things did not work out entirely. As a result, there was no shortage of volunteers, until recently. So many guards applied each year that everyone qualified could have only one turn abroad to give the others in the line-up a chance as well.

Over the last ten years, the queues have become much shorter. Young military policemen no longer seem to be as adventurous as their colleagues of an earlier generation. 'There is a greater desire to put down roots,' a senior member of the military police force told me. 'Our people are balking about moving, wives are working, kids, houses, schooling, income. The trend is to stay home.'

Despite such a trend, the Defence Department is required to supply

External Affairs with a certain number of military guards each year. Other considerations have also been at work, notably the cost of training them for embassy duties. Up until now, a guard's training and experience abroad were lost to the public service as soon as he returned to his original career. A new team had to be chosen, trained, and tried out, at heavy expense, at regular intervals. A way had to be found to retain the guard's expertise and put it to use beyond a single assignment.

'External Affairs liked the job we've done,' Jean-François said, and explained the latest development affecting the postings of all future military guards. A memorandum of understanding was signed in January 1991 between the departments of Defence and External Affairs to cooperate in the creation of a permanent unit of rotational military guards over the next few years. By 1995, 150 positions for military guards in more than 30 missions will be available.

Jean-François and Sharon have been debating whether to join this new team and to commit themselves to permanent rotationality ever since they had decided to stay in Prague for a third year, having greatly enjoyed their second. They had been able to travel to Vienna, Salzburg, Budapest, Belgrade, and even to Greece. During their third year in Czechoslovakia, Sharon went home to Canada to have their third child there – she was entitled under the foreign service directives – and returned with the new baby, Constance, and the two other children to a city that had begun to look familiar. To leave Prague, Europe, and the foreign service altogether will cause some considerable regrets, Sharon told me.

They have been discussing the issue with their fellow guards and wives for some time now. Every one of them appreciates the opportunities foreign-service life offers them, above all, travel, new friends, allowances, and the annual home leave to Canada. But they are also aware of the price they pay. 'We don't put down roots,' they say. Close relations with the extended family in Canada, and with friends and neighbours; owning a house; being part of a community; the children's school; the wife's job – all form a network of roots they are afraid to sacrifice in the course of a rotational life.

Among families with young children, 'the trend is against gypsy life,' Jean-François says. For the sake of their children, he and Sharon will probably decide to follow the trend. But they can well imagine themselves as a foreign-service reserve force, willing to wander once their children are past school age and have themselves put down roots deep enough to sustain them.

Secretary

Cheryl Tanya Overmiller admits that she was in a state of shock for about a year after she had arrived at External Affairs nine years ago, at the age of twenty-two. She could not understand why she had voluntarily exchanged her big, comfortable office and, if not exactly big, at least comfortable salary in the provincial legislative building in Winnipeg for a tiny, drab corner in the Lester B. Pearson Building in Ottawa and a salary so small she could not even afford her own apartment.

The only commodity available in large quantities at External Affairs seemed to be the people who demanded her services as a typist. She was assigned to six different officers at the same time, each of them calling for her with the same degree of urgency. The anger she experienced then is by now clearly mixed with detached amusement: 'There were so few secretaries – people kissed the ground under any one of them. I became a human typing machine. I was so miserable I started to smoke within two weeks of my arrival.'

If it had not been for the divisional secretary, who noticed how unhappy she was and mothered her with cups of coffee, the occasional flower next to her typewriter, and lunch breaks in the cafeteria, Cheryl does not think she would have lasted until her first posting, which finally came after two long years and provided the desperately needed relief from a work environment she had found barely tolerable. Two years in London turned her earlier conviction that she had made a disastrous mistake when joining the foreign service into the certainty that she had made the right decision after all, despite the shortcomings, of which she remained painfully aware.

Born in Swift Current, Saskatchewan, Cheryl had never had any major ambition beyond becoming either an elementary school teacher like her father, a post–Second World War immigrant from Germany who had changed his name Obermuller to Overmiller, or a secretary like her mother, a third-generation Canadian of Ukrainian descent. Having completed high school, she did not cherish the prospect of going to school until the day of her retirement, not even in the slightly more desirable role of teacher. She settled for secretarial school.

After her father's sudden death, her mother returned to her native Winnipeg, a move Cheryl welcomed because she suddenly had the pick of a number of attractive-sounding jobs. For the next four years she was content with her work as secretary to one of the provincial MLAs. But, when the novelty began to wear thin as her tasks grew repetitious, she wondered how much she would continue to enjoy herself in the same job for the next forty years. Besides, the chances of meeting eligible men in her office were not exactly awesome, considering the host of grey spinsters keeping each other company in the cafeteria during their coffee breaks.

Skimming over job-opportunity columns in the newspaper, Cheryl came across an advertisement for foreign-service secretaries. She knew nothing about the service and had never seen any Canadian city other than Swift Current and Winnipeg, let alone a foreign city or country. But the advertisement sounded tempting, and she was eager to try something new, if possible something with a drop of adventure in it. She sent in her application, was called for an interview, underwent a stenography and typing test and an examination by a psychologist, and was accepted. She felt greatly honoured, since this was a nationwide competition and she had been chosen as a member of the small Manitoba contingent.

The national capital struck her as rather provincial, but with metropolitan rental fees. She was forced to share with a fellow secretary a miniature two-bedroom apartment in a gloomy downtown apartment hotel that must have seen its days of splendour half a century earlier. Her salary had dropped by one-third from its Winnipeg level. She could hardly afford a movie on the weekend in order to recover from the week, during which she remained practically chained to her typewriter, except for the occasional break to photocopy documents.

Every three to five weeks she was moved to another division, five of them altogether in her first seven months in the department. She saw External Affairs as a factory with human wheels turning constantly, and herself as a spare cog caught up in a heartless and mindless mechanism. She said she did not know whether to cry or to laugh on the day she found an administrative notice on her typewriter informing her that the department provided the services of a counsellor for cases of emotional and other forms of personal problems.

Cheryl did use the services of counsellors. But the individuals in question had not been officially assigned to that task. Other young secretaries who had joined the ranks at about the same time she had gradually got to know each other, had lunch together – if the workload permitted – and poured their hearts out to each other, establishing a kind of mutual counselling service. Every one of them was disillusioned and considering leaving. Their growing friendship became an oasis in the desert of their office life. A group of older, motherly, single secretaries took pity on the young arrivals, and invited them home to their apartments for dinners and slide shows of their previous postings; they predicted relief once the first overseas assignment came around.

Two years in London did come to Cheryl's rescue. She still did not particularly enjoy her work, although it turned out to be more varied in the high commission than at headquarters, since it included the more entertaining protocol duties. But there were so many attractive sides to her life outside the office that she was prepared to put in eight hours a day typing if she could have the rest of the day and the weekends free for living.

Living for her consisted of the friendship of an ever-growing number of people inside and outside the mission, male and female, Canadians and members of the large international community. It also meant being invited to the homes of people who had lived through the Blitz in London and who had experienced the turmoils of Europe during the two world wars. Cheryl never tired of their stories. There was also a limitless number of historic sites to visit in and around London, not to mention a network of pubs, historic as well as contemporary, that could be visited in the company of jolly local or foreign friends.

With invitations for lunch, tea, supper, picnics, movies, and outings of every conceivable kind pouring in, Cheryl felt like a member of a large family. She no longer had any doubts that she had finally found, if not precisely the ideal job, at least the ideal life, a perfect by-product of an imperfect career.

When Ted, one of her British friends, proposed marriage, she was faced with the choice between him and her foreign-service life. Aware of how much this life meant to her, she opted for it, not for the work, she emphasized. But Cheryl resented the fact that she had to choose at all. Why could she not have it both ways, marriage and career, as so many other women had?

She welcomed a posting to Hong Kong as a new beginning after the emotionally draining experience with Ted, hoping that the wealth of new impressions would help her get over her feelings of pain and guilt and would allow her to forget the whole heart-breaking end of a relationship. But Ted's letters showed that he had not come to terms with her decision. He suggested a compromise. He could ask for a transfer to Hong Kong for himself, a request that would most likely be granted. His stay in the same city would give them a chance to get to know each other a little better. No strings attached, as far as he was concerned – he would not insist on matrimony if Cheryl did not like the idea. Cheryl, still lonely in the large city and homesick for London and all the friends she had left behind, agreed to the arrangement, only to discover eighteen months later that the same painful choice had to be made all over again. She was being posted to Nigeria, where Ted could definitely not be sent by his company.

The first ten months in Nigeria proved to be extremely difficult for her. She came close to an emotional crisis several times. Life in Lagos, the heat, the noise, the food, her apartment, her new boss, even her colleagues in the mission – all of it seemed impossible ever to adjust to. But, hardest of all, she found, was getting used to single life again. In the course of several lonely weekends, she seriously considered phoning Ted to tell him that she would finally accept his standing marriage proposal. But the prospect of a home-maker's existence in a small community outside of London instead of her present life stopped her. On Monday mornings, she usually felt relieved that she had not phoned Ted to bail her out. She knew she would have regretted it.

During a home leave to Ottawa, a year after she had arrived in Lagos, she met Michael, a young administrative officer who had just received his posting confirmation to Nigeria. Both admit that it was love at first sight. They took the same flight to their posting, and three months later they got married. The following year their son, Andrew, was born.

Cheryl said she had never been happier in her life than during that time. She had united under one roof husband, child, and career. Maternity leave allowed her to stay with her baby, but she was not cut off from the mission. Towards the end of her leave, she hired a young Nigerian woman to look after her little boy during office hours and gladly went back to the desk she had left shortly before the delivery date.

Together with Michael and their young son, Cheryl is now back in Ottawa and works in the Legal Bureau at headquarters. She takes turns with Michael picking up Andrew from day care every day and intends also to share with him the next round of maternity leave, to which they will be entitled soon for the birth of their second child. Both of them are pleased with their status as a 'tandem couple' and have put in a request for an assignment to Brussels next, where one of them can work at the mission to the Common Market, and the other at the delegation to NATO.

Many of the 398 rotational secretaries at present employed by External Affairs are familiar with the type of problems Cheryl had to face. Although the majority of them remain single, whether or not by choice, they share with Cheryl an educational background and a training and posting history. A two-year posting rhythm and two or three foreign assignments in a row, alternating with one posting in Ottawa, have been the unwritten rule for secretaries over the past few years.

While abroad, a secretary at Cheryl's level, classified in the hierarchy as 'Secretary 2,' works for two officers simultaneously, typing telexes, letters, and memoranda from dictation or from dictaphones; preparing routine replies to letters of enquiry; making photocopies; looking after the daily calendars for the officers to whom she is assigned; keeping files up-to-date; sorting and distributing daily incoming mail; answering telephone enquiries; taking messages; sending out invitations on behalf of the embassy; and replying to invitations for the officers. She also fills in during the absence of other secretaries.

While in Ottawa, she spends most of her time typing letters, memoranda, and telexes for sometimes as many as six to eight officers. More senior secretaries work for more senior officers and are assigned to small numbers of them.

Contemplating her story, Cheryl is still not entirely without bitterness about the way her first few months in the department were handled. It was a nightmare for her, and in her opinion a completely unnecessary one. None the less, she says, she did meet her best friends during that sad period and she owes External Affairs for having met her husband. She makes it clear that she has remained with the service not because of job satisfaction – there is not too much of that, she remarks, with a touch of contempt in her voice – but because she greatly enjoys travelling, living abroad, and getting to know foreigners.

Cheryl considers herself lucky to be able to combine marriage, family, and work. Many of her fellow secretaries, she tells me, had to choose between marriage and their foreign-service life, and she adds wistfully that she knows painfully well what a cruel choice that can be.

3

The Selection Process

In the late 1980s, a one-page document circulated in the Lester B. Pearson Building, bearing the heading 'Foreign Service Exam.' Among the twelve tasks to be completed were a number of essays on a variety of subjects, among them:

1 A history of the papacy from its origins to the present day, concentrating especially, but not exclusively, on its social, political, economic, religious, and philosophical impact on Europe, Asia, America, and Africa.

2 An evaluation of the emotional stability, degree of adjustment, and repressed frustrations of Alexander of Aphrodisias, Ramses II, Gregory of Nicea, and Hammurabi, based on each of the author's written works and to be quoted from the original language without translation.

3 A thesis on the development and significance of human thought in comparison with the development and significance of other kinds of thought.

Twenty minutes were granted for each essay.

The discerning reader of this document guessed correctly that it was a parody. A group of high-sprited young foreign-service officers who had recently passed the genuine entrace exam could be suspected to be behind this entertaining variation.

The foreign-service selection process is more complex than this 'exam' suggests. A special entrance procedure has been designed for each occupational group.

Candidates for the Officer category are subjected to the most demanding, rigorous, and time-consuming scrutiny that candidates for any job in the public service in Canada have to undergo.

Although an average of 4,000 Canadian citizens write the entrance exam annually – these figures rose in 1989 to 5,165 and in 1990 to an all-time high of 6,013 – details of the nature of this comprehensive test remain shrouded in mystery, giving rise to colourful myths which gather intensity and drama each October when the exam is once again offered by the Public Service Commission.

The entire evaluation process can be compared to an obstacle course. The candidate has to clear five clusters of obstacles, each of them with the potential to disqualify a participant: a written examination, an oral assessment, the final selection, medical clearance, and security clearance. Of the 6,013 candidates who entered the race in 1990, 80 were ultimately hired.

The foreign-service written exam can be taken in every Canadian university and in every Canadian mission abroad. Announcements of the date and exact location are made several weeks in advance in universities, Public Service Commission offices, and overseas missions.

Qualified to sit the exam is every Canadian citizen with a bachelor's degree in any discipline from a recognized university, completed no later than June of the year following the written exam. There is no age limit for participants in the competition, and applicants in their forties and fifties are not uncommon.

In the past decades the written exam has been reviewed and revised every few years to the point where foreign-service veterans are able to entertain each other with stories of their various rites of passage, each of them differing from the next, depending on the vintage year of entry into the service.

Changes to the written portion, among them the need for a written application, were introduced in 1990 for the 'Post-Secondary Recruitment Campaign,' as the Public Service Commission called the cross-country exercise. Until then, applications for admittance to the exam had not been required. Any university graduate was welcome to walk into the examination hall in any Canadian university of his or her choice, pick up a copy of the test paper, and try his or her luck. Only those candidates who wanted to sit the exam at an overseas mission had to notify that particular mission no later than two days in advance. Some of the procedures relating to the exam have changed recently.

As of October 1990, every candidate has to complete the 'Public Service Canada Application for Employment Form' and has to answer questions about his or her education, academic and linguistic achievements, community and volunteer work, previous employment, and general interests. A record of university marks has to be attached to the application, together with a list of the courses taken during the current academic year if the candidate is still enrolled at a university. These documents are to be submitted eight days prior to the written exam to the university or mission where the would-be candidate intends to write the test.

Under the new regulations, the written part of the competition consists of three different tests. The 'Entry-Level Officer Selection Test,' or ELOST, is designed to measure general cognitive ability and to assess a candidate's verbal, numerical, and reasoning ability with 125 multiple-choice questions. The 'Written Communication Test' is an attempt to evaluate a candidate's ability to communicate in writing. He or she is asked to write a 400-word summary of a given 2,000-word text. The quality of that summary is judged on the basis of grammar, spelling, punctuation, style, and content coverage. Finally, the 'Foreign Service Knowlege Test' is intended to measure the candidate's general knowledge of Canada, and of international relations, with 75 multiple-choice questions.

During previous years the written part of the exam was limited to a single multiple-choice test with no fewer than 150 questions on Canadian history, politics, and economics, and on international relations. Subtests were supposed to check a candidate's knowledge of specific political, economic, trade, and immigration issues, as well as his or her knowledge in the area of international development assistance.

Every one of these 150 questions enjoyed the status of a miniature state secret. The Public Service Commission, together with External Affairs, where most of the questions originated, took every conceivable precaution to guard the secrets, especially since, every year, questions from the previous year were used again. If the federal agencies were under the impression the test questions could be considered safe, provided the test papers were not allowed to leave the examination room, they were mistaken. At least one candidate revealed, after sitting the exam, that his photographic memory had allowed him to memorize 132 of the 150 questions. He had then typed them out and passed them on to a few of those intending to sit the following year's exam, of course in the hope that the Public Service Commission would continue its practice of recycling a previous year's questions.

Occasionally, some questions – considered unsuitable or having had too much publicity to be of any further value – are published in handbooks offering details on the foreign-service exam.

Among the 'retired' questions made available to the public can be found a few treasures, such as:

Special Drawing Rights were created by the International Monetary Fund in an effort to:
1. force upward the official price of gold
2. facilitate international payments through the introduction of a new reserve asset
3. inhibit the subsidization of trade in agricultural products
4. facilitate trade between Western nations and the state-trading economies of the Communist bloc.

Some questions acquire instant fame and therefore do not survive beyond one exam session. In the 1987 multiple-choice test, candidates enhanced or diminished their chance of being admitted to the foreign service by their ability to name the Canadian hockey player who had, at that stage, scored the largest number of goals in the history of Canadian hockey. Approximately 4,000 candidates leaked the question, together with the correct answer. Having lost its test value under these circumstances, the question did not reappear the following year. It also remains the favourite example successful and unsuccessful participants use in an attempt to demonstrate the questionable merit of what some of them call a mere quiz.

Most candidates who emerged from this pre-1990 type of written exam say that it is not knowledge that is being tested. No one except the expert would know, for example, what percentage of world wealth is owned by women, or be able to identify the leading Canadian producer of flight simulators. The test, they insist, measures the candidate's intelligence by asking him or her to select the one correct answer from among a collection of subtly or blatantly wrong ones.

Others describe it as a long game of Trivial Pursuit. 'I am a trivia buff,' one candidate told me after he had come away from the written test and all subsequent hurdles with flying colours. He had enjoyed himself enormously, and almost seemed to regret that success had barred him for all time from further pleasurable rounds. Another successful candidate loathed what he perceived to be a mindless guessing-game. He confessed to me that he had seriously wondered while circling correct answers whether he wanted to settle down professionally with people who constructed such primitive measuring devices. Eventually he did settle down in External Affairs, but could not conceal his contempt for the nature of at least the written portion of the exam.

Whether such criticism of the written exam was considered justified or not, in the late 1980s the Public Service Commission and External Affairs seemed to have recognized that the multiple-choice test was, at best, a one-sided and limited measuring device. The decision was taken to broaden the areas in which a candidate's qualifications would be tested. The first part of the newly introduced written exam, the ELOST, evaluated the applicant's quality of abstract and logical thinking in the areas of arithmetic operations, vocabulary, and memory and reasoning power. The 'Written Communication Test' reintroduced appraisal of the art of writing coherent sentences, an essential requirement for foreign-service officers and a severely neglected skill ever since essays had been dropped from school and university test papers in favour of the more objective and more easily evaluated multiple-choice question.

How do candidates fare on the foreign-service obstacle course? The written exam constitutes the most merciless portion of the entire selection process. More than 90 per cent of those who enter the race falter at this first set of hurdles. Candidates who fail can rewrite the exam every year. Many people do write it more than once. A number of young people have sat the exam five or more times before succeeding or giving up altogether.

Those with the highest overall marks, an average of 5 to 7 per cent of all entrants, are invited for an oral assessment. It normally takes place in January or February of the year following the October exam and consists of three parts: a written forty-five minute essay on a political, economic, immigration, or international development subject; an interview; and a group simulation exercise.

All successful candidates agree that the simulation exercise is not only the most intelligently designed part of the exam, but also their favourite, despite the considerable nervous strain it tends to generate. A group of three to five candidates is given in writing a set of data, such as a brief summary of the social structure and political and economic conditions in a fictitious country on an equally fictitious continent. In a recent exam, the country in question had been named 'Erehwon,' which some observant candidates (or fans of Samuel Butler, perhaps) identified immediately as 'Nowhere' spelled backwards. The group was asked to negotiate and propose a solution to a simulated problem in that country.

A team of three or four senior foreign-service officers and a personnel officer watch without interrupting and judge members of each group for their ability to absorb the given data quickly and accurately; the quality of their oral presentations; the judgment shown in assessing the advantages and disadvantages of a suggested solution; the ability to analyse, communicate, negotiate, listen, persuade, propose and defend a position, and compromise with the majority's view; as well as their ability to establish and maintain interpersonal relations with members of the group during several hours of debate.

Candidates and examiners claim that this part of the exam reveals more about the personality of each candidate than any other portion of the selection process. Several successful candidates described to me some members of their group who, in an all-too-obvious attempt to outshine everyone else with a demonstration of dazzling knowledge or leadership qualities, ultimately failed. The examiners are looking for team players, not for prima donnas.

In the course of the personal interview the applicants are often asked why they want to join the foreign service, how they would describe the tasks assigned to External Affairs, and in what way they consider their own abilities and achievements a possible asset to the service. The written essay is expected to assess candidates' suitability for one of the streams – political/economic, trade, immigration, or development assistance – for which they have been preselected based on the results of the written exam.

Once candidates have passed this triple hurdle, the selection committee evaluates all the additional information they have provided, including academic background, summer work experience, volunteer or community work, and, in a fair number of cases, previous employment.

Candidates who have cleared these major obstacles have to undergo a physical and psychological examination and, in the fifth and final round, a security check, a process that can take months and sometimes more than a year if the candidate has lived abroad.

Once medical and security clearances have been obtained, the candidates are handed the coveted trophy, a position as 'FSI-D,' that is, 'Foreign Service Officer 1, Developmental Stage.' The candidates will remain on probabtion for a year and receive training within External Affairs. They will be assigned to several divisions in a row, perhaps starting out in a geographic division, such as Southeast Asia, then switiching to a functional division, for example, export control or fisheries, before moving on to legal affairs. Candidates are supposed to be trained in as large a variety of areas as possible during this initial stage in their careers. Supervisors keep a close eye on performance and decide at the end of the developmental year whether the candidates are fully qualified to be accepted permanently into the foreign-service ranks.

The Canadian Foreign Service Institute was opened in the fall of 1992 to provide, among other things, further training for junior officers.

The academic background of FSI-DS varies. In recent years an average of 38 per cent held Bachelors' degrees, 34 per cent Masters' degrees (10 per cent of them in public or business administration), 13 per cent law degrees, and 5 per cent doctorates. Certain academic disciplines, such as international relations, economics, business administration, law, history, and political science, are usually well represented.

During their first weeks and months in External Affairs, young foreign-service officers speak with a mixture of horror and amusement about their experiences during the selection process. The whole procedure, which can stretch out over a year or two, makes candidates feel as though they are being poked, pinched, twirled, twisted, squeezed, and turned inside out and upside down until External Affairs has shed the last uncertainty about each one of them. The wife of a new officer offered her opinion on why the department needed so much time to make a final decision: 'Obviously they don't want to buy a pig in a poke.'

The screening of applicants for other occupational groups differs considerably from that of applicants for the Officer category.

Candidates for the administrative-officer group have to pass a general aptitude test administered by the Public Service Commission and, if found qualified, are hired on the basis of their post-secondary education, preferably university, or on the basis of previous work experience.

External Affairs has traditionally used the Armed Forces as a recruiting-ground for communicators and electronic technicians. Army graduates have always been considered reliable and well trained and have the added advantage of possessing an up-to-date security clearance, which does not require renewal upon entry into the foreign-service position of communicator or electronic technician. These are the only two occupational groups for whom this rule applies. With the advent of computerized telecommunications, communicators are not being hired, and their numbers are being gradually reduced through attrition.

Electronic technicians continue to be hired. Because of the high degree of sensitivity of their work, candidates who apply from outside the public service not only have to prove their professional qualifications, but are subjected to exceedingly time-consuming security checks. It can take two years before such clearance is obtained. The best chance for a technician to enter the foreign service remains by way of the Armed Forces.

Clerks are recruited in much the same way as secretaries. In order to give as many Canadians as possible the chance to work for External Affairs and to represent abroad the various regions of the country, the Public Service Commission places advertisements in community colleges, universities, secretarial schools, and newspapers in large cities. Applicants have to produce proof that they possess the required qualifications before taking the General Aptitude Test. Clerks take a basic clerical exam, and secretaries have to pass tests in stenography and typing. All candidates have to undergo physical and psychological examinations as well as security checks. Once a candidate has been found qualified, External Affairs offers a job in which the new recruit will remain on probation for six months.

Every time changes to the foreign-service exam are introduced, young Canadians across the country who are ready to jump into the race as soon as the magic date comes around once again wonder whether the new requirements and procedures are nothing more than a rearrangement of the various obstacles, or whether new hurdles have been introduced that are insurmountable except to a handful of high-flyers. The

Public Service Commission, in a pamphlet describing details of the exams, offers these words of encouragement: 'The pass mark on each of the tests will be established at a level which ensures that there is a sufficient number of candidates for the vacancies to be filled.'

4

Foreign-Service Types

'What made you want to join the foreign service?' Few members of any such service have not been asked this question in the course of their career. Most Canadian foreign-service employees first encounter it during their entrance interview. Many of them come prepared with a response: 'I want to serve my country!' Examination officers express weariness with this all-too-common reply. This sort of purportedly self-less motivation, they insist, usually disguises a host of other reasons. They favour candidates who admit honestly to slightly more selfish motives.

Why do people want to embrace a life that is permanently in transition? 'Classification does not explain the individual psyche' – the Swiss psychiatrist C.G. Jung could have had foreign-service employees in mind when he made this statement in his book *Psychological Types*. Members of few professions seem to defy classification into types quite as much as foreign-service employees. And yet, when it comes to one particular aspect of their personality, namely, the reasons behind their choice of career, a large majority of them (by no means all) provide data that point to three key components in what amounts inevitably to a tangled mass of contributing factors for such a decision: 1 / childhood fantasies or childhood experiences involving foreign countries and cultures; 2 / acquisition of professional skills required by the foreign service, whether originally intended for the service or not; and 3 / desire for satisfaction of specific social needs.

Vocational choices are generally influenced by a large number of considerations, such as family history, social and economic background, education, training opportunities in the community, and peer pressure. A close look at individual foreign-service employees reveals more subtle shadings. As recent research suggests, heredity can play an important, if not decisive role in the career decision-making process. Whether as a result of genetic predisposition, family tradition, or a combination of both, an extraordinarily large number of public foreign-service employees have parents and grandparents who were public servants, and a strikingly large number have grandparents who were missionaries. Professional and amateur world travellers are equally well represented among the immediate ancestors of foreign-service personnel.

A remarkable percentage of foreign-service members also mention environmental factors as the basis of their career choice. In many interviews, foreign-service members indicated that the attitude a family and its social environment maintain towards the world beyond the immediate community – in particular, towards foreign countries and cultures – imposes on a child three distinct types of relationships with the outside world. These types can be represented by three creatures noted for their relationship with the world around them: 1 / the oyster, locked in a shell, clinging to a rock, immobile and unaware of its relationship with its environment; 2 / the owl, open-eyed and generally watchful, moderately mobile, and reputedly wise and aware of itself in relation to its surroundings; and 3 / the migratory bird, by definition a world traveller, simultaneously having a bird's-eye view of its environment and a down-to-earth familiarity with feeding- and nesting-grounds wherever it roams.

Foreign-service members of all ages and occupational groups pointed out that their growing awareness during childhood and youth of one of these attitudes in their family and social surroundings strongly influenced their decision to throw their lot in with the foreign service. Stories they tell about their childhood allow for the classification of a majority of foreign-service personnel into these three basic types.

Oyster

'You know, I grew up in Manitoba, a kid playing in the mud on a small farm. And a few years later I stood on Tiananmen Square in Beijing.' Ted radiates contentment. His early years were happy, a prairie boy's childhood: a white-washed farmhouse, the smell of a wood fire, the aroma of home-made bread, a dog, cattle, a one-room schoolhouse, summers rich with harvest and winters filled with sleigh rides. But, as he was growing older, he began to long for the world beyond his father's wheat fields, to go farther than Portage-la-Prairie, the nearest town, which his parents visited once a year, and the farthest they had ever taken him. The radio spoke of huge cities and countries far away, with different languages and entirely without snow, even in winter.

The Army came to Ted's rescue. An uncle had suggested he sign up. Ted remembers a sense of freedom he had never experienced before when he saw the Great Lakes for the first time. He began to dream of oceans. Ten years later, after having moved in Canada from one Army base to the next, he applied to External Affairs. His quiet, so far imagined love for the sea began to flourish. To reach Paris, his first overseas posting, he crossed the Atlantic by boat with his wife and two small sons.

In the course of his twenty-four years in Canadian missions abroad, among them Beijing, Santiago de Chile, Rome, Cairo, and Kuala Lumpur, Ted swam in the Mediterranean, waded in the Indian Ocean, sailed in the South China Sea, and steered a motor-boat off the coast of Chile, not to mention his encounters with other, no less spectacular waters, such as fishing on the Nile and floating in a boat down the Yangtse: 'You don't do this sort of thing on your holidays when you live in Manitoba,' he said and added: 'I have visited sixty countries. I owe a fair amount to External Affairs.'

Not all oysters freed from their confining shells swim quite as easily as Ted. The desire to explore the world is not always accompanied by the ability to live and work in a strange and often hostile environment. Many oyster types initially find it extremely difficult to cope with foreign cultures and usually go through periods of considerable strain before they manage to glide through uncharted waters, especially when hardship posts seem to conspire against them. Not infrequently, a foreign-service employee showing signs of foundering has to be rescued and brought back to the safety of a familiar environment.

More the exception than the rule could be considered the oyster type who eagerly ventures out into the great promising unknown, but grows increasingly intolerant of foreign cultures. One such foreign-service member reached the point where, after sixteen years of foreign-service life and two failed marriages, he found the world, particularly the non-Canadian portion of it, wanting, proclaimed a strong personal leaning towards law and order, dismissed cultural diversity, and retired to his small home town somewhere in western Canada, slamming the shell shut behind him.

Owl

Moira remembers that she had just started Grade 5 when the first immigrant children from rural Sicily arrived at her school, a sensation in the small Irish neighbourhood in Toronto. 'Those kids spoke funny, looked funny, and smelled funny,' she recalls. Moira leaves no doubt about it: the situation had potential for ethnic tension. But her favourite teacher intervened. Mr Hancock deserves all the credit for opening his students' hearts and minds to the little strangers. Thus he not only turned the tide in favour of successful integration of the Italian children – and for the wave of German immigrants on their heels – but awakened in Moira a lifelong fascination with foreign cultures.

Her parents' interests were on her side. Her father had briefly served during the Second World War and had brought back Danish friends, who read Hans Christian Andersen's fairy tales to her, and Dutch friends, a rich source of stories about Britain where they had spent the war. Moira could never get enough of her parents' friends and their tales. As she said, 'They were so different from anything I knew.' With growing enthusiasm she read her way through the public library's complete holdings of books on life in foreign countries.

When she left school at age seventeen, she wanted to experience first-hand what she had only read about other parts of the world. She tried to join the Air Force. But, for some reason, she was turned down and spent seven unhappy years squeezed behind a typewriter in a small industrial enterprise on the outskirts of Toronto, until she came across the advertisement for a foreign-service secretary. The rest is her foreign-service history: twenty-three years of postings to several European capitals, where she finally caught up with the world that had produced Dutch, Danish, British, German, and Sicilian childhood friends and stories, long before she had been able to see their countries of origin with her own eyes. Postings to Asia, Northern Africa, and Latin America have added more friends and tales to her original collection.

Migratory Bird

Richard does not recall a single year during his childhood and youth when he did not head out to yet another foreign country, either to live or to visit. 'My parents moved twenty-one times. I loved it,' he explains, still filled with enthusiasm. His father represented a large international company and went from country to country, exploring the possibilities for opening up new offices. To Richard's delight, each continent had one city as the company's and therefore his family's home base, a place to return to for holidays at least once a year. In Europe, London was such a point of permanent reference. He was born there, and to this day he counts London as his home.

He is no less familiar with the continent. He started school in Paris, completed Grades 1 and 2 in a French school, Grades 3 and 4 in an Italian school in Milan, and Grades 5 and 6 in Madrid, switching easily from language to language throughout those years. During this European period, as he calls his childhood, he saw every European country, except Albania, including such delightful oddities as the principality of Andorra and the republic of San Marino.

The Asian period followed, with two years in that continent's home base of Hong Kong, one year in Bangkok, two years in Tokyo, and two years in New Delhi. Travelling in Asia proved to be more complicated than in Europe. But Richard's parents used every school holiday and every other occasion, winding their way from country to country by car, ship, and plane. When he graduated from a British school in India, his parents returned to North America, switching back and forth between the continental home bases New York, Mexico City, San Francisco, and Toronto while Richard attended Yale University. With a Master's degree in international relations and six languages at his command, he passed the foreign-service exam on his first try.

The passion for travelling instilled in him by his parents still has not left him. But he wants to make it clear that travelling is only part of a deeper love. 'If this passion for travelling were all, I could have opened a travel agency or joined an oil company,' he points out with a slight touch of contempt in his voice. He wants primarily to live in a country, 'to see behind the tourist façade.'

He also enjoys a certain rhythm that allows him to alternate between exploring a new, unknown culture and settling back into the familiar and comfortable world of North America, provided a posting to Ottawa does not last too long. His emotional well-being depends on exposure to other cultures. Foreign countries invigorate him. Sitting at home too long, he says, 'means stagnation and cobwebs.'

The urge to break out of a protective shell that is, at best, experienced as narrow and confining and, at worst, as suffocating; the desire of the owl type to explore a world known to exist and deeply yearned for, but out of reach; the wish to continue a migratory lifestyle instilled in childhood – these vastly different motivations all lead to the doors of External Affairs.

Other considerations play a powerful role as well. During the stage in life in which a growing awareness of needs, interests, abilities, values, and opportunities begins to combine to form a basis for the choice of a profession, a large number of future foreign-service employees shape and mould their interests and aptitudes into marketable skills at school and at university. In many cases, skills that are known to be required by the foreign service are carefully identified in advance and polished.

Each year a broad spectrum of professional expertise is offered to External Affairs by a large number of applicants; in return, External Affairs offers a huge field where that expertise can be used to the benefit of the organization and to the employee's sense of satisfaction and fulfilment. Asked during the interviews which aspect of a foreign-service career promised to satisfy their vision of the most desirable lifetime job, foreign-service employees offered information which permits classification of a majority of them into three further groups, depending on each person's predominant values, interests, and skills: public servant, internationalist-cosmopolitan, and anthropologist-linguist.

An amazingly large number of foreign-service members admitted openly that they had chosen their careers first and foremost because they preferred the secure public service to the uncertain world of private business. Others were seeking the most appropriate forum for their interests in international relations. Yet another group was looking for a chance to study languages and cultures, an endeavour many of them had already started at school or at university. A good many are pursuing in their career a combination of several of these opportunities.

Public Servant

A glow of satisfaction has spread over Betty's face. 'I am the fourth-generation public servant in my family. My great-grandfather started the tradition a hundred years ago,' she tells me. Growing up in Ottawa in one of the comfortable old brick houses around Dows Lake, watching her grandfather wander off to his office in the Finance Department and her father to the Department of Justice, and listening to their conversations about their solid jobs throughout her childhood, Betty never considered working for any employer other than the federal government. Those of her ancestors who had fled the social and political turmoil of Europe in search of a better life were proud of their affiliation with a public service they called trustworthy and honourable. They gently nudged their children into government service. Betty's older brother enlisted in the Air Force; her older sister, a librarian, was accepted by the Department of Industry, Trade, and Commerce.

The question of which department Betty would apply to had not yet been settled when her parents surprised her upon her graduation from Algonquin College with a return ticket to Lahr in West Germany, where her brother had recently been sent. After an exhilarating summer, first staying with her brother's family and then touring the countries where many of her ancestors had come from, she announced to her parents as soon as she had got off the plane that she intended to return to Europe soon. External Affairs would look after the details. Her stunned parents thought for a moment she had got engaged to the young Portuguese student whom she had mentioned in her letters several times. But she had not; instead, she had fallen for the attractions of the Canadian foreign service. A young member of the service coming back from his first posting to Europe had been sitting next to her on the flight from Frankfurt to Montreal and had passed on his enthusiasm about the rotational life to Betty.

Joining External Affairs turned out to be rather difficult. To be precise, it was not possible at all. There were simply no vacancies for someone with Betty's training. The Public Service Commission offered her a job in the Department of Transport instead. A gloomy year followed, during which she did little more than move paper about in great quantities for a pitiful salary. Not prepared to put up with a second year like that, she accepted a job offer with a tempting salary from a brand-new, promising-sounding private company. Within a year, the company had to file for bankruptcy.

To her relief, she had, under pressure from her parents, continued French courses with the Ottawa Board of Education and was thrilled when her second application to External Affairs was accepted on the basis of her bilingual secretarial skills. After her hapless plunge into the world of private business, Betty knew she would never again want to work for a company 'where money is the bottom line,' as she put it. She is not earning much now and could get a better salary in the private sector. But she prefers the federal government. 'I enjoy serving the public,' she says and then adds, as if recanting and making a full confession, 'Especially when it can be overseas every few years and comes with job security and a regular income.'

Internationalist-Cosmopolitan

Jeff recalls clearly that he had been in Grade 4 only a few weeks when his father was called to serve with the Canadian contingent of the U.N. peacekeeping force in Suez. Before leaving for Egypt, his father brought home a globe. Jeff was surprised to see that New Brunswick was a mere dot and that his home, a rural community outside of Fredericton, was not marked, as if it didn't exist at all. Egypt, in comparison, looked huge, as did other countries whose names were unfamiliar to him, like Sudan and Libya. One arm around his son, the other arm around the globe, Jeff's father showed him the route he would be taking. Jeff remembers the moment vividly. On that day, he says, the world moved into his bedroom.

Waiting for news from Egypt, he began to listen to the radio, read newspapers, and pour over maps. He then moved on to memorizing countries and capitals around the world and to collecting travel brochures and airline timetables he picked up at an agency in Fredericton. But nothing distracted him from the issue closest to his heart: his father's role in the peacekeeping mission.

The accounts his dad, upon returning to Canada, gave of his personal contribution to the mission did not have the mythic stature Jeff had imagined. His father, he was convinced, had tried to be modest, a characteristic for which the greatest heroes were noted. History had to be set straight and his classmates would be the first ones to benefit from the truth. He delivered glowing accounts of the acts of bravery and heroism performed by Canadian soldiers, and always concluded his presentation by saying that Canada, having successfully intervened in world affairs, had accomplished a peaceful solution to a nasty conflict that could have led to another world war. He felt his father had been personally honoured when he learned that Lester B. Pearson had won the Nobel Peace Prize for his role in ending the Suez Crisis. Jeff confesses that, on that day, he began to dream of some day working for Pearson.

He started high school at the Canadian Forces Base in Soest, West Germany, where his father had been posted, and spent three years in the heart of Europe, travelling extensively with his parents. When his father was appointed military attaché in Warsaw, Jeff had to remain at boarding-school in Canada. But he visited his parents for the long summer holidays and used the time to explore the city and other parts of Poland as much as travel restrictions allowed. He also began to learn Russian. During a trip to China on the Trans-Siberian Railway, he had the feeling that, in a way, his father was still turning the globe for him. At some point, Jeff knew then, he would want to take the world in his own hands.

At university, Jeff was delighted to discover how many of his fellow students shared his dream of entering the foreign service. 'Everyone in the international studies program at the University of Toronto wanted to live up to the high standards of professionalism Pearson had set,' he mentions. In that context, writing the foreign-service exam was treated as an event on campus. Jeff wrote the exam for the first time after he had earned his BA and the second time after his Master's degree in international relations. He failed both times. Five years later, in possession of a doctorate in international relations from the Sorbonne and fluent in Russian and German, he passed with high marks.

Ever since the day on which an event of historic significance in another part of the world touched his personal life and after years of exposure to Eastern and Western Europe, he wanted to work in a field 'where things are happening,' where he could make a modest contribution to the solution of problems, as his father had in Suez. Lester B. Pearson remains his model. Although Jeff suspects that nobody will offer him a Nobel Prize for his efforts, he loves his profession: 'I simply find what I am doing worth while.' And, after a moment of reflection, he adds: 'I think it is a question of values.'

Anthropologist-Linguist

'My decision to enter the foreign service was my fireman syndrome,' Mark tells me. 'I took it when I was a little boy in Bangkok.' Unlike most boys who abandon their childhood plan to become firemen as they grow older, Mark never changed his mind.

His family has been on the move for three generations. His paternal grandfather, a Presbyterian minister, served as a missionary in Taiwan, where his father was born. To continue the family tradition of foreign birthplaces, Mark was born in Rome, where his father was cultural attaché at the Canadian embassy. He spoke English with his parents, Italian with his nanny in Rome, Thai with his nanny in Bangkok. He did not try to master Amharic in Addis Ababa because his beloved Bangkok nanny joined the family in Ethiopia, bringing with her a suitcase full of children's books in Thai. By the time he was ten years old, he spoke and read Thai fluently. Writing, he admits, he found a bit more difficult.

At the beginning of a four-year posting to Ottawa, his parents bought a house in Rothwell Heights. Mark found Canada yet another fascinating country. After he had made his peace with the cold, he began to enjoy more than anything the informality of daily life. When his father was posted to Hong Kong, he discovered that, in his heart and mind, Canada had moved up in his collection of favourite foreign countries from fourth position, to first place. He remembers vividly how hard he found it to leave the family home, his school buddies, and the neighbourhood. He would have loved to stay on.

In Hong Kong, he enrolled at the International School, and added Japanese to his English and French curriculum. He had never lost his command of Thai. In Ottawa, he had attended the Thai Saturday school, and his parents had paid for private lessons in addition. When he graduated with the International Baccalaureate, he was fluent in four languages. He had also been around the world once and had lived in five countries on four continents.

At the University of British Columbia, Mark majored in East Asian studies, including Japanese and Thai literature and history. His command of Thai began to blossom when he married Panida, a student from Bangkok and, to his delight, a product of the foreign service of Thailand.

A diplomatic career is the only occupation in which he feels he can live with the variety of cultures to which he has been accustomed since childhood. 'I love living in Canada, but after a while I get restless,' he says. 'I couldn't possibly live in the same country all my life.' He confesses that he is somewhat driven to unravel another cultural mystery every few years; to explore the wealth of a country's language, literature, history, philosophy, religion, art, music, and the meaning of the local customs. Language, the gateway to a culture, fascinates him more than anything else. Opening that gate, he cannot emphasize enough, requires dedication and discipline. By now he has worked for ten years on his Japanese; unlike his Thai, which he speaks at home with his wife every day, it still requires constant attention to rust-proof vocabulary and grammar. He depends on daily exercises like a ballet dancer or figure skater in his field. And yet, he regrets to say, his Japanese is rather wobbly right now.

With mock concern he tells me that his career in the foreign service will not be long enough to satisfy his curiosity about foreign countries he has never seen. The 'Itchy Feet Syndrome' has reappeared, now that he has been back in Ottawa for three years. He picks up a book from his desk and wonders aloud if *Teach Yourself Tagalog* is evidence of where he will be going next.

Whereas Oyster, Owl, and Migratory Bird are exclusive categories and do not involve cross-overs, boundaries between Internationalist-Cosmopolitan and Anthropologist-Linguist are fluid, and nothing prevents those belonging to either group from fitting into the Public Servant category as well. Many employees do, in fact, belong to two, and a good number fit into all three categories. The classifications can be further refined by adding a clearly discernible third set of expectations foreign-service members identified as important in influencing their decision to join External Affairs. Most people in search of a profession are looking for more than a job and a salary. Consciously, but primarily unconciously, they yearn for satisfaction of higher social needs, such as belonging to a group, self-esteem, esteem for an employer, esteem from an employer, and recognition and fulfilment of personal potential.

The foreign service is well known for maintaining a close-knit community, even beyond national boundaries, as much as for the prestige attached to membership in this international brotherhood. It also offers, through global mobility, a unique opportunity for its employees every few years to put physical distance between them and their life situation. Quite a number of employees, all of them eager for new beginnings, see this chance simply to get away from everyone and everything, as a particularly desirable aspect of foreign-service life. Many foreign-service members revealed in the course of our conversations that they had been strongly motivated by deep-rooted social needs in the choice of the service. In relation to those needs, three further categories emerged: Joiner, Status Seeker, and Escapist.

Joiner

Réjeanne points to a collection of photographs on her desk and says: 'I am the youngest of nine brothers and sisters. We have always been very close, and we still are.' Leaving her home and her family on the Ile d'Orléans in the province of Quebec at age eighteen was a painful experience for her. But she had made up her mind to get a university degree. She had heard of a small college in Toronto established to train bilingual public servants, and she could hardly believe her good fortune when she was accepted at Glendon College. She loved the atmosphere and speaks highly of the motivation of the students, the hard work everyone put in, and the relaxed relationship between professors and students. It all reminded her of home.

When she had finished her third year of the undergraduate program in public administration, her boyfriend, who had recently completed a Master's degree in history, was notified that he had cleared all rounds in the latest foreign-service exam. A training position as FSI-D was waiting for him in External Affairs. Throughout her fourth year, Réjeanne received exuberant letters from Jean-Philippe. His work, he wrote, first in the minister's press bureau, then in one of the European divisions, was tremendously stimulating. His bosses treated him like a colleague, not like a freshman, and several of his fellow FSI-DS had become friends. External Affairs, he stated over and over, was a great place.

Jean-Philippe had little trouble convincing Réjeanne that she, too, should try her luck. With a sparkling new degree to add to her name, she wrote the exam and failed. She found it a bitter pill to swallow. But, since she had set her mind on a career with External Affairs, she was not defeated by one failed test. Membership in the international foreign-service community, as Jean-Philippe referred to his social environment now, in enthusiastic letters from his first posting in Mexico City, had become irresistible to Réjeanne. If she could not be an officer in External Affairs, she would simply aim at a more modest position. She applied for a secretarial position and was immediately accepted.

'My boyfriend's stories were instrumental in my decision,' Réjeanne admits. She does not deny that the forty secretaries who have university degrees feel intellectually understimulated, unfulfilled, and unhappy as far as the nature of their work is concerned. Réjeanne is determined not to let this happen to her, at least not in the long run. She has every intention of rewriting the foreign-service exam every year until she passes it. There is also the possibility of moving on to become an administrative officer.

In the meantime, she enjoys what she says is rich compensation for rather monotonous work well below her potential: the close friendships with a number of her fellow secretaries. A group of about twelve of them see each other regularly, have lunch together at their favourite table in the back of the cafeteria and exchange the latest news, make weekend plans, and discuss the pleasures and problems of work and life in general. In her office, she says, she has recaptured what she had left behind at home: 'We laugh and cry together and we help each other in emergencies. We are a family.'

Some members of Réjeanne's extended, foreign-service family are now located in various parts of the world. She herself has not yet been posted abroad. But three of her closest friends have been and urge her to visit them. Pakistan and Algeria she finds a bit extravagant for a two-week holiday from Canada, but she has accepted an invitation to spend

Christmas with a member of the cafeteria group who is on assignment in Barbados.

Status Seeker

Herbert is the first member of his family who has ever attended university. His father manages a car-repair shop on the outskirts of Calgary; his mother helps out in the lunchroom at the local elementary school. His parents always wanted something better for their only child and saved every penny for Herbert's education. An honours degree in history from the University of Calgary, they felt, was not quite enough. They would have liked to see Herbert become a doctor or lawyer.

During his last year of law school, a classmate talked Herbert into writing the foreign-service exam. After hesitating for a long time, Herbert agreed to it, provided it was understood 'that it was just for the fun of it.' When he learned that his classmate had passed, while he had failed, Herbert discovered his own sense of ambition. He had never failed a test before. He felt he owed it to himself as well as to his parents to succeed.

He spent the entire summer after graduation from law school in the university library, reading his way through a pile of books on international relations, Canadian history, economics, and the annual reports of the Department of External Affairs for the previous five years. He shrugs his shoulders at the question of whether he thinks there was a connection between his self-imposed summer course and his success in the next exam. 'Probably,' he says.

His parents were jubilant. All their sacrifices had paid off. Their son, a diplomat! They came to Ottawa for the first time in their life to celebrate. Herbert, however, is not entirely sure yet that he has chosen the right career. 'I come from a blue-collar background and all of a sudden I am a diplomat.' At times he feels inadequate and out of place because of his manners, taste in clothes, and way of socializing. He sighs and wonders aloud whether he should not have led an inconspicuous life as a lawyer in a small town somewhere in Alberta, rather than trying to live up to the image of a foreign-service officer. He mentions his European and Asian fellow diplomats and marvels at their ease in any social situation and their superbly polished manners. He feels embarrassed that he might really appear to others to be as gauche as he sometimes thinks he is.

He cannot, however, deny that he likes his work more than anything he has ever done before. He also gets along well with his colleagues and bosses. Maybe he is not quite as much out of place in External Affairs as he fears. But he is not at all sure and mentions a problem he sees as indicative of his inner conflict. He feels torn between his long-time girlfriend in Calgary, a warm and home-minded girl, much like his mother, and his educated and stylish girlfriend in Ottawa, a young lawyer in the Justice Department. His heart, he confesses, is with the girl in Calgary; his mind, with the lady friend in Ottawa. He shrugs his shoulders and wonders where exactly he himself fits into this puzzle.

Escapist

Lisa is adamant about it: 'I should not have been accepted. At least, not at that moment!' Someone in External Affairs should have noticed why she was trying to slip into the foreign service, she insists.

Her life seemed to have come to a screaming halt with her fiancé's fatal car accident. They had been living together for two years and were making final preparations for their wedding when it happened. Lisa did not think she would ever recover. Her family did not provide any emotional support, since they had been opposed to her relationship with the young man from the beginning. In the absence of any close friends, she felt like an abandoned child.

Desperately trying to start a new life and to flee the places in Halifax, Nova Scotia, that reminded her of her fiancé and their life together, she responded to an advertisement for foreign-service secretaries and found herself in External Affairs less than six months later. The first question she asked her personnel manager was how long she would have to wait for a posting abroad. Only the prospect of getting away kept her afloat during the next months in Ottawa. She did not know anyone in the city and did not attempt to make friends. She felt too numb to enjoy any form of social gathering and kept telling herself that her departure – the expected salve for her pain – was just around the corner. There was no point in starting new relationships here. She asked to be posted as far away as possible.

On the day she learned that she was under consideration for Buenos Aires, she began to pack frantically. But the hoped-for relief from suffering did not arrive. On the contrary, the closer her departure date came the more restless and frightened she felt. Something seemed to be holding her back, while she was trying to sneak away. The drive to stay seemed as powerful as the desire to flee. When she was handed her plane ticket, she realized it was too late to change anything. She had to go, and things would most likely fall into place as soon as she was out of the country. Lisa says her worst moment came when the aircraft lifted off. She had the feeling that she had no longer anything to hold on to.

Lisa never set foot in the office that was waiting for her in Argentina. She had to be taken directly from the airport to a hospital. The next twelve months saw her in a psychiatric ward, first in Buenos Aires, later in Halifax, and eventually in Ottawa.

Now, ten years later, completely recovered, happily married and mother of a five-year-old daughter, Lisa cannot understand why no one seemed to recognize at the time that she was using the foreign service as a vehicle to spirit herself away from the reality of her fiancé's death and from the necessary period of mourning. She knows from her own bitter experience that foreign-service employees should check their emotional cargo before climbing on a plane for a foreign posting. Psychological excess baggage can bring down anyone and will be especially dangerous during the turbulence that inevitably accompanies this kind of life.

Not everyone seeking a foreign-service career in order to escape the ill effects of an unhappy childhood; difficulties with parents, friends, or lovers; or any other lingering conflict comes out of the crisis quite as well and wise as Lisa. Unresolved, such problems tend, like hurricanes, to gather momentum and fury as they cross oceans and continents, and eventually catch up with their victims.

Not many members of the rotational foreign-service team fall into the category of Escapist. But those who do carry the potential for a major disturbance that all too often develops into a disaster. Every year, foreign-service members have to be emergency evacuated for a number of reasons, including severe psychological problems related to unresolved inner conflicts.

A number of foreign-service members cheerfully ascribed their career choice to some degree of escapism. But the conflicts they cited and their ease in discussing the issues indicated that theirs amounted to harmless cases, nothing in comparison with the small number of those afflicted with 'Foreign Legion Syndrome,' as one senior member of the service called the phenomenon after having fought an exhausting battle with an obvious escapist among his staff.

The vast majority of foreign-service members fit into the Joiner category. Some of the Status Seeker and Escapist can perhaps be found in more individuals than is immediately apparent. But pure Status Seekers and Escapists are rare. The distinction among these categories points at predominant, but not exclusive personal needs foreign-service members hope to satisfy through an international career.

Why do young men and women want to embrace a life permanently in transition? Classification does not explain the individual psyche. But the three basic groups of clearly discernible motivations and the more detailed nine subgroups might offer one answer to the question of why the foreign service exercises such a powerful pull on such a large number and variety of people.

5

Foreign-Service Directives

Some foreign-service insiders take pleasure in likening the foreign-service directives that govern foreign-service life to the great books of major religious communities. Indisputably of human origin rather than written under divine inspiration, the 'Foreign Service Terms and Conditions of Employment Directives,' generally referred to as 'FSDs,' have been designed to provide for a special system of conditions of employment for foreign-service personnel. Like the great religious books, they play a decisive role in unifying and guiding the community. Unlike their sacred counterparts, the FSDs are changed and adjusted to new circumstances at regular intervals. The National Joint Council of the Public Service, composed of representatives of Treasury Board and External Affairs, renegotiates the regulations and issues a new version of them every three years.

The currently valid directives, effective since 1 February 1989, are a loose-leaf collection in a pale blue cover and consist of seventy paragraphs and numerous subparagraphs, each in both English and French.

According to the introduction of this volume, the purpose of these directives is to offer guidelines and incentives to employees who have been found qualified to carry out government programs outside of Canada. Because working and living conditions abroad are, to a large extent, beyond the control of the Canadian government, the directives, in an attempt 'to minimize variations in these conditions,' apply three principles to the provisions: 1 / 'comparability,' which tries to put foreign-service employees 'in neither a more nor less favourable situation' than they would be in if working on Canadian soil; 2 / 'incentive-inducement,' which recognizes that uncertainties and hardships associated with work and life abroad require monetary incentives in order to attract and retain qualified employees; and 3 / 'program-related' provisions, which are intended to equip employees abroad with the means that will allow them to carry out the assigned government programs.

In 236 pages, the FSDs lay down all possible kinds of rules, from precise instructions, through directives, guidelines, and transitional provisions, to less specific suggestions left to managers' discretion; these rules were devised to cover a multitude of situations that have thus far occurred in the history of the foreign service or might occur in the future and will affect employees and their families as they move and live abroad. Divided into ten parts, the directives address the minutest detail of every possible aspect of life in the posting cycle. A glance at the main issues discussed in each part reveals the scope and complexity of the regulations. Part I focuses on the terms of accountable advances to which an employee is entitled and provides details of repayment. Part II settles all administrative details for preposting medical and dental examinations, posting loans, and travelling expenses for employees and family members before a posting. Part III deals with travelling expenses for family members who go on foreign-language training prior to an assignment, as well as with all the questions arising from management of employees' real estate in Canada during their absence. Part IV refers to financial arrangements in the area of employees' housing abroad, storage of goods employees leave behind in Canada, and accounting for transportation and moving expenses. Part V touches all issues concerning education and general care of employees' children, from education and travel allowances to school holidays spent with the family abroad. Part VI pertains to medical expenses, health-care expenses, as well as medical and dental advances. Part VII takes care of all issues connected with employees' holidays, foreign-service leave, travel assistance, family re-unions, and travel in case of serious illness or death in the family in Canada. Part VIII provides details on allowances and other monetary compensation, such as salary equalization, foreign-service premium, and post-differential allowance. Part IX presents arrangements for departure from a foreign posting in cases of emergency evacuation and death abroad of an employee or a member of the immediate family. Part X discusses administrative issues.

Among the foreign-service population, reactions to the FSDs cover a wide spectrum, from approval to contempt. Where some employees marvel at the generosity of certain provisions and praise them as the best arrangements of their kind of all foreign services they know, others wince at the constraint they feel the directives impose on individuals and families. For a good many employees, 'FSDs' is a word they usually utter with a sigh in order to avoid stronger expressions of discontent.

A common, not entirely unjustified criticism is directed against the legal vocabulary and style, which makes them almost incomprehensible. 'I might as well try to decipher hieroglyphics,' quipped one employee, voicing the opinion of more than one colleague. But, whatever employees' reactions may be, the foreign-service directives constitute one of the basic components of foreign-service life.

The stage is set. Headquarters and 117 embassies, high commissions, consulates general, and consulates are in place around the world. The actors have offered a glimpse of their private lives and have revealed some of their reasons for wanting to join the cast before slipping into the costumes designed for their part. They are considered qualified and feel ready to play the roles assigned to them. The External Affairs Act provides the motivating mandate, the foreign-service directives the ground-rules. The curtain is about to rise on the drama of lives permanently in transition.

PART II

Foreign-Service Life
The Daily Reality

6

Overture in Ottawa

'When will I be posted?' Young foreign-service recruits of all occupational groups inevitably ask this question during the first meeting with their personnel officer. The first appointment abroad, however far away in the future it may be, begins to dominate thought and action of new arrivals as soon as they start to work at headquarters. Like a musical theme whose opening chords are first sounded by a single instrument, then repeated by other instruments, building to fullness until the entire orchestra unites for the complete theme, anticipation of the first assignment structures a newcomer's entire initial period in Ottawa.

Once a novice has struck the chords for the first time by indicating on the post-preference sheet a number of countries to which he or she would like to be sent, the theme of leaving Canada and living abroad within a year or two begins to gather strength and richness. More and more sides of the employee's daily life will be shaped by the impending departure. By the time the official posting confirmation arrives and the responsible administrative divisions have picked up the tune, life will consist of little else but preparations for the first great exodus. But before a young apprentice is entitled to the traditional hallway salute 'Congratulations on your posting,' the Ottawa assignment has to be mastered.

'Ottawa,' says Geneviève, 'was my first hardship post.' She found the national capital as big, sterile, and impersonal as a neighbour in her home in the Eastern Townships had predicted. Until she could find her own accommodation, the administration of External Affairs had put her up in a grey hotel in the inner city. Numb from the cold atmosphere in the office and the merciless pressure on her to type incessantly at high speed all day long, and dreading the dead silence descending upon her in her hotel room every evening, she spent her first few weeks in Ottawa feeling rejected by the world. The only people she met during that time were the officers for whom she operated the word processor, all of them loaded down with as much work as she was, and a dozen superintendents who showed her dark and depressing apartments for rent. She had no one to talk to for weeks on end.

Geneviève is still upset at a discovery she made months later. Four of her fellow secretaries, all of them as new to External Affairs and to Ottawa as she was then, had been staying at the same hotel during that time, feeling every bit as down-hearted as she had been, and for exactly the same reasons. None of them had any idea of the others' existence, and no one in the administration at headquarters had bothered to bring them together. She suspects no one knew that four of them were living under the same roof. A minimum of attention and care for such a detail could have saved five people unnecessary heartache.

Geneviève explains that she had come to External Affairs with the highest expectations, in search of a new life, a new identity, and a new community. In return for such a bounty, she would be completely committed to her work and loyal to the department. But, in the absence of even the slightest sign of support, guidance, or interest in her situation, she felt like a displaced person in the Lester B. Pearson Building and considered abandoning her first independent foray into the world and returning to her mother.

Before admitting defeat, though, she approached her assignment officer. Perhaps going overseas would change everything. She would make friends with embassy staff and foreigners, explore the world, and thus find herself. She did ask the inevitable question and came away from the interview even more downcast. She was doomed to Ottawa for a minimum of one, if not two years. How could she possibly hold out so long in that city and that office? Going back to mother seemed to be the only relief from her unbearable sense of loneliness. But, it would amount to sliding backwards into dependence. Sticking it out in Ottawa would mean a long purgatory, no doubt about that. But, at the end of it waited a foreign posting, maybe even to some tropical paradise.

Geneviève gritted her teeth and decided to hold out, a day at a time. She also made up her mind to look at her life in Ottawa as an unfortunate, but luckily temporary period of misery. Any form of emotional commitment to this place would be a waste of time and energy, and of money as well. She would invest nothing, not in human relationships, nor in an apartment. Henceforth, 'for the time being' would coldly qualify every aspect of her existence, until her real life could begin, once she got overseas.

When Geneviève rented the cheapest one-bedroom apartment she could find, she discovered that, in a sense, she could not even afford that. Before joining External Affairs she had earned $22,000 as secretary in a small industrial enterprise in the Eastern Townships. In Ottawa, her salary had dropped to $18,000. But, because of the local prices, her income had dropped much more dramatically than the figures indicated. Each month her apartment swallowed up $500. Her financial situation, she consoled herself, had become so bad it could only improve. A foreign posting promised salvation from her troubles in that area as well. Abroad she could expect an annual allowance of $2,000.

Until those riches would descend upon her, she forced herself to face daily reality at home. In order to keep people and events at a safe emotional distance, she wrapped herself in a cloak of contemptuousness, demonstrating an unwillingness to be bothered with anyone or anything for any length of time. At best irritable, at worst condescending with colleagues in the many divisions through which she was passed; not interested in building a social life, fleeing to an empty table in the cafeteria for lunch; not concerned about her apartment, which remained largely empty, she waited with growing restlessness for a magic word to be uttered by her personnel officer – London, for example, or Paris, Rome, Vienna, Berne. Any of these cities would turn her life in a happier direction.

Halfway through her first year in Ottawa, Geneviève had to admit to herself that she could not continue to live in complete social isolation. She knew that she had already acquired a reputation for being difficult and could only confirm that she was. She had been passed from division to division at a notably faster rate than other new secretaries. Although she pretended not to care a bit whether she was disliked or not, she felt deeply hurt for being resented by everyone around her.

The temporary structure into which she had forced her life came tumbling down when she realized after eight months that her apartment had become an unaffordable luxury. Since there was still no posting in sight, she would have to share an apartment.

Her notice on the bulletin-board outside the cafeteria in the Pearson Building brought only one reply. Geneviève remarks with a grin that she was on her best behaviour during the first meeting with the prospective roommate, considering the limited choice of possibilities.

Geneviève now sees her financial difficulties at that time as a blessing in disguise. 'We pooled resources,' she explains. Together with Alice she rented a two-bedroom apartment for $650 a month. For her, this arrangement meant relief, not only from a financial burden, but also from the pain of self-imposed isolation. Her new friend, a six-year foreign-service veteran with two overseas postings behind her and a wealth of entertaining stories to tell, convinced Geneviève that she was neither realistic nor wise in treating Ottawa assignments as a penance. She introduced her to her own attitude towards the rotational life. On each assignment, she took with her a few pieces of carefully chosen furniture and personal possessions that reminded her of home or of previous postings; she took a lively and cheerful interest in the city and community in which she happened to be living; above all, she consciously nurtured relationships with family, friends, and a small crowd of fellow secretaries. Their apartment became what Geneviève calls a kind of community centre for secretaries going out on postings, coming back from abroad, or living in their own way through a few years between two assignments.

Although her monotonous work, performed under high pressure, was not what she had originally hoped for, Geneviève felt so content and fulfilled in her private life throughout her second year that she says she was caught by surprise when she learned she was under consideration for a posting to Lusaka, Zambia. Delighted in one way by having shed her initial painful dependence on getting away at all cost in favour of a relaxed view of the first foreign assignment, she felt sad at the thought of leaving Alice, who had assumed the role of loving older sister; the cosy apartment; and a number of close friends. As she was packing her belongings to head out to Africa, she began to look with fondness at the world around her. Ottawa no longer felt like a purgatory at all. In fact, a return to Canada after one or two postings could mean a wonderful break and welcome recovery from the inevitable problems that accompany foreign adventures.

Such feelings were entirely alien to Adam, a young immigration officer in training and friend of Geneviève's who had entered the service one year after she had joined. Ottawa, he told his new colleagues at a two-week orientation seminar, left him cold. He felt indifferent towards the place and was unlikely ever to entertain warm feelings for the national capital. It was not necessary to make an effort anyway, since he would be spending most of his career outside of Canada. His current stay in the city could be safely considered the last obstacle to a more satisfying life abroad.

The announcement by his personnel officer that within five months of his arrival at headquarters he would be sent overseas for a six-week practical training program strengthened Adam's conviction that, in his profession, Ottawa came in mercifully small and negligible portions. He rented a tiny furnished apartment where he counted the weeks left until his departure. His social contact consisted of the occasional movie with Geneviève and gatherings with other young officers in training who seemed to loathe the capital just as much as he did, each for a different reason. Ottawa bashing turned out to be one of the popular forms of entertainment during lunch breaks in the cafeteria. Newcomers, especially those from other parts of the country, outdid each other by trying to demonstrate that the city was not worth anyone's while. Young arrivals from Montreal and Toronto found Ottawa too provincial and bureaucratic, those from Vancouver said it was a sleepy town with an insufferable climate, those from smaller towns and communities called it too big and impersonal.

Watching the snow pile up around the Pearson Building for months on end, the new recruits talked much about getting out as soon as possible. In the evenings, when Adam returned to his apartment building and its stale smell of previous occupants' cigarettes and the more penetrating odour of one of his neighbour's frequent fried-fish dinners, he comforted himself with the thought that life abroad and relief from the triviality of his Ottawa existence were just around the corner.

Four months after he had entered the Pearson Building for the first time, Adam left his office in a royal mood. Furnished with a brand-new diplomatic passport, burgundy-coloured and decorated in gold print with the coat-of-arms of Canada, a wallet filled with rupees, and a suitcase containing his first tropical suit, he jumped defiantly over the latest snowdrift into a taxi and asked to be taken to the airport. Adam was going to India to receive training in how the Canadian immigration laws he had earlier been studying worked in practice. It was good to get out once in while, he told the taxi driver casually, as he was lifting his suitcase out of the trunk, and added: 'I like being Canadian. But I love living abroad.'

Adam says he returned to Ottawa after six weeks in New Delhi as a changed man. The most harrowing experience for him had been the poverty he had seen around him day in day out as he went back and forth between his comfortable hotel and his office in the Canadian high commission. He began to feel guilty for being well fed, well clothed, healthy, and secure. Knowing about Third World problems, he explains, is one thing. Stepping over the poor, the hungry, and the dying on the way to dinner is quite another matter: 'You either die of compassion or you become callous.' Those haggard human beings, he confesses, affected him deeply. They also made him feel that he had been childish, spoiled, and provincial in his petty and narrow-minded discontent with life in Canada. The world he saw was overflowing with hungry and sick people crowding day and night at the gates of Canadian missions in desperate search of nothing more than a decent life, pleading to be admitted as immigrants to a country that, by all standards, is exactly the paradise they perceive it to be. He, Adam, a citizen of that paradise, taking the comforts of his life for granted, had had nothing better to do than complain about life in Canada.

He reached a turning-point in his life when he noticed that an old, wrinkled farmer from Punjab whom he was trying to interview in the course of immigration procedures was quietly praying throughout the translated conversation. Adam says that it is hard to explain what happened inside him, but he was shaken by the incident. Here he was, sitting behind his government desk, endowed with the completely undeserved power to decide the fate of this man; the situation was particularly unsettling since the farmer was so obviously, with the deepest humility, acknowledging Adam's position as superior and all powerful.

Adam found it unacceptable that anyone should exert such power over another's life, guarding the gates of paradise, with wretched applicants for immigration to Canada lining up in front of him. 'That farmer made me feel very humble,' he says, and admits that he has not been able to get the incident out of his mind ever since.

Adam mentions that India has remained on his mind for other reasons as well. He fell in love with a young colleague from the Indian Department of External Affairs. Six weeks in New Delhi had been too short a time for either of them to make a decision. But he had made up his mind during his return flight to Canada to ask for a posting to New Delhi at the end of his training year.

In spite of the sadness of leaving his new love behind, he was most grateful to be able to return to Canada. His attitude towards his country had changed. He had also shed his romantic notions about a pleasurable life abroad. Postings in Ottawa, it seemed to him now, would probably amount to the most comfortable periods in his life, and he would gladly return after a foreign assignment.

When he arrived in Ottawa, the snow in front of the Pearson Building had given way to a sea of bright red tulips. In his apartment building, the neighbour previously devoted to fish dinners either had moved out in the meantime or had changed his dietary habits. Adam spent the second half of his year in training writing letters to his girlfriend and waiting for an answer to his request for a posting to India. He was disappointed to learn that no position at his level would be available in New Delhi. But the high commission in Islamabad had a vacancy. Before turning his attention to Urdu lessons, he suggested to his girlfriend that she ask to be transferred to the same post. Her request was granted. Seven months after his travel overture to India, Adam got off the plane in the capital of Pakistan, where his Indian girlfriend was expecting him.

Less exotic, but no less stimulating were the travel destinations External Affairs had set up for Jean-Marc, a young trade officer from Quebec City, who had entered the service at the same time as Adam. While immigration officers receive some of their training in the large immigration centres around the world – London, Rome, New Delhi, and Hong Kong – trade officers in training are sent on what is known and cherished as the Cross-Canada Tour.

The trip took Jean-Marc and his group of future trade commissioners to fourteen large cities, in all ten provinces. He agreed with his colleagues that not only was the tour the highlight of their training year, but it was also an essential, enabling them to get to know the country they would be representing abroad and to establish personal contact with the Canadian business community.

Because of sharp cuts in their travel budget, they were squeezed into cheap hotel rooms, ate on a tight meal allowance, and rushed from city to city so as not to waste time and money. It turned out to be exhausting. But being able to see the magnificence of their country and being systematically trained to promote Canadian business interests abroad during meetings with representatives of chambers of commerce from coast to coast Jean-Marc found exhilarating. He could not think of a better preparation for his future task abroad of linking Canadian with foreign markets, and returned to Ottawa full of enthusiasm for his first posting abroad.

His long absence had not been easy for Natalie, his wife, who was pregnant. But she soon was caught up in Jean-Marc's exuberant mood and felt as thrilled as he did when they learned that they would be going to Morocco at the end of Jean-Marc's first year. It sounded like an irresistible posting, although the birth of their baby complicated the move to Rabat. Jean-Marc was needed at the embassy four weeks before the baby was due, and most airlines would not accept Natalie as a passenger so close to delivery. Going by boat was not impossible, and Natalie seriously considered making the voyage. Her obstetrician strongly advised her against such a decision. The risk was far too great. Ship physicians were generally neither trained nor equipped to handle difficult births. At sea, the slightest complication towards the end of a pregnancy was potentially disastrous.

It became clear to Jean-Marc and Natalie that the assignment to Morocco meant a separation for a few months, until the baby was old enough to travel to Africa. It was upsetting for them, since they had planned on Marc's attending at the birth of their first child. This posting to Rabat would deprive Jean-Marc of seeing his baby born, and Natalie of her husband's support during the critical hours. Sacrificing this main event in their family life to a foreign assignment seemed more than either of them was willing to do. Jean-Marc raised the subject with his personnel officer. Could not the schedule at the embassy in Morocco be adjusted in an exceptional case such as this? Unfortunately not, Jean-Marc was told. A Canadian trade mission, led by the minister for international trade, had to be prepared well in advance. Jean-Marc was urgently needed in the commercial section of the embassy to assist in the delivery of Canadian trade policy in Morocco. What about my assistance in the delivery of our baby? he wondered aloud. Ironically the arrival of the trade delegation in Rabat, he learned, coincided with the baby's due date. With sadness, Jean-Marc and Natalie accepted the verdict and immediately tried to console each other with the promise that both of them would attend the birth of their second child, even if it meant giving up a choice assignment abroad.

Until Jean-Marc's departure, they concentrated on preparations for their new life, carefully absorbing all the information the Posting Briefing Centre in External Affairs had available on Morocco and Rabat, attending evening seminars on life in northern Africa, on formal entertaining, stress management, and the intricacies of the foreign-service directives. An older member of the department, an expert on the directives, spent an entire evening deciphering and interpreting some of the key rules for a group of newly posted colleagues of Jean-Marc's and their spouses.

Jean-Marc and Natalie had already embarked on language lessons as soon as they had received official confirmation of their assignment. The department had engaged the Algerian-born wife of a foreign-service officer. Three evenings each week Jean-Marc returned to his office after dinner accompanied by Natalie to study the subtleties of Arabic. At home Natalie attached with Scotch tape a new lesson of vocabulary and grammar to the cupboard next to her kitchen sink each morning, going about her chores to the mumbling of Arabic words and phrases. Performing her duties outside the kitchen, she carried her Walkman around with her, listening to language tapes. Only the roar of the vacuum cleaner took precedence. Natalie prided herself on learning thirty new words and a few new sentences each day, and made rapid progress. It was hard work and required dedication and concentration, but she found this part of her preparations stimulating, unlike the innumerable details of the move.

Natalie was shocked at how complicated the transfer of her household was. She had moved before and thought she knew what was involved. To get ready for this intercontinental version of her previous moves she had conscientiously studied all the relevant paragraphs of the foreign-service directives. But nothing had prepared her for the most gruelling job of all: making a complete inventory of all their possessions in accordance with the FSDs for insurance purposes.

Every single item she and Jean-Marc owned had to be listed, age and condition described, the purchase value noted, and a separate replacement value calculated. A depreciation formula had to be applied to every shirt of Jean-Marc's, to every skirt of hers, and to every book and record they owned. Saddled with this task because her husband was tied up in the office all day, Natalie painstakingly worked her way from cupboard to closet, from room to room.

In order to list prices accurately, she spent whole days phoning stores to find out the exact value of china, silverware, and household goods they had received as wedding gifts. When asked by an impatient saleswoman whether she wanted to know how much her wedding guests had spent on her, Natalie decided to give up her phone calls and to take her goods to the stores. Some items posed even greater problems. Antiques Jean-Marc had inherited from his grandparents, paintings, engravings, etchings, carved boxes, and silverware, had to be taken to antique dealers and assessment certificates obtained. Natalie remembers that she must have carried about half of all her mobile belongings through Ottawa for evaluations, when a compassionate saleswoman mentioned that she herself had just been through the same heartbreaking experience in the case of her own divorce, also far too soon after the wedding. Was dividing up all those lovely gifts of happier days not the most painful part of the separation? And being pregnant at that? Natalie made up her mind to abandon her visits to the stores and resort to educated guesses for her remaining 'personal effects.'

An additional difficulty arose for which neither Natalie nor Jean-Marc had been prepared. All their possessions had to be allotted to four categories: those items, mainly furniture, that would stay behind in Canada and go into long-term storage; heavy household goods that would be packed into a container and sent to Rabat by ship; lightweight items, such as clothing, which would be sent ahead of them by air; and Natalie's personal goods and everything needed for the baby – crib, changing table, carriage, and clothes – which would remain with her while she stayed in Ottawa at her parents' house before and immediately after the delivery. This last set of belongings would eventually be shipped to Rabat by plane, once she and the new arrival were ready to go.

After two months of taking the household apart, preparing the inventory, attending language lessons in the evening, and spending every remaining hour practising her Arabic, Natalie was exhausted. In a weak moment she could not resist remarking to her husband that dividing up the possessions for a divorce looked a lot easier than getting ready for a move with the foreign service.

When the movers swarmed into the apartment and began to carry out their furniture, marked in huge letters 'LTS' – 'long-term storage' – Natalie had to fight back her tears. She knew she would not see the familiar pieces for years and would be living with impersonal government furniture. With her bed, sofas, armchairs, and bookshelves removed, the sense of security that had marked her life until then seemed to be gone as well. Within two days, the entire contents of their apartment had disappeared.

The prospect of a long separation from Jean-Marc, the impending birth of their baby in the absence of its father, the unknown life awaiting her, the uncertain living conditions in Africa for her newborn child – all this weighed heavily on her, and combined with Jean-Marc's fatigue from too much office pressure, intensive language training, the thousand administrative details to look after regarding the move, concern for his wife and baby, and worries about the family separation created an atmosphere of tension between them they had never experienced before. When they had locked up their empty apartment and moved the remaining suitcases into a hotel, they both felt too numb to savour the three days left before Jean-Marc's departure. Natalie admits that, during the last six weeks of the move, they had argued more frequently and more severely than during three years of marriage. They had even gone as far as to question the wisdom of their decision to get married at all.

As soon as Jean-Marc had phoned from Rabat to announce his safe arrival and to tell Natalie how beautiful the apartment was that would be waiting for her and the baby, Natalie settled down comfortably in her parents' house near the Civic Hospital. The familiar world at home was a balm for the wounds the last few months had inflicted on her. She remembers that she woke up for the first few mornings thinking 'I don't need to work on the inventory and I don't have to move today, either.' That alone had healing powers.

As she was gradually recovering her bearing under her family's care, Natalie was beginning to wonder how Paul and Jennifer were holding up in the turbulence of their move. The communicator and his wife had been taking Polish lessons in the office adjacent to that in which Jean-Marc and Natalie had been studying Arabic. The two couples had seen each other regularly, had tried out on each other their first hellos and goodbyes in their new languages, had exchanged information about their forthcoming postings, and had advised each other on how to cope with the foreign-service directives. In the course of sixteen years of service with the Armed Forces, Paul, together with his wife and children, had moved eleven times within Canada before joining External Affairs. Warsaw-bound now, they were as much newcomers to international rotationality as Jean-Marc and his wife. Natalie decided to phone them.

Jennifer had just arrived in a downtown hotel and was to leave for Poland in three days. Whereas Jennifer had seemed vigorous and cheerful to Natalie at the time of their language lessons, Jennifer's voice over the phone showed signs of weakness. This move, she told Natalie, was the most painful one in their nineteen years of marriage. It had seen the dissolution of the family. She had spent the previous day saying goodbye. Within twenty-four hours she had had to separate from her husband and their two eldest children. In the morning, she had taken Paul to the airport, as he was urgently needed at the embassy. At noon, she had put their son on the bus to Kingston, where he was to start his first year at Queen's University. In the afternoon, she had returned to the same bus terminal, this time with their daughter, who had to leave for boarding-school in Toronto as there was no adequate schooling at her grade level in Warsaw. When the tears of the sixteen-year-old girl began to flow, the two younger children, a girl of six and a boy of three, joined in, immediately followed by their mother, who had been fighting her own tears bravely and successfully until that moment. With a heavy heart and two weeping children in the car, she drove back to the hotel, too weak to do anything except cry. But she had to pull herself together for a last desperate attempt to solve the overwhelming problem of their house.

For the three months since they had been told where they would be going, Paul and Jennifer had run advertisements in several newspapers to rent their house. Almost every day they had shown prospective tenants around in the middle of the chaos of the move. For some reason no one wanted to rent it. Now that they were on their way to Warsaw they had no choice but to turn the house over to the care of a rental agent. His enormous fee would cut deeply into their hardship allowance, which they had planned to use for their son's education. In fact, they had volunteered for this hardship post with an eye on that very allowance. The sum would enable their son to start university without having to spend a good part of his time working as waiter.

According to the foreign-service directives, they had to pay the government a substantial sum of money each month for their apartment in Warsaw, exactly the amount their house in Ottawa cost them each month in insurance, property tax, and maintenance. Unless they found a tenant whose rental payments would cover the costs of their house, they would have to finance two residences at the same time. Within a few months they would be bankrupt. Admittedly, in special cases the FSDs allowed for a waiver of payments for the apartment in Warsaw. But this was possible only for a maximum of six months. In the meantime, their house in Ottawa had to be heated, adding yet another large expense. The rental agent had suggested they reduce the rent by 25 per cent. They had agreed, although it meant that tax and insurance on the house would cost them more than they could collect. They would be losing money on the house even if they could rent it out. At that rate, the house threatened to swallow up the entire hardship allowance, the only reason for voluntarily exposing the family to the difficult life in Eastern Europe. The alternative, forced maintenance of two residences at the same time and inevitable financial ruin, was worse. It was all too horrible to even think about.

Natalie had fallen silent during the telephone conversation. Compared to what Jennifer and her family had to go through, her own move had been a trifle and her circumstances, enviable. She and Jean-Marc did not own a house and had simply ended the lease on their apartment. Their overseas allowance would be secure, and they had planned to save it towards a down payment on a house in Ottawa upon their return from Morocco. After listening to Jennifer's story, she was wondering whether it would be worth the trouble to own a house at all.

Jennifer's catalogue of difficulties did not end with real estate. The human problems, she told Natalie, were even harder to bear. Their two younger children, unlike the older ones, had not taken part in the many family moves while Paul had been with the Armed Forces. They were not used to pulling up roots every eighteen months and starting a new life in a strange house, neighbourhood, school, and community. But the older ones had always remained within a familiar culture. The little ones would have to cope with a foreign culture, and seemed already devastated when they discovered that their beds were being carried out of their house and their toys had vanished in huge crates. Although she and Paul had prepared the children for this enormous change in their lives, their obvious anxiety caused her as much pain as it caused them. After the family had walked for a last time through the echoing emptiness of the house that had been the little ones' nest for as long as they could remember, and after they had all gotten into the car, the youngest child, clutching his Teddy, had looked back at his home and had said quietly, 'Goodbye, house.' Three of the four children had burst into tears. She and Paul were wondering whether they should not have given up the nomadic life long ago for the sake of the children. Had they been acting in a responsible way when they joined External Affairs, and particularly when they had volunteered to go abroad?

Jennifer also felt deeply concerned about her parents in Saskatoon. Both were in their late seventies and not at all well. Paul and Jennifer had managed to visit them at least once a year, sometimes twice when travelling across the country during their frequent moves or when living within a day's drive from Saskatoon. Now it would be very difficult to see them, and Jennifer felt guilty, as if she were abandoning them. Her parents were distressed about the enormous distance the posting would put between them. Jennifer had tried to console herself that the directives provided for her to fly to Saskatchewan in case of serious family illness. But a physician in Saskatoon would first have to confirm that the situation was critical before she would be entitled to make use of the compassionate travel privilege and go home with financial assistance from the government. Besides, she could hardly use this regulation in the FSDs to offer comfort to her parents now that she was leaving.

Natalie thought of her own parents. Both in their early fifties, in excellent health, and full of adventurous spirit, they had already announced their intention to visit Morocco to babysit their first grand-child and to allow the young couple to get away for a few days before heading out themselves to explore Rabat and other parts of Morocco and northern Africa.

When Jennifer finished telling her story, it was midnight. She told Natalie how good it had been to unload and how much better she felt already. Things would probably work out somehow. Natalie, wondering how such enormous problems could ever find a satisfactory solution, expressed her admiration to Jennifer. Was there anything she could do to help? Jennifer was deeply grateful for adult company now that Paul had left and for two extra hands to assist with the children. She gave Natalie her schedule for the next three days. Natalie, completely free from duties, set out the following morning and drove Jennifer, who no longer had a car, and the two children to the clinic of the Department of Health and Welfare for the last in a series of hepatitis shots, and afterwards from one shopping centre to the next for innumerable last-minute purchases, among them a year's supply of children's shoes. It was an exercise in patience to find, in the sweltering August heat of Ottawa, a store selling heavy winter boots. A hundred administrative details still had to be attended to, and were, with Natalie's help, accomplished in time.

Jennifer seemed to be recapturing some of her natural cheerfulness. At the airport she could not thank Natalie enough for her practical and moral support. Embracing each other, they promised to stay in touch. As soon as she and the children had passed through the metal detectors and had grabbed their carry-on bags, Jennifer waved her passport and boarding-passes and called out to Natalie in Polish: 'Do vidzenia. Z bogiem!' Natalie waved back and replied in Arabic: 'Bsalama!'

7

In Transition Abroad

Between Two Worlds

'Do svidaniya,' the Russian version of *au revoir*, was lingering in my mind as the coast of Canada faded behind us. An Air Canada flight was taking my husband, me, and our two little sons to the Soviet Union in the summer of 1973. Six months of intensive language training had left their mark. We had begun to think in Russian and were expecting to graduate to dreaming in Russian soon.

Ever since our new posting had been confirmed nine months earlier, we had been living between two worlds. Although we remained physically in Ottawa, our minds had already left for Moscow. We still went through the motions of everyday life at home, a particularly draining experience, since preparations for this transatlantic move required more complex motions than we could have anticipated in even our most apprehensive moments. But life at home had ceased to have any value of its own. Every day in Ottawa seemed harnessed to the service of our future days in Moscow. The present had abdicated in favour of the future.

As the plane was calmly following its course between two continents and the twilight of the summer evening turned into night, the tension that had been building up within us during the previous nine months slowly began to leave us. Throughout this period, we had been trying to keep our balance between our present life in familiar surroundings and the demands of our future life in an uncertain environment. At times, we had felt as if we were standing with one foot at home and one foot abroad. Now the end of this divided existence was in sight. With Canada receding into the background, we would immerse ourselves with the necessary single-mindedness in a new type of life in the Soviet Union. The tyrant future would finally loosen its grip on daily realities and hand over the reins to the present. The present would be reinstated.

But the past claimed its share of our attention as well. An era in our family history had come to an end all too suddenly. Gone forever would be a young family's profoundly peaceful and private life in familiar and comfortable surroundings. Unsettling questions appeared out of the darkness. Had we acted responsibly when we had dragged our three- and one-year-old sons, Robin and Jeremy, out of their cosy home and beloved garden in Ottawa to thrust them into a high-rise apartment with a parking lot as playground in the centre of a polluted city? Did our fascination with Russian culture and Soviet politics justify the predictable hardships to which we would be subjecting our children and ourselves? How would we bridge the warm family life in complete privacy we had voluntarily given up with the chillier existence of diplomatic life that awaited us at the end of this flight?

The night separating the Canadian from the European shore appeared to be long and dark. Sleep would not come. Robin, too excited about the magnificent aeroplane he was riding in and too occupied with his new toy planes and miniature cars, only dozed for a short while. Jeremy could not sleep at all. He entertained his parents throughout the night, wiggling about in his seat, opening and closing the blinds on the window a thousand times, crawling around in the aisle, examining sleeping passengers, and paying visits to the flight attendants. He drank innumerable bottles of milk and juice and never tired of the subsequent diapering excursions to the washrooms.

With the dawning of the new day, Europe appeared below us, looking as grey and leaden as we felt. When our plane, after ten hours in the air, with a brief refuelling stop in Copenhagen, descended on the outskirts of Moscow, we caught our first glimpse of the fabled white birch forests. Nine months of waiting and working hard for this moment had come to an end. Philosophical considerations about past, present, and future would have to be put on hold. A new chapter in our family's life was about to begin.

As soon as we had made our way to the plane's exit door, armed with two small boys and bags full of empty bottles, we were struck by the powerful reality of our new surroundings. At the bottom of the stairs to the tarmack, a group of heavily armed Soviet frontier guards had taken position. We had, indeed, arrived in a different world from the one we had left behind.

Exposure to local customs and traditions began right at the airport. Faint with fatigue and heat, eight hours outside of our time zone, and trying to comfort our crying sons, we were introduced to a local variation on one of the principal activities of Soviet citizens: queuing. Only two of the booths for passport control were manned. The others remained empty, while those obviously supposed to man them were engaged in a brisk game of cards. It was one and half hours before our passports were checked and stamped.

The much-needed silver lining appeared on the other side of the dark passport horizon. Our embassy colleagues Claire and Phil Reynolds greeted us with encouraging smiles and open arms: 'Zdrávstvuite!' They had not limited their welcome to words. Claire, by that time a six-month veteran of Moscow shopping practices, had queued for us in the local stores, had filled the refrigerator in our furnished apartment with whatever edible goods the Soviet economy had churned out at that point, and had raided her own supply of pots and pans to provide us with essentials for the kitchen.

Claire also handed us an invitation to a dinner she and Phil were giving in our honour so that we could meet colleagues from other Western embassies. If we had any lingering doubts as to where we belonged during those first hours in our new domicile, at least we knew that life between two worlds had come to an end. With this invitation we had been admitted to the brotherhood of Kremlin watchers, and that meant entry into an exclusively Soviet orbit.

Departures and arrivals and the period in between constitute important stages in the posting cycle. Foreign-service members and their families remember vividly the circumstances under which they left Canada, travelled, and landed in a foreign posting. They give impassioned, colourful accounts that convey their deeply emotional engagement in the events. Many know that this particular change amounts to a turning-point in their lives. Not all of them are aware that it is also a time for high hopes, illusions, and anxieties. Their vulnerable emotional state inevitably coincides with a condition of extreme fatigue following weeks, if not months, spent dissolving a household in Canada; preparing personal goods for a move across oceans and continents; cleaning out desks, files, and offices to make room for a successor; and trying to acquire, through intensive language training, at least some of the linguistic competence necessary for the assignment abroad.

Because the last days before departure are hectic, the journey itself usually is the first opportunity for energy to be directed towards psychological preparation for the move, a task as essential as the many practical ones that precede a posting change. Some of the wiser foreign-service members use their trip to contemplate the life they are leaving behind, to disconnect and attune themselves and their families to the future environment. It can be a time of uncomfortable suspension in mid-air or in a no-man's-land, but it can also be a period of calm and recovery between two storms.

Often the discomforts of travelling deprive migrants of such a possibility for reflection. Crowded airports and planes, radical climate and temperature changes, jet lag, and other unsettling conditions combine to create a new set of problems. Foreign-service employees who have enormous distances to overcome are entitled to stopovers for twenty-four hours on the way to their destinations, a provision greatly appreciated as a chance to rest, catch up on sleep, gradually adjust to time zones, and recover a certain amount of physical and psychological equilibrium.

Departure and arrival stories foreign-service members tell to entertain each other about first assignments abroad indicate that some joyful event with family and friends to mark the beginning of this new stage in the life of a young nomad is generally welcomed by those who are leaving, for reasons similar to the ones that inspire young couples to invite family and friends to their wedding. While some employees like to slip out quietly the first time around, others prefer a certain amount of fanfare. Still others want to be seen off in style to the blare of trumpets acknowledging the great occasion in their lives.

In some cases, bells serve as a trumpet substitute. Michael, a twenty-five-year veteran of the foreign service, and his wife, Kate, look back with a mixture of amusement and nostalgia on the evening they left Ottawa on their first foreign assignment. It was their wedding day. A few months earlier, under the pressure of the impending posting and in order to avoid a long separation, Michael and Kate had decided to convert their eight-month-old relationship into marriage prior to Michael's departure. The traditional wedding going-away ritual culminated in the young couple's boarding a plane, Africa-bound, watched and photographed by the entire wedding party. Celebrating the start of their honeymoon during a night flight to Rome – the first leg of their journey – they found champagne before dinner high above the sparkling lights of Montreal a splendid and appropriate beginning to a life that could be expected to be exciting and wonderful.

When they arrived in Rome the next morning, the city was resounding with Sunday church bells. But Kate and Michael were too exhausted to interpret them as the Eternal City's contribution to their wedding. All they wanted was a quiet place to sleep. For the rest of the day the noise around them and their anxiety about missing their connecting flight prevented them from getting any sleep at all. The overpowering amount of work, the race to get everything done, and the chaos of the previous weeks had been too much and too instense suddenly to vanish without a trace. Both of them were tense and tired, and jet lag had left its mark. They knew of that strange phenomenon everyone who had travelled a great distance talked about, but neither of them had expected to be overcome by such paralysing fatigue. After a few cups of strong espresso in the hotel, Michael felt a little more energetic. But Kate seemed to have crumbled. Without eating or drinking anything, she sat without much sign of life in her seat during the long flight to East Africa, staring out of the window and barely responding to Michael's enthusiastic comments on the spectacular landscape below.

By the time the plane landed in Dar es Salaam, Kate was so weak Michael had to support her on their way down the staircase to the airport bus. As soon as their suitcases had been brought up to the hotel room they would be occupying for the few weeks before their apartment was ready, Kate collapsed on the bed. Never in her life had she experienced such desperate tiredness. Was she ill? Or had wedding, move, and jet lag been a bit too much to deal with all at once?

Twenty-five years later Kate and Michael say the answer is 'yes' to both questions. Kate did, in fact, get very sick shortly after their arrival in Tanzania and was ill for a good part of their two years in the posting.

It seemed to be a complicated tropical disease. But, during their first few days there, exhaustion, they think, had been the main problem. It would have been less glamorous, to be sure, but much wiser, to have scheduled the wedding some time earlier than the move to Africa. Starting a marriage amounts to a major project even under the best of circumstances, and should not be undertaken with a task of such magnitude as trying to cope with daily life in a totally different culture, and in a hardship post at that. Their marriage survived the strain, but neither Kate nor Michael would want to mark their departure for a new life in the same way and do not recommend it to any of their colleagues.

The question of how to coordinate a wedding with embarking on his first overseas assignment presented itself to Ross in a different form. Himself a bachelor intent on sampling independence to the fullest during his forthcoming posting to Dhaka, he could not entirely escape the sound of wedding bells either. A friend in British Columbia and his fiancée, after moving their wedding date around a bit, had been able to fix it for the day on which Ross could stop in Vancouver for twenty-four hours on his way from Ottawa to Bangladesh. The pleasure of the company of this old friend and new foreign-service member was requested by the entire bridal party so that he could act as best man and display his well-known talents as master of ceremonies.

Ross's friend's wedding had been scheduled to accommodate him, but External Affairs had made no such effort before assigning him to Dhaka. The department had simply informed him of its decision. He would never have volunteered to go to that hot and humid part of the world. But he was determined to make the best of a thoroughly unwelcome first marching order. A beautiful June wedding would usher in his first going away. The reunion with family and friends in his much beloved home city would be exactly the tonic he needed and longed for after the strenuous move and before an even more strenuous life in one of the most sweltering corners of Asia.

As he was proposing the toast to the bride while looking at all the faces that had been familiar to him throughout his life, Ross felt acutely aware for the first time of how much his family and friends meant to him. He had always taken them for granted. They had simply been part of his personal landscape, much in the way the majestic mountains were part of the spectacular skyline of Vancouver. The airline ticket to Bangladesh in his wallet reminded him that everyone and everything familiar to him was about to fade from sight for a long time. He would have dearly loved to hold on a little longer, and hoped his flight would be delayed. But it left on schedule.

Three days after the wedding, following a day of sight-seeing in Hong Kong, Ross landed in Dhaka. Lethargic from the intense heat and humidity, he spent the first day lying on his bed in a darkened hotel room, feeling discouraged and rather depressed. If only there weren't that gnawing loneliness! His thoughts drifted back to the wedding. The stopover at home had been the best event in the entire year since he had joined External Affairs and certainly the most important part of the period of transition between his familiar surroundings in Canada and the strange environment he had been thrown into now. His family and friends had – unintentionally and without being aware of it – revealed to him the sense of security they had instilled in him since childhood. But he had been surprised to discover how much he seemed to need them as an adult as well, provided he was as much of an adult as he thought he was. Maybe his dependence on them only proved how much of a child he remained, despite his august status as a foreign-service officer.

Ross could not quite make up his mind whether he should be moved or amused by the discovery that he had been suffering from nostalgia for family, friends, and home all the while he was being celebrated as the dauntless hero on his way to conquering – well, if not the whole world, at least the Asian portion of it. Next to the bride and groom, he had definitely been the centre of attention. A certain aura seemed to be surrounding him because of his new status and his exotic destination. He had also noticed that some of the younger female wedding guests who had never paid much attention to him when he was a student suddenly had been eager to engage him in lively conversation. Was it possible that he had graduated to the 'eligible' rank?

Now, three days later, he felt weak, lonely, and sad. How could he live up to the image his family and friends had of him? To make matters worse, it was an image he liked as being rather soothing to his ego, but knew was not deserved. What should he make of all that? There was no one with whom to talk about his predicament. It would take a long time to make friends with whom to discuss such a complicated matter.

How much he longed for the loving and admiring company he had been in only three days earlier! No doubt, they would be watching him lovingly from afar. But this did not change the fact that they seemed light years away when he needed them most.

Ross shoved aside the mosquito net, got up from his bed, and began to search in his suitcase for the framed photos of his parents, brother, and sister. He arranged the pictures the family had given him as a fare-well gift on a small bamboo table where he could see them from his bed. A year from now, during his first home leave, he would tell them all about his life in Asia, he thought as he was slowly drifting off to sleep to the monotonous hum of the ventilator above his head.

Arrival: Housing and Health

Our new home in Moscow greeted us in the summer of 1973 with all the grace of post-Stalinist architecture. A sixteen-storey grey concrete apartment building in the farthest outskirts of the city rose in front of us out of an endless field of sun-dried mud and a sea of nettles and weeds like the trunk of a prematurely aged elephant. The high-rise had been recently erected in such deliberate isolation to separate foreign heretics from the local Communist faithful. The latter were huddling at a safe distance on the other side of a broad thoroughfare in houses of the same grey concrete, but of less monolithic proportions.

In spite of its monumental ugliness and its forlorn position, 83 Vavilova Street enjoyed high prestige among members of the foreign-diplomatic *nomenklatura*. By Moscow standards, it was 'an address.' Not quite a Russian variation of one in Mount Royal, Rockcliffe Park, Rosedale, or West Vancouver, but one of the finest accommodations in the Soviet capital. It was not the neighbourhood that had lent class to the address, it was the nature of the building itself. Built as a home for diplomats, foreign correspondents, and businessmen, the structure was reasonably modern and contained large apartments with huge windows and good-size balconies.

Knowing that most Moscovite families were crowded into one-room apartments, we had been most grateful to learn that the only apartment allotted to our embassy by the omnipresent state-run Foreign Service Bureau that enjoyed a reputation for being palatial by local standards had fallen to us because we came not only with two small children, but with a nanny as well. Three normal Russian-size apartments had been joined into one and had been furnished with Canadian government appliances and household goods.

Although the rooms looked rather barren and the sheer size of the flat, I thought, would make it quite difficult to create a warm atmosphere and a feeling of cosiness, our little boys quickly came to the conclusion that the hallway had been designed specifically for tricycle races. As soon as these treasured vehicles arrived from Canada, they could be used in a manner our three-bedroom house in Ottawa had not been suitable for.

Encouraged by the prospect that the air and sea shipments of all the familiar items that had surrounded us in our pre-Vavilova existence would arrive shortly, I felt confident that I could establish a homey atmosphere here. The moment the goods were delivered I would set to work to shorten the period of transition as much as possible. After having surveyed our new territory one last time on that first evening in Moscow, we decided to fortify ourselves for the tasks ahead with urgently needed sleep. I had noticed that the kitchen floor had begun to spin around me and had ascribed the extraordinary motion less to a sophisticated feature of this new example of Soviet domestic architecture than to the total lack of sleep during the previous forty hours. We tucked our sons into their beds in a barren room all too far away from our own bedroom, and recommended happy dreams about tricycle races and subsequent banquets for the champions in their new home.

The home as castle: foreign-service transients attach extraordinary importance to their residences abroad. In a strange country, and even more so in a hostile environment, home becomes a refuge and a fortress where the nomad is monarch in a realm of familiar rules and customs, living in a state of harmony and peace determined by its owner.

Furnished apartments or houses the government either owns or rents from local owners and offers to the foreign-service employees for a fee are not always a source of harmony for the tenants. For economic reasons, to simplify the complications attached to housing and to control the quality of accommodation in foreign countries, the government decided some years ago to buy or to rent apartments and houses before leasing them to government employees, furnishing them and acting as landlord rather than paying enormous sums of money to move furniture around the world every time an employee moved into or out of privately rented quarters. The results of this policy range from very good to bad. In the 1960s and 1970s, a majority of employees would have emphasized the negative. After 1981, however, following the report of the Royal Commission on Conditions of Foreign Service, headed by former ambassador Pamela McDougall, the housing situation improved dramatically. Many of the housing horror stories therefore go back to pre-McDougall days.

It remains an almost impossible task to accommodate the large variety of needs, wishes, standards, and expectations foreign-service members maintain for their residences abroad. The administrative section of each mission is responsible for acquiring, furnishing, and maintaining all staff quarters for a never-ending succession of personnel. Regardless of the efficiency of the administrative officer, the mission is at the mercy of local markets, which vary strikingly between such cities as Tokyo and Lima, Oslo and Lusaka. Poor-quality housing, housing shortages, or exorbitant prices are rampant throughout the world. To match local realities with the standards and expectations of new arrivals at an embassy can be a challenging undertaking. A comfortable apartment or house with pleasing furniture has the power to offset the negative aspects of a hardship post, just as an undesirable dwelling can spoil an otherwise attractive posting. Whether at the positive or the negative end of the scale, housing constitutes a powerful component in foreign-service life.

Inseparably linked with the contentious issue of what standard should be applied to determine the degree of comfort Crown-owned staff quarters should maintain is the principle of equity enshrined in the foreign-service directives. It states that each employee is entitled to housing comparable to accommodation used in Ottawa. A rate, based on Ottawa housing fees and depending on the number of members in the family, has to be paid to the government, regardless of the quality or the nature of the dwelling abroad. The government pays the local fees, whether they are below Ottawa rates, as in some Third World countries, or high above Ottawa rates, as in many highly developed countries. It seems natural that employees paying Ottawa rates for their residences abroad expect Ottawa standards of housing, a feat impossible to accomplish in a number of capital cities around the world.

Foreign-service employees, even more so their spouses who often spend most of their time at home, told me that accommodations, appliances, furniture, curtains, and carpets have the power to make or break a foreign assignment. One employee reported an outbreak of rage that kept flaring up throughout his two-year posting in a Middle Eastern country when he walked into what he called 'a concrete shell of a house' that was supposed to be his family's home for the duration of their stay. Almost barren, except for beds, tables, chairs, and kitchen appliances, it cost him '500 bucks a month,' a hundred dollars more than his considerably larger and much more comfortable furnished house in Alta Vista had cost him. He wondered what had happened to the principle of equity in his case. The rental share, as the FSDS call the monthly payment, became his monthly irritant, breaking out like an allergic reaction every time he received a written notice that the amount had been deducted from his salary. House and rental share, he told me, served as constant reminders that he and his family in fact had no home for their two-year assignment. More than a decade after he had left the post and the house, he still sounded angry.

Another employee's housing, this time on a posting to Paris, had caused distress as well. A young couple with two small children, one of them a baby, had been allotted an old, severely neglected, gloomy house on the outskirts of the city in a miserable neighbourhood. Paris lay splendidly on the horizon, while they suffered through the most depressing posting in their entire career. Living within the boundaries of one of the most beautiful cities in the world, they remained imprisoned in their house and depressing neighbourhood because they could not afford a car and lived too far from the centre of the city to bundle up their children and simply head out to admire the sights. Restaurants in town or babysitters at home were out of the question, for financial reasons. In their case, the supposed castle had felt more like a dungeon.

Not much better fared a young employee on the west coast of Africa. His house, he said, was tiny and practically empty, except for his bed, a few chairs around a table, and some form of a closet. He described with considerable eloquence the metal library shelves on which he kept his few possessions. His domestic situation did not, however, bother him. He told me that the magnificent location of the house, right by a glorious beach, made up for all the shortcomings inside the walls. Years later he still brushes the insufficient interior decoration of the house aside with laughter and a shrug of his shoulders. He is convinced that anyone who saw the setting would have reacted the same. Admittedly, he said, he was a bachelor, and had he had a wife and children, his attitude would have been different.

At the positive end of the satisfaction-dissatisfaction scale are foreign-service members who call themselves lucky to arrive in a new, well-furnished, completely equipped apartment or house that they say is more comfortable than anything they have ever owned themselves. Young employees who went out on a first assignment in the post-McDougall era, after 1981, who had not earned enough money in Ottawa and had also not seen the need to establish themselves comfortably in an apartment or house before embarking on the first foreign adventure, were quite easily satisfied with the housing their government-landlord offered them.

From tiny, suffocating apartments in overcrowded, heavily polluted cities, to houses or apartments with all windows and doors barred for security, to generous houses with large gardens in balmy climates, foreign-service members are exposed to such a variety of residences that it can strain their ability to adjust from one set of circumstances to the next.

In Moscow we had the unexpected and questionable pleasure of studying at close range a variation on the housing theme: the residence as status symbol. But, before getting tied up in that unnecessary tangle, we were hit with our first serious emergency.

The post report External Affairs had prepared about living conditions in Moscow had warned us against the dangers of the local water. We had followed instructions given by old Moscow hands and had boiled every drop of water for at least ten minutes. Even the water for brushing our teeth we had conscientiously prepared. But, five days after we had landed in the Soviet capital, Robin and Jeremy showed the first unmistakable signs of what was to lead in a short time to a violent battle with a parasite known to be thriving in the Moscow water. The symptoms resembled those of dysentery: our little boys' temperature soared. They could keep nothing in their stomachs, not even the mineral water we fed them by teaspoons. The process of dehydration was so rapid we could watch their eyeballs sink deeper and deeper into their sockets.

I had to overcome a paralysing sense of helplessness and fear. In a familiar environment there would have been no question about what to do. But, here, everything that needed to be done seemed impossible to accomplish for one reason or another.

It was a Saturday morning when the symptoms had become alarming. The embassy was closed. We lived thirty minutes' drive from the centre of the city, but we had no car. The old one had been left behind in Ottawa, and the new one was waiting to be picked up in Helsinki, a twenty-hour drive from Moscow. We did not know a single physician in town, nor did we know the location of a hospital. I was horrified at the thought of having to rely on a Russian ambulance, a local hospital, Russian doctors and nurses. Even without these doubts, hospitalization would have involved leaving the children in an environment in which they would be unable to communicate with anyone because of language difficulties, which would have caused them immeasurable distress in addition to their dangerous illness.

The rapid deterioration of our sons forced us to venture into the unknown and to face the local health-care system. A telephone call to the guards manning our embassy day and night produced information that sounded too good to be true. The British embassy had its own resident physician. Everything now depended on him. What if he was out of town, on a call, or not available for other reasons? I dialled his number and held my breath. Dr W. answered the phone himself. Within forty-five minutes, he rang our doorbell, the life-saving medication in his bag. He administered the drugs, and I was left to worry about whether the boys, especially the delicate one-year-old Jeremy, would be able to hold out until the medication took effect.

Whether Dr W. wanted to keep a close eye on his patients during the critical hours, intended to reassure the panic-stricken parents, or was acting out of professionalism combined with human kindness, he recommended immediate evacuation of parents and patients from the barrenness of our quarters to the living-room of the home he shared with his wife on the grounds of the British embassy residence, the comfortable converted stables of the former town palace of a Czarist noble family. When the huge gates to the walled embassy compound, wooden structures big enough for feudal horse-drawn carriages to pass through and now guarded by Soviet militiamen, shut behind us, I had the feeling Dr W. had locked out the reaper.

I remember with the deepest sense of gratitude the afternoon and evening we spent in his sitting-room. The atmosphere of security his calm, competent, and kindly manner created and the impact it had on all of us cannot adequately be described. He kept a constant eye on the children, checked their pulse and temperature, and fed them mineral water, teaspoon by teaspoon. Towards evening, the fever broke, their breathing grew more regular, and eventually both fell asleep peacefully. As Mrs W., every bit as warm and kind-hearted as her husband, served tea, the last rays of the setting sun lit the gilded domes of the Kremlin cathedrals a short distance across the river.

Now that tragedy had been averted, Dr W., without leaving the side of his little patients, administered to their parents a dose of healing comedy.

Before arriving in Moscow, he had been engaged in a personal power struggle with his future neighbours in the Kremlin. An avid astronomer, he was the proud owner of a Questar, a telescope powerful enough to enable the user to observe the stars at close range. Someone using an instrument of that quality was able to examine not only the firmament above the Soviet capital, but the red stars decorating the Kremlin towers and to put the lives of those working in the shadow of their dim light behind the Kremlin walls under the equivalent of a microscope.

All his efforts to assure the Soviet authorities that he was not interested in what was going on behind the lace curtains of the Kremlin windows and that he was an astronomer in his spare time, not a Peeping Tom, failed to convince his neighbours on the other side of the Moskva River. By all accounts already weary of being studied and analysed by foreigners, Soviet officials simply refused to grant permission for the deployment of a high-powered telescope at the Kremlin gates. What looked like a harmless device for astronomical purposes could secretly double as the agent in more sinister schemes. It might even become instrumental in revolutionizing and – God forbid – improving Kremlin-watching methods. The Questar was declared 'instrumentum non gratum' and was refused entry into the Soviet Union. That struggle Dr W. had lost.

When Robin and Jeremy woke up after a long sleep it was clear that they were on their way to recovery. That decisive battle, Dr W. had won.

Not every foreign-service member exposed abroad to serious illness escapes with nothing more dramatic than emotional bruises, as we did. Children, especially young ones, are highly vulnerable in countries where the quality of water and food, sanitary conditions, and health-care facilities are well below Canadian standards. A two-year-old girl was lost to a tropical disease and, twenty years later, her parents are still inconsolable. A toddler injured in an accident died because of a strike of hospital personnel. I found that the subject of serious illness or death of a child remains so painful to parents that they hesitate or refuse to talk about it, even years after the event.

Few foreign-service members get through their careers without being hit, more or less seriously, by one of the diseases for which their respective postings are noted. Each family's story includes a long chapter on illnesses. Unsanitary living conditions, inadequately trained medical staff, and primitive medical facilities are responsible for a large number and variety of sicknesses inflicted on foreign-service members who know that they would have never come down with the disease if they had not been assigned to the country or region in question. Those who recover often admit that they should not have taken the risk; others have no regrets and insist that the good sides of this posting outweighed the bad sides, even the danger inherent in local illnesses.

Individuals or families suffering irreparable damage are reluctant to discuss the issue most likely because the guilt that remains is as powerful as the sorrow. In general, foreign-service members rarely volunteer much specific information about medical crises. But Health and Welfare physicians who are familiar with the health of their charges in External Affairs confirm that foreign-service personnel are at high risk in many foreign countries and succumb to diseases at a dramatically higher rate than Canadians staying at home.

In one family alone, the spouse of an employee in a tropical posting caught hepatitis, one son suffered from malaria, another son contracted a virus that rendered him deaf, and a daughter came down with cholera. Several foreign-service members were lost as a result of inadequate medical care, although they could have been saved in a Canadian hospital. What would be treated in Canada as a blatant case of malpractice is often shrugged off abroad by representatives of the local medical establishment as an inescapable act of Nature or God's will. An ambassador died in a developing country because of an incorrect diagnosis. One of the saddest cases in the entire history of the service involved one of its most senior members. Minor surgery incompetently performed abroad led to permanent, severe brain damage.

The AIDS virus has added considerably to the dangers to which foreign-service personnel are exposed overseas. AIDS is common in a good part of central Africa. Up to one-third of the population of some countries are said to be carrying the virus. To avoid the risk of catching it through blood transfusions, the evacuation of foreign-service personnel to hospitals in Western Europe has now become the rule in cases where surgery is required. But patients who cannot wait for evacuation to another continent because they require emergency surgery remain at high risk.

Foreign-service members are taught preventive measures against diseases. Vaccinations prior to a posting against yellow fever, malaria, hepatitis, smallpox, and many other diseases are standard practice. The advice not to drink local water without boiling it or to drink only mineral water is followed by everyone. And yet, amoebas, parasites, viruses, and a host of other problems cannot be entirely avoided in many parts of the world where the general health education and observance of basic rules of hygiene fall well below Western standards. As one of the sixteen Health and Welfare physicians who look after foreign-service personnel in Ottawa and in some of the largest capitals told me, you can vaccinate yourself silly and boil your drinking water for hours, but nothing will prevent you from getting seriously ill if your local maid rinses your drinking-glass in the toilet bowl.

As our sons' illness had shown us, even the most stringent of precautions did not forestall the risk to health and life. Returning from our medical evacuation to our apartment with two pale boys, we were fiercely determined to avoid a repetition of such an attack. Robin and Jeremy were obviously over the worst. They were asking for toys and a bite to eat. The desire for toys could be satisfied. Supplying food proved to be a more difficult task.

In order to cook, I needed water. There was none. The opened taps produced coughing and choking sounds, but not a drop of water. Our next crisis had arrived; it was nothing in comparison with what we had just survived, but it was a major trial.

A phone call to our embassy disclosed that our distinguished address had two weaknesses: the water pressure went down in the summer because of drought, and water could be expected to vanish altogether for a few days each August while the pipes were being cleaned. One or the other was the cause of our current dry taps. The Moscow-experienced guard at our embassy suggested we investigate the pressure at some level below the fourteenth floor, where our apartment was located.

A kingdom for friends in low places! We had earlier met an Australian colleague who lived on the fifth floor. A quick ring at his door and we had secured access to the most precious natural resource we could think of, even though every drop of it required ten minutes of boiling to turn it from poison into something drinkable.

Transportation of the treasure was the next hurdle. Nine floors and one tiny elevator for a host of occupants of this high-rise lay between our well on the fifth floor and our apartment on the fourteenth. We gathered the few pots and pans we had been lent by our colleagues, filled them with the slow-running water, carried them back to the elevator, and waited our turn in the seemingly endless queues. Eventually we had enough to cook some kind of supper.

It was, however, not possible to use a washing-machine, flush a toilet, or clean the dozen cloth diapers we had brought with us on the assumption that our air-freight shipment, which included enough diapers for a regiment of toddlers, would arrive in Moscow at the same time we did. The shipment, contrary to all promises, had not made it on time, and we were stuck with no more than six diapers per sick child. With water and washing-machine intact, this would have been no predicament. But we had approximately one cup of water available for each diaper. Disposable diapers had not been introduced to the Soviet economic plan yet.

The next day became diaper day. We knew that our embassy had a washing-machine in its basement, but we had no car and no way of transporting the diapers back and forth. I cannot recall who drove us to the embassy in the morning, but I do remember leaving our cheerfully chattering little boys in the care of the nanny and cradling a pail of dirty diapers in my lap, as my husband and I set out on this important mission into the centre of Moscow. I thought I had never seen water flow so abundantly as in the basement of our chancery. Never before, I was convinced, had a washing-machine performed such miracles. But our deliverance was incomplete: the embassy had no dryer. Colleagues who had heard of our dilemma had invited us to their apartment for tea and had offered the services of their own dryer.

Some friendships are made during a crisis. Drained from the months of chaos before our move and discouraged to discover that the innumerable problems we had solved prior to our arrival had been only a prelude to the fierce onslaught of much greater trouble here, we felt like shipwreck survivors being led to the redeeming shore when Henry and Ann Wealdon welcomed us with open arms to the haven of sanity over which they presided. Their small apartment, filled with books, carpets, and paintings, breathed an atmosphere of comfort and peace. I had not seen so much order and beauty since we had started to dismantle our own house months ago. To sit with them, to tell them details of our sons' serious illness and merciful recovery, to unload much of our misery, and to absorb their warm and compassionate hospitality was like a balm on our wounds. Eventually we collected the cleanest and dryest diapers the Soviet capital had seen in a long time and returned home to our boys, feeling refreshed and encouraged. The short-term project was to change diapers, the long-term project to convert our apartment into a home as quickly as possible.

A few days later, our air and sea shipments arrived and I did what every foreign-service member considers to be his or her first major task in a new posting: to unpack in order to settle down in the strange environment and to get on with a life that had been interrupted for too long. Opening boxes and taking out familiar objects that had been part of our life in Canada felt like a reunion with beloved old friends whose presence would bring warmth to even the coldest surroundings. Exactly seven weeks after we had set foot in the apartment, everything was in place, and the rooms had begun to look a little bit like home. Family life could be resumed where we had left off months earlier. Robin and Jeremy had completely recovered from their illness and were their boisterous selves, in spite of having been transplanted to different soil.

During the week that I had indicated in my personal calendar marked the successful completion of our move, we learned that our prestigious address and the size of our apartment had captured the imagination of the wife of a newly arrived senior colleague. Shocked by the size of the apartment she and her husband had been allotted, especially in comparison with the splendid accommodations they had enjoyed in the previous posting, she had enquired about other possibilities and had been told that a junior officer was occupying a more desirable apartment. She demanded to inspect it, found it up to her standards, and announced that we would have to relinquish our apartment since her husband's senior position in the embassy made our quarters a necessity for the two of them. Both my husband and I found it hard to believe that anyone would act in such a way towards colleagues. But we decided to give in graciously in order to avoid petty squabbling and felt somewhat consoled when most of our colleagues in the mission expressed their sympathy to us and admiration for our good-humoured retreat in the face of such bullying. It was the only case of narrow-minded prestige seeking that we ever encountered personally, but judging by the accounts of other foreign-service members, it was not the only incident of its kind.

Once we had learned that we were to be tossed out of our brand-new home and thrown into 7/4 Kutuzovsky Prospect instead, we began to list the disadvantages of the old and the advantages of the new apartment. We still had not seen the new place, but we knew that it was located in the centre of the city and within walking distance, admittedly long walks, of the embassy, shops, and the Kremlin churches and museums. We could also see the windows of Ann and Henry Wealdon's apartment in the middle of our high-rise slums, a reassuring neighbourhood.

To stress these positive aspects of the new address was an important exercise at that point because the apartment presented considerable problems to a family of four with a nanny. It consisted of two small apartments, separated by a public hallway. This hall had to be experienced to be believed. In the centre an elevator that looked like an iron cage and doubled as a urinal for some of the building's occupants rattled and scraped its way up and down eight floors all day long. Across from the elevator door a garbage chute served as a favourite haunt for the local cockroach population. Each of these features competed for our attention with their own distinguishable scents. A hundred times a day we would have to cross over to the other apartment, unable to escape the thick odours from all sides.

But, for me, the most difficult aspect of this move was the unsettling effect it would inevitably have on our children. As if it had not been hard enough for them to leave their house in Ottawa, the ground was to be taken out from under them again, only seven weeks after they had begun to settle in the Vavilova apartment.

My other concerns about the move turned out to be justified. Our goods, which had been packed in Ottawa by professionals with the greatest care and had arrived in the first apartment in immaculate condition, were now simply thrown by untrained Russian packers into boxes and transported across town. I watched with horror as the last of our local moving trucks – all of them converted Soviet Second World War army vehicles, still painted dark green – came to a halt in front of the new building. The last two items taken out of the Vavilova apartment and tossed into an open box found themselves serenely united on top of the truck: an eighteenth-century oil painting of a German king pierced by the tip of a broomstick. Whether by coincidence or by the design of a discriminating Russian mover, only the king's jacket, and not his face, had been blemished. To this day the German king bears his Russian scars, a reminder of countless works of art and other treasures irretrievably lost to our colleagues each year in the course of merciless moves.

Foreign-service employees often move from one staff quarters to another within the same city. Because of tight housing markets and a never-ending stream of personnel leaving and arriving, staff quarters tend to be rotational as well. Each foreign-service member who is unhappy with the first accommodation will be looking for something more suitable or desirable among the apartments and houses the embassy has at its disposal as soon as something becomes free after an embassy member has left and before the replacement has arrived. Some employees are forced to stay in hotels for the first days, weeks, or sometimes months of their assignment before an apartment either becomes available or is ready for occupancy. In the aftermath of the McDougall Commission, a housing committee was established in each mission to determine the allotment of houses and apartments.

Whatever verdict such a committee may hand down, housing constitutes one of the key elements that determine success or failure of an assignment abroad. Trying to cope successfully with that issue can be as exasperating as contending with another key component of the local daily reality: the quest for food. Our own struggles in that area represent the experience of hundreds, if not thousands, of our colleagues all over the world.

Food

Food, or more precisely the scarcity or absence of it, has been the subject of jokes in Russia since time immemorial. During our years in Moscow, the story was often told of a long-suffering comrade who entered a store and asked for a quarter-pound of butter. The saleswoman replied: 'This here is the store without meat. The shop with no butter is next door.'

As I found out on my first shopping day, the food situation in the Soviet capital was indeed grim. A great dearth seemed to have spread to every store in the neighbourhood. The post report prepared by the embassy in Moscow for newcomers had warned us about shortages. Old Moscow hands had told similar stories. But no written or oral account had adequately described the stark reality of the local food scene.

A tiny fruit and vegetable store in a dark and musty-smelling basement somewhere near our apartment displayed a few shrivelled heads of cabbage, some misshapen balls resembling red beets, and a collection of sickly-looking potatoes and carrots. A wooden bin half-filled with small, spotty apples represented the fruit department. This disheartening sight was surpassed only by the window of the general food store where innumerable cans of Bulgarian peas had been arranged dramatically into huge pyramids. On the shelves inside the shop more pyramids had been erected of tins of green beans from Bulgaria, alternating with jars of pickled cucumbers from Poland. Apart from grey paper bags containing sugar or flour and several other bags filled with indefinable contents, there was not much else.

An excursion to the market for goods from the state farms did not produce the hoped-for results. Row on row of old women dipped into huge wooden containers to reveal almost triumphantly the fruits of their efforts: pickled cucumbers and pickled white cabbage. The crowds of Moscovites shuffling past this array of goods were also offered potatoes, carrots, and beets, not different from the ones I had seen in the basement store. Here they were available in great quantity. One stall specialized in onions. And there were more of the tiny spotty apples I had seen in our neighbourhood. They all seemed to have fallen off the same neglected tree. How could I wean our children from the variety and quality of Canadian food to a sad diet of withered apples and pickled cabbage?

I decided to survey the territory for other essentials. Bread was available in abundance, every bit as dark, moist, coarse, and tasty as Russian 'chleb' was supposed to be. But it had a taste that needed to be acquired and I was not entirely certain that our children would ever adapt to it.

As urgently needed as bread, milk had to be secured. The thick, creamy, yellow substance sold in heavy glass bottles as 'moloko' contained 6 per cent butter-fat, a hair-raising proposition for anyone who had grown up on skim or 2 per cent milk. Life in Canada had convinced me that any Canadian nutritionist would have been horrified by the amount of cholesterol in each bottle. If our children could be persuaded to like this cream, they would turn into little barrels of fat. It was decidedly undesirable to acquire a taste for the local milk. But what should they drink instead for the next two years?

Fellow Canadians in the embassy and previous generations of foreign-service families had already done pioneer work on the milk front and provided us with the tested and trustworthy recipe for Moscow milk, Canadian style: Boil water for ten minutes, refrigerate until cold, mix equal amounts of 6 per cent milk and boiled water, stir thoroughly, and refrigerate overnight. The alternative was simply to make do with Western milk powder.

The third possible source of milk for our children we dubbed the 'Finnish solution.' A department store in Helsinki shipped frozen 2 per cent milk to Moscow. The milk was known to be of the finest taste and quality. Unfortunately, it also fetched the finest price. We decided to keep the milk from Helsinki as our last resort and to experiment with our own production.

Whenever possible, we turned milk brewing into a family event. Robin and Jeremy, armed with egg beaters and wooden spoons, stood on kitchen chairs and mixed and stirred with a passion. The grand finale was always the sampling of our concoction, just before it was stowed away in the fridge. Ageing over night, as we had learned from Moscow veterans, had the same mellowing effect on milk as ageing in barrels or bottles had on rebellious young wine. All four of us soon developed the ability to distinguish, like experienced connoisseurs, between the various milk vintages. But our expertise surpassed that of any wine producer. Our taste buds became attuned to differences so subtle that we could tell from one sip whether we were drinking the Monday, Wednesday, or Friday creation. Thus peace was quickly established on the milk front and I could devote myself to a more complex theatre of war: the food scene.

When in Russia, do as the Russians do – this motto, with local variations, is the watchword for many foreign-service members. I was dedicated to absorbing as much of Russian culture and traditions as possible, and that included Russian cuisine. If Russian children had been raised on *borshch* and still grown up to become Pushkins and Chekhovs, or even astronauts – the last-named of even more impressive stature, as far as Robin was concerned – then there should be no reason why Canadian children should not thrive on it, especially since we could rely on the luxurious version of the Russian national dish, which included meat.

Judging by the almost empty meat stores in Moscow, which all resembled showrooms for tile manufacturers, meat was clearly a luxury for the average Soviet citizen. In order to provide foreign diplomats with meat and other scarce articles the Soviet authorities had established special shops for foreigners. By Soviet standards, these two or three places in the centre of the city were overflowing with nutritional treasures. Behind permanently lowered blinds and protected by a guard against stray unprivileged comrades, diplomats had a chance to purchase beef, mushrooms, butter, and the occasional orange. By Western standards it was a pitiful selection, but we had at least precious protein to enrich the diet of bread, potatoes, and cabbage.

The red beets, white cabbage, onions, and potatoes I turned into the classic *borshch*. Served with equally traditional sour cream, it seemed to be a hit. Robin and Jeremy ate it, concentrating on the chunks of familiar meat and tolerating the other parts. I quickly congratulated myself not only on having introduced my family to a local dish but on having successfully initiated the process of cultural adaptation.

I was soon to find out that this *borshch* would be the last the children would eat. They seemed to have acquired tastes and eating patterns at ages one and three that were difficult to change. After the first few experiments with local dishes, they retreated to eating only dishes they had known in Canada. In the absence of fresh fruit and vegetables and anything beyond the most basic goods, we were forced to import food from abroad.

I had to admit with dismay that living off the local economy is a principle more easily espoused than practised. I had always been convinced that cooking and savouring local dishes made of local ingredients should be part of any foreign-service member's immersion program into any culture. However, in Moscow, every food store seemed designed to demonstrate that my principle could be pursued with more delicious results in some postings than in others. There was only so much *borshch,* Stroganoff, *kulebiaka,* and *kolbasa* the family was willing to eat.

A colourful, glossy catalogue from a supplier in Denmark promised relief from the grey monotony of the Moscow fare. Proudly advertising its status as 'Purveyor to H.M. the Queen of Denmark's Household' and displaying the Danish crown on its cover, the catalogue offered the finest choice of any type of food, together with the reassuring information that it had been shipping its goods to diplomats all over the world for twenty years. Anything could be ordered that was displayed on 1,000 pages: baby food, canned meat and soups, rice, pasta, cake mixes, sweets, tinned seafood, and Chinese, Japanese, and Indian dishes. All the magnificently arranged and photographed delicacies could be packed and dispatched to any destination in the world.

Altogether, it was a mouth-watering array. Unfortunately, filling out one of the conveniently attached order forms was bound to have a draining effect on family finances. In spite of the tax-free status of all items, the prices were regal by Canadian standards and considerably higher than their counterparts in the average grocery store at home. Costs for transportation and insurance were extra.

Fresh produce, which was not included in the Danish catalogue, was offered in Helsinki by one of the finest department stores we had ever encountered. Crisp heads of lettuce; golden, spotless bananas; lush parsley – any conceivable type of fruit and vegetable could be ordered by telex through our embassy and would arrive in Moscow exquisitely wrapped and packaged and looking immaculately fresh even after the sixteen-hour train ride from Finland. However, going to the train station once a week to pick up groceries from Helsinki was following the road to ruin on a Canadian salary. To satisfy our needs and wishes, we could have spent most of our hardship allowance on the juicy and tasty treasures from a Western grocery store, but we settled for a compromise. The basic goods available in Moscow would be cautiously supplemented by a modest amount of fresh produce and occasional allowances for such luxuries as bananas, oranges, lettuce, tomatoes, and parsley, all at about two or three times the Canadian price.

During the short summer months the private farmer markets in Moscow offered strawberries, cherries, and fresh beans at Helsinki prices. It was impossible to resist such temptation. I remember consoling myself one day when I had just paid the equivalent of five dollars for a kilogram of potatoes with the thoroughly satisfying thought that I had not only honoured private initiative, but supported the 3 per cent of all arable land in private hands from which came more than 25 per cent of the Soviet economy's total agricultural output.

Two types of foodstuff were considered to be such essentials that even Canadians behind the Iron Curtain could not be expected to do without. In the middle of December each year, Air Canada flew turkeys into Moscow to provide for a proper Christmas meal for embassy staff. In April, the new harvest of maple syrup was flown in. We paid, of course, for the goods. But the tab for the air freight was picked up either by Air Canada or by the government. This special delivery for the Moscow shut-ins was greatly appreciated, and the arrival of the goods from home was celebrated each time as a joyful event.

Shopping from Swedish, Danish, and Finnish catalogues in addition to the daily struggle for food in the local stores complicated life and wasted enormous amounts of time. Catalogues had to be studied, prices compared, order forms filled out – all months in advance, since it took months for orders to arrive in Moscow. For anyone who had cherished the chance in Canada to limit the time and energy spent on shopping to one or two hours a week and thus gain time for more stimulating pursuits, the constant preoccupation with local and long-distance shopping amounted to a particular form of hardship.

And yet, we had much to be grateful for. In the mid 1970s, our situation in Moscow could be considered comfortable compared with those of colleagues in some other parts of the world, or with life in the Soviet capital ten or twenty years earlier. Thereza Ford, the wife of our ambassador, who had lived with her husband in Moscow during the Stalin era, used to entertain us with anecdotes about her days as housewife at that time. Her stories were amusing during the relative affluence of our sojourn, but would have been harrowing at the time of the greatest shortages twenty years before.

If diplomatic suppliers outside the Soviet Union had already been established in the late 1940s and early 1950s, Stalin and his advisers would have been unlikely to believe in them. Members of the few foreign governments represented by embassies in Moscow were completely cut off from any source of food from abroad. For years, they had to get along on bread, potatoes, cabbage, and red beets, just like the average comrade. Many of them felt lucky to have even that fare.

Two of Thereza Ford's tales remain in my mind. During a rare visit to postwar Berlin, she had obtained a whole, fresh, and rather large fish, a breath-taking delicacy by Moscow standards. If it was to brighten their grey diet in the Soviet capital, it would have to receive royal treatment on the long journey from Germany to the heart of Russia. In order to assure the well-being of the priceless cargo and to shield it against the unwelcome attention of fellow passengers, the ambassador's wife spent the seemingly endless trip in a converted Soviet Second World War plane cradling the treasure in her lap or taking it for walks up and down the aisle to give her neighbour a chance to breathe more freely.

Another incident took place in an even more delicate atmosphere. One of the ambassadors accredited in Moscow, briefly hospitalized, received a joint visit of half a dozen of his fellow envoys. When, after a few hours of conversations around his bed, lunchtime arrived, each ambassador unwrapped the sandwiches he had brought along. The only person in the circle who had nothing to unwrap was an uninvited guest whose presence had been nevertheless quietly tolerated. He was known to be the agent assigned to this meeting by the local authorities. The congregation of ambassadors passed a plate around and collected enough from everyone's sandwich to feed the starved KGB agent too.

Together with the issues of housing and health, food ranks high on the list of priority concerns of foreign-service members and their families. In many of the hardship posts, the procurement and quality of food represent some of the great uncertainties of daily life. Except for postings in North America and Western Europe, the utmost flexibility is required for transients. They are well advised to leave dependence on Mother's cooking behind and to bring adventuresome and tolerant taste buds and stomachs along if they want to participate to the fullest in the local culture, and remain healthy and in good spirits at the same time.

Delight in the discovery of new delicacies is one of the hallmarks of foreign-service living. Many families take great pleasure in the change from their usual diet that a new posting offers. Canadians posted to Western Europe never stop marvelling at the quality and variety of breads they eat and report losing their taste for traditional Canadian bread. Asked about some of the best sides of their life in a far-away country, foreign-service members are quick to refer to the most delicious seafood in Asia and Latin America; wholesome, wonderfully tasty, unrefined grains in central Africa; the distinct flavour of Chinese cuisine; and the subtleties of Japanese cooking. Luscious fruit in many parts of the world, and colourful markets overflowing with vegetables and fruit continue to cheer Canadians up wherever they are shopping for ingredients to vary and enrich their menus.

As mouth-watering as exotic dishes may be to one group of people, a lot of novices to a foreign culture are unable to adjust to what is locally produced or eaten. Children especially tend to be more conservative than their elders in matters of the palate. Many foreign-service parents confirmed my own experience: mouths and stomachs of smaller children simply close up at the sight and smell of unknown dishes. With the reserve they showed to Russian menus, our sons' taste was typical of Canadian children of all ages who, sitting down to a meal of bird's nest soup, roast octopus, or *Hortobágyi palacsinta,* long for hot dogs, hamburgers, and spaghetti with meat balls. If the children's wishes cannot be fulfilled, parents have to resort either to cunning or to force in order to ensure a reasonably balanced diet for them. Under such circumstances, family meals can be more a draining experience than a period for physical and emotional restoration. Our own experience with four children over more than twenty years illustrates what hundreds of our colleagues report about their children.

On the evening of our arrival in Budapest, our daughters, Julia and Alexandra, seven and nine years old at that time, expressed horror at the sight of warm milk decorated with floating scum. They took one sip, shuddered, and refused to drink a single drop for the following week. Faced with the prospect of watching them go entirely without milk for the next three years, we found the solution in chocolate powder. Stirred into cold milk – the cook had been persuaded in the meantime not to heat the milk – the powder blurred the distinction between Canadian and Hungarian milk. For the first few months, parental lectures on the importance of milk dominated our meals, a topic of conversation loathed equally by children and parents. It took a full year before our girls were willing to be weaned from chocolate milk and to graduate to pure Hungarian milk.

During our initial months in Budapest, the local beef, pork, bread, apples, and a large number of other items seemed as insufferable to Julia and Alexandra as the local milk. In most cases, it was not possible to disguise the distinctive taste with chocolate powder. We decided to exploit shamelessly our daughters' passion for After Eights. A certain amount of meat, vegetables, and fruit eaten per meal fetched a certain number of these chocolate mints. Dinner conversations now alternated between the subjects of the importance of drinking milk and the importance of eating a well-balanced diet. All of this stretched the parents' patience to the limits. But the bait worked worders. Without the prospect of such wonderful rewards, our girls might have continued their self-prescribed diet of ice water and toast with black currant jam well beyond the first week in the new posting. We could have been strict about the issue, but out of deference to the uprooting they had just experienced, decided against that approach. Throughout the period of After Eights therapy, we dreaded the moment at which they tired of the bait. To our great relief they never did. One evening they ate their meal and forgot completely about the chocolate mints afterwards. It was a moment of quiet victory for their hard-pressed parents.

Not every foreign-service member is able to overcome aversion to unfamiliar food quite as easily. In some cases it is difficult to distinguish between a person's simple rejection of strange-tasting dishes and the rejection of this particular assignment or of foreign-service life altogether. Eating disorders are not uncommon among foreign-service personnel. The ease or difficulty with which foreign-service members cope with constantly changing food deserves attention as one of the key indicators of a person's general adjustment to a specific posting, or to the rotational life as a whole.

Eating outside the home while living abroad can be one of the great delights of a posting. I have yet to meet a foreign-service member who does not rave about some of the delicacies he or she has sampled in various countries. Some street vendors in Beijing are said to sell the most delicious noodle soup and moon cakes in the world. Moscow ice cream brings back happy sighs of longing from any child who has ever licked through a scoop of it. All our children found freshly baked hot waffles sprinkled with icing sugar at open air markets in Brussels tantalizing.

Restaurants – whether a converted *dacha* in a village outside of Moscow, a tiny seafood tavern by a beach in a Greek or Chilean fishing village, a pub overlooking a firth in the northern part of Scotland, a splendid establishment on the European side of Istanbul in full view of the Asian continent across the Bosphorus, or a gourmet restaurant in the Belgian capital – can be a most pleasurable introduction to the host culture in any part of the world.

Not all experiences with a country's food culture lead to a happy ending. Canadians in many postings report suffering short or prolonged illnesses after having sampled local dishes in a restaurant or private home. One ambassador recalls trying to reach by telephone some of his colleagues the morning after the foreign minister of the host country had given an official dinner. Every one of the previous evening's guests was sick in bed. Comparing notes later, they discovered that the entire party was suffering from the same intestinal problem.

Foreign-service members encounter, perhaps more often than members of any other profession, the close link between food and disease. Illnesses contracted through eating in other countries, especially in hot and humid regions, abound. Dysentery, food poisoning, salmonella, and amoebic infections rank high on the list of occupational hazards and have claimed more than one life.

The same mixture of delights and disasters potentially inherent in foreign foodstuffs descends on international migrants in the form of a large variety of climatic conditions that force them to come to terms with yet another challenge of the daily reality of life abroad.

Climate

Father Frost, the personification of Russian winter, entered Moscow six weeks after the city had suffered a summer shortage of water. Huge snowflakes came tumbling down reluctantly, as if not yet certain about their destination and the timing of their arrival. From the balcony of our fourteenth-floor apartment, the grey concrete houses below us seemed to be wrapped in graciously moving white sheets. The air was filled with the smell and whispers I remembered from the first snowfall each year in Canada.

Father Frost lived up to his reputation. The snow he had so abundantly spread across the city on the official first day of fall remained on the ground, assisted by bitterly cold temperatures. The sudden change of weather provided an occasion for Canadians to discuss with their Russian colleagues the eternal question of whether Ottawa or Moscow qualified as the colder capital. Ulan Bator, the capital of Mongolia, had once and for all won the title as coldest capital in the world, but the Canadian and the Soviet capital were forever competing for second place. During the period of the Cold War, this contest had been a safe subject to debate at East-West diplomatic cocktail parties. In September 1973, the Soviet capital, under a blanket of snow and sparkling with ice, was undoubtedly in the lead as Ottawa was probably basking in a long Indian summer. The distinctive Moscow climate could be expected to be a reliable companion throughout our two-year assignment.

Three weeks later, in the middle of October, when I returned from a visit to West Germany, where a warm and golden autumn had convinced vineyard owners that the 1973 vintage would become one of the wines of the century, I was struck by how thoroughly winter had established himself during my brief absence. It was bitterly cold, and darkness had settled in. A strange grey light lay heavily over the city. It grew rapidly darker until, by the beginning of November, we needed the lights on in our apartment all day long.

After the chaos of our move to the Kutuzovsky apartment was over, I had a great desire to be free of the demoralizing routine of taking down tents and rebuilding them, as I had done twice during the past four months. Now that the Kremlin and the shopping district of the Arbat were within walking distance, I would be able to explore the city and combine this adventure with outings for Jeremy while Robin was attending morning classes at the French nursery school. The idea was exhilarating. I would finally have a chance to study the everyday life of Soviet citizens, practise my fledgling Russian on location, and meet people. I would be able to do many of the things for which I had worked so hard during the upheaval of the previous months.

To my dismay, I discovered, after having pushed Jeremy in his stroller through the heart of the city for a few hours, that his little face was covered with a layer of tiny black particles. Under close examination, they turned out to be soot. Moscow was polluted, that much I had known before we came. But I had had no idea how serious the problem was. I was horrified at the thought of what Jeremy's lungs looked like after this excursion in search of fresh air for him, and Russian culture for myself. The pleasure had been cruelly taken out of future walks. The air in our apartment was probably healthier than the air outside, although even that was a contentious assumption, judging by the daily accumulation of soot on our windowsill, behind closed windows.

Except for some weekend outings into the Lenin Hills for a modest amount of cross-country skiing and the occasional ice-hockey tournament with our two-man midget team in the parking lot of our foreigners' compound, we settled into our apartment for the longest and gloomiest winter I can remember. It was the all-embracing darkness that made the Moscow winter so much more difficult to enjoy than winters in Ottawa. I wondered whether we were perceiving the darkness as particularly powerful for psychological reasons, as emblematic of the dismal political and economic system and the suffering of the people. A look at the maps of Russia and Canada revealed more convincing reasons. Ottawa, sharing the latitude of Milan, qualified as a southern city by European geographic standards. Moscow, at about fifty-six degrees northern latitude, was about ten degrees farther north than Ottawa, which would put it somewhere between northern Quebec, the centre of Hudson Bay, and the city of Petersburg in Alaska. Similar temperatures and average snow accumulations aside, the quantity of sunshine each city received during the darker months of the year created dramatically different kinds of winters.

Once in a while, just after a snowfall, the all-pervasive white in the centre of Moscow would reflect the amber façades of some of the Kremlin palaces and turn a unique pale yellow. The air would adopt an almost golden hue. Against a grey sky, heavily laden with more snow, this pastel tone created a mood of harmony and beauty, which had caught my attention in films, photographs, and slides I had seen of the city. But those days of gentle golden light surrounding the gilded domes of the Kremlin churches were rare.

Darkness seemed to be even more pronounced in the Baltic republics, which I visited with my husband in December. Throughout our week-long stay in Estonia, Latvia, and Lithuania, the automatic light meter in my camera confirmed my own impression. The amount of light available was insufficient to take photographs. Even at the height of day, dusk hung over Tallinn, Riga, and Vilnius. I treated the information my light meter gave me not as advice against taking pictures, but as an invitation to try to capture the mood. The photos and slides I took preserved the all-encompassing greyness.

Helsinki, however, farther to the north than the Baltic republics, had somehow managed to brighten streets, hotels, restaurants, and shops with such cheerful colours and brilliant artificial light we never noticed the natural darkness there.

Darkness hung over Moscow until March. By that time we had been without any visible sun for almost six months. One day, in the middle of March, the grey sky opened and revealed an almost blinding light. It was such a staggering event I heard that friends phoned each other to share their excitement. I remember looking out of the window and feeling a sharp, stinging pain in my eyes. The two-year-old son of one of our colleagues had burst into uncontrollable shrieks of joy when he saw the sun for the first time that year, his mother told me. But it was the middle of May before anything resembling spring made its appearance. The May Day Parade of Communist workers, all of them proudly passing our foreigners' compound, featured thousands of Soviet citizens in heavy winter coats, hats, and boots, enthusiastically waving giant paper carnations.

When the sun finally forced Father Frost to retreat, the result was as dramatic as it was enchanting. Moscow had been transformed in one day. For the following months, darkness seemed to have been shut out entirely. The days were filled with endless hours of glorious sun. Even the nights received a copious amount of light. I remember returning with my husband from a dinner some time after midnight in the middle of June under a glowing pale pink sky. Could it be that the sky was already lighting up for the new day? I wanted urgently to find out. We settled down on the balcony and watched. After long and careful observation, we had to admit that we would not be able to find out whether we had seen the light of the previous or of the new day. At no point had there been darkness in the sky. The two days had merged invisibly. When we left our balcony at around two o'clock in the morning, 'Eos was spreading her rosy fingers' – as the ancient Greeks described their own sunrises – across the sky high above the roofs of the Soviet capital, brightening up memories of the previous months.

Different, but no less distinct and dramatic, were the summer nights in the city that was still called Leningrad at that time. Located farther north than Moscow and situated on the shore of the Baltic Sea, it had been celebrated in literature for its 'white nights' ever since Czar Peter the Great had raised the new capital out of the swamps. During a visit to St Petersburg, we found what we had been looking for. Whether caused by air-sea interaction or by any other phenomenon science could explain, the city had wrapped itself in a mysterious milky light throughout the midsummer night we spent there. A magic mood held everything under its spell.

Whenever they talk about their postings abroad, foreign-service members usually point out that climate, in all its manifestations – temperature, precipitation, humidity, wind, air pressure, and clouds – is one of the most important elements of the overall effect any foreign assignment has on them. Some well-defined aspect of local climate contributes to the first impression foreigners receive as they set foot on foreign soil and leaves a final mark as they climb on a plane at the end of their posting. During the intermittent years, the local climate possesses – according to experienced foreign-service personnel – the power to turn an assignment abroad into a pleasure or a problem.

Foreign-service members have to learn to adjust to the whole range of the world's climate types and to develop the flexibility to switch, within the shortest possible time, from a posting in the equatorial and tropical climate in central Africa or Southeast Asia, to an assignment in the desert climate of North Africa, or from the temperate climate of Central

Europe to the Mediterranean climates of southern Europe, California, South Africa, and southern Australia. Monsoon climates in Asia, with their daily floods of rain, demand adaptation as much as do tropical grassland climates south of the equator in Africa or other tropical highland zones.

Reactions to climates vary considerably. What qualifies as pleasant or unpleasant, good or bad climate is a matter of individual taste and physical constitution. The same type and degree of heat may be perceived as a paralysing and mind-numbing torture by one person, and as sustaining and revitalizing by another. One person's merciless, mind-splitting cold may be another's invigorating source of general well-being.

The advent of air-conditioning and central heating has made temperatures in office buildings and staff quarters largely controllable. Beyond control remain natural disasters, earthquakes, typhoons, hurricanes, and floods, to which foreign-service members are frequently exposed. Several colleagues told me how they sat shaking through minor earthquakes in Latin America, watching the contents of their apartment or house moving about and wondering whether this was the end. One young mother described to me in the most vivid terms her terror as the high-rise apartment in which she and her husband were living with their two small children suddenly began to sway. That nightmarish experience contributed to the couple's decision to leave the foreign service and seek a more stable profession and life.

Hurricanes in the Caribbean and typhoons in East Asian postings cause horror among foreign-service employees who are unaccustomed to such spectacles. If all the stories of natural disasters told by foreign-service members were collected, they would form a multi-volume work.

An equally sizeable publication might emerge if the encounters foreign-service personnel have had with local animals were anthologized. A country's fauna, closely linked to the surrounding climate, can cause reactions as strong as those to its climate. Generations of foreign-service members have struggled with mosquitoes, grasshoppers, and insects of every conceivable type. Snakes and other univited guests have wound their way into Canadian staff quarters without showing the slightest respect for diplomatic immunity. Cockroaches, rats, and vermin of many kinds, including enormous, and sometimes poisonous, spiders, have strained to the limits the nerves of Canadians abroad, especially those with small children.

When the local fauna detracts from the comfort of a posting, the local flora is bound to fill in. The first letter a close friend of mine wrote to me shortly after her arrival in Australia represents the joy and delight hundreds of foreign-service members express about the local vegetation. Her letter read like a hymn to the tropical trees, shrubs, and flowers in her huge garden accompanied by the never-ending concert of innumerable exotic birds.

While I listened to the stories foreign-service families told me about daily life abroad, I came to the conclusion that the majority of them had either brought with them or acquired extraordinary flexibility in adjusting to unusual climatic conditions and had responded to the sometimes overwhelming challenges with a degree of equanimity that deserves to be called professional.

Flexibility and adaptability are, however, sometimes not enough when one has to cope effectively with some of the more sinister aspects of daily life in the foreign service.

Security

One evening, while we were living in Brussels, my husband was urgently called to the official residence. The burglar alarm was wailing and, in the absence of the ambassador, the chargé d'affaires had to authorize the Belgian police to enter and search the building, since it was under diplomatic immunity. A small contingent of policemen, followed by the chargé, worked their way from room to room. The house looked empty and untouched. There was no sign of who or what had set off the alarm. Equally mysterious remained the location of the switch that would silence the high-pitched siren. For more than an hour, the policemen tried to track down the magic knob as more and more neighbours congregated outside, eagerly anticipating some form of spectacle. After the shut-off mechanism had been discovered, an almost deafening silence descended on Franklin Roosevelt Street.

Shortly after this incident, the ambassador found a bullet hole in one of his children's bedroom windows. No one ever determined who had fired the shot or with what intention. The incident had occurred during a period in which European public opinion was strongly against the Canadian government for the killing of seals for commerical puposes. Every day bags bulging with letters of protest were carried into the embassy in Brussels. Several of these contained threats to the safety of Canadians working in the mission, including the ambassador and his family. One of these documents announced retaliatory measures against Canadian diplomats living in Brussels unless the killing of seals stopped, and culminated in the statement: 'Seals are human beings too!' The question of whether Canadian diplomats and their families qualified on the same count had not been addressed in the letter.

The embassy never discovered whether these separate events were connected or whether they were at all linked to the European crusade for the rescue of Canadian seals. The episodes did, however, underline the fact that the safety of foreign diplomats was threatened everywhere in the world, even in the civilized environment of the Belgian capital, and that social or political causes adopted by fringe or more organized terrorists served as an excuse to single diplomats out as the target of their fury.

Diplomatic communities anywhere are under attack from two different sources and for two different sets of reasons. Ordinary thieves and robbers focus on foreign diplomats because they expect to find money, jewellery, electronic equipment, and other treasures in their apartments and houses. Especially in countries with extremes of wealth and poverty, diplomats serve as a favourite target for criminals attempting to redistribute material goods to their own benefit.

Local and international terrorists look to foreign diplomats for other reasons. Kidnapping, hostage taking, and threats to the lives of foreign envoys are often undertaken in the hope of a hefty ransom. If no money is forthcoming, there is always the benefit of international attention to the social or political cause the terrorists claim to embrace.

After guerrillas in Latin America started to kidnap, hold hostage, and even kill foreign diplomats in the late 1960s, foreign services developed a set of security measures. Particularly after the Iranian hostage crisis, governments have made enormous efforts to spare their employees the fate of falling victim to international disputes.

The Department of External Affairs supplies all rotational foreign-service members and their families heading out on a foreign assignment or travelling abroad on offical business a thick volume containing detailed information on how best to avoid confrontation with criminals and how to behave in emergencies caused by robbers or terrorists. For obvious reasons, these recommendations have to remain confidential.

Because the private apartments and houses of diplomats, including the ambassador's official residence, are favoured by intruders, as is the chancery, External Affairs has taken elaborate measures to protect all buildings. Chanceries and residences anywhere in the world are now surrounded by high iron fences whose gates are locked. The residence and chancery in Budapest are illuminated at night with floodlights. Military policemen guard the chancery around the clock. In an apartment in the basement of the residence lives the gardener, who acts as the permanent guard for the house.

Video cameras are placed in strategically important spots around the chancery, and a set of monitors allows the military guards to keep an eye on the grounds and exterior of the building complex. Inside the house, access to the secure zone, the inner sanctum where confidential papers are kept, is possible only through a heavy iron door with a keypad lock that can be opened by a code known only to Canadian employees of the mission and is changed frequently. It is virtually impossible for an unauthorized person to enter this safe haven. In cases of attack from the outside, it serves as refuge for all personnel. Recently, further security measures have been introduced in the building complex. Any prospective terrorist studying the premises for future operations should be sufficiently discouraged to try his luck somewhere else.

The safe haven of the residence consists of a few rooms and a bathroom, all separated from the rest of the house by a series of bullet-proof doors. Balcony doors are secured against the outside with iron chains.

The safety measures taken at the residence in the capital of Hungary are as modest as the local threat to the safety of the ambassador. In many socially and politically less stable countries, residences and chanceries have been equipped with more elaborate devices. Where local conditions are deemed to present a permanent threat to Canadians, all staff quarters are provided with a secure zone. It usually consists of the bedroom area and a bathroom completely surrounded by an iron grill that can be closed and locked at night. In such postings, all windows are covered with iron bars. As a result, many Canadian staff quarters abroad look like a fortress at best, a prison at worst. Their occupants often feel that a life behind bars is a steep price to pay for security.

Before such extensive safety measures were introduced, and, in some cases, afterwards, Candian diplomats often faced thieves and terrorists. In an African country, a robber, after having entered a house, grabbed a small child and held a gun to his head until the mother handed over her valuables. In several Latin American postings, employees frequently found themselves face to face with intruders.

Foreign-service members have been robbed while abroad so often no one has bothered to keep count of the cases. Everyone who has come across one or more thieves in his or her house points out that being robbed is bad enough, but the robbers are often armed. Even if the thief is a frightened novice, the possibility of being injured always exists.

Terrorists on a mission are always armed. In March 1989, the Toronto *Globe and Mail* published, under the headline 'Canadian Diplomats in the Hot Spots,' a series of articles in which former ambassador Sidney Freifeld listed some of the cases of terrorism involving Canadian diplomats. According to this report, Jim George, ambassador to Tehran in the late 1970s, called his office from the residence one day and heard an unfamiliar voice saying: 'Mr George, I am going to kill you!' When the ambassador asked for details, the man on the other end of the line added that he was being paid to kill him. Before the ambassador could leave the country, a twenty-four-hour guard was assigned to him. Eventually he learned that terrorists had chosen him as next-best alternative after they had failed in their attempt to kidnap the American ambassador, who had previously been head of the CIA.

The same article described the case of two officials of the embassy in Amman who had been moved out of war-stricken Lebanon to a hotel in what appeared to be a more peaceful spot in Jordan. Around ten o'clock one morning, bullets began to fly through the windows of the mission and the sound of machine-gun fire was heard. H.S., one of the two officials, locked himself in the bathroom and, as bullets sprayed the hotel room, settled down in the empty bathtub. The second official, R.V., had fled to another bathroom, where she spent two hours with three consular visitors and two hotel employees. H.S. managed to squeeze out of his bathroom window, crawl over the rooftop, and slide down a drainpipe to safety. R.V. and her companions were unable to escape. Two and half hours after the attack had begun, they were freed by Jordanian troops, who ordered them to raise their hands, took them to an army post, and eventually released them. Shortly afterwards, the officials resumed their activities, the bullet holes serving as a reminder of the event, if a reminder was necessary.

Acts of terrorism have caught up with Canadians outside embassy premises as well. Sidney Freifeld included in his account of such incidents the story of our predecessor in Budapest, Robert Elliott, who had been ambassador in Cairo when, in 1980, President Anwar Sadat of Egypt was killed. Robert Elliott had been sitting close to the Egyptian president to watch a military parade when Muslim fundamentalist soldiers left the parade and began to shoot into the reviewing stand. Beside President Sadat, the acting Coptic pope was killed, as were a number of other dignitaries. The Canadian ambassador escaped unharmed, but the call had been close.

Frequent travel exposes foreign-service members to airports and planes, some of which are the favourite haunts of international terrorists. In his newspaper articles, Sidney Freifeld reported several close calls various foreign-service members had had while travelling abroad. In 1982 a counsellor at the embassy in Ankara, seeing his wife and daughter off at the airport, learned that their flight to London had been delayed. They followed the airline manager's advice and settled down in the airport restaurant; moments later Armenian terrorists launched a sub-machine-gun attack on the check-in area the Canadian family had just left. One of the terrorists, using the airline manager as a shield, stormed the restaurant. The Canadians hid under a table for three hours. When the siege was over, twelve people were dead, including the airline manager, and seventy injured. The counsellor remembered vividly that 'Auld Lang Syne' had been playing over the airport sound system.

Canadian couriers scheduled to board the Air India flight in 1985 which ended with 329 passengers being killed and the Egyptair flight in the same year that was hijacked to Malta and left sixty passengers dead had rebooked on later flights at the last moment.

Even without terrorists, the travel schedules of foreign-service personnel take their toll. A young officer on his first assignment abroad perished on a flight that vanished between Hanoi and Saigon in 1963. No one ever found out what happened to the plane and its passengers. One of my husband's closest friends posted to the Canadian mission in Hong Kong was the only Canadian on a flight from Hong Kong to Delhi that crashed in June 1972 as it was approaching its destination. Wayne Hubble was on the way to his wedding, scheduled to take place in New Delhi two days later. His fiancée was at the airport when it was announced that the plane had crashed. We learned about Wayne's death on the CBC morning news. A pair of silver candlesticks acts as our permanent reminder of this tragedy. His fiancée brought them to us in Canada all the way from India as a memento of our friend. She had bought them to place on the altar during the wedding ceremony.

On 10 January 1977, the secretary of state for External Affairs together with a plane load of senior public servants and journalists had a close brush with death. For months, an official visit to several South American countries had been arranged for the minister. On the morning of their departure date eastern Canada was struck by what was later dubbed 'the snowstorm of the decade.' Schools and offices were closed and radio warnings were issued, urging people to stay at home. To everyone's surprise, the special military plane that was to carry the minister and entourage, including a television crew, received permission to take off from Uplands Military Base, although all eastern airports had been closed. According to later reports, the pilot was forced to make an emergency landing as soon as the plane had taken off. No longer able to tell where the runway began and ended, the pilot attempted a blind landing. The plane was stopped by a huge snowdrift only a few metres from a wall of airport power installations. According to some of the passengers, the pilot emerged from the cockpit after a few minutes obviously in a state of shock. Eventually the Armed Forces came to the rescue of the passengers stranded in the middle of the raging storm. Members of the television crew volunteered to get out first, positioned their cameras, and filmed the distinguished group's graceless exit from the plane. It was later confirmed that, as some passengers had suspected, the aircraft should never have been given permission to take off.

Preventive measures to protect foreign-service personnel abroad are also taken by host governments. The Canadian government is committed to the protection of foreign diplomats in Canada just as other governments are responsible for the safety of Canadians accredited to their country. During the seal campaign or when threats had been issued against Canadians while we were living in Brussels, the Belgian police took the matter seriously. Whenever I picked my husband up at his office and found a Belgian policeman wearing a bullet-proof vest and holding a sub-machine-gun posted at the entrance to our embassy, I knew that some militant organization had once again targeted Canadian foreign-service personnel. Under such circumstances, police and weapons became a welcome sight.

The twenty-four-hour guard at the entrance to our foreigners' compound and at the gate to our embassy in Moscow, by contrast, was a more contentious local security measure. Members of the foreign community were convinced that the purported protection these militia men were to guarantee disguised two more important functions: preventing Soviet citizens from entering and establishing contact with foreigners, and keeping a close eye on the activities of foreigners.

Two of the uniformed guards occupied a small grey hut whose windows were covered by curtains. An occasionally open door revealed mirrors everywhere on the inside, giving a panoramic view of the outside. The hut was also equipped with telephones. Whenever we left our compound or arrived at the gate, the militia man standing in front of the hut would inevitably go in and reach for the receiver, while his partner took over the outside watch. Someone was apparently being kept up-to-date on our activities at all times.

We received evidence of such surveillance one day after we had run out of gasoline while driving through a quiet residential area in Moscow, far away from any of the foreigners' compounds. Good fortune had depleted our tank close to one of the few telephone booths in the city. As we were coming out of the booth, having called a taxi to take my husband home so that he could pick up some gasoline, while I remained to guard the coveted removable parts of the car, such as its windshield wipers and tires, we discovered a policeman investigating our vehicle. He must have arrived on the scene only a minute or two after our car had stopped, brought to this unlikely spot by superior insight into our whereabouts. He looked relieved when we told him the reason for our presence in that particular neighbourhood. It was quite clear to us that we had been suspected of having evil intentions, for example, secretly visiting Soviet citizens who were not authorized to receive foreign guests, especially Westerners.

Two further connected incidents offered us a glimpse into the range of duties assigned to our militia men. A few weeks after we had landed in Moscow, I was alone in the apartment when the phone rang. My husband had left only minutes earlier and the nanny had just taken her little charges for a walk. A young male, speaking with an immaculate British accent and oozing charm with every word, identified himself as 'Andrei, your familiar.' I remember clearly being surprised by his use of the word 'familiar' as a noun. Andrei went on to tell me that we had recently met in the British Club and that he very much wanted to see me again. I had never set foot in the British Club and told him that he had obviously dialled the wrong number. No, he said, it was his mistake. Now he remembered, it had not been the British, but the American Club. At that moment my suspicion was awakened. I had never set eyes on the American Club either, and I told him. He was apparently ready for that piece of information, too. Ascribing his undeniable confusion about the exact location of our alleged first meeting to emotional turmoil following the magic event, he pleaded with me for a reunion. Any place would be all right. Please! I can't recall what I muttered before putting down the receiver, but I do remember that my knees were shaking. Having an agent of the KGB on the line was a questionable thrill I had never had before in my life.

When I later described the conversation to my husband, he burst into laughter at the crude methods still used by the secret police in an attempt to compromise foreign diplomats or their wives and to elicit cooperation in return for silence about embarrassing events of the past. We also discussed the word 'familiar.' It struck me as the only flaw in the caller's superb performance, unmasking it as a script written with a dictionary in hand. My husband agreed with me. Turning on his heels in our living-room, he shouted into every corner in which we could safely assume microphones had been installed by Andrei's colleagues: 'The word "familiar" is used as an adjective, not as a noun. The correct noun to be used is "acquaintance, acquaintance, acquaintance."'

A few weeks later – it was again one of the rare occasions when I was alone in the apartment – the phone rang. Another male dripping with artificial tenderness whispered: 'This is Pavel, your acquaintance.'

It sounded too good to be true. The microphones were clearly in excellent condition. And the language lesson given to Andrei had been a success with Pavel as well.

I could not help but suspect that one of the militia men's duties consisted of alerting individuals like Andrei and Pavel to moments suited to their purposes. The same guards who allegedly protected us against possible attacks from the outside were, in fact, isolating us from the local population against our will, while attempting to funnel into our compound a tiny trickle of carefully selected individuals on a special mission.

As Russian history books confirm, isolating foreigners in special enclosures to better control their interaction with the local population was a security measure of Russian, not of Soviet origin, taken in a culture where suspicion of foreigners was inextricably linked with suspicion of the local population.

Such incidents only added to my fascination with the singular characteristics of the surrounding culture and strengthened my desire to switch my attention from the all-consuming struggle with the trivia of daily life to an exploration of the unique world outside the walls of the local diplomatic version of a maximum-security prison.

But hardly any time was at my disposal for such pleasures. Like hundreds of my fellow Canadians and thousands of foreign-service spouses all over the world, I was harnessed into the diplomatic team, and that focused my attention on large-scale entertaining.

8

Official Hospitality

Entertaining at Home

In December 1969, the two largest political parties in West Germany, the Christian Democrats and the Social Democrats, had formed a government known as 'The Grand Coalition.' The third party, the Free Democrats, who had been coalition members in most previous governments, had been cast in the role of a small, weak opposition. Hostile exchanges and shouting matches between members of the government parties and the opposition had been heard in the Bundestag for months. Knowing that several members of the West German parliament were no longer on speaking terms with each other, we decided to invite our acquaintances from all three parties for a romantic black-tie dinner.

A hundred candles had turned our apartment, which overlooked the spectacular ruins of the medieval castle of Bad Godesberg, into a fairyland. Baroque music wafted through the rooms together with a small group of waiters who served nectar and ambrosia. I had recently completed my university studies, and had used all the time and energy suddenly available to take an intensive course in gourmet cuisine. Every dish I had prepared was meant to be a work of art for the eyes as well as for the palate, every flower arrangement an Ikebana creation.

Not one of the guests could resist the magic mood. Parliamentarians from all three caucuses were talking and cheerfully toasting each other. When one of the senior Free Democratic opposition members, Hans Dietrich Genscher – until 1992 the longest-serving of all European foreign ministers – asked for a soup spoon and, to the applause and good-natured laughter of members of the government parties, used it to retrieve what remained of the sour cream-and-dill dressing of my salad masterpiece, I had the feeling that we had created the right atmosphere for a relaxed and friendly exchange of ideas. Late at night, as our guests left, several remarked that a young Canadian diplomat and his wife had accomplished in the course of this evening what for months had looked impossible in Germany: peace among parliamentarians. They called it *Die Groesste Koalition,* 'The Largest Coalition.'

In the Belgian capital, during the early 1980s, divisions and hostilities between the Flemish-speaking part of the population and the French-speaking Walloons burst open at irregular intervals. The small, but beautiful and elegant house that came with my husband's position as minister-counsellor at the embassy, we thought could serve as neutral ground where productive conversations could be conducted in a harmonious environment. To signal to our guests that they could expect a special evening, we asked them to dine in formal dress.

A carefully selected group of influential Belgians from all walks of life – members of the Flemish community, Walloons, academics, leading politicians of the largest parties, and widely read journalists – sat down in groups of eight at small, round tables. The seating arrangement had been carefully planned. I had filled graceful wicker baskets with bouquets of flowers and had distributed floral arrangements and candles all over the salon and dining-room. The menu was intended to please even the most discerning of palates – a challenge, since the Belgians enjoy the reputation of having produced more gourmets than other countries noted for such expertise.

After our posting to Moscow, where I had had to make do largely with what was available from our assorted suppliers in other countries, I had now graduated to menus of my choice. As a devoted Canadian foreign-service wife, I favoured what I called 'patriotic' meals. Our guests marvelled at the Canadian treasures I had managed to procure in the heart of Europe: Pacific smoked salmon or Atlantic crabs in dill sauce or filet of Alberta moose garnished with wild rice and fiddleheads, which I had bought frozen at the Canadian Forces Base in Lahr in southern Germany and which my husband and I had driven, first, to the safety of my family's freezer in Bonn for a period of overnight recovery and then to their final destination in our freezer in Brussels. The culinary feast culminated in a maple mousse fit for a king. At some point in my cooking career, I had obtained the governor general's recipe for this dessert, which was often served at Rideau Hall and had become a favourite of royal visitors to Ottawa.

Encouraged by French wine, conversations in English, French, Flemish, and German flowed abundantly. We took part in the most animated and peaceful discussions. Our guests, who represented dramatically different political viewpoints, seemed to be trying sincerely to understand their opponents' position and to explain their own stand. Clutching the handwritten menu cards I had decorated with a photo I had taken of one of my favourite spots in the Gatineau Park where trilliums grew in great profusion, our visitors departed in the early hours of the morning with the comment that it had been an evening of enchantment and of a very useful exchange of ideas.

In extending our invitations to German politicians and leading Belgians, we had neither intended to intervene in German or Belgian politics nor tried to comfort local political opponents with a charming meal. For foreign-service officers whose duties include the representation of Canadian interests abroad, official entertaining provides a most important opportunity to establish and maintain contact with influential citizens of the host country, to gather valuable information about developments in the country, and to present the official Canadian position on current issues. Such occasions also allow Canadian diplomats to try to steer foreign governments' impending decisions on political, social, or economic questions in a direction beneficial for Canada.

Such social and culinary battles, often gallantly fought to the point of exhaustion and sometimes triumphantly won, are known in the administration of External Affairs as 'official hospitality.' A special entertainment allowance tailored to the particular role a foreign-service officer plays in the hierarchy of a mission is granted under the condition that the money be used exclusively to further Canada's interests. In order to prevent personnel entitled to such funds from wining and dining their buddies at taxpayers' expense, the administration demands a detailed accounting for every social occasion paid for out of the official hospitality budget. Name and occupation of every guest are to be listed, together with meticulous accounts of the cost of food, drinks, flowers, kitchen help, waiters, and any other expenses.

In many capitals around the world, the whirlwind of receptions, cocktail parties, luncheons, and dinners has somewhat subsided. In a period of widespread need for financial restraint, the number of such gatherings has decreased, and their character seems to have undergone subtle changes as well. Over the past twenty years, diplomatic functions appear to have been converted from social occasions used by diplomats to do business into primarily, if not exclusively, professional meetings.

Gone altogether are diplomatic parties arranged for the sole purpose of socializing. Diplomats no longer entertain without specifically stating the reason on the invitation card. Newly arrived embassy members have to be introduced to their colleagues in other missions since they will be working closely together. Diplomats leaving a post often use their farewell reception to present their successor to local dignitaries in order to assure continuity in their working relationships. Delegations visiting a foreign capital have to be put in touch with their counterparts. In general, diplomats now issue invitations only to people who are considered professionally relevant to the host and are seen as important acquaintances, capable of promoting the interests of the host mission.

Diplomats now congregate mostly without spouses. A majority of embassies have moved the reception to celebrate their country's National Day from evening to noon, thus turning what was previously a huge occasion, lasting for hours and attended by hundreds (sometimes thousands) into a brief gathering with colleagues for a 'vin d'honneur' before everyone heads back to the office or on to a business lunch.

The Women's Movement seems to have promoted this fortunate development. Few independent professional women appreciated standing around at cocktail parties, wasting their time in polite, superficial conversation. The schedules of their own careers rarely permit them to attend luncheons and most cocktail parties, anyway. Even dinners are often scheduled to allow diplomats and their guests to continue earlier working sessions, although the official dinner, the last remaining traditional diplomatic gathering, still sees husband and wife performing as a team.

During our four years in Budapest, we have had neither the time nor the money in our official hospitality budget to entertain colleagues or any other influential personalities just for the sake of a pleasant reunion. All our luncheons, cocktail parties, and dinners have served a specific purpose. I have discussed this issue time and again with our foreign friends and learned that their situation does not differ in any way from our own. No one can afford the luxury of trying to live up to the image diplomats have outside their own circle as martini-glass holders and canapé pushers. For diplomats, social life has become an extension of their long working hours – a demanding and strenuous extension at that.

Teas and coffee mornings remain the exclusive domain of non-professional wives or those who cannot practise their profession while on assignment abroad with their husbands. Many such occasions serve a purpose as well. An invitation for a ladies' gathering often rings in a diplomatic wife's special project, a charity bazaar or some cultural event. Much admirable and important work has been done for decades by such women. Tens of thousands of dollars are raised each year for refugees, hospitals, orphanages, and the poor. In Budapest, the International Women's Club has performed small miracles to generate money for important social causes in the best tradition of work by generations of foreign-service wives throughout the world. Their dedication and achievements deserve the highest esteem. In pursuit of charitable goals, they move to centre stage. However, for most foreign-service wives, a posting abroad means stage management: they are the true power behind the official hospitality scene, an invaluable asset to their husbands' official endeavours, and often accurately described as head of the foreign service's domestic support staff.

All diplomatic wives find themselves, willingly and, in increasing numbers, unwillingly, presiding over a smaller or larger hotel and restaurant business. The restaurant part of the establishment tends to be more heavily frequented than the hotel portion, but – as I know from my own experience and that of my colleagues – there is no shortage of official house guests in such households either.

In the course of my interviews and informal conversations with diplomatic wives, I found confirmed time and again that preparations for large parties and the event itself could be likened to pregnancies and deliveries. The inevitable gestation period is followed by the actual delivery of what has been taking shape until then. The particulars vary, but in general the foreign service has put us all in the same boat. My own years of experience in setting the stage for official hospitality and eventually bringing forth the fruit of past labour represents theme and variations on the accounts given by hundreds of my foreign-service sisters.

What kind of expertise is required of professional hostesses? And are those women who suddenly find themselves invested with authority to entertain on behalf of their foreign service sufficiently trained to master the task? The wife of a European ambassador, herself a lawyer, complete with a doctorate, summed up her situation and the dilemma of most diplomatic wives: 'I should have studied gastronomy!'

In my case, university degrees in philosophy, literature, and political science proved to be of limited value when it came to feeding what, by now, after almost twenty-five years in the business, amounts to tens of thousands of official guests in Bonn, Moscow, Brussels, and Budapest. On the evening of my university graduation, a friend encouraged me to throw myself into the hitherto unknown world of cuisine. Anyone who knows how to read, he remarked casually, can be a gourmet cook. It made sense to me. And because I had been in the reading business for a while, I thought I had a chance. I went out and bought ten cookbooks.

After I had cooked my way through the first volume, a gem with the charming title *Cooking in Order to Be Loved* containing delectable treasures for two, my husband, who had volunteered his services as guinea pig, pronounced the results of my culinary efforts superb. Since he also called them 'promising,' I felt inspired to turn my attention to the remaining nine volumes. From then on, I struggled through cooking techniques and recipes, until I felt confident enough to face the world of professional eaters.

Cooking, I soon noticed, constituted only one portion of the entire entertaining process, and not necessarily the most demanding part of it. Throughout my career as a foreign-service wife, I found confirmed what I had discovered early on, that a perfect dinner party requires one week's preparations. As soon as my husband and I had sent out invitations for a dinner three to four weeks in advance, a miniature time bomb began to tick. The countdown began for me always a week before the event.

In Moscow, where most of the menus required ordering many of the ingredients months in advance, the talents of a clairvoyant would have come in handy to determine what to order when and for which social event. In all other postings, however, my shopping could be done without catalogues and telex machines.

The sheer amount of food necessary to feed twelve to twenty-four guests a four-course meal posed a challenge. I did not have a driver's licence in Bonn, and in Moscow was too intimidated by the traffic to use the newly acquired document; so, it was imperative to break the shopping expedition up into two or more phases. First, I procured all the non-perishable goods, including drinks and wine, an enormously heavy load to carry home on foot. In Moscow, an embassy car and driver took the non-motorized wives to the grocery store once a week and brought them and their cartons back to their apartments. But all other shopping remained my own responsibility. I often walked for miles to reach a farmers' market and then lugged around shopping bags as heavy as lead.

I set half a day aside for polishing mountains of silverware, cutlery, serving plates, bowls, candlesticks, and coffee- and teapots. Another half-day went into rewashing and drying, all done by hand. A minimum of a hundred glasses were needed for twenty-four guests if I was serving predinner drinks, white wine, red wine, water, and post-dinner drinks.

Washing, starching, and ironing by hand several white linen tablecloths and the matching napkins consumed almost another half-day.

At that point in the preparations, I usually felt I deserved a reward for having struggled through these rather mindless chores. I devoted myself for a few hours to one of my favourite jobs: the menu cards. Strictly speaking, they amounted to an unnecessary luxury, but, if beautifully done, lent a festive touch to a dinner. Guests invariably asked whether they could take them home. The production of menu cards became my own cottage industry. In Brussels I bought huge sheets of raspberry-coloured or bright red, lightweight cardboard, spread them out on the dinner table, and measured and cut out each card. Photographs I had taken in Canada of nature scenes close to my heart I glued on the cardboard as a frontispiece. The actual menu was placed inside, on a separate sheet of white paper.

Depending on the language of the majority of our guests, I wrote the menu in English or French. Tongue in cheek and in mock imitation of pompous-sounding menus, I added to every main dish a significant 'à la ...,' followed by the name of a distinguished personality or noteworthy locality in Canada. Lakes with authentic Indian names provided the fictitious origin of the wild rice we had imported from home. 'Riz sauvage Wapikamaski' became one of our specialties. A rural community in the heart of New Brunswick I had located on the map and whose name appealed to me became our fiddleheads' provenance. I chose a forest in Alberta as home of the imported frozen moose meat. Our maple mousse, of indisputable origins, could sincerely be dubbed 'Rideau Hall.' For a vast array of other dishes, my husband and I used whatever literary, historic, geographic, military, or political Canadian allusion that sprang to mind. For specifically Russian meals, we searched the atlas for names of little-known cities or towns in order to convey the presumed subtlety of the dish. One dessert known to have been served at the court of the tsar I dubbed 'Tsar's torte,' or '*à la* Winter Palace,' '*à la* Romanov,' or '*à la* Peterhof,' depending on the mood of the chef. A dash of humour added to the seriousness of eating would be a spice, I thought, to which none of our distinguished guests would be allergic. As it turned out they all loved it.

I spent hours writing the list of dishes and wines twelve or twenty-four times. Then I tied the red cardboard cover and the white menu sheet together with a white or gold ribbon.

Once this aesthetic interlude was over, I had to turn to the less amusing task of cleaning all the rooms in which the dinner guests would be moving about. In a household with small children, this was an enormous undertaking. When I had finished, I always had the urge to lock and seal or at least cordon off the official area against the invasion of children with bags of Lego, glasses of milk or juice, particularly crumbly chocolate-chip cookies, or Play-Doh.

Days three and two of the countdown were taken up with the second shopping expedition, this time for fresh goods – fruit, vegetables, salad greens, and meat – followed by a day and a half of non-stop cooking. Dishes that would benefit from ripening in the fridge were prepared first.

Day one usually began early, with an excursion to the flower market, in Moscow with uncertain results, in Bonn, Brussels, and Budapest with a predictably glorious outcome. Arranging bouquets for the several round dinner tables and for all the other barren places normally took three to four hours.

Laying the tables on day one kept me busy the entire afternoon or evening. At that stage I began to enjoy the fruit of my earlier labour. I felt I was bringing in the harvest. Everything was clean, beautiful, and ready, and just needed to be assembled: impeccably pressed table-cloths and napkins, gleaming silver, sparkling glasses, colourful flower baskets, and my entertaining menu cards. I savoured the pleasure of that afternoon as a well-deserved reward for my efforts of the previous days.

Day zero was and still remains my favourite phase of the countdown. With this type of long-term planning, all the hard work had been done and I had time to relax and to deal with the unexpected. Luckily, last-minute problems rarely surfaced, except in one or two dramatic cases, which we now cherish as family lore.

Party preparations did not, of course, mean that ordinary family life could be suspended for a week. The daily routine of household and children continued as if nothing else were happening. The two projects ran parallel to each other, and I had to tend to the needs, first, of two, then of four children, as well as to those that accompanied extending official hospitality.

Regardless of how long and how bravely they have been fighting the entertainment battle single-handedly, at some point in their lives abroad foreign-service wives have to recruit domestic help. Depending on the nature and number of parties an officer must give, staff, cleaning personnel, waiters, or the occasional cook may be enlisted. In countries of the Third World, where housekeeping methods have not changed for hundreds of years, every foreign-service member, including Canadians whose duties in the mission do not extend to official entertaining, depends on servants. Cooks are indispensable in countries where procuring and preparing food amounts to a full-time occupation, whether the Canadian employer is entitled to an official hospitality allowance or not. The servants foreign-service members employ abroad often are, especially in developing countries, poorly educated, slow workers on a small salary, who are noted for their inefficiency and unreliability.

At the same time tales of warm and loving nannies; of maids and manservants deeply devoted to their Canadian employers; of superb cooks, dedicated to their masters as much as to their art; of domestics who help foreign-service personnel abroad for decades, make their lively and colourful rounds wherever foreign-service members congregate. Swapping humorous stories and tales of horror can be amusing once the events being described have been relegated to the past and some of the more objectionable servants themselves are at a safe distance.

Ambassadors', high commissioners', and consuls general's households occupy a special position. External Affairs considers domestic staff in official residences an indisputable necessity. While all other foreign-service members hire help on a private basis – even if a small allowance is offered for such a purpose by the administration – a cook, a maid or two, a gardener, and a chauffeur are employed at official residences by the Canadian government. Their contracts carry the signature of the chief administrative officer of the mission, and their salaries are paid by the mission as well. No one who has ever watched life at an official residence for any length of time will doubt that a staff made up of a cook, maid, driver, and gardener represents the absolute minimum required to help the ambassador and spouse carry out their official duties.

Nannies are a necessity in households with one or more small children. There is hardly a foreign-service family that has gone from post to post without at some stage sharing their life with a nanny, and thus enriching their collection of entertaining tales by a few anecdotes.

The long procession of our own domestic help abroad was headed by Luba, a sweet-natured, intelligent, and educated girl with silky, golden hair falling down to her waist. Born in Canada of Russian-born parents, she was thrilled about the opportunity to return to her family's beloved roots while remaining in the familiar and comfortable environment of a Canadian household. Her family seemed as delighted to have found us as we were to have met them. In order to give everyone a chance to get acquainted and to help us survive the madness of our move, we asked Luba to join us in Ottawa for our last few weeks there, before we all headed out to Moscow together. With the proverbial Russian warmth, she proved to be a most loving nanny for our two small boys in the middle of our domestic chaos. She could be expected to be a conscientious, reliable, and loving member of the family under the much more difficult circumstances in the Soviet Union as well. Eager to let her continue her Russian studies, we promised her two free afternoons a week for language training in addition to all her weekends off.

When we arrived in Moscow, Luba threw herself whole-heartedly and with our full approval into the rich cultural life of the city. Watching the ballet of the Bolshoi Theatre gave her the idea to enrol in a ballet school. Would I mind if she took lessons? Of course I did not mind. On the contrary, I would have loved to come along! The only problem was the school's location: it happened to be at the other end of town. Only Moscovites can imagine what that means in a city with eight million inhabitants. A two-hour round trip would encase a one-hour ballet lesson. She would not be available for another half-day. Since I wanted her to benefit from her year in Russia as much as possible, I also agreed, somewhat reluctantly though, to time off for horseback-riding – another half-day with travel time.

At some point I realized that between two afternoons a week for Russian lessons, two mornings for ballet and riding lessons, and Saturday and Sunday off as well, our so-called full-time nanny was at home and at the family's disposal for no more than three days per week.

As I was pondering the problem, I got a phone call from a good friend, the wife of the minister-counsellor of our embassy. 'Christine,' Huguette said, with cheerful determination, 'you are spoiling the prices!' Through the English-speaking nanny network in Moscow, word had got around that our Luba was rolling in free time. The corps of nannies had informally united during the previous weekend, and the membership was now exerting considerable pressure, not only on Huguette, but on several of our colleagues in our own and other countries' embassies, to live up to the exemplary standards and conditions of employment I had set for Luba.

Huguette, relieved to discover that I had already begun to regret my generosity, suggested a joint policy to be introduced by all Canadian employers of nannies. We agreed that time off for Russian lessons should be considered sacred and untouchable, but should take up no more than half a day each week. Another half-day should be free to pursue interests and hobbies in addition to free Saturdays and Sundays.

Before I had mustered enough courage to enforce the new rules, Luba got tired of ballet and riding lessons and dropped both. To my relief she did not ask to use the two mornings for other activities, and we were back to Huguette's suggestion of two free afternoons a week, which Luba did use for language lessons. It certainly was a much more satisfying arrangement, but we still had her in the house for no more than four weekdays. She remained her sweet self and a warm and loving mother substitute for Robin and Jeremy whenever I was occupied with a thousand chores or when we had to go to Helsinki to shop or have our car serviced. When her year was up, she returned to Canada, much to our regret, and she continued to write to us about the happy time she had had with our family.

How to find a substitute for Luba to see us through our second year? Close friends in Munich, themselves just retired from the German foreign service and old hands in the business of hiring nannies in the most unlikely corners of the world, offered to put an advertisement in the local newspapers. To find a Canadian nanny in Europe was an impossible task. A German nanny seemed to be the obvious alternative.

On our return trip to Moscow after a summer holiday in Italy, I accepted an invitation to stay with our friends in Munich and to interview some of the young women who had replied to our advertisement. A flood of letters had poured into the house. I had to sift through more than fifty applications before calling the ten most suitable-sounding girls. In the course of our meetings I tried to paint the most realistic picture of what was awaiting them in the job, omitting none of the gloomier aspects. I made a deliberate effort to scare off the best candidates and told them openly that this was my intention, hoping, of course, that I would not succeed. To my mind only someone who knew exactly what she was getting herself into and was happy to come in spite of it all should get the job.

Of the amazingly large group who had firmly replied to my warnings 'I still want to come!' Sieglinde withstood the closest scrutiny. As outspoken as Luba had been soft-spoken, Sieglinde talked with intelligence, charm, and a remarkable sense of humour. Hair cut very short and dressed in jeans and t-shirt, she looked to me like a teenage tomboy. She had been briefly married to an American who had gone off to work in the oilfields of Kuwait. The separation did not seem to bother her. Neither her husband nor she, herself, had been particularly serious when they had got married, she told me, with an impish grin.

Sieglinde acted more like a devoted older brother than like a nanny towards Robin and Jeremy. She never tired of playing games with them, and could be every bit as noisy and wild as the two young fellows demanded. She read English and German books to them, sang with them American and German folk songs, and took them for long walks from which all three usually returned in the best of moods, full of amusing stories about small incidents that had crossed their path. Our sons loved her. We appreciated her uncompromising devotion to the well-being of her charges and her intelligent way of getting household jobs done efficiently and with never-failing good humour. In the course of our frequent cheerful conversations over countless cups of tea, she told me how glad she was that I had not succeeded in my attempt to talk her out of joining us in Moscow; I always replied that I was equally delighted by my failure on that front.

Her three passions in life – parties, alcohol, and the other sex – eventually led to her departure a month before her time was up. She had taken a fancy to a young American foreign-service officer, a bachelor whose boyish good looks and lanky figure had captured her imagination. She pursued the unsuspecting victim with never-ending ardour. Since Russian women were out of bounds for him, the man in question had to rely largely on the local nanny population. A young Irish woman with cascades of curly, chestnut-coloured hair and a shapely figure had caught his eye. He ignored Sieglinde completely, although she moved in the same circles as he did and always exchanged her jeans for a tight miniskirt and bright red pantyhose whenever she expected a sighting. Her best bet, she told me, would be to keep a close eye on developments with the Irish nanny. The redhead was trailed by other men in their group as well. If she found the charms of one of the American Marines irresistible, then Sieglinde's Romeo might finally come to recognize that a Juliet, hitherto unnoticed, had been waiting for him all along.

She began to spend a lot of her time on the telephone with fellow nannies, hoping for a bulletin on the young American's planned weekend activities and the role the Irish girl would be playing in them. On weekend evenings, she dashed to whatever location the grapevine had assigned the young man. If she did not find him there, she kept close to the Irish nanny's entourage, assuming that sooner or later the tall figure would be making an appearance.

Her weekends became so fraught she needed a growing number of weekdays to recover from them. For a long time I was lenient, hoping that her passion for the fellow and his group would subside – that she might settle down with one of the Marines who occasionally seemed to be making headway with her, or that her love would get engaged to the redhead or at least run away with her for a while. But nothing like that happened, and Sieglinde wore herself out with alcohol, sleepless nights, and weekend activities of which I had no desire to know the details. One Monday morning, when she did not turn up for breakfast, as had happened a little too often since the young American had descended upon the nanny world, I felt the time had come for her to depart. She left, clearly regretting the sad end of our relationship as much as we did.

As is the case for all foreign-service families with small children, a nanny was an indispensable part of life, unless I was prepared to ignore my social duties. For some reason, the Soviet authorities did not permit their own citizens to live in the homes of foreigners, or to stay overnight to babysit. For families who depended on such help, a foreign nanny was the only answer. However, live-out domestic servants were made available by the local authorities.

After we had got along with only a nanny during our first year of large-scale entertaining, my husband and I decided that our five-person household, spread over two apartments, and the large number of parties we would have to give in our second and final year would require a full-time maid in addition to the nanny. Our hardship allowance would largely disintegrate under this new financial load, but the alternative amounted to an overpowering burden that could not be measured in rubles and kopeks.

The Soviet authorities had prepared themselves well for foreign diplomats' domestic needs. UPDK, a central government agency, had recruited suitable staff and had trained them to perform as maids, cooks, waiters, gardeners, and handymen in addition to their other roles as spies reporting on their Western employers. UPDK decided who among their personnel would be most appropriate for a particular position offered by a diplomat and then sent their choice off for an interview. The woman who would come to present herself to us, we were sternly told by the agency, was the only candidate available. It was either her or no one at all.

As soon as I had opened the door for Nadya, I had the impression of a puppet gone crazy. Like a wound-up toy, she began to roll her eyes, to twist, turn, and wiggle her entire body and gesticulate wildly with her arms and hands, all the while pouring over me a flood of Russian. After I had asked her to sit down, she relaxed a bit, and it became possible to ask a few questions. Her chaotic pitch-black hair and her equally dark eyes dominated a prematurely aged face, heavily marked with harsh lines and a wild expression. In a hoarse voice and once again using her filthy hands to gesture ferociously, she told me that she had been born in Baku, Azerbaijan, was a Muslim, and was noted for her honesty. She had sworn at her grandfather's coffin always to be honest and had kept her vow. In support of her claim she lifted up one hand and showed me her thumb and index and middle fingers. I had no reason to doubt her honesty, but her desperation to assert it made me suspicious.

When she heard my husband enter the apartment, she jumped up and the whole process of twisting and turning started again, but this time with a variation. She straightened her blouse, pulled down her skirt, and began to freshen her make-up. Neither my husband nor I was very impressed with her, but she was the only candidate.

After three nerve-racking months with Nadya, I became convinced that no maid at all would be better than one more day with her. Everything she did looked like a grotesque caricature of ordinary human activity. When the telephone rang, she would race, almost panic-stricken, across the room, tear the receiver off the hook, and announce in a high-pitched voice, as though proclaiming some religious truth that had just been revealed to her, that the caller had the honour of having reached the residence of Mr and Mrs Derek Fraser of the Canadian embassy in Moscow. This proclamation was accompanied by convulsive curtsies and subservient bows directed simultaneously at the owner of the telephone and at the caller on the other end of this obviously very distinguished line. In spite of this grand display she could never remember the name of the caller or the purpose of the call.

Several times she knelt down in front of me and tried to kiss either my shoes, since my feet could not be reached directly, or the hem of my dress. She never got close enough to succeed as I managed to escape and pretend that nothing had happened. It was difficult to lead a normal life while she was around. Robin and Jeremy refused to go near her, and I noticed a growing urge in myself to flee the apartment. Whenever I came back from one of my shopping and queuing expeditions or from an attempt to get away from her for a while, she had worked hard in the household and proudly showed off her accomplishments, pleading for praise like a child. Deep down I felt terribly sorry for her and wondered what childhood horrors had produced this absurd behaviour.

A bottle of rum was her eventual downfall. When I asked her to fetch me the bottle I had recently bought for a dessert that needed a few tablespoons of the Jamaican specialty, she suddenly erupted into a hysterical attack, screaming that I suspected her of having drunk the rum. Even though she had brought me the unopened bottle, she continued to yell, her voice growing hoarser, that I had not trusted her.

When heavenly silence descended upon the kitchen after I had simply fired her, I stood marvelling at the thought of never having to see Nadya again and wondering why my completely innocent request had precipitated such an aggressive attack.

A few weeks later, Galina, a calm, kindly, barrel-shaped grandmother, took Nadya's position and stayed with us until our last day in Moscow. She was the personification of sanity. Her entire body shook with laughter when I told her that she had the pleasure of being Nadya's successor. Had I never noticed, she asked me, that Nadya was an alcoholic? Everyone in the agency knew about it. She had a reputation of guzzling from morning till night. Had I not checked the level in our liquor bottles? I certainly never had! Had I not smelled the alcohol on her? What I had smelled was a permanent cloud of sickly sweet perfume. Nadya had always mentioned the beauty of the scent, just in case I had failed to notice the bouquet that surrounded her. It had not only accompanied her wherever she moved, but lingered in the apartment long after she had left for the day. Although I felt greatly relieved to have found Galina and to be able to put the whole Nadya episode behind me, I was thoroughly annoyed at UPDK and the tyranny that had inflicted Nadya on me and my family in the first place.

Whether someone in the state agency had been repentant and had offered a conciliatory gesture by sending Galina to us, I never found out. Always friendly, cheerful, hard-working, she was an excellent cook and housekeeper, and brightened the remaining part of our second year in Moscow. What made her especially amiable was the soft spot she had for our little boys. In her eyes they simply could not do anything wrong. One of her greatest joys was to watch them eat. She stuffed them, and I discovered late that, between meals, she slipped them a handful of candy whenever possible. She actually chided me for keeping our children on a diet that was too low in sweets. It was impossible to get upset about it.

Galina accorded Jeremy the distinction of Russifying his name. The suffix 'ushka,' traditionally added to a small child's name as a form of endearment, converted the little Canadian fellow into 'Jeremushka,' a name pronounced slowly and in a deep guttural Russian voice. 'Robinushka' did not seem to sound quite right to her ear, and she returned to 'Robin.' I can still hear her say in a warm and throaty tone: 'Jeremushka, my darling, be ca-ree-ful!'

Her English vocabulary did not reach much beyond this sentence, except for a few words she needed in the kitchen. It took me several days to decipher the meaning of 'ist,' a mysterious product she kept asking me to buy for some of the Russian dishes she wanted to prepare for us. The ingredient, I eventually discovered, was also known as 'yeast.'

With Galina, I practised my Russian, talking and listening during seemingly endless preparations for countless official dinners. She had been working as cook and maid in diplomatic households for decades and lived with her husband, who was a woodcarver, on the outskirts of Moscow. They were owners of one of the greatest treasures a Russian can possess: a small wooden house surrounded by a little garden, where Galina raised potatoes, cabbage, carrots, beans, and strawberries and produced honey from her own bees. We would have loved to visit her there, but the local authorities took a dim view of such unauthorized forays of Westerners into the countryside. It was in her own interest that we limited our contact with her to the foreigners' compound. Everyone in the family was very fond of her, and she seemed content with us too.

We all have equally warm memories of Gwenda, a young woman from the Philippines, who lived with us for more than two years in Brussels. Any household with four young children, two of them toddlers and the others boisterous young men of nine and eleven years, can be taxing. But if frequent official entertaining is added, the load can be overpowering at times. Not once did Gwenda get impatient or angry. She remained her calm, friendly, humorous, and completely reliable self, whether dealing with our children or going about her chores.

When she left us to pursue a career better suited for someone with her intelligence and education, and much better paying as well, we were deeply sad, although we understood completely her decision. She moved to another part of the world, where one of her many relatives had found a job for her. We realized right away what we had lost in her, but the extent of the loss was driven home during the following year when we had to face a procession of successors, each of them a greater disaster than the previous one.

Successor number one, fresh off the plane from Manila, stole silver and had to go. Number two claimed to be allergic to soap and water, and left the day she arrived. Number three came down, after a few promising weeks, with a mysterious disease from which she never recovered for more than three or four days at a time. Number four hid behind a clan of Philippine aunties when she came for an interview; the women's incessant chatter was all too transparently an attempt to disguise the fact that their niece did not speak a word of English. Since my command of their native Tagalog was limited to a few words and counting from one to ten, communication with her would have been reduced to zero, an unacceptable proposition. The remaining parade of mother's helpers marched into and out of service so rapidly I can remember neither their names and faces nor the reasons for their hasty departures.

After we seemed to have exhausted the possibilities in the large Philippine community in the Belgian capital, the only reply to our newspaper advertisement came from a German girl, Helga, who sounded coherent, warm, and good-natured on the phone, but appeared a lot less attractive in the course of the interview. She recounted at length the details of her unhappy life: an alcoholic father, an equally unpleasant stepfather, and an uncaring mother had driven her out of her home in a little town in northern Germany and directly into the arms of her boyfriend, a waiter in an Italian restaurant in Brussels. She did not say so, but she was clearly in need of a family to make up for the painful loss of her own, in particular, her mother. I had been searching for a nanny and a maid and not an additional child, but I was prepared to give her a try, less for charitable reasons than for lack of an alternative. She immediately set to work and displayed a high degree of devotion to our little daughters, and the whole household. By some unspoken agreement, she and our sons kept away from one another.

Helga followed me around whenever possible, and always brought up the subject of her miserable childhood. A few weeks after she had arrived, she told me how happy she was to have found a family for the first time in her life. She seemed to identify with our little girls, and I thought I could detect in her the need, perhaps even the ability, to recover from early emotional injuries through the love she said she was experiencing in our family life. She sat next to me, watching with growing excitement and delight as I sewed long dresses for Julia and Alexandra to wear to a costume party at their nursery school; they had decided to go as characters from their beloved Grimm's fairy tales. When the dresses were finished and their owners could not get enough of admiring themselves in the mirror, Helga looked as happy as if all the sewing and fitting had been done for her. On such occasions I had the feeling that she was beginning to recover from her childhood misery. The help she was giving us appeared to have healing powers for her as well.

Her boyfriend seemed to be the stable centre in her life. I had just begun to think kindly of him, although I had never met him, when he made an ill-fated attempt to contact us through Helga. He offered his greetings, and a request to buy, through us, duty-free alcohol. My husband and I were furious, and sent back the reply that we had no comment to make about such an impudent proposal.

A few weeks after we had conveyed this message, we had a break-in during the night. Helga reported that she had found a downstairs window open in the morning. My husband's wallet, which he had left in his jacket in the dining-room, had been stolen, together with all his money, cheque-books, European and Canadian credit cards, passport, and driver's licence. We did not exclude the possibility that Helga or her boyfriend might be responsible. But she displayed such convincing signs of loyalty and devotion to us that I began to feel guilty for ever having suspected her.

Several weeks later, after my husband's passport and driver's licence had been found on a neighbour's lawn (the cheques had been cashed – with the help of the Eurocard – in various fine banks in London on the day after the break-in), I was standing in the kitchen, icing a chocolate cake for my husband's birthday dinner that evening. I remember the moment vividly. Helga, slicing mushrooms to go with the steak, seemed to be once again in the mood to confide in me. A few days ago, her boyfriend had discussed with one of his buddies the possibility of kidnapping our daughters for a good ransom.

My knees buckled. Before I could say a word, Helga assured me that she had opposed such a project and had also refused to cooperate if the two gentlemen went ahead against her better judgment.

There was only one thing to do – send her packing to her boyfriend that very evening, minus the key to our house. I left the icing unfinished and asked her to gather her belongings and to leave as quickly as possible. I finally mustered the courage to phone her mother, and was told a very different version of Helga's past history. I learned, to my horror, of Helga's previous record of theft and of her shady boyfriend's connections with the Brussels branch of the Mafia.

Within an hour or two, Helga's room in our house was empty. Its previous occupant was on her way to the Italian restaurant where her boyfriend worked, all locks in the house had been changed, and Julia and Alexandra were under twenty-four-hour parental and fraternal guard.

The blame for this nightmare rested, of course, solely with the little girls' mother, who had failed to check the nanny's credentials and had been all too trusting. I should have called Helga's mother before hiring the girl, not after firing her. Tragedy had been averted, but only just.

A few weeks after I had come to the conclusion that we should not attempt to find a replacement for Helga, Gwenda suddenly appeared at our front door. I thought she was an apparition, or that I had lost my mind and had begun to hallucinate, seeing what I wanted to see. To my joyous shouts, all the children came running. Embraces and kisses proved that I had not gone mad and we were not to be haunted. Gwenda was real. Everyone congregated around to listen to her story. The computer job had turned out to be less desirable than she had expected. She had also missed her life in Brussels. Could she come back? The prodigal son could not have been given a happier welcome. Gwenda stayed with us until the day we left. I still remember the tears she shed when we said goodbye to her.

Comparing notes with foreign-service colleagues on the subject of domestic staff led me to the conclusion that each account sounds a familiar theme. All of us have had a group of servants whose human qualities and professional qualifications ranged from excellent, through good to mediocre, to unsatisfactory. Our personal experience with either a loving parent substitute for the children and a reliable companion for the family or someone whose unresolved inner conflicts overshadowed his or her work to the point that he or she became more of a domestic problem than a help is familiar territory for foreign-service personnel. Many had had servants of the calibre of Luba, Galina, and Gwenda; many had had their share of Nadyas and Helgas. All of them agreed that official entertainment at home depends to a considerable extent on the competence, dedication, and loyalty of domestic staff.

Official Representation outside the Home

Official hospitality is not limited to luncheons, cocktail parties, and dinners given in Canadian diplomats' private homes or in ambassadors' official residences. A great many other events, also designed to help diplomats represent their country's interests, establish and maintain friendly and close contact with foreign officials, or express appreciation for cooperation and help, are part of the diplomats' program.

In the course of my career as foreign-service wife, I have taken part in a variety of social functions. My first unforgettable National Day reception in 1966 at the ambassador's residence was followed, in 1967, by an extraordinary form of celebration. To mark Canada's hundredth anniversary in a special way, the embassy in Bonn had invited a huge crowd of German dignitaries and foreign diplomats, more than a thousand guests and far too many to entertain in the residence. The embassy had rented the American Club in Bad Godesberg for 1 July 1967. Located on the banks of the Rhine, overlooking the river and the local romantic landmark, the Siebengebirge, the seven mountains where Snow White and the Seven Dwarfs were said to have originated, the club was ideally suited for a great birthday party.

The day was blessed with glorious sun and warmth. The crowd of guests were chatting, laughing, toasting the venerable country, and strolling the lawn and building, where an exhibition told Canada's story in colourful photographs. The mood was as splendid as the day itself. At noon, a German band played the Canadian national anthem, for me a moving moment under any circumstances, but even more so when 'O Canada' is sung and played abroad. The complete silence after the last chords had faded away lasted only for a few seconds; then, suddenly, out of nowhere, a formation of Canadian fighter planes appeared, roaring directly above our heads and vanishing into nowhere as quickly as they had appeared. It was my first fly-past and I joined the guests in the thunderous applause, which was unfortunately lost to the ears of the pilots, who were probably one or two countries away by that time, given the size of European states.

In the meantime, inside the club, a gigantic white birthday cake, complete with a huge red-icing maple leaf, waited. Cutting this work of art deserved to be celebrated. The Canadian military attaché in Bonn, dressed in a spectacular ceremonial uniform, raised his shiny sword and, as the crowds around him watched in breathless silence, slowly and solemnly sank it into the sweet concoction. A new round of applause followed, this time not lost to the ears of the main actor, and immediately turned into waves of laughter when the distinguished colonel pulled out the sword and licked the icing off the blade.

In 1972, when Team Canada was playing against the Soviet hockey team, the Canadian embassy in Moscow sent complimentary tickets for the various games to Soviet officials as part of the hospitality program. Few invitations for lunch, cocktails, or dinner could have delighted the recipients as much.

Visits abroad by Canadian orchestras, choirs, theatre and ballet companies, and distinguished soloists are often used by members of Canadian missions as an excellent opportunity to extend invitations to influential contacts in the host country and in the local international community and to nurture important contacts.

While we were living in Brussels, the exquisite Canadian Orford Quartet visited. Their interpretation of Beethoven, surrounded by the opulent Flemish splendour of the Rubens House in Antwerp – a building the painter had designed for himself and his eighteen-year-old bride in the style of an Italian Renaissance palazzo – proved to be a wonderful opportunity to celebrate with invited prominent Belgians the close cooperation between Belgium and Canada.

One of the most unforgettable events in our entire foreign-service career took place in May 1990 when the Royal Winnipeg Ballet came to Budapest. On three consecutive evenings, this outstanding company danced classical and modern ballet in the gilded grandeur of the State

Opera House, captivating the entire local ballet establishment and the hearts of amateurs as well. During the intermission, we recognized the stars of the Hungarian ballet in the audience and felt deeply satisfied and proud when the applause at the end of each performance surpassed any we had previously heard in that building.

For each performance, the embassy had bought, for official-hospitality purposes, as many tickets as the Hungarian organizer was prepared to sell to the mission and had sent the treasures to a select, yet rather large group of Hungarian officials and artists. Several cabinet ministers, senior politicians, prominent members of parliament, and other eminent personalities attended the opening night and the gala reception following held in one of the magnificent salons in the Opera House. Our guests, without exception, expressed their gratitude for the invitation and their admiration for the ballet company's superb artistry.

The presence of distinguished guests added considerable pleasure to each performance for the dancers as well. We saw the artistic director, the general manager, and the music director and conductor every day while the company was in Budapest and told them which local dignitaries would be in the audience each evening. At the opening night, my husband and I took the Hungarian minister responsible for the recent restoration of the building to its original Imperial beauty backstage to meet the entire cast. He seemed as delighted to talk to them as they were to shake hands and have their pictures taken with the man who had managed to restore the Opera House to one of the most spectacular auditoriums they had ever danced in. A cordial thank-you letter to us from the artistic director of the Royal Winnipeg Ballet stated: 'Our performance in front of so many politicians and ambassadors gave us a tremendous sense of purpose.' Long after the Royal Winnipeg had left, Hungarians and foreigners alike would continue to refer to the company's unequalled performances on stage and to the indelible impression the Canadians had left behind in Hungary.

Representing Canada abroad is, however, not limited to issuing invitations for social occasions inside and outside the homes of Canadian diplomats. A huge portion of foreign-service members' time has to be spent at parties given by influential personalities of the host country or representatives of the foreign diplomatic and business communities.

The variety of functions at which Canadian foreign-service officers are called upon to represent their country is, quite simply, limitless. Ambassadors, high commissioners, and consuls general are flooded with invitations: to attend the local head of state's New Year's reception; opening sessions of parliament in the host country; National Day receptions; major religious, political, cultural, academic, and sports events in the country of accreditation; and a host of parties given by their colleagues of other foreign services.

Every member of the foreign-service team cherishes his or her own collection of anecdotes about official hospitality. Stories abound of guests who arrived a day or a week early or late, did not arrive at all, forgot all about a formal sit-down dinner, or brought uninvited friends. There is no end to the number of tales about guests who behaved in an unforgettable way, to put it mildly, and who seemed to follow more individual than local or international standards in their eating and drinking habits, conversations, choice of clothes, or conduct in general.

Some hostesses delight in accounts of formal meals that turned out to be a disaster. One such epic culminates in the moment at which a suckling pig, the main culinary event of the formal dinner somewhere in a capital in the heart of Africa, was placed, in all its roasted glory, on a silver platter in the centre of the dining table. The table collapsed under its weight, onto the knees of the assembled guests.

Other colleagues specialize in stories about servants whose quick intelligence rescued a cocktail party or luncheon, or whose stupidity turned a dinner or any other function into a farce. Those families whose assignments had taken them to countries with extreme climates usually maintain a rich supply of sagas about heat or cold, rain or sun, sand- or snowstorms, typhoons or hurricanes playing havoc with carefully and lovingly arranged social gatherings.

One of our closest friends actually contributed to the incident that eventually became one of the all-time favourite yarns to make the rounds in External Affairs. On posting in Cairo, and a bachelor at the time, the young foreign-service officer was employing an Egyptian, Abdul, as butler, maid, cook, and waiter, all in one. One day Abdul had found a juicy cut of beef at the local market, just in time for an official dinner. He prepared the entire meal himself, expressing particular satisfaction with the results of his efforts in the meat department. Glowing with pride, he carried the magnificent roast, surrounded on a silver platter by mouth-watering delicacies, into the dining-room. All eyes turned towards him and his creation. At the next step he stumbled over the carpet and fell to the ground, the delectable load scattering all over the floor.

Our friend's guests, too polite to notice such a minor domestic detail, resumed, after a moment of silence, their conversation. The host, equally politely trying to keep his eyes off the floor where Abdul was crouching in an attempt to gather what could be rescued, also tried to find his way back into the animated discussion at the table, all the while wondering how the meal would proceed.

After an amazingly short time Abdul reappeared, looking even more triumphant than he had the first time. He was carrying a plump, golden, roasted turkey on a silver platter. Our friend had had no knowledge of the presence of such a bird in his household. As if nothing had happened, he helped himself to what looked to him like a miraculous conversion of disintegrated beef roast into a spectacular fowl and awaited eagerly the departure of his guests so that he could find out what magic Abdul had performed.

Abdul, well plugged into the servant network within the apartment building where our friend was living, had remembered as he was scraping up the beef from the carpet that a dinner happened to be in progress in the flat a few storeys up, where his friend Gamal was working as a cook. A quick ring of the doorbell produced the information that the guests had not yet been served their main course and that a turkey was waiting to make its grand entrance. After a brief discussion, including the promise of later compensation, the reassembled roast moved up three floors, and the turkey moved down. Guests on both floors had expressed their delight with their dinners, as Gamal and Abdul later assured each other. The question of how his neighbours interpreted the transformation of their turkey into a beef roast, our friend usually answers with a mysterious smile.

In a Southeast Asian posting, the last course of a dinner proved to be a more dramatic than delicious ending to a formal diplomatic gathering. The local servants were to add the final touch to the ready-made dessert by sprinkling liquor over it and lighting it. The hostess had demonstrated earlier how to do it, and the staff had succeeded in rehearsal. Nothing could possibly go wrong. When the dish was carried to the table, the traditional gentle blue flicker had been replaced by roaring red and yellow flames. A fire extinguisher had to be brought to the table. One of the servants later confessed to resorting to gasoline when the liquor had failed to rise to the occasion.

My own collection of anecdotes includes one about the fire department of the Belgian capital. About two hours before twenty-four guests were to arrive for a black-tie dinner, I discovered the intensifying smell of burning electric wire between the kitchen and dining-room. It was undoubtedly coming from the wall behind our kitchen appliances, which were operating in high gear. What to do? On the one hand, I loathed the prospect of drama; on the other, I wanted to avoid disaster. Finally caution won out.

The fire department arrived in full force. A regiment of Darth Vaders in huge, shiny black coats and hats swarmed through the house, snaking through the arrangement of small round dinner tables laid with china, crystal, and silver, and decorated with baskets of flowers, in search of the threatening smell's source. I knew that the two worlds represented in our dining-room during those tense minutes would not mix well in the long run. Either the firemen would turn their hoses on my dainty tables to prevent them from going up in flames, or the crisis would pass with their voluntary retreat, house and tables intact. To my indescribable relief, they quickly discovered the origin of the smell, shut off one part of the overburdened electrical system, pronounced house and inhabitants safe, and, before leaving the scene, posed for a few pictures to grace my family album. I cherish those photos still of black, shiny giants surrounded by the fragile paraphernalia of a diplomatic dinner. Our guests, who made their appearance shortly after the fire trucks and their crews had left, found the story highly entertaining and expressed regrets that I had deprived them of the pleasure of the company of firemen in full regalia.

During our years in Brussels, the biennial heads of post meeting took place in the Belgian capital. At that time, ambassadors serving in Eastern Europe got together regularly in Western Europe to exchange information and ideas without being overheard. My husband and I gave a dinner in their honour. I had just completed two courses in Chinese cuisine and had acquired a few unusual and attractive recipes, together with some Chinese cooking techniques.

Knowing from my own experience that Communist countries in Eastern Europe were, for lack of ingredients, not necessarily noted for the refinement of their cuisine, or for the culinary connections with their Chinese comrades, I prepared a small feast fit for mandarins of any public service, including Canadian ambassadors. My own favourite soup and one that our previous guests had enjoyed was Suan La Tang, a creation from the southern province of Szechuan; I intended to follow it with Ching To Sho Liun, shrimps with snow peas; Tong Ku Tse Pien, chicken with Chinese mushrooms; and How Yo Nu Lo, beef with oyster sauce. I had been able to obtain the appropriate ingredients from Chinese grocery stores in Brussels, and, to add authenticity, bought a set of Chinese bowls, plates, and the indispensable chopsticks. When I had cooked all the dishes, two hours before our friends were to arrive, my husband phoned to remind me that one of the guests had recently developed a serious allergy to, among other things, yeast, flour, wine, and soy sauce. My heart sank. I had completely forgotten his affliction in my enthusiasm for the menu. What on earth could I do if I wanted to avoid first torturing and then starving an old friend?

I got the car out of the garage and raced off to the stores, arriving as they were about to close. I purchased single servings of shrimp, chicken, beef, and other items; rushed back home; and cooked a completely new version of each dish for one person only, omitting the offending ingredients. Minutes before the guests arrived, I had completed the special order, and the assembled ambassadors could not praise my achievements enough. Our friend told me much later that the allergies he developed in Brussels had been the result of a meal somewhere else. He insisted that my delicious Chinese meal could not possibly have been responsible for it.

Attention to detail in promoting Canadian products abroad! The only ingredient I never managed to find in Brussels, a city known as a gourmet's paradise, was fresh dill. When I decided to treat guests to Canadian crab in dill sauce, I had the choice of asking External Affairs to assign us to a posting where the tasty herb was readily available or importing it from abroad. I settled for the latter solution. Abroad, in this case, amounted to the neighbouring capital, Bonn, where the farmers' markets were overflowing with dill throughout the year. From Brussels, Bonn could be reached by car within two hours. By train, it took considerably longer. The mail needed several days. But I had found out that express letters made it in thirty-six hours. Good-quality dill should be able to survive such a trip.

My brother's wife, Barbara, after twenty years in Bonn, was well acquainted with every greengrocer in town and volunteered her services as foreign supplier of the precious herb. By long-distance phone call, we worked out the strategy. Barbara would buy the dill first thing in the morning on the day before our party, pack it in a plastic bag, and send it off by express mail. It was bound to be delivered well before the guests were to arrive and could be immediately incorporated as a final touch into the waiting crab entrée. We had given ourselves a few hours' grace. Confident that our plan would work, I wrote the menu cards, promising our guests crab in dill sauce.

The morning before our dinner, Barbara phoned to report the successful completion of her part of the operation. The finest dill had been dispatched as an international traveller in support of Canadian official hospitality. The rest was up to the German and the Belgian mail service. Thirty hours after the little parcel had been sent on its way, I began to listen for the doorbell and to check the time. By four o'clock in the afternoon I began to worry. What if the package arrived in time for dessert or as the guests were leaving? Should I toss out my lovingly written menu cards or simply cross out 'dill sauce'? I was reminded of one of my favourite incidents in Thomas Mann's novel *Buddenbrooks,* in which a rather uncouth suitor of the heroine, in the absence of a calling-card of his own, presents that of the owner of the company for which he is working. Having crossed out the owner's name, leaving only '... and Co.' intact, the hapless suitor tries to introduce himself to the heroine's patrician parents as a man of credentials. My carefully planned entrée was also in danger of suffering a lack of credibility if deprived of one of its main components.

About two hours before the guests were to turn up, the doorbell rang. The unmistakable helmet of the special messenger promised the safe delivery of the cherished ingredient. One glance at the parcel confirmed that our guests would be able to enjoy the promised fare. The mailman told me that usually he did not get such a heart-warming reception at other houses. Barbara, whom I phoned immediately, was thrilled to learn that our German-Canadian joint venture had been a success, and our guests amused by the dramatic story that garnished their meal.

The Belgian capital was also the backdrop for one of the more extraordinary incidents in our entertaining history. One of our visitors, a very influential man, vanished from our house in the course of a dinner. He had got up discreetly and gone to the washroom. When he did not come back, I sent a waiter to check. The washroom was empty, but the window was wide open. He had apparently climbed out and fled. We had no idea why he had left. The next time we invited him, he pretended nothing had happened. So did we. Throughout the evening, I waited for a repeat disappearance. But he stayed clear of the washroom and departed late at night by way of the front door.

Under official-hospitality rules, a reception or party of any kind is not over when the last guests have gone home. The final act is considered by most hosts to be the most unpleasant one. It consists of accounting for every dollar, mark, yen, rupee, forint, shekel, franc, krone, guilder, or lira spent on the event. A detailed list, complete with receipts for expenditures on food and drink, flowers, candles, cigarettes, cigars, and waiters and other personnel, has to be prepared; it will be checked by the local ambassador and then filed for further scrutiny by an auditing team that visits missions abroad regularly. In my nearly twenty-five years as foreign-service wife, I have probably spent altogether several months writing up accounts for official entertaining at home.

In postings such as Moscow and even Budapest, where much of the supplies are purchased abroad or from sources other than the local economy, accounting becomes complicated and time-consuming. While on post in Moscow I bought goods in Helsinki with Finnish currency, in Stockholm with Swedish currency, at the Danish diplomatic suppliers for American dollars, and in Moscow itself with rubles and kopeks. The amount for every item I had spent had to be converted into the same currency. In Brussels, matters looked relatively easy in comparison, although I did have to convert everything we had purchased in Lahr with Canadian dollars or German marks into Belgian currency.

In Budapest, accounting is extremely tiresome. Our groceries come not only from Hungary, but also from Britain, Germany, Denmark, and Austria. My bills and receipts show the grand total in forints, British pounds, Canadian and American dollars, German marks, and Austrian schillings. It is bad enough to have to count every can of beer; every bottle of wine, whisky, and gin; every carton of juice; every pound of meat, mushrooms, and rice consumed by official guests. Having to list all of this in four or five different currencies is a great burden.

At times, the bookkeeping turns out not to be the unpleasant ending to a pleasant party. Thank-you notes, the guests' accounting of the event, arrive, and are usually a lot more fun to read than subtotals and final figures. One of these letters, from a British colleague and friend, occupies a favourite place in my private record of our official activities. After eloquent praise of one of our dinners she had attended with her husband, she stated that no one in the local international community could live up to the high standards we had set for diplomatic hospitality. For that reason, she added, tongue in cheek, they were glad to hear that we were about to leave the posting.

9

Friendship, Marriage,
and Family Life Abroad

Friendship and Marriage

For senior members of the group of approximately eight hundred foreign-service officers, official hospitality usually absorbs every free
moment left over from the host of other duties. Younger officers on
their first or second assignment abroad have more room for a private
life, although severe cut-backs in foreign-service personnel introduced
over the past few years have imposed a heavy workload on junior officers as well, reducing the time available to devote to private and family
life.

The majority of foreign-service employees – the approximately 2,700
members of the administrative support staff – remain entirely free from
official representational obligations. If they wish, they can enjoy abroad
the same type and degree of privacy they enjoy during postings at home.
But most of them are eager to point out that they have not joined the
service in order to lead private lives. Their yearning for foreign countries and cultures amounts to a yearning for people, friendship, and a
rich and varied social life.

Few of these transients return from a posting abroad without a set of
new friends from at least one of the three different cultural environments in which they have moved: Canadian, international, and local.

A large number of foreign-service members are single. Not only
young clerks, officers, and secretaries arrive on their first posting without a spouse and children. A considerable number of middle-aged or
older personnel have either chosen the single life or return in growing

numbers to single status after separation or divorce. In the course of long interviews, many External Affairs singles explained to me that the rotational lifestyle can bring more satisfaction or dissatisfaction to single persons than to married couples or families. An active social life with a growing number of friends in constantly changing parts of the world is widely seen as superior to a stationary existence with limited social contacts and fewer opportunities to strike up friendships. But loneliness is also cited as a typical foreign-service problem. Many singles told me that the restless rushing from place to place actually prevents the development of deep and lasting relations. Foreign countries and cultures, they say, are all very well, but, in the final analysis, amount to poor substitutes for permanent and sustaining friendship and love.

Singles in all occupational groups who emphasized how important the prospect of a vigorous social life was as a motive in their decision to enter the service are not always aware of the degree to which they hope that the acquaintances they are looking for will fill the void left by the social network and support system provided by family and friends during their childhood and youth. In a county the size of Canada, a job in Ottawa makes regular visits home an unaffordable luxury for a lot of foreign-service members. Physical distance often means a weakening of social bonds. A considerable number of colleagues admitted that their transitory life had, in fact, terminated old friendships with Canadians who had opted for a more stationary life.

Foreign-service employees who arrive at a posting without the portable security blanket that a family provides tend to move towards the cultural environment that promises to satisfy their needs for security, recognition, self-esteem, and a sense of belonging. Places in the heart and mind left empty by parents, brothers, sisters, friends, and neighbours who have stayed behind in Canada demand to be filled again. Although each foreign-service member follows his or her own unique path in pursuit of higher social needs, patterns of socializing and establishing human relationships exist within the three basic environments.

In all our foreign postings, I observed that, during those first weeks of confusion, for many foreign-service members, the local Canadian mission played the role an oasis plays for an exhausted desert traveller. And yet, most Canadians thrown together in an office abroad are initially strangers. Getting to know each other and getting along requires a lot of effort and goodwill. Indifference towards each other, dislikes or animosities, whether open or hidden, do exist and are not always overcome. But, in many overseas postings, the cultural differences between a newly arrived Canadian and representatives of the local culture prove to be so enormous that dissimilarities within the Canadian community fade. At such an early stage in the course of a posting, the common culture tends to act as a powerful bond.

Experienced travellers will appreciate how much comfort can be derived from a familiar language; gestures; ways of thinking, feeling, speaking, and acting; and the essence of home that characterizes a Canadian office when every aspect of the world beyond this island of the known looks new, strange, and at times unpleasant and threatening. Such circumstances promote friendships within the local mission.

Edna, a young single woman on her first overseas posting, never tried to venture beyond the Canadian community throughout her assignment in an Arab country. Uneasy in the silence of her apartment and equally uncomfortable with the incomprehensible language around her and the wild gestures of the local population, she fled to the embassy early in the morning and left her desk in the evening as late as possible. The office and its staff served as her refuge from a world she perceived as hostile. She desperately longed for her parents. Her obvious misery and her shy and awkward way with embassy staff prevented her initially from making friends, even within the mission. She could never escape the feeling that she was invited to social gatherings out of a host's sense of duty or out of pity for her.

Eventually a middle-aged couple arrived at the mission. Separated from their only daughter for the first time, they began to invite Edna over, and soon informally adopted her as their substitute child. Trailing her fun-loving newly acquired parents, Edna soon found herself on a never-ending round of Friday-night 'happy hours,' potluck suppers at the homes of embassy staff, brunches, and gatherings to celebrate an endless list of birthdays. Once in a while, all three of them decided to do some sightseeing in the city or in the countryside. But they found travelling in the merciless heat a tremendous strain, and the local food in the few restaurants did not agree with them. Their contact with the local population remained largely limited to pointing at the fruit, vegetables, and meat they wanted to buy from the vendors and to a few fleeting encounters with the owners of some dry-goods stores. As full-time members of the tight-knit Canadian community, they were completely content with their limited social life.

When Edna was cross-posted to a Scandinavian country, she felt confident enough to handle the next two years without her adopted parents. In spite of the loneliness she had initially suffered in her first assignment, she insisted that she would not have wanted to miss the experience. It allowed her to recognize a similar type of loneliness in a fellow secretary who arrived a year after her and with whom she eventually established a close friendship in the course of trying to help the newcomer get over familiar signs of alienation.

As she was leaving the Arab world, she suddenly realized that she knew as little about it as she had known upon her arrival. She began to regret that she had never made a serious effort to learn the language and to meet the people. Her own life in this country had run its course without ever touching the life of anyone in the local population. It was too late to do anything about it now, but she could take a different approach in her new posting. She made up her mind to open up to the new language and culture waiting for her and to try to overcome her shyness with foreigners.

Edna's case is not an exception in the foreign service. An amazingly large number of Canadians seem to remain satisfied with the company of their fellow countrymen, regardless of where in the world they live. Some cultures and societies appear difficult to penetrate. I was told many times that the natural urge to explore the world beyond Canadian cultural boundaries does exist, but that obstacles such as language, religion, customs, and traditions seem insurmountable. For Edna and her group, a tiny Canadian enclave anywhere in the world serves as a comfortable vantage-point from which to view the hustle and bustle of surrounding foreign cultures without the complication of participating in the spectacle.

Foreign-service members who are endowed with a more developed sense of curiosity often use their command of English or French to gain access to the inevitably large international community in their posting.

As Winston discovered on his first overseas assignment, his mother tongue, English, was the key to open the doors of many embassies. Shortly after his arrival, he announced in the Canadian embassy that he had not come to this country to spend his time mingling with Canadians. He declined invitations to formal gatherings from embassy staff and turned his attention to the International Club, a community of American, British, and Australian diplomats; representatives of European embassies; and American businessmen. A few weeks of language training had convinced him that the local language was not worth the enormous amount of work he would have to put in to speak it reasonably well. As far as the culture itself was concerned, it appeared as impenetrable under close scrutiny as it had looked from afar. Because of the country's regrettable role during one of the more recent wars, he made up his mind that he would not be able to embrace the population as a whole or develop warm feelings for any individual representative of the local community. They were quite simply too different.

He led a busy social life. Whenever possible, he dined at the club. The taste of local food was not to his liking, and he could not communicate with the waiters, anyway. There were plenty of amusing English-speaking people around, so there was no need to struggle with someone else's language. The club had so much to offer – tennis, squash, bridge parties, movies, and above all dances. Once in a while, Winston, accompanied by his friends from the club, went sightseeing. It was important to him to take photos and slides in order to show his family and friends back home what the world outside Canada looked like. When he left the post, he had made many friends in the International Club and had acquired a reputation as bridge player, gourmet cook, and dance partner. He had also made enemies. Single girls in various embassies agreed that he had been a bit too friendly with too many of them. The Canadian staff in his own embassy had not appreciated his open display of indifference towards Canadians and his exclusive socializing with foreigners.

Lucien, by contrast, represents a large number of young and single foreign-service employees who enjoy cheerful relations with members of their own mission, while moving with the same ease in the local international community. Fluently bilingual, Lucien was his embassy's man about town, the darling of every social gathering of Canadians and closely connected with English- and French-speaking missions as well. His Canadian colleagues and their spouses knew that they could always count on him if they needed a single man at a dinner table or someone to fill in for a guest who had dropped out at the last moment. Without thinking too much about it, he felt equally at home in the Canadian and international communities, but had no desire to venture much beyond these two worlds.

Edna, Winston, and Lucien represent the group of foreign-service members whose life abroad revolves around familiar points of reference. A considerable number of rotational employees, however, go abroad in order to direct their attention systematically to the local culture.

When Francine arrived in her first posting she had already studied modern Greek intensively for several months. Getting to know the country and its people had been her main interest when she had asked for this assignment. She knew that fluency in the language would be her access to the culture, and she was determined to experience Greek culture and get to know its people as soon as possible. Although her colleagues in the foreign ministry in Athens all spoke English, French, or both languages fluently, she made a daily effort to conduct her conversations with them in Greek. She read the newspapers, listened to her car radio, watched local television, and, above all, kept her evenings free whenever possible to go over her self-imposed daily quota of vocabulary and grammar rules. The effort paid off. Within less than a year of her arrival, her command of Greek allowed her to discuss the preparation of Greek dishes in her favourite restaurant, to talk about politics with her greengrocer and her colleagues in the foreign ministry, and to follow the plot in theatre productions. She began to feel integrated into the world around her and found her work inside and outside the Canadian mission a growing pleasure.

Blonde, beautiful, and single, Francine did not need to wait long for her social life to take off. Invitations landed on her desk for official functions, as well as for private ones. Acquaintances from all walks of life in Greece asked to take her out. To play it safe, she went out to concerts and restaurants with two or three men at the same time. She explained to me, with amusement in her voice, that several of her escorts were, after all, local officials. She was representing Canada. A certain amount of reserve, even on the weekends, should be considered appropriate under such circumstances.

A group of assorted eligible men who had invited her for a weekend outing to celebrate sun and sea unwittingly became actors in an incident that still makes the rounds in External Affairs. In the course of a day of swimming, boating, and water-skiing, Francine's turn came to be pulled on the water skis. Nothing quite matched the delight of flying over the water, dressed in a pink bikini, to the admiring glances of a boatload of attractive young Greeks.

Whatever may have caused her fall, Francine suddenly found herself underwater, her lofty flight prematurely terminated. When she came back up, the motorboat with her escorts was already speeding towards her for a rescue operation. When she was assisted onto the boat, she noticed an unforgettable expression on the face of every one of her friends. Obviously they had been impressed with her athletic prowess. Looking down, she discovered that the top of her bikini was missing, lost in the bottomless sea, as Homer would have put it. She had emerged from the waves somewhat like Venus from the oceans.

The story reached Athens with Marathon speed and made the rounds of every government department and every cocktail party. For the remainder of her stay in the Greek capital, Francine was hailed as the person who had done more for the establishment of cordial Greek-Canadian relations than any of her predecessors.

Not too many foreign-service members are given such an opportunity to further international understanding. But Francine represents the large number of those who use every foreign assignment as a chance to explore a new culture in a systematic way. Language lessons are the unavoidable first step to getting to know and to understand a country and its people. Friendships are bound to follow as every foreign-service veteran who has ever invested time and energy in learning a new tongue will confirm.

Those who eagerly set out to study the new world into which they have been thrust often benefit greatly from a close friendship. The company of a Canadian friend during the trials of foreign-service adventures can generate in single nomads a sense of security similar to the one offered by a happy marriage or a loving family. An understanding, reliable, and familiar companion often does wonders to help overcome the uncertainties of an unknown road.

Malcolm, a young, single officer on his first posting, struck up a friendship with his colleague Cole as soon as he had arrived in the large

Canadian embassy in Paris. Cole, also young and single and as intent on examining every aspect of French culture as was Malcolm, had come a few months earlier than Malcolm, but had not quite recovered his equilibrium in order to throw himself whole-heartedly into the surrounding world. With a new friend sitting in an office down the hall and living in the same arrondissement, within walking distance of his own apartment, Cole's loneliness and listlessness disappeared. He had the feeling that Paris and all of France had suddenly begun to smile at him.

The plan to capture, first, the French capital and, then, the countryside was born on the day Cole's sea shipment had arrived from Ottawa. He had invited Malcolm to browse with him through his books. Malcolm was thrilled about the large collection of volumes on history. He had studied history and art history and could hardly wait for his own library to turn up so that he could share it with Cole. The strategy they worked out for a conquest of the unknown territory around them was simple. They would use their lunch hour during the week to discuss and select the sights they were going to see on the following weekend. Cole would consult his history books, Malcolm his volumes on art history, and they would lecture each other.

Their post-graduate seminar became an instant success. The second-hand Peugeot they bought jointly, and dubbed 'The Fifth Republic' in view of its delicate state of health and frequent signs of exhaustion, provided transportation; the grocery stores in their quartier supplied baguettes, cheese, and fruit; and the two friends, strolling through museums, palaces, galleries, and churches, took turns delivering the information they considered essential to understand the significance of what they were looking at.

After a few months the travelling history and art history seminar doubled in size, when two French students from the Sorbonne, both female, joined the all-male Canadian team. They produced an astounding number of relatives and friends who invited the foursome to their apartments and houses in and around Paris, where the conversations were as French as the food. Eventually the group set out on more extensive excursions and used short and longer holidays to criss-cross the country from Calais to Montpellier and from Brest to Chamonix.

Thirty years after they met, Cole and Malcolm still agree that their four years together in Paris not only amounted to an immersion course in French culture, but gave them the best of two worlds: a Canadian government office with absorbing and stimulating work and a fascinating foreign culture. Their close friendship added a personal dimension to their job, and made their explorations the most enriching and invigorating part of their entire time in France. At that stage in their lives, both had come across the main components of what they considered the ideal life: a desirable job, a good friend, and an all-consuming interest in other cultures. Although they were not yet aware of it, their years in Paris served as model for the next decades of their private and professional lives. Each of them married a woman who shared his passion for foreign countries, thus acquiring a permanent friend in the house with whom to explore other parts of the world in a similar way. Eventually the young couples had a few children to bundle up and take along on the adventures.

Cole and Malcolm have extended their friendship to include both families. Although their respective postings took them to different countries, their good fortune kept them on the same continent for most of the next thirty years. Their wives received a retroactive promotion to the status of honorary member of the Paris seminar on the basis of their distinguished overseas service to husband and children. To everyone's delight, the second generation has become friends too. They are discussing a plan to travel through Europe together. Some of them seem to have picked up their parents' professional enthusiasm for other countries. It looks as if a foreign-service officer might be in the making in the younger generation of each family. Cole's and Malcolm's eldest sons, now both at the University of Toronto, are debating whether they should write the exam once they have completed their studies.

Not every friendship between foreign-service members resembles that of Cole and Malcolm. Theirs represents an ideal case in which two compatible personalities share values and interests, pursue common goals with great ardour, and thrive on promoting each other's growth. But a large number of their colleagues in the service, both male and female, maintain similar types of relationships. All of them are intended to satisfy higher human needs, a complex cluster of powerful desires for security, stability, continuity, structure, order, belonging, affection, self-esteem, achievement, recognition, and dignity. The rotational lifestyle of foreign-service employees poses a serious threat to the fulfilment of many of these needs. Under such circumstances an affectionate and reliable friend in a stable and secure relationship can perform miracles in countering the profoundly unsettling impact rotationality has on foreign-service members.

Friendships seem to be one of the foreign-service hallmarks. They come in all combinations. Single women cherish warm and loving relationships with other single women. Sometimes a mother-daughter bond acts as a model; in other cases, sisterly ties develop. I have talked to a number of single women who have limited their friendships to one or two other women, a substitute mother or sister, and I have listened to the stories of many other single women, usually younger ones, who thoroughly enjoy friendships within a larger group as well.

A few middle-aged and older single women had much to say about the subject, after having experimented with various kinds of friendships for years. Young single women have admitted openly that they have joined the foreign service in search of friendship and love. Although such an admission won't go down well with their liberated sisters, some of them say the chances to meet people, to socialize and to go to parties, are better in the foreign service than in most other work environments. Young women who, for some reason, do not end up married after a few years sometimes pride themselves on being liberated. They hurry from one light-hearted and easy friendship with someone of the other sex to the next, and leave the posting for another assignment when relationships begin to get too complicated for their taste, turn sour, or become repetitive. Such independence is often considered an asset by young singles, although their outlook on life tends to change when invitations to parties become scarcer. In hindsight, much of the partying abroad with other foreign transients appears suddenly to be superficial and nothing more than a futile attempt to cover up a deep-seated sense of loneliness. At that stage, older single women feel the need to nurture relationships with a small group of women in a similar situation, if they have not committed themselves to such a surrogate family already.

Loneliness is regularly cited as one of the foreign-service trade marks. More women than men seem to be suffering from it. Many of them claim that there is no such thing as a busy social life for them, neither at headquarters, nor abroad. I have heard bitter complaints from young women who sat in their first foreign posting, waiting for the invitations to parties to pour in, and nothing happened. They spent all day at their desks in the mission and went home in the evening to lonely apartments, wondering where the myth about all the socializing and partying had originated. In a few sad cases, loneliness and the resulting misery increased with every new posting. The victims did not find a solution to their problem, and sank deeper and deeper into depression.

Such cases, however, remain rare. Most foreign-service members do adjust in some form or another to the shadowy sides of a life they may have expected to be filled with brilliant sunshine, and continue their search – consciously or unconsciously – for bonds that promise to satisfy their deep-rooted needs.

Friendship and love between men and women remains the most popular form of human relationship among rotational foreign-service personnel. An extraordinarily large number have met their spouses through their work. Precise figures are not available, but as many as 40 to 50 per cent may have been introduced to their prospective spouses while abroad, through the Canadian, the international, or the host culture.

The Department of External Affairs acts unintentionally like a marketplace for eligible men and women. Headquarters and Canadian missions abroad with a constant stream of rotational personnel bring together, in a short time, a large number of people. The question 'How did you meet?' is frequently answered with the remark: 'We were both working at the embassy in [any of the 117 missions].'

Noreen and her husband, Martin, first set eyes on each other at the consulate general in Seattle, where Noreen worked as secretary in the commercial section. Martin had spent a freshman year at the local university before being hired by External Affairs as a clerk. They saw each other every day in the office, went out to dinner on the weekends, and soon began to talk of marriage. When Martin received word from Ottawa about an impending posting to Bogotá, and Noreen learned that she was under consideration for the embassy in Tehran, both of them knew that the time had come to act. They sent a telex to their personnel managers at headquarters, announcing their engagement. It was not necessary to add that they would henceforth require the type of attention accorded by the department to other 'tandem couples.'

This done, they went off to buy engagement rings and to celebrate the occasion with a dinner in their favourite restaurant. While they were waiting for a verdict from Ottawa on their next appointment as husband-and-wife team, they had to choose a city in which to get married. They had given themselves the options of Vancouver (Martin's home), Ottawa (Noreen's), and Seattle (where all their friends were living at the time). As soon as they had opted in favour of Seattle, the countdown to the wedding began. It all had to be done quickly. Their next posting was waiting for both of them. The job offers for Bogotá and Tehran had been withdrawn and replaced by a joint assignment to New Delhi.

Noreen had always envisioned a slightly more romantic wedding than the one she finally celebrated. Although she felt happy about the presence of all their colleagues from the mission, and their American friends, she greatly missed her parents, who had been unable to travel across the continent for financial reasons. But, worst of all proved to be the maddening rush in which wedding preparations, tidying up the office for her successor, and the move to Asia had to be accomplished. There was not even time for a honeymoon. They spent the day after their wedding packing Martin's goods. He was the first one of them to leave for India. They found themselves caught between two official delegations. Martin was urgently needed at the high commission in New Delhi before the arrival of a parliamentary delegation, while Noreen had to stay in Seattle until after the departure of a trade delegation. Three days after they had got married, they found themselves separated by the rigours of official timetables. After Noreen had seen Martin off at the airport, she returned to her twelve-hour days at the office for the following three weeks. Every free moment left over from the administrative fall-out of the invasion of Canadian businessmen, she needed to get her own and Martin's personal effects ready for the move to their first shared apartment halfway around the world.

The circumstances under which Noreen and Martin met, got to know each other, and settled for matrimony and the status of two-career couple resemble the conditions under which a rapidly growing number of young foreign-service couples meet abroad. The family atmosphere in a Canadian mission often promotes the development of friendships both in the office and during social gatherings. Large missions, like those in London and Washington, lack a close-knit community, but are responsible for more marriages between Canadian employees than are smaller missions because of the sheer numbers of staff and the huge annual turnover of personnel.

At times, future husbands and wives have already met at headquarters or worked together in a division before they find themselves, by coincidence, posted to the same mission. Romantic relations that don't seem to have much of a chance in the impersonal environment of the Pearson Building begin to blossom in the more intimate social surroundings of a small Canadian island in a large foreign sea. But insiders insist that a remarkable number of friendships turned into love and marriage even in the somewhat chilly and emotional climate at headquarters. Marriages between foreign-service employees not only are numerous, but also seem to be growing in number, and may account – according to insiders' estimates – for as many as 10 to 15 per cent of the entire married foreign-service population.

International communities abroad – and, to a lesser extent, the international community in the Canadian capital – are prized by foreign-service members as promising alternatives to the Canadian community as a source of spouses. Foreign embassies are usually well staffed with young single employees in various occupational groups and cooperate closely with each other. Meeting members of the other sex takes place through official contacts as easily as on social occasions. Foreign-service employees tell eloquent stories about formal meetings between two officials that moved with remarkable ease into more private gatherings. For a considerable number of foreign-service men and women, the road from cocktail party to wedding altar turned out to be surprisingly short.

Among the many foreign embassies around the world that have provided the Canadian foreign service with a splendid collection of spouses, Commonwealth missions have rendered outstanding services to their Canadian cousins.

Pamela and Gregory represent a sizeable group of foreign-service members who owe their marital happiness to personnel management of another country's foreign service. Pamela, born in the heart of Scotland and on her first overseas assignment with the Commonwealth Relations Office, arrived at the British high commission in Nairobi, as Gregory, born in the middle of the Canadian prairies and on his first posting with the Canadian foreign service, was settling down in the Canadian high commission in Kenya's capital. One year after they had been formally introduced to each other at the reception to celebrate the National Day of India, they were exchanging marriage vows in the presence of most members of the British and Canadian missions and a considerable contingent of colleagues from the Indian mission who deserved recognition as originators of the happy union. The wedding reception turned out to be a truly international gathering. Pamela's and Gregory's friends represented no fewer than sixteen nationalities, and many of them had donned national costume. The brilliant colours of saris, Japanese kimonos, and Scottish kilts shimmered under the glaring African sun. Not everyone, though, opted for national costume. One of the groom's Japanese friends still remembers today, more than thirty years later, that the formal pearl-grey morning suit he had bought years earlier in Ottawa during his first overseas posting had obviously been designed to provide warmth in an Arctic climate and decidedly not to shield its wearer against the heat of Africa.

Marrying a foreigner soon put an end to Pamela's career, although it was marriage within the Commonwealth. The British service would have been happy to keep her on, but the Canadian service demanded her resignation. A compromise was worked out. She remained at her desk in the British mission for a year. When their first child was born, she retired to the nursery and transfered her loyalty and talents to Canadian causes.

Embassies of France throughout the world and several other French-speaking embassies have done for French-Canadian marriages what Commonwealth missions have done for English-Canadian marriages in the foreign service.

Pierre, orginally from Chicoutimi and on a posting to the embassy in Mexico City, recalls with pleasure one of the first tasks to which he was assigned in his new job. He had to discuss a complicated and time-consuming consular case in the French embassy. Dominique turned out to be his counterpart. For him the dreaded negotiations became a pleasure, while Dominique remembers that all disagreeable aspects of the case seemed to fade under the gaze of Pierre's blue eyes. Eight months later, Dominique gave up her maiden name and career in the French foreign service to settle down to domesticity. When Pierre was called back to headquarters for a home posting, Dominique and their two little boys travelled to Canada for the first time in their lives. Dominique admits that she loathed the prospect of having to live in the Canadian capital and dreamt of Paris throughout the flight from Mexico City to Ottawa.

In pursuit of prospective spouses, Canadians do not limit their field of action to embassies whose personnel is fluent in one of the two official languages of their country. A good number of embassies outside the English- or French-speaking realm have also rendered invaluable services to eligible Canadian diplomats.

Hugh, six months into a posting with the Canadian mission in Ghana, and Margareta, one year into her assignment at the Norwegian embassy in Accra, were introduced to each other by a mutual friend from the Danish embassy not at a cocktail party, but beside a swimming pool. Two years of dating separated this first meeting in bathing suits on the west coast of Africa and their reunion in full regalia in a snow-covered, wooden country church on the coast of Norway. From the outside, the wedding appeared to be the beautiful ending to a romantic courtship. But, for both Hugh and Margareta, the joy was mixed with several bitter pills.

The bride, surrounded by family and childhood friends, felt ill at ease in a small rural community outside of Bergen to which she did not seem to belong any more. A previous posting to Southeast Asia and her years in Africa had changed her. Throughout her wedding day, she felt as if she had tried to slip into a dress she had outgrown a long time ago. The world of her childhood seemed insufferably narrow and provincial to her, and, at the same time, she felt guilty for not sufficiently appreciating the simple kindnesses expressed towards her and her new husband. Not one of her colleagues and close friends who shared her ideas, values, and professional life had been able to spend the day with her. How much she missed their familiar faces and the international perspective they represented!

Hugh, although kindly received by his new in-laws, regretted deeply that his parents and two sisters had been unable to afford the trip from Calgary to Norway. Not one member of his family and not one of his friends from Accra had managed to come north for the occasion. His brother-in-law, whom he had met only a few days earlier, acted as his best man. As he did not speak any English, and Hugh's Norwegian was limited, they communicated largely by smiling at each other.

But none of this was as bad as the news Margareta received on the day before the wedding. The position at the Norwegian embassy in Canada for which she had asked would not be available for the next few years. If she wanted to follow her husband to his new assignment in Ottawa, she had to resign from the Norwegian foreign service and give up her career, at least for the time being. Margareta wondered how happily ever after she would be living.

Hugh and Margareta represent a growing number of foreign-service members who marry colleagues from another country's foreign service. Sooner or later, one of the partners has to give up his or her career. It is usually the woman who yields and settles for the joys of marriage and motherhood in Canada or wherever the husband happens to be sent with the Canadian foreign service.

In the 1980s, a handful of wives of Canadian foreign-service members succeeded in retaining their positions in another country's foreign service. Lawrence and Muriel are the couple who introduced to the Canadian service the idea of two different services in one marriage. They met in Ottawa, while Lawrence was serving at headquarters and Muriel was working as political officer in one of the Western embassies. Each of them had to apply for permission to marry from their foreign ministries. Both permissions were granted, and they briefly worked for two separate foreign services as a married couple. But they knew from the beginning that the days of such an amicable arrangement were numbered. As soon as Muriel was transferred from Ottawa to her own service's headquarters and Lawrence asked for a posting to the Canadian embassy in the same capital, Lawrence learned from External Affairs that a conflict of interest would prevent him from holding the position in the Canadian mission for which he had applied.

A policy paper presented by External Affairs in 1985 stated that the Canadian foreign service was willing to tolerate career couples, but only if the Canadian partner served at headquarters. He or she would not be allowed to serve in embassies abroad. A policy paper issued by Muriel's service on the same subject ruled that she could pursue her career in every mission in the world, except in her husband's country.

Implementation of the contents of these two policy papers would have been the end of either Lawrence's or Muriel's foreign-service career if Muriel's service had not made an exception and granted her a second assignment to Ottawa. During that period, however, her service brought in a complicated new set of rules to deal with similar cases. Lawrence explained their uncertain circumstances to me at a time when these new regulations had taken effect, while Muriel remained under the protection of an earlier, more generous and tolerant arrangement. Neither of them knew then what kind of long-term solution their respective services could be expected to devise in the future. Both are convinced that the problem can be solved with goodwill on both sides. They also point out that their situation has been too volatile for comfort ever since they got married. Every new assignment for either of them can bring down the delicate structure of two professional lives. They advise against trying to put two foreign services under one marital roof. One foreign service per marriage, they insist, is struggle enough.

Most Canadian foreign-service employees who propose to foreigners seem to be heeding this piece of advice and do stay clear of members of other foreign services. Such caution does not exactly qualify as a daunting task. Each foreign posting offers almost limitless possibilities to meet representatives of the other sex in the host culture. Besides, Canadian foreign-service personnel can rely on the expertise and traditions established by some of their forebears who had earlier acquired a reputation for bringing home foreign-born wives. Although generally not carried off as booty, or introduced to husband and home as the Sabines had been, many of today's Canadian wives entered their new country as war brides. Wherever Canadian troops had been stationed around the world during the First and Second World War, local women found themselves wooed, wed, and whisked off to Canada.

Whether foreign-service members have been intent on practising well-tested ancestral traditions, are expressing deeply felt devotion to a local culture, or are merely attracted to the surrounding charm and beauty, one-third of all foreign-service employees have married foreigners. The number of those who marry more than one foreigner – one at a time – grows with the number of divorces.

While war grooms never seem to have set foot on Canadian soil in great profusion, female foreign-service employees see to it that a growing number of foreign-service grooms do. The influx of numerous foreign-born husbands made a terminological adjustment necessary: one now speaks of foreign-born 'spouses,' or, informally, 'spice.'

Except in countries where Canadian security regulations discourage or prohibit private socializing with members of the other sex, a large majority of single foreign-service employees date men or women of the host culture. As the crowd of foreign-born spouses suggests, many of these relationships lead to marriage.

While we were living in Bonn, most young and single Canadians were dating Germans. Within one year, the embassy acquired two German-born wives. While our own fate was being sealed at the registrar's office in the city hall of Bonn, a colleague of my husband's exchanged vows with his bride at the registrar's office in Munich. There had been a small stream of German brides beforehand, and they still keep coming. No one has counted the nationalities represented among the foreign spouses, but I have been assured by the experts that as many as fifty different nationalities may be adding their particular flavour to the Canadian foreign service.

Bicultural couples are asked time and again how much of the mutual attraction they would ascribe to cultural differences between the partners. If an accurate answer could at all be given it would, of course, vary from case to case. But those members of the service who are happily married to a foreign-born spouse insist that cultural differences exercise a strong pull.

Canadian foreign-service members have courted their future spouses on all continents and in all conceivable climates, during moonlit rides on horseback at the foot of the pyramids, while walking through the parks of Seoul, in boats on the waterways of Bangkok or on the Seine in Paris, in seafood restaurants on the beaches of Chile, at barbecues in the Australian Club down the street from the Canadian embassy in Ankara, in the pounding heat of New Delhi, and in the gentle warmth of spring in Madrid. Marriage has been proposed under the cherry blossoms of Tokyo and Washington and in castles and vineyards along the Rhine. Wedding bells have rung for foreign-service members and their brides and grooms from Copenhagen to Pretoria, and from Hong Kong to Amman. Vows have been exchanged in innumerable languages, and ceremonies have been conducted in exotic religious and secular rites.

Canadian-born husbands and wives, however, still constitute the majority of foreign-service spouses. They either met their partner before he or she joined External Affairs or during a posting at home or abroad.

Whether the spouse is Canadian- or foreign-born, sooner or later most couples will be joined by a particular species of descendants who are known in External Affairs as foreign-service children.

Children

Without stories of the children, many foreign-service tales would be incomplete. No other parental profession shapes a child's life quite as much as the foreign service. For parents who pursue an international career, a child's wellbeing must be of utmost concern, long before the birth. Personnel officers consider the plight of an unborn child a vital administrative detail, powerful enough to determine or even change elaborate posting plans.

In January 1979, five months before our daughter Julia was due, we were offered a choice of postings, to either a particular country in Africa or Latin America. Both parts of the world attracted us greatly. But the medical situation, I feared, was anything but inviting. I consulted my obstetrician in Ottawa, and he strongly advised against either assignment as local physicians, nurses, hospitals, and child-care facilities would be inadequate. External Affairs accepted his judgment, and we remained in Ottawa, where Julia was born under the superb care of my obstetrician and his staff. Whenever I took her, during her first year, for routine check-ups and vaccinations to the pediatrician, I wondered whether she would be in as good health if we were living in either Latin America or Africa.

A year later, while we were expecting Alexandra, the department asked us to go to Brussels. This time, I did not need to seek the obstetrician's advice. We knew that in Western Europe the standards of health care did not in any way differ from those in Canada. A small army of Canadian children had been born in the Belgian capital. Local water, milk, baby food, and city air could be relied on to be fine for our one-year-old girl and baby. We gladly accepted the assignment. The timing of our departure was dictated by Alexandra, the youngest and as yet unborn member of the family.

Hundreds of foreign-service children have been born abroad, ever since foreign-service families began to live in other parts of the world. The accounts given by their mothers about their experiences range from very positive to extremely negative.

The story of Anthony's birth in Bangkok bears all the characteristics of a happy delivery. American-trained obstetricians decided on delivery by Caesarian well in advance and reserved a comfortable private room for the young family. The future father not only was invited to witness the birth, but was treated as a full member of the fledgling social unit. After Anthony's safe arrival, mother, father, and child were expected to spend a few days together to celebrate and to get acquainted. A beautiful suite was provided. Several years after the event, Anthony's parents still rave about the experience. They can't think of a more desirable way to begin family life. All their needs were generously satisfied, and they could devote themselves to each other whole-heartedly. The hospital reminded them of a first-class hotel that for some inexplicable reason was swarming with first-rate physicians, nurses, and other accomplished personnel, including superb cooks. When they took Anthony home, they had the feeling of returning from a long and restful holiday.

Amy was born in Hong Kong under slightly less favourable circumstances. Her parents were living in Beijing at the time. But hospitals in China did not meet Canadian standards. Amy's mother was entitled, according to the foreign-service directives, to have her baby in a modern hospital outside of China. But this well-meant clause in the government regulations had a bitter rider. To comply with airline rules, Amy's mother could fly no later than six weeks prior to the due date. She was forced to leave her first child, a three-year-old girl, in the care of a housekeeper, while she herself spent most of her time sitting in a lonely hotel room in Hong Kong, longing to be with her husband and child. Finally the baby was born. It was a normal birth, and Amy was healthy. Her mother received adequate medical care, but she felt desperately lonely. She did not know a soul in the city. No one ever visited her. Eventually her husband came to pick her and the new arrival up and to take both of them to Beijing. Amy slept throughout the flight, but her mother told me that she herself cried from take-off to touch-down. The thought of having to face life in China with a new baby seemed almost unbearable. She held on to the irrational hope that some miracle would divert the plane to her home town, Regina. But it touched down in Beijing instead.

'A nightmare,' Jason's mother called the events surrounding her son's birth in a Mediterranean country. Minutes after the delivery, the doctors announced that the mother urgently required a hysterectomy.

Because of language difficulties neither Jason's mother nor his father understood the reasons. There was no time to get a second opinion, so they accepted the physicians' verdict. It took the young mother months to recover from the delivery and operation, but she never completely regained her inner equilibrium. Jason was born retarded. Doctors in Canada later told her that the hysterectomy amounted to a monumental case of charlatanism. Even if malpractice suits were a possibility in the country in question, she would not have sued the doctors, she said. A court case would restore neither her nor her son to complete health. She has sadly resigned herself to her fate.

In order to prevent such cases in the future, all foreign-service wives are now entitled to fly home at government expense and to have their babies in Canada. Many wives make use of this provision and spend the last six to eight weeks before the delivery with family and friends. Some of them even manage to have their husbands with them during the critical hours. The government recognizes a father's right to attend his child's birth and pays for his trip to Canada as well. But not all fathers arrive on time. Too many can get away from the mission only a few days prior to the date or after the baby has arrived. Those, however, who carefully arrange their annual leave around the most likely date and whose babies cooperate with the timing often make it for the decisive moments, even if they have to be rushed to the delivery room in Canada directly from the airport.

The hospital at the Canadian Forces Base in Lahr, Germany, is widely seen as an alternative to a hospital in Canada. Foreign-service wives in European and even in some African postings sometimes consider a sojourn in this Canadian enclave in the heart of Europe more convenient than a prolonged stay with relatives in some remote part of Canada, especially if the final weeks before the birth coincide with the depth of winter at home.

Medical standards in many foreign postings, notably in the United States, Western Europe, Australia, and a few Asian countries, live up to Canadian standards, and a good many wives have their babies in local hospitals. Going to Canada for a delivery inevitably means a long period of separation for husband and wife and a lonely stay in a hotel or a crowded one with relatives or friends in Canada for the young mother. Even more complicated is the situation for mothers with other children.

If no grandmother, aunt, or friend in Canada can look after the children, should the mother take them along and keep them in the hotel with her, or should she separate from them and leave them abroad in the care of a babysitter or housekeeper? Neither is an acceptable solution. A delivery in Canada also involves a long and exhausting trip, sometimes halfway around the world, first in an advanced state of pregnancy and later with a newborn child. Under such circumstances, many mothers are grateful if doctors and medical facilities in the host country spare them the upheaval surrounding a delivery back home.

But more than half of all overseas postings that qualify as hardship assignments are classified as such for a variety of reasons. Among them are often the poor quality of water, air, and food, and low standards of medical care. Pregnant foreign-service wives in these parts of the world have no choice but to set out on a trip to a safe hospital, in Canada, in Lahr, or in another country, and to cope with all the complications such a trip adds to the birth of their child.

Regardless of how safe delivery and post-partum care have been in a modern hospital, mothers returning to one of the more than sixty hardship postings around the world have to face a harsh reality for their pink and blue bundles. In Africa and some Asian and Latin American countries, dangers to the well-being of a small child, especially a newborn, can hardly be overestimated. To protect the delicate new life from the onslaught of innumerable hidden and overt enemies in the environment can be an all-consuming task. All foreign-service mothers who have guided children through their first years of life in a hardship post deserve the highest esteem of their sisters in Canada who are able to raise their little ones in comfort and security.

Data from the Outside of Canada Health Care Plan confirm what experienced foreign-service members have known for a long time: while on postings abroad, personnel come down with many more illnesses than during assignments in Canada. In the course of our four years in Brussels – one of the healthiest and safest cities External Affairs can offer to its employees – we could have served as a painfully convincing example. Our family, so seldom sick in Canada that our sons' school commented on our never-absent children, required medical attention for four solid years. We could have won a competition for the number, variety, and quality of our diseases. Our predecessors had already warned us before we set foot on Belgian soil to expect a dramatic increase in sickness. Ears, noses, and throats especially were bound to come under heavy attack in the rainy and damp climate. But we were not prepared for what was to hit us.

A family physician whom we got to know shortly after our arrival in Brussels, when one of our sons had fainted at school, became a weekly, at times daily, visitor to our house. We must have provided him with one of the most colourful collections of sicknesses under the permanently grey skies of Belgium: enormous bee stings, dramatic skin rashes, stomach flus, allergies, an uninterrupted series of ear and throat infections, and a host of other more serious illnesses, including scarlet fever. With almost reassuring predictability, at least one member of the household would be coming down with the next minor or major malaise the moment someone else had completed his or her turn. We could also offer with beautiful regularity more than one patient at a time. A sense of brotherly or sisterly solidarity saw to it that some of the more impressive ailments were shared.

The long-suffering parents still don't know what they would have done without two young physicians in a suburb of Brussels who never tired in their effort to track down the source of a malady and to rout bacterial and other types of culprits with the united forces of the local pharmaceutical industry. One of the doctors held the fort in a shared office; his partner made house calls. Often he would reach our home within ten minutes of our alerting him, carrying a satchel full of medical wizardry. Whatever his magic bag did not contain could be procured in one of the pharmacies that graced every street corner. Altogether I must have bought tons of pills, potions, drops, creams, salves, and ointments.

The services we received from the entire medical establishment in the Belgian capital, including emergency wards of hospitals, were outstanding. In the absence of Canadian physicians who make house calls, we would have loved to import both Dr DeJonghe and Dr Robijns to Canada, and we told them so. But they expected business to remain brisk even after our departure and decided to stay at home. It turned out to be just as well. They could not have made a living out of us. As soon as we got back to Canada, our illnesses vanished.

Like many foreign-service families, we survived our overseas postings without any long-term damage to our children's health. But not every family is as lucky as we were. Children of all ages have suffered serious and irreparable damage.

'Foreign-service life is very hard on children,' one of the most distinguished members of the Canadian foreign-service told me in a letter. 'Where were you, when I needed you?' had been one of his sons' bitter questions in response to years of boarding-school. The father admitted to feelings of regret and guilt, but pointed out that his sons eventually saw their life in a more favourable light, thus absolving him from responsibility for the misery they had earlier ascribed to long periods of separation from their parents.

Life between two worlds consists for children of a wealth of possibilities and of a multitude of limitations. In few areas is this more apparent than in the wide field of schooling and of a child's general education. During more than twenty years in the foreign-service community I have had plenty of time to witness the exposure of our colleagues' children to the whole range of opportunities and restrictions. The story of the education of our own brood of four sums up the experience of hundreds of foreign-service children.

In Moscow we encountered an unsatisfactory situation. The only English-language kindergarten was filled and had a long waiting list. Because we did not want our three-year-old son, Robin, to salute the picture of Lenin every morning and to march in a Soviet kindergarten, we had the choice of an overcrowded French kindergarten or none at all. If it had not been for our eagerness to raise a bilingual Canadian, even if the project had to be started in the heart of Russia, we would have abandoned the idea of any schooling until Robin's name came up on the waiting list for the English system. But, as we considered bilingualism a pressing matter, we registered him in the French school.

We soon discovered to our dismay that the mornings in his new environment were not Robin's idea of happiness. For the first few weeks, he looked gloomy and withdrawn when he came home. I thought I should find out more about his class and asked the director's permission to sit in one day. I quickly understood why he always referred to 'the angry teacher.' Faced with an overwhelming crowd of small children of all colours and creeds in two tiny rooms in one of the grey downtown high-rise apartments that would have qualified as a slum in the West, the poor woman displayed all the signs of tension and suppressed anger that were so apparent in the entire local population. I felt great sympathy for Madame l'Institutrice and was certain that I could not have coped with half of what she had to put up with. For most of the morning, the children ran around uncontrollably, screaming and shouting. It seemed impossible to bring order to the pack or to get them to do anything sensible. From about ten o'clock on, the sharp smell of urine, coming from a tiny, windowless washroom next to the playroom, began to spread across the rooms where the running and yelling continued. Eventually, the crowd began to calm down a bit and the teacher could get them to follow her instructions. By one o'clock, it was all over for the day. We decided to take Robin out of school, if he asked us to, but he never did. He seemed to cheer up and make peace with the lot that fate had dealt the young Canadian patriot abroad. How much French he actually learned was never clear to me. He refused to speak the language at home or anywhere else outside the school. But his report cards suggested that he had become a member of the community of three- and four-year-old Francophones in the Soviet capital.

While Moscow represented all the limitations Canadian children face in the selection of their schools abroad, Brussels stood for all the educational possibilities. A vast array of nursery schools and kindergartens had sprung up all over the city in the 1970s. When Julia and Alexandra were old enough, we had an impressive collection to choose from. The enormous size of the Belgian capital narrowed our options somewhat, unless we wanted to spend hours each day driving our little girls to school. I was delighted to find a German nursery school only minutes away from our house. It was run by a tender-hearted young German woman, married to a Belgian, who, in the absence of children of her own, had lovingly adopted each one of her little charges. She had redecorated an entire floor of her house and had converted it into a small paradise for children. She played and sang with them, read fairy tales, took them for long walks, and taught them countless skills. As much as Robin had tasted a rather oppressive atmosphere, Julia and Alexandra sampled an open and enriching environment. They thrived on their teacher's warmth and on the company of a small group of other two- and three-year-olds.

With the German border no more than an hour's drive away and the constant back and forth of family and friends between Bonn and Brussels, our children were surrounded by the German language. All German television stations could be picked up in Brussels as easily as the Belgian, French, and British networks. Our daughters began to mix German into their fledgling English. The songs they were learning every day at nursery school became part of their rapidly growing vocabulary.

The number of schools and types of school systems open to Robin and Jeremy in Brussels were almost limitless. American, British, French, German, and international schools, and the distinguished European School, offered a menu of languages that would have made the mouth of any linguist water. Although eager to see our older children benefit from the French environment we came to the conclusion that a transfer to a French *lycée,* in addition to all the other unsettling changes the move had imposed on our ten- and eight-year-old boys, was more than they should be expected to handle at that stage. We therefore enrolled Robin and Jeremy in the British School of Brussels, where they enjoyed the comfort of a familiar language, while trying to come to terms with a new, strange, and at times rather uncomfortable world around them.

As chaos gradually gave way to order and as the turbulence each individual and the family as a whole had experienced slowly subsided, we began to introduce the prospect of a French *lycée* to our sons. After talking the matter over and over, we finally got their full agreement to switch them to the French school system at the beginning of our second year in Brussels. They recognized the posting to Brussels as their opportunity to become fluent in French. They wanted to return to Canada as good, solid, bilingual citizens.

Like two novice divers who discover that the distance between them and the water seems a lot more dramatic when they are looking down from a diving board than when they had first surveyed the situation from the water, looking up, Robin and Jeremy stood in the schoolyard of Le Verseau one wet, chilly, windy September morning, shivering a little and gathering courage for the cold plunge into the sea of shrill French sounds surrounding them. Compassion and a motherly urge to return her young ones to what felt like a warm and cosy pool at the British school briefly struggled with the forces of reason and courage. When a harsh bell rang, the latter forces had won. I renewed the promise my husband and I had made earlier: every day we would be waiting for them, with towels and dry, warm clothes, figuratively speaking, provided they did the jumping and swimming. They grabbed their blue airline bags, threw them over their shoulders, and quickly disappeared into the building.

Three years of daily diving into bitterly cold waves followed, not only for the two boys but also for their parental coaches. We had to be immersed every bit as much as they were.

Le Verseau, located in the small rural community of Wavre on the autoroute between Brussels and Namur, was the only school in Belgium, and as far as we know the only one of its kind in Europe, that offered a curriculum that fulfilled the requirements of both a French-language *lycée* and a British school at the same time. Designed to give the large number of Anglophones residing in Brussels the best of both worlds, the school used French as language of instruction for all children, Belgians and dozens of other nationalities alike. For Anglophones, one hour a day was reserved to meet the demands of the British system. Since it was entirely impossible to accommodate studies of English language, literature, grammar, history, and geography in an hour, the teachers, who had been hired in Britain for this demanding job, could only touch on all the subjects, leaving hours of work to be done at home each day, in addition to all the homework in the main subjects taught in French, such as French grammar, literature, history, geography, mathematics, and Latin. Robin and Jeremy needed daily coaching and study during their first year to enable them to reach the French reading and writing levels of their classmates.

Towards the end of the third year, it became clear that all our effort had paid off. Robin and Jeremy felt as elated as their worn-out coaches to learn that they had accomplished the nearly impossible. Teachers at Le Verseau, with whom we had by then developed the kind of relationship team members in a hospital's intensive-care unit enjoy, told us that our sons would now be accepted at any French *lycée* and at any British school. A reward for two exhausted pupils and their personal instructors was not long in coming, and at least the British portion of Le Verseau's prediction soon proved to be correct. Shortly before leaving Brussels to return to Ottawa, my husband and I decided to make long-term educational plans. If another overseas posting after three or four years in

Canada took us to a country with an inadequate senior high school, boarding-school would become a necessity for our boys. We felt we should prepare the children for such a drastic change in their life well in advance, even several years prior.

On the basis of their achievements at Le Verseau and after an extensive interview with the headmaster, Robin and Jeremy were accepted at one of the most demanding boarding-schools we knew of, an institution in Scotland noted as much for its high academic standards as for the strong emphasis in its curriculum on the development in students of a sense of responsibility and social service. We were delighted. So were all the teachers at Le Verseau. 'We told you so,' they said, and assured us again that our boys would find the same wide-open doors at a French *lycée* anywhere in the world.

Upon their return to Ottawa, they received a royal welcome to the French-immersion program. Beyond their fluency in French they had acquired, under extremely difficult circumstances in a foreign country, a sense of direction and purpose as well as a set of valuable work habits – assets less likely to be secured in a familiar and less-challenging home environment.

Adjustment to the educational situation in any of their postings is one of the main tasks of foreign-service children and their parents. Many of them treat it as a challenge, take a constructive attitude, and manage to make much out of little. If parents convert a problem into an opportunity for learning and growth, their children are bound to go along, provided they can count on parental support. A large number of parents with whom I spoke confirmed what we had discovered. Their children had ultimately benefited from having to overcome obstacles, regardless of how insurmountable those obstacles had looked initially. Others, however, pointed out that one or more of their assignments had forced their children to move rapidly from one unsatisfactory school to the next, leading not only to profound unhappiness and insecurity, but also to a patchwork education.

For parents who are eager to make their children fluent in both official languages, schooling can be a knotty issue. French schools abroad, in which many French and English Canadians enrol their children because the quality of education provided is unquestionably high and because of the continuity the French system guarantees, are not noted for the quality of their English-language instruction. English-language schools abroad, whether British or American, are generally not known for outstanding French-language training. I have talked to English-Canadian parents who, out of an ardent desire to introduce their child to French as early as possible, put him or her into the French system for the first few years of schooling, only to discover upon returning to Canada that the child did not know how to read or write English. Other parents told me that English-language schools neglect the French language to the point where their children find themselves way behind Canadian children, who enjoy at least one hour of French every day from kindergarten on.

Most foreign-service parents, however, emphasize that their children have emerged from a patchwork of school systems with a broad education of good quality.

At some point in their career, most parents have no choice but to put a child into boarding-school. Foreign-service families have been discussing the advantages and disadvantages of life at boarding-school, as compared with life at home, for decades, and continue to do so. Only complex opinion polls and refined statistical analysis would be able to determine whether the pro–boarding-school forces outnumber those opposed. Judging superficially by the debate at a seminar I attended a few years ago in External Affairs and during which half a dozen young boarding-school veterans spoke about their experiences, it looks as if, from about sixteen years of age on, children consider such a form of schooling, and its lifestyle, an attractive alternative to living with their parents abroad. However, the participants qualified their statements by pointing out that success or failure of this life depends on a large number of factors. Thus, any general conclusion in favour of or against boarding-school would turn a blind eye on a multifaceted reality.

As in almost every aspect of the rotational life, opinions range from the extreme positive to the extreme negative. I have talked to teenagers who loved the independent life away from home, while thoroughly enjoying regular visits with their parents. I have listened to parents point out how much boarding-school promoted their child's development towards self-reliance and responsible and mature adulthood. Some younger teenagers confirmed their parents' verdict by calling it a mixed bag of good and bad, an assessment to which a majority of experienced foreign-service parents and their children would subscribe. In a few cases, boarding-school can spell disaster. One mother told me the story of her son who had tried to take his life at boarding-school. He was sixteen years old when his parents decided that eleven different schools on five continents had been enough and that it was time for a bit of continuity and quality education in a Canadian environment. The boy had never lived in Canada for any length of time and felt desperately lonely and homesick for his parents, who were on a posting in Latin America.

The way children respond to the challenge school in a foreign country presents often reveals the way they react in general to demands made on them. In many families, children's academic performance can serve as an important indicator of their attitude towards the posting and of their overall ability and willingness to come to terms with life in a strange environment. Parents, at times under the inflence of perceptive and experienced teachers, recognize school marks and behaviour as telling information about their offsprings' general response to the host of uncertainties surrounding them. Asked how their children fared in a specific post, or in the rotational life as a whole, most parents reported that satisfactory overall development is usually accompanied by good report cards, discounting the normal ups and downs in a pupil's record.

I have met dozens of highly intelligent and broadly educated foreign-service children who display all the signs of a well-balanced, harmonious, and mature personality, and I have listened to hundreds of parents whose children seemed to fit into the same category. A large number of mothers and fathers pointed out to me how much their children had especially benefited from exposure to overwhelming social and economic problems, which they had been able to observe at close range while being posted to countries in the Third World. They came away, not only with a sense of gratitude for living conditions in Canada, but also with a strong sense of broad responsibility and a desire to contribute personally to the redressing of social ills in other parts of the world. Independence and self-reliance are most often cited as the chief characteristics of foreign-service children who have adapted well to their fate.

Frequently, a child's poor standing at school goes hand in hand with behaviour problems, both at home and in the classroom. Parents who are able and willing to see that such a child is unconsciously trying to convey a message about his or her negative response to a particular posting or to foreign-service life as a whole normally take some form of remedial action. Depending on the nature of the child's unresolved inner conflict and on the parents' insight into a complex situation and degree of responsibility, they re-examine and adjust their family life, seek professional help, decide to go on a long home posting to give the child and the family a period of rest and recovery from an overdose of challenges, or take a radical step and leave the foreign service altogether. Two of our friends gave up promising diplomatic careers because one of their children went into a prolonged state of distress with every move. As soon as the family had settled down for a life of continuity, the children recovered. Both of them are blossoming not only socially, but academically as well. I know of several other foreign-service employees who changed professions to accommodate the needs of their children.

Not all parents, however, are prepared to sacrifice their careers for their children. Some of them refuse to see a connection between a child's academic and emotional problems and their own profession and resulting lifestyle. They may send their offspring to a psychologist, or even agree to family therapy, but they will not consider as a viable option saying farewell to the foreign service.

I have listened to mothers and fathers who told me that their children's dilemma at home and at school was attributable to poor personnel management at External Affairs. Their continued presence in the rotational service was not to be blamed, but the organization: bad postings, poor climate, inadequate housing, unsatisfactory teachers, and a host of other factors. Those parents simply shut their eyes to unpleasant realities. Some parents went as far as to pronounce their children 'thriving on foreign-service life' even though the kids' social and academic record contradicted such a claim.

In the course of my interviews, I came across a small number of parents who saw no avenue open to them outside External Affairs and remained on the constantly turning merry-go-round, even though their children showed clear signs of dizziness and motion sickness. Some of them rely on a dangerous form of home-made remedy. In the hope that a child's predicament will disappear with a change of scene, they rush from one foreign assignment to the next. If the trouble is minor, it may vanish in a different environment; however, more serious problems tend to worsen under the impact of further uncertainties and disruptions. Each posting places a set of demands on a child; unless they are met with the help of newly acquired skills, life in each of the subsequent postings is bound to be seen to have the same shortcomings as the previous ones, with the result that the sense of failure only grows.

The academic and social problems of foreign-service children have to be seen in a larger context. Psychologists and psychiatrists confirm that the unsettling nature of rotational life is frequently only of secondary importance and that the primary problem lies within the family. Unresolved individual, marital, or other conflicts often prevent an entire family from benefiting from the many possibilities foreign-service life offers.

Countless conversations with families suggest that children's emotional well-being is a highly sensitive indicator of how the social unit copes with the exceptional demands of rotational life. Young children are especially vulnerable. They can't speak for themselves and may therefore resort to unacceptable social behaviour to give their parents the message that a specific post, or this kind of life in general, is more than they can take.

Too many young parents are blissfully unaware of the pitfalls of foreign-service life that are masked by its surface attractiveness. Years, sometimes decades, after they first joined the service, they express deep regrets for not having understood earlier what they know now, and for not having been warned about the perils by experienced members of the older foreign-service generation. I have come across a number of parents with seriously troubled children who could have avoided some major mistakes if they had received the necessary training in foreign-service-life skills. But, even when parents are prepared, the rotational lifestyle holds many risks for children of all ages.

Fortunately, most parents are aware of the dangers inherent in their lifestyle. They prepare their children carefully, monitor them daily, and help them lovingly to overcome obstacles and to acquire the social skills that will allow them to adjust to forever-changing surroundings. One mother's dream prior to a new posting represents the unconscious concerns of foreign-service wives for their young ones. She told me she had dreamt she was waiting for a train that was to take her and her little son and daughter to Africa. For some reason the continent could be reached from Canada by ViaRail. As she was standing with her children on a narrow platform between two train tracks, suddenly, out of nowhere, two gigantic engines came racing towards them from opposite directions. She felt paralysed with fear of being squashed between them. Grabbing the tiny hands of her little ones, she was even more horrified to feel the roaring monsters brush against her clothes as they passed on either side. Any moment, she thought, the children could be torn away from her. But the trains disappeared as quickly as they had come, leaving all of them unharmed. She has never forgotten the nightmare.

In fact, few foreign-service children are endangered by the momentum of rotational life. Those who insist that the advantages of this kind of life outweigh the disadvantages seem to be in the majority. The sixteen-year-old daughter of one of my colleagues expressed in a letter to me what many other foreign-service children had indicated during earlier conversations:

I think that the diplomatic life is for children a very rich experience and ... has its positive and negative sides. I am still not sure if it is a very good idea to live in a place just long enough to get attached to it and then have to cut oneself off from that place, perhaps permanently. This sort of thing only worsens as children get older. On the other hand ... I would not exchange places with anyone who has lived in the same city, or even country, all their life, because I feel that my experience will be of great use to me, now and in the future. Of course the greatest advantage of this mode of life is to get to know a culture other than your own well, if not intimately ... You make friends among them ... I believe that children of diplomats have a special responsibility to tell others about their experiences and to carry them into whatever they do in their lives ... International schools really are valuable; I think they contributed greatly to my development ... The best thing of all is the student body itself. So far my best friends – met at these schools – have been from India, Cameroon, Austria and Hungary. Each one has helped me approach problems in a different way. There is a peculiar kind of family relationship in these schools. All of these things have – I hope – given a richness to my life which would not have been there otherwise. On the other hand, there is one way in which we suffer overwhelmingly. If you have been away from your own country six years – as I have, from the ages of nine to fifteen – you may have no real relationship with your birthplace ... Now I am living in Ottawa and everything is strange ... I am unused to the taste of milk and water. I am also apprehensive about entering a very large high school, where I only know one girl. And then there is the fact that you have to say goodbye to friends almost every year. The places where my friends live are very far away ... Apart from that, I really loved life as the child of a diplomat.

Home Leave

Whether child or adult, most members of the foreign-service community cherish their right to home leave while living abroad. Each employee and his or her immediate family are entitled to such a trip once in the course of each non-hardship posting, twice during a minor hardship posting, and once a year in a major hardship assignment. Experienced foreign-service members are very familiar with recurring feelings of alienation and rootlessness while abroad, and many of them know that such a reaction to life in a succession of foreign cultures is often best treated with renewed exposure to home.

A sense of homelessness can build up gradually and strike as suddenly and powerfully as lightning. We learned that lesson a few weeks after our arrival in Budapest from our daughter Alexandra. During a leisurely walk back to our house from Julia's and Alexandra's school, where we had attended an open house, Alexandra discovered in the soft light of the early evening a small black and white cat sitting under a garden fence. After she had played with it for a few minutes, Alexandra announced she was going to take the cat home. When my husband and I pointed out to her that this cat belonged to someone and that we could not take it away from this area, Alexandra, with uncharacteristic high-pitched drama in her voice, pronounced the kitten 'homeless.' She, Alexandra, would be the one to give this animal the desperately needed home. A flood of tears followed.

Even our most gentle attempt to persuade her to leave the cat failed. She simply informed us with an almost cold sense of determination that she intended to stay with the little fellow right there throughout the night if we refused to let the cat come home with us. She would not abandon the poor thing. After a long and fruitless discussion, we finally picked Alexandra up and carried our inconsolably weeping child back to our house. Never before in her seven-year life had she been in what appeared to be a state of distress.

Without immediately understanding the reason for my own reaction, I felt strangely shaken by the incident long after Alexandra had fallen asleep in my arms. She had looked and acted bereaved when we had separated her from the kitten. Could it be that the homelessness she ascribed to the cat was a projection of her own feelings after the recent separation from her brothers and home in Canada? Since the feeling of bereavement could not have been caused by the need to part with an animal she had known only for a few minutes, was it possible, then, that she felt deprived of the chance to make a home for the cat as a substitute for the home she craved for herself? Was the cat supposed to fill an emotional vacuum left by her beloved and painfully missed brothers? I was once again hit by feelings of guilt, which I knew very well from earlier postings. Was it not irresponsible and cruel to tear our children out of their home every few years and throw them mercilessly into a strange world? Should we leave the foreign service?

Whatever the deepest reason for Alexandra's grief had been, and whatever decision we would make about our life in the foreign service, my husband and I agreed on two things: we would get a pet for our daughters and we would begin to discuss with them the prospect of our home leave in Canada the following year.

A few days after this unsettling incident, I used a free hour during Julia's and Alexandra's ballet lesson and drove to the outskirts of Budapest where a member of our embassy had located a cat breeder. I will never forget the moment when I was able to put a tiny, cream-coloured, pure-bred Persian kitten in the arms of two little ballerinas as they were emerging from their class. Alexandra whispered: 'Whose cat is this?' I barely managed to whisper back, 'It is yours' before my emotions caught up with me at the sight of tears in Alexandra's eyes. Words are insufficient to describe the expression on Julia's and Alexandra's faces. Surrounded by other miniature dancers, both of them seemed to be floating along the dignified dark halls of the National Ballet Institute, tenderly holding the tiny treasure as if it might break any moment or vanish like a dream.

Our daughters called the little fellow 'Sneakers' and demonstrated what they meant by making a home for a cat. They never ate until he had eaten, fed him with the finest food they could find, cleaned and brushed him, played with him, cuddled him, carried him through the house, and sang him to sleep after he had settled down for the night in a blanket-lined doll's bed. Alexandra, a born veterinarian, removed expertly and patiently from his coat a small army of ticks whenever he returned from his forays into the wide world of our garden.

Sneakers quickly captured the hearts of every member of the household. In the morning, my husband invited him to his study, poured part of his cup of hot Ovaltine into a saucer, and watched him lap up his portion as both listened to the six o'clock BBC news. He curled up at my feet when I worked at my desk and came tearing down from any part of the house as soon as he heard the sound of the piano. He rushed back and forth between his favourite place under the keyboard and an equally cherished location in the kitchen, where the cook kept chicken liver and other delicacies for him. In return for his family's affection, Sneakers began to act like a contented baby. He continues to cuddle up with anyone he can find in the house, waits patiently at the door for us when we have been out, and spends most of his time either sleeping or purring peacefully, unless, of course, his feline duties call him into the garden where he keeps a close eye on moths and butterflies.

Judging by his obvious happiness, Julia and Alexandra had succeeded in giving Sneakers a home. But I suspected that their attempt to create a friendly and familiar world for him had only partially satisfied their own need for the kind of warm and intimate environment that 'home' in Canada had meant for them. In spite of the new love and joy he had brought to their life in Budapest, too much of what had been part of their happy life in Canada was still missing, above all their brothers. One evening I found Alexandra burying her tearful face in Sneakers' fur after a phone call from Robin in Toronto had brought his voice back to the family for a few minutes. The all-too-short transatlantic conversation had torn open the barely healed wound of separation.

Both Julia and Alexandra felt that the family had been cut to pieces. Alexandra was more outspoken about the matter than her sister. I still keep in my desk a small piece of paper on which Alexandra had scribbled a message while I was talking to Robin on the phone with the request to pass it on to Robin. The note reads: 'Four in the family is not enough!' It was her way of saying that the family remained a fragment as long as her brothers lived on a different continent.

Another notice from her to me, written a few days before Sneakers had joined us, combined a request for a pet with the statement: 'In Canada I was never sad.' It was clear to us that our new furry addition to the family could console our little girls to an extent, but could take away the longing neither for their brothers nor for the world they had left behind in Canada. Alexandra admitted that, sometimes, at school, during recess, her tears began to flow when she thought of Robin and Jeremy and of her life at home. Julia and Alexandra placed on their bedside tables a small Canadian flag together with a piece of paper on which they had printed: 'Canada – I love you! Canada – I miss you!' I felt certain that these extraordinary little shrines had been created more out of yearning for the lost paradise than from patriotism.

After countless previous conversations with foreign-service colleagues on the subject of what exactly constitutes 'home' for them, I counted myself lucky for having long ago established a consensus within the family on what 'home' meant and for having enjoyed long years in a setting that the entire family had consciously experienced as 'home.' A home leave would allow us to reassemble the key components of which our undivided realm had consisted. Regardless of how brief such a holiday would be, the possibility of returning to a clearly defined, harmonious universe and a reunited and complete family on Canadian soil brightened our days. Visits to our house, calls on neighbours and other friends, a Sunday morning at our church, a day for the girls in their former school, the sounds of familiar language around us, the smell and taste of long-missed food and drink – all combined promised to serve as the oasis we were dreaming of while trudging through a desert of which our life at the early stage in our new posting reminded us. In gloomy moments during the first winter, we entertained each other with glowing accounts of our previous existence around hearth and home and of equally wonderful things to come as soon as we returned. Now, one year after we had left Ottawa for Budapest, I landed with Julia and Alexandra in Canada. World travellers and expatriates know the indescribable joy of stepping on familiar soil after a long and difficult absence.

I suggested that we live every moment of these precious two weeks to the fullest. We started that project at the airport in Ottawa. The best way to celebrate this first hour at home, my girls told me, would be at McDonald's, the one we would be passing on our way into town. After all the turmoil we had experienced in the past year, it was reassuring that the restaurant was still standing in the same place. As I watched Julia and Alexandra dig into their hamburgers and Chicken McNuggets I reminded them that their brave daily struggle over the past year under sometimes very sad circumstances should be seen as the shadow side of the sunny hours we were able to enjoy now. Was not the thrill of having breakfast in Hungary, lunch in Switzerland, and supper in Canada, all on one day, a reward for their courage and conscientious work in a strange country? In spite of all the hardships we experienced, were we not lucky to be able to explore other parts of the world and still have a wonderful country to come home to? Sucking on their strawberry and chocolate milkshakes, both agreed. Being back in Canada made up for a lot of the previous year's difficulties. And one thing was certain too, they told me: if they had never left Canada, they would not be half as happy to be here as they were now.

I had carefully arranged our holiday around the Thanksgiving weekend. Jeremy spent four days with us in our downtown apartment hotel, Robin arrived from Toronto, and even my husband managed to get away from his merciless Budapest schedule and join us in Ottawa. For three magic days the family was reunited in Canada. At times, we felt as if we had never left.

One of the key components of our happiness had moved within reach. The doors to our house had been opened wide. Marilyn and Marvin, our tenants, and foreign-service colleagues and friends at the same time, had invited us for a lovingly prepared, festive Thanksgiving dinner. For the first time after a year's absence, we stepped back into our house as guests in familiar rooms full of unfamiliar furniture.

Reunions with neighbours and friends followed. Phone calls, invitations, and visitors poured into our small rented apartment. We were celebrated like long-lost children, and accorded our friends similar treatment. Julia and Alexandra spent a day in the school they had attended before leaving for Hungary and a day in the school they were scheduled to enter after our return. They lounged on cushions in their favourite bookstore on Sussex Drive, selecting treasures to take to Budapest with them. They accompanied me on my calls, after having fortified themselves against their mother's rather long conversations with a fine assortment of books and bars of chocolate.

I had made appointments by letter for routine medical and dental check-ups for all of us. Even in the various doctors' offices, we received the warmest welcome. The physicians were most eager for first-hand accounts of the exciting political events we had been witnessing in Eastern Europe.

Expeditions to buy shoes, clothes, and other goods unobtainable in Hungary took us to familiar shopping centres and stores. The eleven years our family had spent in Ottawa altogether between various postings had filled the city with happy memories and we felt completely integrated into the world around us. The days were long and exhausting, especially since neither the girls nor I could adjust to the time change and woke up around four o'clock most mornings. But not even fatigue could bring down our high spirits.

Huge, dark clouds began to gather in the sunny skies of this glorious Indian summer, however, on the day we had to say goodbye to my husband, who had to fly to Budapest; to Robin, who had to go back to university; and to Jeremy, whose school holiday was over. Within six hours, the family had been cut in half. Alexandra and Julia looked as downcast as I felt myself when we opened the door to the empty and silent apartment. We had to start packing for our return to Hungary. The next morning Alexandra announced that she was not going back. She would be staying in Ottawa. Her home was here and nowhere else.

I realized immediately that we had been hit by a crisis. It was one of those moments in which the merciless requirements of international mobility appeared irreconcilable with the ordinary needs of a human being. I knew from hundreds of conversations with foreign-service personnel that everyone in the service is familiar with such a dramatic clash of two sets of conflicting demands. If such moments are recognized for what they are and dealt with in a responsible and realistic way, they can form a genuine turning-point on the path towards a reconciliation of seemingly incompatible forces. If, however, such vital messages are ignored, covered up, or simply played down as being nothing more than childish outbursts, the consequences can be disastrous. I was determined to face the crisis head on and to discuss with Julia and Alexandra their own needs in relation to the harsh realities of rotationality. For an eight- and nine-year-old, such a discussion would be best couched in terms of a comparison between the good and the bad aspects of foreign-service life. I dropped the plans I had made for the day, and settled down with my little girls for a long conversation. I still remember the uncomfortable, mustard-coloured hide-a-bed on which we spent hours talking.

I thought it would be best to invite lamentations first of all. Both threw themselves into the open arena and presented me with a long list of what they felt were the main problems of their present life. The worst thing was the separation from Robin and Jeremy and the overwhelming distance between them and us. The occasional phone calls made matters worse, as far as they were concerned. Having to leave their cosy rooms, our lovely house, and the Gatineau Park behind followed closely in the register. Then came the separation from neighbours, friends, and school buddies. Canadian food had been moved entirely out of reach: milk, juice, their favourite cereals, bacon, chocolate-chip cookies, and what about maple syrup?

The isolation in Budapest due to the language barrier they found particularly hard. They did not like the big, impersonal official residence. It was everything but cosy. They resented the loss of privacy occasioned by the presence of servants everywhere in the house, the thick pollution of the city, being locked up in the garden behind a high fence instead of having the run of the Gatineau Park. I had no trouble listening to their complaints since I felt at least as disheartened over the separation from half of the family and about the rapidly approaching end of our home leave as they did. After we had explored their views, I added my own collection of grievances to the pile.

Eventually the three of us ran out of examples of what we saw as the darker side of foreign-service life. We decided that it was time for tea and hot chocolate, left the mustard-coloured sofa, and moved into the kitchen to prepare a snack. The cheerful whistling kettle and the glorious aroma of chocolate-chip cookies baking in the oven ushered in the second part of our session: an enumeration of the brighter aspects of international mobility.

In order to set the record about our posting to Hungary straight, I reminded my daughters that a certain amount of boredom with daily affairs in Canada had clearly crept into the house and established itself months before the news of a possible assignment to Budapest had reached the family. One of our girls had greeted the prospect of moving to Europe with particular enthusiasm. She was tired, she had one evening informed everyone sitting around the dinner table, of having to look at the same old walls of her room all the time. Four years had already passed since our return from Brussels, an appropriate moment to change walls and to move on. I had not forgotten my reaction then to this unmistakable symptom of 'Itchy Feet Syndrome' and I remembered vividly how surprised and amused I had been to watch a seven-year-old child display signs of an affliction I had always associated with foreign-service veterans of slightly more venerable age.

I used all the eloquence at my disposal to recapture the atmosphere of happy anticipation that had accompanied the months of preparation for our great Hungarian adventure. Even their brothers' exodus from home had looked to them like a wonderful event. A new and independent existence for Robin at university and for Jeremy at boarding-school had captured their imagination. The period of separation from them would be short and negligible. Within four months both boys would fly to Budapest for Christmas holidays with the family. As far as the girls themselves were concerned, had they not felt inspired and delighted by the prospect of a new house, a large garden, a new international school with students and teachers from all over the world, newness and freshness all around, and an entirely different world to explore?

Did they recall the beginning of that promising life: the flight to Europe? It certainly was not necessary to remind my girls. At that moment, Julia and Alexandra were the ones who became eloquent. Not for anything would they have wanted to miss the plane trip across the ocean, the comfortable seats by the window, the view of Toronto from the air, dinner high above the clouds, all in the company of their white teddy bears. The flight attendants had entertained them with several new games and had brought candy and chocolate. Mommy had taken photos of them cuddled up comfortably with a small stuffed zoo while, outside, the night over the Atlantic floated by.

Admittedly, they had felt too tired to eat when a breakfast tray had arrived. Their legs had felt like lead when they staggered out of the plane, and their plump teddies seemed to have gained an enormous amount of weight overnight. The same fate had obviously befallen the bags they had taken on board, filled with books, crayons, and a few favourite bunnies. What had been casually flung over the shoulder in Toronto was being dragged through the Frankfurt airport.

But things had picked up quickly. On the lower level of the airport building, the shiny, blue Lufthansa Express had been waiting for them, and they had had their first train ride. Medieval ruined castles, vineyards, villages, towns, and cities appeared out of the September fog as the train raced along the banks of the Rhine. Trays with grape juice and fresh buns had arrived too, a chance to make up for missed opportunities on the plane. At the station in Bonn, their overjoyed grandparents had greeted them with chocolate and bouquets of roses.

Julia and Alexandra were trying to outdo each other with details of the three days in Bonn that had followed. The cosy hotel in the heart of the old city where the crunchiest warm rolls in the whole world were waiting for them every morning together with hot chocolate served in silver pots – all of this in full view of an ancient, half-timbered house that reminded them of Grimm's fairy tales. And then there had been the visit to Beethoven's house, where they had seen the tiny low-ceilinged room in which he had been born, his grand piano, his manuscripts. Seeing the university where Mommy had studied, the places where Mommy and Daddy had dated, and the city hall and church where they had gotten married had been lots of fun, too. But the ultimate event in Bonn had been the excursion to a huge toy store filled with treasures beyond imagination, where a stuffed dappled dog and three tiny puppies had been invited to accompany the family on the posting to Hungary.

Both girls held similarly happy memories of the day of their arrival in Budapest: the welcoming ceremony with Hungarians and Canadians held next to the plane; the car sporting a small Canadian flag; the first ride through the city; the castle of Buda high above the Danube; the arrival at the residence, where in front of the house in an ordinary Hungarian street a huge Canadian flag was flying; the warm welcome extended by the line of servants at the entrance door, and the flowers they presented.

Recollections of our first year in Budapest and all the extraordinary things they had done followed. They still remembered with great joy their first visit to the castle; the ride in a horse-drawn, open carriage along the cobbled streets of the small late-medieval town surrounding the former Hungarian kings' palace; going to see the crown jewels; the day we spent wandering through a historic village, the Hungarian equivalent of Upper Canada Village; how fascinated they had been by the tiny white-washed peasant huts with thatched roofs, by wells with long pole handles for wooden buckets to bring up the water, the open-air clay ovens for baking bread, the wattled fences to keep in geese and ducks that formed a fairy-tale landscape.

One of the greatest attractions of that year had been the many evenings the family had spent in the magnificent Opera House where, for less than the price of a movie ticket in Canada, a front-row seat was obtainable. We had seen Mozart, Verdi, and other classic operas and had watched superb performances of ballets, including *The Nutcracker, Giselle, Swan Lake, Sylvia,* and *Romeo and Juliet.*

When I gently suggested that, without their daddy's work in the foreign service, they probably would never have seen Budapest, as many operas and ballets, their family in Bonn and Vienna, the emperor's palaces in the Austrian capital; never have spent four wonderful weeks in Greece, visiting Athens, Delphi, Mycenae, Sparta, Mystra, and Olympia; never have met Nina, their closest friend in Budapest; never have cuddled Sneakers; and, above all, never have had the unforgettable joy of picking Robin and Jeremy up at the Budapest airport for Christmas and summer holidays, I gathered from the expression on their faces that the tide had turned.

Finally I asked Julia and Alexandra the question I had asked myself many times before and I knew foreign-service members keep asking themselves all the time: Would they decide in favour of or against this kind of life if they had the choice after having experienced both aspects of it? I got a resounding and unanimous 'in favour.'

To bring the discussion from such theoretical heights down to reality, they asked me whether I would take them, once we returned to Budapest, to see *The Nutcracker, Romeo and Juliet,* and, best of all, *Sylvia,* a second time. Now that foreign-service life had received a vote of confidence, I was more than eager to prove that it held as many rewards as it promised and that they had cast their ballot wisely.

I had tried to be as honest with the children as possible by admitting my own concerns and doubts about this life. Without intending to impose my opinion on them, but knowing all the same how a mother's attitude influences that of her children, I told them that I would not have wanted to miss out on the events and experiences we had listed, but that I missed their brothers, our home, our friends, and our familiar, comfortable, and private life in Canada as much as they did. My own formula for dealing with the sometimes breathtaking odds was to enjoy consciously and intensely the large number of positives and to accept the negatives as unavoidable by-products of an otherwise attractive kind of life. As far as the issue of 'home' was concerned, our home was in Canada. But I was convinced that we could create a form of 'home' in Budapest, or wherever we happened to be living, and have a chance to get to know other countries. With goodwill, intelligence, work, and patience we could turn the unfamiliar into the familiar and enrich our lives in the process. Was this not what we had accomplished to a modest extent in our first year in Budapest?

Two voices chimed in. Ottawa, they told me, would always be waiting for us. But if we stayed here now, rather than return to Budapest, they would never again see our house, our rose garden, their lovely pink bedroom, their friends at school, the Opera House, or Sneakers.

The discussion had taken several hours. We had looked at our life from all angles and had come to the conclusion that the sunny sides by far outnumbered the darker ones, and that shadows had to be expected in the presence of light. It was quite all right to complain about shadows once in a while, provided they were put in their proper perspective and not regarded as an insurmountable obstacle; similarly, the brilliant sunshine could not simply be taken for granted. In order to celebrate the end of a wonderful home leave and the impending happy return to Hungary, I invited the participants in this strenuous seminar on the pros and cons of foreign-service life to a Chinese restaurant. Two days later, we flew back to Budapest, all three of us in an excellent mood, refreshed and renewed, and eagerly awaiting familiar sights.

In the absence of my husband, who was attending a CSCE conference in Bulgaria, our driver, Sandor, greeted us at the airport. How glad he was to see us, he said. He did not like it when we were away as everything felt a bit empty. During the long ride into town he filled us in on all the events of the past two weeks. Erzsebet Bridge and the castle were lit up and seemed to glow under the evening sky. Sneakers was waiting for us at the door. Julia and Alexandra almost suffocated him with embraces. Our maids, Jutka and Valeria, had lovingly put flowers on our bedside tables and desks. Endre, our cook, had baked a chocolate cake and had decorated it with white marzipan roses and the message 'Welcome home.'

After I tucked my travellers into bed and had assured myself that the cat was presiding over their sleep with appropriate purring, I settled down at my desk to record in my diary the successful completion of our home leave. Considering the joy we had felt throughout our stay in Ottawa and the pleasure upon our return to Budapest I asked myself whether we were in the process of accomplishing what I saw as one of the most desirable goals that foreign-service parents could set for themselves: namely, to give their family a sense of being at home, regardless of where in the world fate had deposited them. Was it possible that the strong sensation of being at home we had just experienced in Canada could be re-created anywhere that a close-knit, warm, and cheerful family had a comfortable house, friends, and fulfilling work in a peaceful environment? I also wondered to what extent the sense of security and tranquillity we all seemed to gain from our haven of stability and continuity in Canada gave us the strength to venture out into other corners of the world, and to try to build a home in its image wherever External Affairs dispatched us.

Aware that foreign-service life might amount to nothing more than homeless and aimless drifting from one assignment to the next, to which I had watched some colleagues succumb, my husband and I had decided early on in our marriage to buy a house in Canada during our first posting to Ottawa and to make this home a family stronghold to which to return from our foreign adventures. Our first house in Ottawa had been a beginning, but had quickly proved to be too small for the growing family. Our second house, nestled in the Gatineau Hills, fulfilled exactly the function we had originally intended. Entirely my own design, its salutary effect on the family began while it was under construction during our last six months in Moscow. We returned from the Soviet Union to that brand-new family sanctuary and spent five peaceful and happy years there before heading out to Brussels.

During our only home leave from Belgium, we came to recognize what a powerful anchor the house and our roots in the surrounding community had become. In the summer of 1983, three years after we had left Canada for Europe, we chose to forgo the lure of Switzerland and Italy and to travel to Canada. Because we knew that we would be returning to Ottawa the following year for a home posting, we wanted to re-establish our bonds with the house and its surroundings, our neighbours, the Canadian branch of the family, and our friends.

This world had been familiar territory for my husband and our sons before we had moved to Belgium. For our daughters, however, it was a somewhat unknown realm. Julia, born in Ottawa, had been a year old when we had left the country. Alexandra, born in Brussels, had never set foot on Canadian soil. It was therefore most important to us to introduce our daughters on this home leave to the visible dimensions of the family universe. Furthermore, we wanted them to experience the return to Canada the next summer as a genuine homecoming. As it turned out, we had instilled in our two youngest children a sense of where they ultimately belonged that proved to be more formidable than we had realized.

The morning after we had landed in Ottawa, the entire family set out on the expedition that had been declared to be the main point of the holiday: the pilgrimage to the family sanctuary and the initiation of Julia and Alexandra to the world that constituted their home. Excitement ran high as we drove up into the Gatineau Hills. The house seemed to us to stand more securely and firmly in its familiar place than ever before. The deep silence of the forest embraced us. Alexandra and Julia climbed out of the car and stared at the house for a few moments. Then Alexandra turned to us and declared with the forceful conviction of her two and a half years: 'It hasn't changed!' Julia immediately agreed with her sister's assessment and insisted that she, after all, should know, considering she had spent the first year of her life in the house. She claimed to remember it all well and we did not try to talk her out of this obviously precocious idea.

The incident has remained in my memory as one of the highlights of our foreign-service life. In our daughters' emotional and mental universe the house was such a familiar and beloved sight they simply dismissed the suggestion that Alexandra had never set eyes on it, and Julia had never knowingly seen it.

As we watched our four children happily lost in the sight of their house, I had the feeling we were reaping the fruits of having quite consciously set out to create a kind of cult of our house. In Moscow I used to make large-scale detailed drawings of the building for our sons. The success of this kind of entertainment let us graduate to another art form. With the help of coloured construction paper, I re-created the pink-red brick and light brown wood of the outer walls and added paper versions of the Gatineau Park, complete with trees and trilliums and moon and stars for final touches. Many times we had sat on the floor of our apartment in Moscow and erected the structure out of wooden building blocks.

The boys had loved this game so much at the ages of three and four and maintained such happy memories of our house-building bees that they resurrected this form of family pastime when Julia and Alexandra reached approximately that age. To amuse their sisters, Robin and Jeremy modelled our house from a huge collection of wooden blocks of all sizes, shapes, and shades. The most elaborate and subtle version they fashioned out of Lego. All four children used to spend weekend afternoons in Belgium happily lost in our house and life in Canada. Once the outer walls had been raised, building blocks and Lego served as windows, doors, beds, tables, and chairs. Not only the house, but the family's comings and goings in it had been brought to life. At times, the floor of our living-room could not be used because one part was needed as a construction site for a Lego model of the main floor of the house, while, in another corner, family life was in full progress in the building-block version of the second floor.

Photos in albums and on the walls showed the house, inside and outside, during all seasons, surrounded by ferns, blooming trilliums, and huge shade trees; the foliage of autumn; and the veil of snow and icicles. Our never-ending attempts to celebrate the family home as a symbol of our roots, of stability and continuity, seemed to have developed and nurtured in our children an invaluable sense of home and belonging. The house had certainly given my husband and me this feeling. Knowing that parental attitudes tend to be accepted by younger children, we assumed that we had successfully conveyed our views on the all-important issue 'home' to our brood.

After the initial moments of gazing, one of the kids yelled: 'Let's go in!' It sounded like a signal to storm the barricades. We rang the bell.

The chimes had remained tuned to the familiar pitch. Excitement could barely be contained. The door opened slowly to the familiar sound of slight scraping and our tenant appeared. It must have been the look of horror on his face that stopped our children from darting into the hall. No, we could not come in, he said and invoked an obscure clause in our lease that gave him the right to forty-eight hours' notice in the case of the owner wanting to inspect the premises. We tried to calm him. We had no desire to inspect the premises, we told him. All we wanted was to show our children their house. He shook his head and muttered something about a lady friend who had arrived from abroad late the previous night and needed a long rest. Our request for a peek at the inside once the lady friend had recovered, perhaps sometime in the afternoon, was turned down. He would open the doors after the legal forty-eight hours, and no earlier. With that, he closed our door.

Our children were devastated. Julia and Alexandra could not understand why the door to their own house was shut in their faces. We tried to explain, but had little success. Sadly we wandered around the outside, let our hands slide over the rough surface of the bricks, and picked a few ferns. Forty-eight hours later we were sitting on a plane that was taking us to the family summer cottage in the interior of British Columbia. Here the doors were wide open and so were the arms of all members of the Canadian branch of the clan. After four weeks, we flew back to Europe for our fourth and last year in Brussels. Our children were overflowing with happy memories of their holiday on Kootenay Lake, surrounded by grandparents, uncles, aunts, and cousins of all ages. Being denied access to our house in the Gatineau Park, however, was a wound that did not heal until the following summer, when the drawbridge definitely came down for us and stayed down throughout our four-year assignment to Ottawa.

Stories about home leaves to which I have listened in the course of my foreign-service life and during more formal interviews appear to be as varied as the lives of those who tell them. Many of our fellow transients seem to cherish their home leaves as much as we do, regardless of the particulars.

A single secretary from a large French-Canadian family told me that, for her, home leave means a hero's welcome by a crowd of admiring parents, sisters, brothers, nieces, and nephews at the airport in Montreal, coffee served in bed in her childhood home by a doting mother, and weeks of relaxation during which she passes on to family, friends, and neighbours the tales and treasures she has accumulated between Buenos Aires and Beijing. It doesn't matter to which hardship post she must return from this scene of domestic peace and comfort, she says. She always arrives at her desk, in Pakistan or Peru, feeling refreshed and with her emotional equilibrium restored.

Home leaves for a young clerk and his wife and two small children mean his parents' farmhouse in a rural community outside of Charlotte-town, Prince Edward Island. This safe port usually also serves as the last stop whenever the budding family departs for an exotic tour of duty and as the first for each new member born here. It is the place where they can count on a loving welcome upon arrival from the steamy heart of Africa for a snowy Christmas or from a wintry Australia for a summer holiday.

For a middle-aged technician and his wife, home leaves consist of reunions with grown-up children and two grandchildren in their large, winterized cottage on the Rideau River. A procession of friends also winds its way to this retreat when word has got around that the travellers are back in the country, loaded with photos, slides, videos, and stories. He mentioned to me how important it is for him and his family and friends to catch up on one another's lives. They consider the nurturing of precious human bonds to be a vital element in any satisfactory life and an essential component in the lives of transients.

A single officer in his early fifties normally spends half of his home leave with relatives in the prairies, and the remainder with foreign-service friends in Ottawa. He uses the second portion also to touch base at headquarters. As he has no family of his own, he feels particularly close to one or two of his colleagues and their families with whom he has served abroad and whom he has known for more than twenty years.

Not every home leave leads to weeks of unparalleled harmony and contentment. In fact, tales of woe abound.

A young administrative officer remembers with a shudder the first home leave he took in the middle of his posting to a Southeast Asian country. In the hope that long-lasting tensions between him and his parents could finally be dissolved now that he was securely settled in matrimony, he took his new wife of Asian origin to his home in northern Alberta. The holiday, he said, turned out to be a painful experience. Behind his parents' polite faces he recognized not only the old familiar disapproval, but a new level of it, directed at his wife. He emphasized that his parents had remained courteous to his wife, but she strongly felt the rejection, and her in-laws' hostile attitude made her adjustment to Canada particularly difficult. His parents have mellowed a bit, he told me, but they still have not entirely reconciled themselves to having an Asian daughter-in-law or an adoped Asian grandchild. The young couple now keeps home leaves with the husband's family down to a few tense days, then rushes to Ottawa to relax in the home of colleagues with whom they shared their Asian posting. These friends, the officer said, are for him and his wife what the Canadian Legion is to his father. Common values and experience under exceptional and sometimes extremely difficult circumstances act as a powerful bond between them. The importance of that kind of fellowship is hard to understand for people who have never lived the foreign-service life, or belonged to the military in two world wars, he added.

Separations and divorces complicate home leaves for a growing number of foreign-service families. One separated employee pointed out to me that he has nowhere to go in Canada. With his parents in a nursing home, his former wife unlikely to welcome him, and his children hostile and scattered across the country, he takes his home leave in Ottawa and negotiates with his personnel officer his next assignment, sees his lawyer about settlements in the pending divorce, visits his dentist, and deals with complicated financial matters at the bank. He can't call such weeks a home leave, or even a holiday, he stated with a touch of bitterness in his voice. They are really just business trips, but at least they grant him a change of scene. He admitted that he is usually glad when home leave is over and he can return to the posting.

Even under the best of circumstances, home leaves carry potential for problems. The thorniest issue is, for most families, finances. According to the foreign-service directives, the government pays a full-fare economy return ticket from a posting to Ottawa for every member of the immediate family who lives in the posting. Children at boarding-school or university are not included. Every other expense connected with home leave is the responsibility of the foreign-service member.

Those expenses can be astronomical. Unless parents, other close relatives, or friends open their apartments, houses, or cottages to the invasion from abroad, costs for accommodation alone can drain the bank account, leaving little for transportation, food, and a hundred incidentals. During our own home leaves – if we don't head to our cottage in British Columbia – we stay in Ottawa in a modest hotel in tiny rooms with Spartan furniture, bath towels the size and softness of newspaper, and grass-green bedsheets laced with holes of assorted shapes and proportions. Although, by all accounts the cheapest of its kind, the hotel costs a small fortune for a family. So does a rental car, an absolute necessity during home leave. Colleagues told me that basic expenses for a two- to three-week holiday in Canada can wipe out years of savings, especially if a family's accommodation is not equipped with a kitchen and restaurant bills have to be added to the long list of other expenses. I knew only too well from my own experience how accurate this observation was.

Financial difficulties, though, don't seem to be the predominant reason that home leaves can turn into regrettable interludes. A distressing human void, the complete lack of close and warm human relationships in Canada, can be a shattering discovery. On such occasions, a considerable number of foreign-service members come to mourn not only the loss of their original home base and ties with neighbours and the local community, but human bonds they failed to establish or to nurture in Canada because of their itinerant lifestyle. Intensely occupied with the foreign-service culture to which they are exposed, and expected to change constantly in order to adapt to a never-ending succession of different environments, they often undergo such fundamental changes in themselves that they have less and less in common with their family and friends at home.

Veteran foreign-service families, children as well as adults, pointed out to me that their exposure to the overwhelming social, political, and economic problems in other parts of the world and the deep suffering they have witnessed among peoples in the iron grip of inhuman ideologies and dictatorships cause them to perceive the preoccupations and concerns of Canadians at home narrow and petty, and neighbourhoods and communities of their childhood and youth as boring and provincial.

This weakening of human relations is not solely the responsibility of the transients; those who stay behind frequently react negatively to the travellers. 'I am a homebody. I can't understand why you do this to yourself' was the remark condescendingly thrown at me by a casual acquaintance. My light-hearted reply that a certain amount of masochism might be a necessary characteristic of every migrant elicited the contemptuous-sounding comment: 'Obviously!' Many foreign-service members have encountered in Canada milder or stronger forms of rejection. Negative reactions from homebodies, whether family or friends, range from a complete lack of interest in the travellers' experiences – 'I don't care about all that foreign nonsense' – to treating the nomads either as oddballs or as show-offs, and frequently as a combination of both. Foreign-service children suffer this kind of treatment in Canadian schools. A good number of employees mentioned an astounding lack of curiosity among their fellow Canadians for the world outside and wondered whether it was a genuine absence of interest in foreign countries that prevented them from asking any questions or whether it was perhaps fear of appearing to be ignorant.

Whatever the reasons behind mutual reserve shown by homebodies and international migrants, foreign-service members agree that the different course their own lives and those of their family and friends take frequently have adverse effects on earlier relationships. Home leaves, I learned from more than one family, tend to make such a sad development painfully clear.

I have listened to home-leave stories of individual employees and of couples and children that are too distressing to recount. In all cases the persons were suffering from acute feelings of rootlessness and being rudderless and adrift. Such feelings were not entirely alien to them, they admitted, but seemed much more difficult to endure in an environment they had expected to offer them a sense of home and belonging. Women and children, in particular, seem to be afflicted, and reported that serious attacks of alienation from the world around them can hit harder during a home leave in Canada than at any other period in the posting cycle.

Because of the enormous expense and a heavy emotional toll, some foreign-service members don't often make use of their right to such a holiday. Others take advantage of a provision in the foreign-service directives that allows them to travel to a destination other than Canada. This regulation is especially appreciated by couples in which one spouse is foreign-born and who often call two countries in the world their home. Not all employees who trade their full-fare economy ticket to Ottawa for an Apex ticket to Bali or Florida do so because they can't afford a holiday in Canada or because they have nowhere to go in their own country. Frequently, it is an indication of nothing more than a desire to exchange a holiday in Canada for a vacation in another part of the world and an irresistible opportunity to travel. But, in more than a few cases, the decision is prompted by the absence of emotional ties and human bonds with their country of origin.

A large majority of foreign-service employees, however, gladly take their home leaves in Canada. According to their own accounts, most of these holidays range midway between the happy and the miserable. Foreign-service members to whom I talked shortly after they had returned from a home leave cited positive as well as negative aspects of their sojourns at home: the joy of being reunited with relatives and friends, but the crowded conditions in other people's house and an exhausting social whirlwind; the pleasure of finally being able to buy everything that they could not get in their overseas posting, but the sudden flood of enormous bills; the delight of being back in familiar territory, but the disturbing discovery that the travellers no longer quite seem to fit into the local scene.

One common theme was that of real estate. Houses that appeared to be in excellent condition when put up for rent prior to the owners' foreign posting suddenly need expensive repairs to the roof or plumbing as soon as the owner arrives on home leave. Tenants who appeared to be respectable while signing the lease revealed seedy sides when the landlord turned up unexpectedly, or have vanished altogether. The precious weeks of home leave are often needed to look after a house or apartment, to sell a piece of property, or to get rid of unacceptable tenants and find new ones.

Foreign-service members who use their home leave to fight a real-estate battle often return to the posting feeling as exhausted as their colleagues who have spent a leave looking after ageing and infirm parents. One ambassador mentioned to me that he had devoted his much-needed home leave from an African hardship post to attend to the needs of his ninety-year-old father.

For many travellers, the joy of being back home is mixed; they discover that the home shore is exposed to gales as well and does not necessarily offer the safe haven of which they dreamt as they were being tossed about by high winds on a sea of insecurities. Foreign-service members have no choice but to weather storms that rage abroad and at home, and to focus on two worlds simultaneously.

Once Again between Two Worlds

The ancient Romans depicted Janus, their god responsible for doors and city gates, as a head with two faces gazing in opposite directions. As guardian and protector of entries and exits, he had to keep an eye on the world inside and outside of passageways. If rotational foreign services had been invented at the time of his reign, Janus should have been the Pantheon's most appropriate candidate for the position of patron of international transients. Permanently either on the way in or on the way out, foreign-service personnel would have approved wholeheartedly of Janus's appointment to the portfolio. Furthermore, the image of their patron would have been considered a most accurate depiction of the foreign-service members' outlook on life. Whether at home or abroad, they cannot avoid following the example set by Janus; they glance back at the door gradually closing on one assignment, and peer ahead at the slowly opening gate to the next appointment.

Approximately one year before a posting is due to end, foreign-service staff usually begin to divide their attention between the present and a future assignment. Last year's vistas recede almost imperceptibly into the background, and new avenues either at home or in another country appear on the horizon.

In the course of a two-year tour of duty, this process can set in as early as one year after arrival. Home leaves often provide an opportunity to discuss prospects. Employees tend to return from a visit to headquarters with news about challenges awaiting them in another part of the world. If, however, stories about the most recent home leave are accompanied by tales about newly bought condominiums in New Edinburgh or houses in Orleans, colleagues on posting abroad can safely assume that the ground for a few years in Ottawa is being carefully prepared.

Once foreign-service members see new roads open up in front of them, they can look at their current situation from the perspective of someone whose countdown for departure has begun and who no longer feels quite as hopelessly submerged in daily trivia. Employees and their families confirm that, under such conditions, the final year, whether it is their second, third, or fourth in the posting, often turns out to be the best year of all. This rule seems to apply most to hardship assignments. With one foot in the present and one in the future, nomads generally are able to take a more relaxed and balanced view of their host country and their own position in it than they were capable of earlier, when no new day seemed likely to dawn on the other end of a long, dark tunnel.

Many foreign-service members described in detail how much they usually enjoyed a sense of accomplishment in the course of the final year in one of their postings. They may have mastered the local language sufficiently to do all the shopping without running into difficulties. Others are able to use the local tongue for their work and their social contacts. A large number of men, women, and children mentioned their pleasure in having adapted to the host culture in a hundred different areas of daily life. Practically all of them had made new friends; many had travelled extensively, had learned new skills and discovered that they had dropped old prejudices and stretched their minds in a few years abroad more than in a decade of life in an all-too-familiar home environment. The open-mindedness, tolerance, and humour they had developed in the process of adjusting to a totally different world struck them as one of the greatest treasures they would be taking with them on all future postings. One veteran foreign-service spouse summed up her feelings on this issue in a most eloquent way. If anyone can overcome the rather common North American attitude best expressed in the exasperated question, 'Why can't Africans / Asians / Latin Americans / any other people be more like North Americans?' then all the struggle surrounding the daily reality of foreign-service life has been worthwhile.

In many of the less treacherous assignments, particularly in the comfortable four-year postings, where it is often easier to come to terms with language, people, culture, and customs, foreign-service members tend to experience poignant final years filled with painful farewells. 'We have fallen in love with the people and the country' is a remark I have heard hundreds of times. Those who make them are the same foreign-service employees who will ask for a year's extension if the thought of leaving behind what may have become a second home turns out to be too distressing. External Affairs does grant extensions if the request makes sense to the department.

In households with more than one member, difficulties that may have been suppressed in the course of a posting sometimes come to the fore during the final year. One family member's delight in the assignment may have meant misery for someone else. A job abroad that offers a professional challenge and perhaps a chance for promotion to the employee may amount to nothing but daily drudgery for a spouse who would have preferred to pursue his or her own career in another country or in a home posting. Employees who wish to get a year's extension might meet with resistance from other members of their household. Tensions arise out of such conflicts of interest within a family.

Equally problematic are the family situations in which the parents greatly enjoy many aspects of a foreign posting, especially the social rounds, but children suffer because parents, most notably mothers, are away too much. An amazing number of mothers told me quite cheerfully that they preferred having babies while living abroad to having them during home postings because they had so much more help abroad to take care of them. Of course, many mothers are totally dedicated to their children and give them top priority, whether domestic help is available or not, and despite the siren call of the social whirlwind. But some mothers think nothing of passing their little ones on to au-pair girls, nannies, ayas, and servants in order to be able to head out in almost full-time pursuit of coffee mornings, ladies' luncheons, afternoon teas, bridge parties, cocktail parties, charity bazaars, and dinners. For mothers who favour foreign assignments for the sake of social activities, bidding farewell to parties in order to go back to Ottawa to the plain existence of a public servant's wife may not be a happy time. Such cases, however, were more common a few decades ago than they are now since spouses receive far fewer invitations to official functions and have more opportunities to pursue some form of career, even abroad.

A lot of foreign-service members mentioned that their feelings about leaving a posting often consist of a mixture of relief and sadness: relief, because the daily struggle is finally coming to an end, and sadness, because they have invested an enormous amount of work and emotional energy in getting to know the country and its people and must say goodbye at exactly the moment at which the world around them has begun to make sense for them.

Only an almost negligible minority of foreign-service employees and their families to whom I talked had remained indifferent to the places in which they had lived. Even those who had earlier tried to convince themselves that they had not wasted any emotions on a particular country or its people discovered to their surprise – as they were packing paintings, sculptures, carvings, china, carpets, and other treasures acquired in the posting – that the culture had, in fact, not left them untouched. At the latest, when the movers arrive, a sense of attachment to place begins to set in. Surroundings that had gradually and invisibly merged with the self are being withdrawn. Friends are torn apart. Many foreign-service members claim that a small portion of themselves always stays behind in a posting. Anthropologists and linguists among them express regrets because so much remains to be explored, studied, and understood.

Whatever sentiments an impending departure elicits, all foreign-service members, especially their long-suffering spouses, loathe the last months before a move. Every item must once again be listed, described, and evaluated. Records have to be established of all goods that will be insured by the government. Everything beyond the allotted amount has to be listed for private insurance. Separate shipments have to be packed for sea and air transportation.

Once all private possessions have been sealed in containers and sent off to their next destination, foreign-service staff live out of the so-called pack-up kit, a box the mission provides with essential dishes, glasses, cutlery, pots, pans, bedsheets, and towels. The contents of the box are a familiar sight, last used in the first weeks spent in the posting prior to the arrival of personal effects from the previous post.

Last days in a foreign country carry their special flavour. The familiar environment is beginning to fade; the present is about to become part of the past. A new life is about to begin in another part of the world or an old life in Canada is to be resumed where it had been left off a few years earlier. Departures are generally perceived as memorable landmarks in the posting cycle. Most foreign-service members carry around with them their own unique collection of stories of final days in a posting in which half-empty apartments or houses play leading roles.

To reduce the strain of a move, foreign-service employees are entitled to three days in a hotel once their personal effects have left the country. I have always greatly appreciated this provision of the directives. The prospect of a tidy, clean, and well-functioning hotel at the end of weeks of domestic turbulence and makeshift living offered the haven of sanity that helped me maintain my good humour during the ordeal.

I felt the salutary effect of this hotel privilege in 1970 when I moved for the first time as Canadian foreign-service wife. Physically exhausted from the ordeal of transferring our household from Germany to Canada, I was comforted and strengthened to know that an inviting hotel down the street would receive the refugees from a disintegrated world with utmost graciousness.

The Redoute in Bad Godesberg, a small Rococo town palace built in the eighteenth century as gathering-place for the court of the Prince Electors of Cologne, had seen many distinguished guests, among them Mozart and Haydn. After the war the interior had been restored to its original splendour. Recitals and receptions had been resumed, regrettably without Mozart and Haydn though. The attic, initially the realm of the Princes' domestic staff, had been converted into a charming hotel. Everything in the upper part of the building was as tiny as everything on the main and first floors was of majestic proportions, probably reflecting the physical size as well as the social significance of those who moved about on the different levels. In our quarters, the picture-windows resembled those of a doll house. The ceilings were slanted and the door frames low. From the moment my husband walked into our miniature suite, it became clear to us that the eighteenth-century German architect had not taken the frame of a twentieth-century Canadian into account.

Our stay in this otherwise delightful retreat rapidly developed into a trial for my husband. Every time he passed through one of the doors that separated bedroom, sitting-room, and bathroom, he hit his head. To prevent severe head injuries, I decided to take unorthodox measures. I taped a row of long stretches of toilet paper to the upper part of all door frames. As soon as he approached one of them, he found himself confronted with a softly swaying pink curtain. It looked like a tissue version of the beaded screens in the doors of Mediterranean homes intended to keep the flies out. The extraordinary installation served its purpose and reminded him to duck. The success of my intervention encouraged me to explain to the waiters who brought breakfast up to our refuge the meaning of this unusual sight. I thought I should set the record straight lest they jump to conclusions about Canadian home-decorating traditions.

We spent a few poignant days among the pink hangings, saying goodbye to family and friends. We ate in the salon downstairs where, two hundred years earlier, dinner guests in powdered wigs had been serenaded by the Princes' chamber orchestra. The hotel not only provided us with a little island of peace, but granted us a last, gentle brush with local history, a happy ending to our years in Bonn and a harmonious period of transition before we jumped into the next phase of our posting cycle, a stage known to foreign-service personnel as 'home posting.'

10

In Transition at Home

WELCOME TO CANADA – BIENVENUE AU CANADA! The huge sign at the airport in Montreal intended to greet immigrants, foreign visitors, and returning Canadians alike touched me for the first time in 1970 when we came back from my husband's assignment to Bonn. During his four years in Germany, he had, among other things, converted one of the local students into a Canadian foreign-service wife. According to the immigration laws of that period marriage had entitled a native German, although on foreign soil, to the status of 'landed immigrant.'

In the course of the next twenty years, I discovered that the story of my own first years in Canada closely resembled the tales of a large number of my fellow spouses. This was particularly true for the approximately one-third of all foreign-service wives who were born abroad. Many of them delivered eloquent accounts of initiation into their new home, which suggested that this period in their life had been also an intense emotional experience that had set the stage for their attitude towards their chosen country also during all subsequent home postings.

Like most newly arrived immigrants, I had no home in Canada. We had no idea where we would be living and, worse than that, we did not know a soul in the city. My husband remembered a few names and faces from a brief assignment in External Affairs years ago. But they were bound to have been scattered all over the globe in the meantime.

We touched down in the national capital one afternoon in the second half of March. I remember a world of almost blinding sunlight. After Bonn, where spring had set in at the beginning of February, where trees had been heavy with buds and stores had been filled with spring flowers, I was amazed by the mountains of snow piled high on the sides of the Parkway all the way from the airport to the centre of town. I was well familiar with the combination of snow and brilliant sunshine from the Austrian Alps, but I had never seen a large city overflowing with snow and sparkling with sunlight. The sky looked to me as blue as the violets that were already blooming in Germany. It struck me as being bitterly cold.

The administration of External Affairs had rented for us an apartment in an old, gloomy downtown apartment hotel. Two small rooms and a kitchen contained the necessities of life: beds, a table, chairs, dishes, cutlery, and a few pots and pans. We had a prime view of rusty iron ladders belonging to the red brick house next door. I learned that they served as fire escapes. My favourite view, though, was that of a colourful bouquet of spring flowers my husband's parents had sent from British Columbia to welcome us.

As is not uncommon among newly arrived foreign-service wives, an as yet unborn and rather tiny Canadian citizen had accompanied the immigrant. In the chaos of our move I had left my first pregnancy unattended longer than planned. Not knowing the name of a physician in Ottawa, I had inquired at our embassy in Bonn about an obstetrician in the national capital. 'Why not the best?' Shirley, one of my closest Canadian friends, had asked, and had given me the telephone number of a physician. As soon as we had put down our suitcases in the apartment hotel, I called his office and asked to see the doctor. His nurse gave me an appointment for six weeks later. When I described my situation to her, she promised to have the doctor call sometime later in the evening. My European experience had taught me that patients call physicians, not the other way around. I found it hard to believe that he would ring me up. But he did, and gave me an appointment for the next day, thus establishing in my mind once and for all the superior services of the Canadian medical establishment.

By telephone, we reported back to the family fold on the west coast, to various of my husband's friends in other parts of the country, and, of course, to the local authorities, in this case the Department of External Affairs. We then turned our attention to the house we were intending to buy in order to give our family a home in Canada as quickly as possible. Other close Canadian friends whom we had met at the embassy in

Bonn had written a letter of introduction for us to one of the local real estate agents. The lady took one look at us, read the letter, and announced she had a house for us. Five days after I had set foot on Canadian soil, my husband and I were the delighted owners of a small home in the west end of Ottawa. The property included a garden with trees. Flowers could be expected once the snow had melted. This would be the family's safe haven to which to return from the storms of our foreign-service life. But we could not move into the house for another three months. So, like many of our foreign-service colleagues who return from an overseas assignment and are trying to establish themselves at home, we had to spend a long time in the apartment hotel.

My life as a foreign-service wife had entered a phase typical of the fate of my foreign-born fellow spouses. I had the impression I was listening to a variation of my own story when they told me their tales.

After nine years of total immersion in my university studies – a stage of my life that had come to an end only with this move – I was eager to become a housewife, and a full-fledged Canadian one at that. I had to justify and excuse my about-face to a few liberated women and lost a certain amount of their respect, but this did not bother me. I felt sufficiently liberated to settle down to contented domesticity and motherhood, if perhaps not forever, at least for a good number of years. I began to engage in all the activities that I associated with honourable Canadian homemakers. I studied the newspapers for advertised specials on canned tuna, dishwater detergent, and paper towels, and rushed to the store to buy in large quantities. In the morning I usually walked from Metcalfe Street to the Byward Market and procured the fresh groceries for the day. I carried the heavy load back to our apartment and spent the rest of the morning trying to convert the ingredients into a Canadian dish, assisted by a cookbook that contained recipes from all parts of the country, *a mari usque ad mare*. To sample the concoction my husband put German-Canadian relations on hold for an hour and sauntered down Metcalfe from his office in the Langevin Building during his lunch break. In the course of the afternoons I read *The Globe and Mail* with great care and worked my way into the Canadian political scene. I also took the plunge into Canadian history and literature.

Except for my husband's brief midday visit, the days seemed rather long. I enjoyed the chance to read, but after a while I began to miss my family and friends and having someone to talk to. I resorted to more books and added *Chatelaine* and *Maclean's* to my pile of required Canadian reading.

I did not know at that time that my sense of loneliness was small and negligible compared with the feeling of isolation the new wife of one of our colleagues was experiencing only two or three floors up in our apartment building. We found out fifteen years later that we had been living in the same building at the same time. By the time we made this discovery, we had been the closest of friends for more than ten years and felt like crying about the missed opportunity then and laughing at the absurdity of the situation. Every hour we had spent together over the previous ten years had been stimulating and heart-warming. If we had met during our initial weeks in Ottawa, life then could have been a delight.

At the time of our arrival in Canada from Bonn our friends had just got in from a Mediterranean posting. The young foreign-service officer had met a local graduate student three weeks before his departure from the country and had married her two and a half weeks later. After the balmy southern shores where she had spent all her life, the young bride shuddered at what she could make out from the plane, as it landed in Ottawa. Surely, all that greyness and dirty snow below was a regrettable exception, evidently a bad year. Did people actually volunteer to live in such a place? she asked her husband. It turned out to be a rough landing for her after the whirlwind courtship and wedding. Years later she suggested with hearty laughter that she might not again opt for the national capital in the month of March as the location and season for a perfect honeymoon.

Unaware that salvation lay two or three storeys above me, I continued my monotonous forays into the world of Canadian newspapers and magazines. A refreshing relief from my repetitious activities in the dark and barren apartment came from a lively young colleague of my husband's who invited us for dinner. Barney and his wife, Iona, welcomed us in a most cordial way as the latest addition to the foreign-service family in Ottawa and treated us to an evening of superb food and wine, serious and light-hearted conversation, and, above all, to the feeling that we were part of a group, judging by the warm and cheerful reception they and their guests accorded us. We all seemed to share the same type of education, interests, and fascination with foreign cultures. The gathering at their home was the beginning of a friendship that has lasted for more than twenty years now and has been celebrated frequently during joint assignments either in Canada or in Europe.

A snowstorm of major proportions interrupted the cold, grey, dismal month of April. Never before in my life had I witnessed such a blizzard, and it left a deep impression on me. The morning after the white fury had abated, the city woke up to a sky as brilliant and blue as that of my first day in Ottawa. Huge branches had been torn off the trees and thrown across the streets. A thick blanket of immaculate snow had spread over the entire world around me. Even the rusty fire escapes had turned a dazzling white. I abandoned my history books and the pre-blizzard edition of *The Globe and Mail*, grabbed my camera, and ploughed my way through the snow drifts to capture the beauty of the day.

Four weeks of home leave followed. At that time 'home' for a foreign-service employee was a place in Canada with which he or she maintained ties either because it was his or her place of origin, or because parents or other close relatives lived there. An employee's choice of 'designated home-leave centre' had to be approved by External Affairs. This provision was later changed, and Ottawa was made home-leave centre for everyone.

According to the foreign-service directives issued for 1970, we were entitled to a home leave in British Columbia after my husband had completed his four-year assignment to Germany. We decided to fly only as far as Calgary. My parents-in-law greeted us at the airport and whisked us off to the splendour of Banff and Lake Louise. Jasper turned out to be inaccessible because of a snowstorm. We headed to British Columbia, where family, friends, and neighbours welcomed the landed immigrant to the western portion of her chosen country.

We had earlier asked External Affairs whether we could return to Ottawa by train instead of plane. I wanted to see as much of Canada as possible. The three-day journey between Vancouver and the national capital remains one of the great events of my life. From our comfortable compartment I gazed at spectacular mountains, rivers, lakes, the prairies in their serene beauty, and eventually the Canadian Shield, with its rocks, birches, and beaver ponds. I fell in love with everything I saw and could not understand why anyone would call the prairies boring. The trip also marked the beginning of a love affair with the works of the Group of Seven; their paintings captured for me what had instantly become a familiar and beloved landscape. A massive snowstorm moving slightly ahead of our train had spread a thick, white cover across the country. The weather report confirmed what we were able to make out ourselves: the blanket reached from Calgary all the way to the east. When we got off the train, Ottawa did not seem to have dug itself out from under the April blizzard that had struck four weeks earlier. By now it was the middle of May. We settled down in another apartment hotel and waited for news about the fate of our sea shipment from Bonn and for the arrival of spring.

The latter never quite made it. Without giving its gentle herald a chance, summer burst on stage with dramatic temperatures only two weeks after the last snowstorm had hit. Our goods from Germany, however, did arrive. On 1 June a moving truck rolled into the driveway of our new house. It was a joyful reunion with our possessions, and both my husband and I were surprised to discover how attached we had become to our furniture, books, pictures, carpets, china, silver, and a thousand other personal items. After a quarter of a year's wanderings from our apartment to the hotel in Bad Godesberg, to Paris, London, Ottawa, Banff, Rossland, Seattle, Victoria, Vancouver, and back to Ottawa, we would finally settle in one place and live a well-ordered life in our own house and surroundings. Six weeks after the movers had poured the contents of their truck into our house, the chaos was sorted out. A clean, tidy, and, to our mind, very beautiful home was waiting for our baby. Robin was born four days after we had quietly declared the house and its occupants ready for the new arrival.

Once the administrative side of our move had been cleared up and all the insurance papers had been completed, we were released from our pledge to abide by the foreign-service directives, returned my husband's diplomatic passport to External Affairs, and withdrew to a blissfully private and quiet life with our new son. He was, of course, the most wonderful child the world had ever seen. Nothing could lure me away from him, not even the invitation from one of the universities in Ottawa to take on a full-time teaching position. I felt delighted and honoured by the offer, but I was not prepared to do more with it than to thank the professors who had expressed their confidence in my abilities and to frame it and hang it up over our baby's changing table or the stove where I created health-food dishes *à la* Adelle Davis for our little boy and slightly more adventurous menus *à la* Julia Child for ourselves.

During those three years of our first home posting, the other side of our foreign-service existence, diplomatic life abroad seemed very far away, and we did not miss any part of it. I devoted myself entirely to our baby, and two years later to our second son, Jeremy, another magnificent child, comparable only to his brother. Our pediatrician shared my prejudices and called the two little fellows the 'Gerber' babies whenever I took them for routine check-ups and vaccinations. I read and sang to them, kept the house, and continued to hunt for specials to protect the integrity of the budget and to pay off the mortgage. When the children were sleeping I took piano lessons or read my way through a modest library on Canadian history. I also devoured Canadian literature. We led the life of an average Canadian family and loved it.

One year after I had landed in the country, I became a citizen, swore allegiance to the Queen, and voted for the first time.

Every now and then posting bells would ring for colleagues in External Affairs and we would get together with them to say goodbye. Old friends from the embassy in Bonn returned, and we welcomed them back home. But our own existence remained at a happy distance from overseas assignments. My husband had to go to Europe once in a while to visit his parish and attend a NATO meeting. To me the Old World felt slightly inconsequential at that stage. There was so much to discover and to learn here. But we both knew all along that this idyllic life would have to come to an end sooner or later, and we began to ask ourselves where we would want to go next, if we were given the choice.

Eventually two years in Moscow followed, and when we came back from that assignment, I realized how much Canada had become home to me in the short five years that had passed since I had landed as a stranger. I felt elated to be back, and so did my husband and our two little boys. Ottawa had become a city full of happy memories, and it was a pleasure to show Robin and Jeremy the world of their early childhood: the bookstore in the National Arts Centre where we had spent many entertaining Saturday mornings browsing through the publications while our baby was peacefully asleep in his car bed among the books; the National Gallery, where I had first admired the Group of Seven with Robin securely established on his daddy's shoulders and Jeremy snuggled up with his mommy; the toy store where Robin had fallen in love with a bright blue Volkswagen and had refused to let the cashier look at the price; the downtown funeral home which Robin had identified as a Greek temple after seeing a drawing in a children's encyclopaedia; Parliament Hill where both boys had saluted the governor general's footguards; the canal; the market; the arboretum; the Experimental Farm – in short, the entire city seemed inextricably linked with our family history. Personal events became almost synonymous with special places in town.

Upon our return to Ottawa from Moscow I was introduced to an aspect of life in Canada that most Canadians seem to take for granted, but which strikes most foreign-born spouses as a noteworthy and especially attractive side of the daily reality of a home posting: the loyalty and friendship of neighbours. When I compared notes with other foreign-service spouses who had also come from crowded, or overcrowded, corners of the world, I found my own impression confirmed: whereas 'neighbourliness' had an intrusive connotation in our home countries, in Canada it was sustaining and valued.

The area in which our house was under construction in the summer of 1975 revealed itself to be not only a nature resort but a small social paradise as well. Our friends Gerald and Ilham from External Affairs, through whom we had got to know this part of the Gatineau Park, had already introduced us to some of our future neighbours two years earlier, as we were on our way to the Soviet Union. War veterans arriving home after a gallantly fought and victorious campaign could not have received a warmer welcome than we did upon return from our daily skirmishes on the Russian front. On the day of our move into the brand-new house three of our neighbours had combined their talents and lovingly prepared a dinner for us. In the middle of the worst chaos the doorbell rang for the first time and Karen arrived with a full hot meal for us. We soon found out that the home-delivery service was only the beginning; generous hospitality was extended to us by the entire community of about twenty families whose houses are scattered over fifty acres of privately owned land between the hills and among the trees of the Gatineau Park. In the almost ten years we have lived in our house, our neighbours have invited us to candle-light dinners, rustic barbecues, salmon and champagne vernissages, barn-raising feasts, baby showers, English high teas, New Year's dinners and dances, cheese and wine parties, children's poetry and piano recitals, house concerts, a last-mortgage-payment party complete with ceremonial burning of the mortgage papers, Swedish mulled-wine gatherings, Christmas parties with hours of carol singing, wedding anniversaries, house-warming parties, birthday parties for children and adults alike, and the traditional Hallowe'en party given each year by Graham and Karen, the community's five-star hosts. Around a roaring fire on a clearing in front of their house, local goblins, witches, ghouls, ghosts, and other horrifying creatures of all ages and sizes ate, drank, and performed acts of magic and spookery, before being transported by another neighbour's tractor from house to house in pursuit of trick or treat. Thus we were adopted as the latest addition to the neighbourhood family. Their friendship contributed decisively to our feeling of belonging to a community, and I can only confirm what most foreign-service members can't emphasize enough, that cordial human relations with neighbours and friends is one of the best things that can happen to international transients when they return to the home turf for a few years of rest and recovery.

My own family's contentment throughout each one of our three postings to Ottawa did not mean that our life was miraculously free from difficulties. We had our share of the problems the average Canadian family knows only too well: a strict budget for six people living on one public-service salary and with a mortgage to pay; one car for a crowd of half a dozen; a car accident; emergency races to the Children's Hospital following a dog bite and a fall from a tree, and at the height of an alarming attack of the croup; a chimney fire; power failures that lasted several days, in the heat of summer and in the icy blast of winter; lightning striking our electric water pump, which is buried 300 feet down in the rocks next to our house; and a hundred minor disasters. But that was not all.

According to rotational foreign-service employees, the workload at headquarters is so overpowering, it has the potential to ruin life in Canada for them altogether. Many of them view an Ottawa posting as a strait-jacket, and try to get abroad as soon as possible. Others simply accept it and see it as the cost of the pleasure of living at home for a while.

The intense pressure in my husband's office in the course of every assignment to Ottawa – in External Affairs as well as during a second-ment to the Privy Council Office – added a lot of strain to our family life. However, I refused to let the demands of his work and his many absences from home for NATO meetings, sessions of the Organization of American States, and visits to his respective parishes in Eastern and Western Europe interfere with our family life. Our days proceeded calmly and in an orderly way, and, if possible, cheerfully, whether he was at home or roaming around in obscure parts of the world. The fre-quent traveller greatly appreciated his family's independence and pointed out that he was aware that not every wife was as sanguine about a hus-band's absences. Friends and neighbours knew that I had to function much of the time as single parent, and they were used to inquiring about my husband's itineraries. 'He is in Siberia,' I told a neighbour while my husband was accompanying a federal cabinet minister on an official visit to the easternmost part of the former Soviet Union. 'What has he done to deserve that?' he replied, in mock horror.

The children and I actually found some pleasure in these journeys. Besides the occasional phone call he placed to us from remote locations that had to be looked up on the map, he always came back with half a suitcase full of small treasures for every family member: tiny figurines carved out of walrus tusk, beautiful dolls, polished stones from the Black Sea or the Bering Strait, piles of books, and, best of all, tales about the countries and the people he had seen.

While we succeeded in keeping the impact of the merciless schedule at headquarters on our private life to a minimum, political develop-ments in Canada placed a heavy burden on our hearts and minds. Six months after I had landed in the country the FLQ crisis erupted, Pierre Laporte was murdered, and the War Measures Act was invoked. In 1976, one year after we had returned from Moscow and had settled in Quebec, the Parti Québécois – a party committed to the separation of the province from the rest of Canada – won the provincial election. The months preceding the 1980 Quebec Referendum on separation took a heavy toll on the emotional well-being of the whole family.

But, despite the political tension in the country, each of our assign-ments to Ottawa deepened and strengthened each family member's feel-ing that Canada was our home and that a posting here surpassed anything that even the most desirable foreign posting could offer.

Judging from my interviews and extensive conversations with foreign-service members of all ages and from various occupational groups, many lead lives during their home postings that resemble ours in some form or another. Most people to whom I talked could identify with the kind of ordinary existence that characterizes our years at home. They expressed satisfaction with their Ottawa assignments and gave the impression that they had mastered the art of 'repatriation,' a term used in the department to denote the complex process of reorientation and reintegration into life in Canada after years of exposure to foreign countries and cultures. Although it is impossible to determine how many foreign-service members fit into this category, more than half seems a safe estimate.

Each foreign-service life lived at home between two foreign postings is, of course, unique since a host of variables combine in myriad new constellations. And yet, foreign-service employees and their families who manage to land on their feet whenever the merry-go-round drops them on home soil seem to constitute a more homogeneous group than do those for whom the variables of foreign-service life conspire in a hundred different ways to turn a posting to Ottawa into a minor or major hardship assignment, if not an outright disaster. The difference between these two groups can be likened to the distinction Leo Tolstoy makes in the first sentence of his novel *Anna Karenina:* 'All happy families resemble each other; each unhappy family is unhappy in its own way.'

For foreign-service personnel, however, happiness or unhappiness is of only secondary significance. The primary issue is how well an international migrant and his or her family are able to cope with various ordinary-life problems, all of which tend to be exacerbated by the extraordinary turbulence of rotational life, and the additional problems generated exclusively by the foreign-service lifestyle.

Female and male singles as well as employees with families who express contentment with this kind of life as a whole are also the first ones to describe their home postings as happy periods in their posting cycle. Stories abound of single employees of both sexes who are pleased to return to what they perceive as genuine home, who emphasize that they feel content wherever they are but appreciate particularly the comfortable, secure, and predictable life in Canada with extended family

and friends after years of adventures, difficulties, or considerable hardships. One single secretary in her thirties told me she needed to feel
unchallenged for a while, and safe as well, following three consecutive
hardship posts in Asia, Latin America, and the Near East. She had had
her purse stolen in broad daylight and her earrings torn off her ears in
the crowded centre of a Latin American capital, and, on another of her
assignments, a full-scale war had been in progress just a few hundred
kilometres away.

A married couple with grown-up children and two new grandchildren expressed the same degree of satisfaction during each one of their
postings to Ottawa. Over a period of more than twenty-five years, husband and wife have kept in mind that family life in the foreign service
requires constant attention. They have consciously synchronized their
attitudes and reactions towards the main variables of their life; have
accepted in good humour every posting; and have a long record of contentment within their marriage, with their children, and with life
abroad as well as at home. They explained to me that life in Canada is
always a particular treat because they can move about in familiar territory, unlike so many other corners of the world in which they must
tread cautiously, as if crossing a minefield. After a few years of comfort
and security, they always feel they have gathered enough strength to
take on another distant challenge. Reorientation and reintegration into
the home scene never presents the slightest problem for them because
they remain integrated into their family's, friend's, and country's life,
even while serving abroad. Their marriage and family operate as a portable home and allow them to settle wherever they go. But in Ottawa,
they say, this is accomplished with greater ease than anywhere else.

Most of the foreign-service families I talked to describe their own
feelings and experience in similar terms. But, what struck me was that
employees and their spouses and families who call their home postings
difficult or genuinely troubled are more negative about foreign-service
life in general. They tend to become enmeshed in the complex tangle of
everyday predicaments and specific conflicts caused by the lifestyle
imposed on them. At times, both kinds of problems reinforce each
other; on other occasions, incompetent or irresponsible ways of trying
to solve them make matters worse.

Foreign-service employees and families for whom an assignment to

Ottawa represents an undesirable experience have usually fallen victim to one or more of a series of specific foreign-service afflictions: 1 / they have failed to recognize that the rotational life requires special measures to cope with ordinary life problems as well as with particular stumbling-blocks unique to foreign-service life; 2 / they assume that the foreign-service lifestyle will ease everyday difficulties; 3 / they have allowed extensive periods abroad to affect their willingness to take life at home as seriously and thus are less able to dedicate themselves to complicated tasks while on a home posting in view of the temporariness of the assignment; and 4 / they find themselves confronting the disastrous fall-out of a high-risk life for which they may not have been sufficiently prepared. A considerable number of foreign-service employees and their spouses and children with whom I spoke experienced difficulties with postings to Ottawa that could be traced to at least one of these typical foreign-service malaises.

Heading the current list of knotty points is the problem of spousal employment. It is no longer the contentious issue it was a few decades ago. Everyone in the service seems to agree that spouses should be given a chance to work whether they are on a posting at home or abroad. But rotational life constitutes a prime obstacle to the rapidly increasing number of spouses who want to pursue a career outside the home for personal-fulfilment or financial reasons. An assignment to Ottawa may spell disaster for a family in which the spouse holds a satisfying and reasonably well-paying job abroad, for example, as a teacher in an international school or as a private language instructor. Such spouses often resent a return to the home shore, if the prospects of finding a job in the Canadian market are as dismal as usual. Countless spouses told me that their free time on home postings was taken up entirely with futile attempts to find employment. 'As a spouse of a rotational foreign-service employee, you are basically unemployable' was the typical response to job enquiries, and the futility casts a dark shadow on every assignment at home.

Accommodating two separate careers within a marriage in which one partner is committed to the foreign service is an almost impossible task. For every spouse who has better job opportunities abroad than at home, there is a spouse who is, in some form or another, professionally established in Ottawa and will be facing unemployment in a foreign posting.

Foreign-service employees who prefer the varied and stimulating duties a mission offers have to find a compromise between their own preferences and their partner's if the latter can be employed only in Ottawa. Similarly, employees who are convinced that careers are made at headquarters and who are willing to struggle for years in a huge, impersonal bureaucracy in the hope of a promotion have to accommodate a partner whose career prospects are more promising abroad than at home. In either case, accommodation is a tall order.

The Department of External Affairs has been making an effort to support spouses in their attempts to find work and to build careers through an open-minded spousal employment policy. But, for the majority of foreign-service spouses, little has changed. In extreme cases, where the partners' job opportunities simply cannot be reconciled in one city or country, the marriages collapse.

Ottawa has developed a bad reputation among foreign-service members for reasons other than its poor employment opportunities. It is often seen as an insufferably provincial backwater by those who return from large and colourful cosmopolitan capitals around the world. But young Canadian spouses who grew up in Quebec City, Montreal, Toronto, Winnipeg, or Vancouver are not over-enthusiastic during their first few years in the national capital either. Foreign-service couples and families on their second assignment to Ottawa, however, are bound to point out how much they have come to enjoy the city and the peaceful family life that is possible in the community. Especially in cases where repatriation means return to an apartment, a condominium, or a house bought in the course of an earlier home posting, re-entry means reunion not only with familiar territory, but also with neighbours and friends. Most foreign-service members with whom I spoke cherished the experience of home-coming, although some of them admitted that they had not felt that way on their first home posting. It satisfied, they told me, their basic need to belong to a place and to feel integrated into the social surroundings, a project on which they had worked in the course of previous assignments to Ottawa.

A handful of male employees surprised me with the remark that they did not understand what people meant by 'all that "home" and "root" business.' The subject seemed to annoy them, as if, in not sharing the sentiment, they had failed to measure up. These cases appeared to be the exception that proved the rule. The vast majority of service personnel, married and single, spoke about the importance of roots, and a fair number of them expressed regret about having, so far, been unable to establish a sustaining root system anywhere in the world, least of all in Ottawa.

For couples with children, reintegration of the family unit into a community that is expected to be home and often feels as strange as a foreign posting is a complex process. It is difficult enough to coordinate the attitudes and reactions of two adults in a constantly shifting environment; it is an even more demanding task to satisfy the special needs of children during the many stages of their schooling and their general development.

Not all parents realize how much a child adopts their outlook on a home posting. Such unawareness does not present much of a problem if the parents are happily disposed towards assignments in Ottawa. However, those parents who, for whatever reason, loathe life at home pass this message on to their children in a hundred different ways. By imposing their own prejudices on their offspring, they prevent the natural development of emotional bonds in Canadian surroundings and, in the long run, deprive a youngster of a vital home base and of the stable centre around which a satisfactory foreign-service life must rotate.

An aversion to home postings often begins during a first assignment to Ottawa, when a young family who has just experienced a satisfying first foreign posting cannot come to terms with a somewhat more ordinary life. Statements such as 'Ottawa is a downer,' 'We hated to come back,' 'We never unpacked completely,' and 'We can't wait until we get our next posting' come mostly from those in their twenties and thirties. Unless they join the rather large crowd of converts who later call their initial Ottawa resentment 'silly' and 'unjustified,' they form the core group of those foreign-service members who will always feel miserable in Ottawa and find reasons for never-ending complaints. They will accept any foreign assignment just to get away and stay away.

Such families will remember their first posting to Ottawa as a failure; will decide against buying property, or in favour of selling it, when their second stay in Canada comes around; and will launch themselves on an endless round of cross-postings. A number of families with seriously troubled marriages and children with severe emotional problems had a long record of miserable home postings that displayed symptoms of deeper unresolved conflicts. Whenever they had spent a period of a few months or a year or two in Ottawa, life, they claimed, had comprised a succession of insurmountable obstacles. Housing, schooling, limited budgets, the office grind, and the feeling of aimlessness had conspired to make Ottawa feel like the worst hardship post. Foreign countries, so their reasoning went, at least had the advantage of providing a change from the dreariness of life at home and required a family effort to make a go of it, a project that kept everyone busy.

In such families, it was often the case that marital discord or children's emotional, social, and academic problems had appeared during a first Ottawa posting, after the joint project of adapting to the demands of a foreign posting had been removed. Unwilling, and perhaps unable, to admit to themselves that not everyone in the family was thriving on the rotational life and that problems were brewing that might be the direct result of foreign-service life and require re-examination of the family's foreign-service membership, the parents wrongly diagnosed Ottawa as the source of discontent and prescribed diversion, in the form of a series of foreign assignments, the more exotic the better, as the cure.

Needless to say, parents who prescribe such treatment for their family act out of ignorance, not ill will. Such cases are not numerous, and don't always lead to disaster, but too many foreign-service children are left to the mercy of parental incompetence and irresponsibility. The results are school phobias, serious behaviour problems, eating disorders, more or less severe depressions, and, in extreme instances, suicide attempts. The magnitude of individual and family suffering under such conditions can hardly be overestimated.

My own efforts to understand why some Canadian families sank deeper and deeper into trouble with every new assignment at home or abroad while most others managed reasonably well, and still others thrived, led to conclusions I found later confirmed by the findings of a team of German psychologists. The Hormuth Study of 1988, a scientific investigation into the impact of frequent international mobility on foreign-service children, commissioned by the German foreign ministry, states that geographic mobility alone does not cause emotional disturbances. Rather, the combination of rotationality and unresolved individual or family conflicts increases the risk of emotional illness.

Repatriation represents one of the critical points in the posting cycle, where the course that a foreign-service life will eventually take is often determined and where much can go wrong. This rule applies to foreign-born spouses more than to any other group within the service. The term 'repatriation' is somewhat ironic for them. They have left 'patria,' their fatherland, behind somewhere in Africa, Asia, Europe, or Latin America. With homeland, they have given up their family and friends, culture and customs, jobs and professions, and in many cases their language as well. Like trees, not all of them survive transplantation. Many of them have long, deep, and complex root systems that can be damaged irreparably in a move.

Foreign-born wives told me that the initial weeks and months in Ottawa are not the worst. The demands of the move, the rent or purchase of an apartment or a house, and the task of setting up a household keep them running, and leave little time to be stunned by the strange world around them. Disorientation sets in only when the turbulence begins to subside.

At that stage another problem arises. Several wives mentioned that they had discovered during the first years in Ottawa, subtle, but none the less unsettling changes in their husbands' personalities. The vivacious, outgoing, and generally cheerful foreigner they had known abroad seemed to be withdrawing and turning into a quiet and somewhat moody fellow. Asked to what circumstances they ascribed such changes, they cited the fact that he was no longer living in the challenging and stimulating environment of a foreign culture, but in the undemanding and somewhat grey home culture and was trapped on the impersonal treadmill of headquarters rather than moving freely in the more lively and colourful world of a Canadian mission abroad. Those wives whose husbands succumb to what wives may perceive as the 'Local-Boy Syndrome' or who are confined by office routine frequently report experiencing a sense of isolation and alienation themselves. During such spells, they miss not only the easy-going husband they knew in their first years of marriage, but also their family, friends, and home country and culture. Even wives whose husbands remain relatively unaffected by their Ottawa postings suffer pangs of homesickness and loneliness. Whether language barriers, cultural differences, or shyness prevents them from knocking at a neighbour's door, many foreign-born wives find it difficult, sometimes for years, to break out of their solitary confinement. A sense of having been rejected may exacerbate feelings of isolation if attempts at social contact remain unreciprocated.

Their sense of worth and their dignity often suffer at the hands of prospective employers as well. Training, diplomas, degrees, and professional experience acquired in their country of origin generally count for little or are not recognized at all in their new home. Often, the wife discovers that she is unemployable, which can deal a blow to self-respect as well as to the young couple's income.

A number of foreign-born wives pointed out to me that the accumulation of such problems is more than an average person can cope with. Marital tension, sickness, and depression visit such households. I have talked to several young wives who volunteered the information that, at this particular stage in their lives, they had turned to professionals for help in working through their conflicts.

Those foreign-born wives who, in the first six to twelve months after what more accurately could be called 'patriation,' do not sink into bewilderment or sadness and who manage to stay afloat with the support of strong inner resources and a loving husband, often discover that the new world around them begins to look a lot more familiar and friendly. In many cultures, mourning rituals suggest that adjustment to new circumstances – that is, loss – takes a minimum of a year. Foreign-born wives don't generally don black clothes as they enter Canada for their first home posting, but they do mourn – consciously or otherwise – and their loss is enormous since their entire world has been taken away. If they come from countries in Asia or Africa, it may be years, even decades, before they can get back, and they never know for sure whether they will see their families and friends again. Many of them, though, have regained enough of their equilibrium by the time a year has passed in their new home that the black mood of the previous twelve months can be put aside, like mourning attire, and replaced by a more joyous and hopeful state of mind.

Some of the wives with whom I discussed the issue of their first year on a home posting recalled with gratitude the help they had received from a variety of sources: a kind and understanding husband who was aware of his wife's difficulties and attentive to her needs and who considered the first anniversary of the joint entry into Canada an occasion for, say, flowers and a special dinner; a loving family in her country of origin who eased their daughter's entry into her new world with letters, phone calls, and visits; supportive in-laws; and, if not a stimulating and paying job, at least a chance to learn and master new skills.

By all accounts, a baby usually helps its mother out of isolation, or prevents her from getting caught up in it in the first place. Whether children arrive with their parents for a first home posting, or are born afterwards, they have a way of introducing their mothers to a small community: future mothers in prenatal classes, brand-new ones in the maternity ward, and seasoned mothers on sandbox watch in play-grounds and on nursery-school ferrying duties.

But discussions with foreign-born wives revealed that all too many of them had not been able to pull themselves out of their initial misery in Ottawa, with or without baby. Either the inner resources had been lack-ing or outside support from husband, family, friends, colleagues, or neighbours had never materialized, or both. After two or three years in Canada they greeted the announcement of a forthcoming overseas assignment like a commutation of a prison sentence. In such cases, the first home posting was a trauma to be recovered from. The thought of ever having to come back was insupportable. A series of foreign post-ings, they hoped, would postpone that nightmare indefinitely. As it turned out later, it required much goodwill, hard work, and patience during a long second round at home to undo the damage the first assign-ment had done. After one contented posting in Ottawa, such families have usually mastered the art of repatriation and express satisfaction or even joy at the prospect of another home posting.

In some cases, however, the obstacles to living a contented life in Canada appear to be insurmountable. Foreign-born husbands seem to fare the worst in this regard.

Giuseppe Dotti met his wife, Monique, a young foreign-service clerk, on her first overseas posting. He was working as a waiter in a small restaurant in Rome near the Canadian mission. He had left his home in Sicily a year earlier to seek his fortune in the tourist industry of the Ital-ian capital. A fortune was certainly not to be made there, he told me, but he had an income. Six months after he had met Monique he became a Canadian foreign-service spouse and moved into his wife's staff quarters. Monique's and his salaries remained modest, but combined seemed an impressive sum. For the first time in their lives they could afford to buy everything they needed – no luxuries, as they pointed out, but genuine necessities. Their comfortable circumstances lasted one year. The letter from External Affairs asking Monique to report back for duty in Ottawa early in the summer arrived shortly after Monique had found out that a baby was on the way.

As soon as the young couple had landed for the first joint home posting, both of them were struck by a flood of unexpected problems. The cheapest apartment they could find to rent would devour a good portion of Monique's pay-cheque. They owned no furniture. Monique had shared furnished accommodation with a friend on her previous posting to Ottawa and had never bought a bed or table for herself. They urgently needed basics for themselves and a crib and changing table for the baby. For all that, they depended on having a second income. But Giuseppe's skills as a waiter proved to be less marketable in Ottawa than they had been in Rome. He spoke a bit of French and was fluent in Italian, but had hardly a word of English. Job hunting turned out to be a humiliating experience for him. The few positions available required fluency in English. Even the local Italian restaurants were not satisfied with a unilingual Italian. Desperate to pay off a small bank loan they had taken for essential household goods, he accepted jobs in restaurants about which he hesitates to talk.

Shortly before the baby was born, Monique went on maternity leave at 75 per cent of her salary. The first eighteen months of their home posting was a period neither of them wants to remember. But the worries and strain of that time are impossible to forget. During the second year in Ottawa, Monique never left out an opportunity to remind her personnel officer that she and her husband were more than eager to go out again. A hardship post would be most welcome as it came with a special allowance of $2,000 a year. Giuseppe, of course, would have to be able to find a job there, too. When the longed-for phone call from Personnel Branch reached Monique with the offer of a posting to Nigeria, she felt relieved. Their nightmare – money worries, her husband's demeaning night-time jobs, his inability to adapt to the harsh climate and homesickness – would be over. They put their modest collection of furniture into long-term storage, packed up their little daughter, and set out for Lagos, vowing that they would make use of Monique's right to three consecutive two-year postings abroad. They would save every penny Monique would receive for overtime work and as much of what Giuseppe hoped to be earning in one of the large international hotels as they could in preparation for their next term in Ottawa. For the moment, however, they did not want to think of that far-away day. Any foreign assignment at this stage in their life sounded better than another year on a home posting.

Lizandro Casas had to face a similar situation after he had married a Canadian foreign-service officer in Buenos Aires. He had known Vivian for almost three years when she told him that she had finally been offered the job in Ottawa on which she had had her eye for some time. She would be leaving within three months. Lizandro responded with a proposal. Getting married, closing down two households, taking Lizandro's thirty-year roots out of Argentinian soil and transplanting him at seventy-five degrees latitude farther north were accomplished in the three allotted months, but at a heavy cost. Both of them began to doubt the wisdom of their hasty decision as Vivian found herself all but chained to her new desk at headquarters while Lizandro sat in an apartment hotel day in, day out, in growing despair.

He spoke neither English nor French. Spanish, the language he spoke with Vivian, was of no use. His advanced engineering degree from an Argentinian university counted for nothing. He had held a responsible and well-paying position in Buenos Aires, but, in Ottawa, he was unemployable. Language difficulties meant he could not even look for an apartment during Vivian's seemingly endless office hours. The only area where he could be of help to his wife was on the domestic stage. He did the cleaning, shopping, and cooking and wondered whether he would ever be able to return to a more demanding career.

An employment agent suggested that he go back to university and requalify with a Canadian engineering degree. Lizandro could not see how his wife's salary, barely enough to pay for the necessities of life, could carry such an enormous additional load, or how the language barrier could be surmounted. He applied for a job with the embassy of Argentina and a few other Latin American missions where he could use his Spanish, but he was turned down in every one of them.

Two years after their arrival in Ottawa Vivian gave birth to a son. Her maternity leave, she told me, became an oasis for both of them. For the first time since they had got married, she had the feeling that she was living rather than racing. However, domestic tranquillity was short-lived. When she returned to her office, she was caught up in the merciless grind of a division permanently in a state of crisis because of a severe staff shortage. She spent ten hours in the office each day and often had to go back to her desk on Saturdays and Sundays. Lizandro sat at home, lovingly tending the baby and resigning himself to the fact that he had no future as a professional.

The family is now on its way to Venezuela. Lizandro, in the meantime having become a Canadian citizen and fluent in English, will have a much better chance of finding employment in that part of the world than in Ottawa. If no job should turn up in the local market he might find a position as locally engaged staff in the Canadian mission, although he would be working well below his capacity and at a small local, rather than Canadian, salary.

Speaking lovingly and with deep admiration of Lizandro's integrity and patience during three extremely difficult years, Vivian is adamant that her and her husband's decision to stay abroad as long as possible is the right one. Unless Lizandro, who is already in his mid-thirties, should decide to go back to university in order to find a job suited to his qualifications, Ottawa remains for them nothing more than the embodiment of insoluble problems and painful memories.

Raymond Duclos feels at times that he has taken the conflicts of all foreign-born husbands onto his shoulders, and a few other difficulties in addition. When he married Rachel, a secretary with the Canadian Embassy to the Common Market in Brussels, he had been employed as an accountant with the French embassy in the Belgian capital for fifteen years. He had also just come out of a divorce, and was still bruised, figuratively speaking. Rachel offered not only the patience and love he needed, but a home; he had lost his in the divorce settlement.

Raymond and Rachel think of the year after their wedding with nostalgia as they are now struggling with overwhelming odds in Ottawa. Raymond's teenage sons from his first marriage opted to live with their father when Rachel was posted back to Canada. According to the foreign-service directives, her husband's children qualify also as her children and are entitled to the same benefits as the couple's daughter, who was born shortly before their arrival in Canada.

The list of his unresolved and in many ways unresolvable problems is so long he needs the fingers on both hands to count them. He hardly speaks any English. His Belgian training as an accountant is not useful in Canada. He has no job and no income, and adds with a bitter laugh that it does not require the expertise of an accountant to understand why three children constitute a poor substitute for a regular pay-cheque. His wife's salary is too small to support a family of five. The only employment he can find are part-time jobs as a waiter during lunch hours. If he wants to work at that time of the day, however, he has to leave his baby daughter in the care of an expensive babysitter sent by an agency. The fees would swallow up a good part of his earnings and tips. His prospects of finding work in his area of expertise are minimal and so are the chances ever to have the desperately needed second income.

The only way out of their trouble is a posting abroad, he says. It should be somewhere in French Africa, where he might find employment and where the family would have the hardship allowance. As far as Raymond and Rachel are concerned, a home posting has all the negative aspects of a serious hardship post, but without the hardship allowance that could help to make things bearable.

My conversations with foreign-service members and their families indicate that reactions to home postings can range anywhere between delight and despair. Those who express positive feelings about the initial phase of reorientation usually maintain their attitude throughout their assignment to Ottawa. A satisfactory first home posting tends to cast a bright light on all subsequent repatriations, although all foreign-service members point out that shorter or longer periods of adjustments should be considered normal and ought to be dealt with in a relaxed way. Those who take home postings in stride also respond positively to almost any assignment abroad, and to foreign-service life as a whole.

On the negative side of the scale, some employees and their families struggle with considerable difficulty during the first months after re-entry into home orbit but manage to overcome problems gradually in the course of the first year. For some singles as well, the first Ottawa assignment is such a negative experience that a second round at home is needed to help them revise their views about postings to Canada.

A small group that deserves more attention and support than it receives finds itself lodged farther towards the negative end of the scale. Among them are those for whom life in Canada can be even more difficult than life in a hardship post. Families with foreign-born spouses, who encounter sometimes overpowering problems, fit into this category.

A small group of singles and families spend much of their energy in Ottawa complaining about difficulties that are simply part of life, self-created, or imagined. Such people belong to the club of incorrigible grumblers, and its members can be found everywhere. They claim that life abroad is always wonderful, and life in Canada – in Ottawa, particularly – always terrible. Their moanings about an insufferable existence at home reveal more about their unwillingness to come to terms with ordinary life in Canada than about Ottawa's purported shortcomings. To satisfy the demands of this negligible group of people Ottawa would have to be converted into a full-scale paradise and even then they would manage to find fault and demand transfer to a distant, and therefore innately superior, Garden of Eden.

The majority of foreign-service members, however, are well settled around the middle of the positive–negative continuum. They describe home postings as initially complicated. Reintegration takes time, they say. After six to twelve months, the turbulence of the move subsides and life regains its familiar equilibrium.

Once foreign-service lives in Ottawa reach a level of security and predictability and the boredom threshold can easily be crossed, most foreign-service members start to get restless. In search of new challenges, languages, cultures, and continents, they ask for an assignment abroad. 'We clean out and go,' a veteran wife said, summing up her own feelings and those of many of her fellow nomads at such a moment. Thus, another round in the posting cycle begins.

11

Retirement
The Posting Cycle Closes

Every foreign service employee reaches the point where the posting carousel stops to let the rider and his or her family off, for good. No further rides will be available. Some transients jump off before the carousel comes to a full stop, more than willing to forgo further dizzying rounds; others drag themselves off at the last moment, watching longingly as a younger generation of riders climbs on. Most, though, leave the scene with a mixture of relief and regret.

The process of retirement from the foreign service elicits from its members as many eloquent reactions as does foreign-service life itself. Withdrawal from such a distinctive type of life can be as all-consuming a task as leading the kind of existence that is being given up. One foreign-service employee voiced the opinion of a large number of his colleagues: 'Retirement from the service is like an overseas posting – it depends on what you make of it.' Comparing their life in retirement to previous assignments either at home or abroad is an approach many foreign-service members take.

Terence considers his retirement the best appointment he has ever had. He and his wife, Evelyn, had known the exact date of that event for some time and had brightened the difficult years of their last assignment in a hardship posting with enthusiastic planning of every detail of their retirement. An ambassador in his last three postings, Terence had invested carefully. He and his wife had saved enough, after putting their children through university and financing the weddings of two daughters, to build a modest summer house in Portugal, 'in quest of the sun,' as Evelyn put it. They had sold their family home in Ottawa and had bought a small house in the English countryside, an hour away by train from London.

After a retirement party organized by the staff of their own embassy, a succession of formal dinners, and a farewell reception given in their honour by eighty fellow ambassadors, the Canadian ambassador and his wife were seen off at the airport with a formal ceremony arranged by the host country. Although not much of a man for pomp and circumstance, Terence appreciated all these occasions and the speeches given in recognition of his work and achievements. He saw them as the highlight and symbolic closing of his thirty-five years in government service.

The welcome in London for Terence and Evelyn by their eldest daughter, son-in-law, and three small grandchildren turned out to be as informal as the farewells had been formal. The former head of post and his wife had had a surfeit of semi-public life, and were delighted to return to complete privacy. For the first six months of their retirement, they concentrated on settling into their new house, located half-way between their daughter's home and London. Then they began to spend their time either visiting their children and grandchildren or going to London to shop, visit museums and galleries, and call on a good dozen old friends with whom they had shared, on five continents, much of their foreign-service career.

When winter descended upon Britain, they handed the keys for the house to their daughter and headed to Portugal. The house there was finished, but it had yet to be furnished. With the help of a lively community of British expatriates, they found themselves quickly established in their second home. As soon as the balmy Portuguese spring began to change to blistering summer heat and news arrived that the first rosebushes in their garden in England showed promising buds, they handed the keys for their southern residence to their younger daughter and son-in-law, who had arrived with their twin sons from New Jersey two weeks earlier, and returned to Britain. Within six weeks their son, just graduated from Wilfrid Laurier University in Waterloo, would eventually make his way to Britain too.

Ten years into their retirement, Terence and Evelyn still cherish the freedom from schedules, deadlines, formal entertaining, official delegations, and especially the rigours of life in a hardship post. With two permanent homes in completely different environments and climate zones and the freedom to come and go whenever they please, with children and grandchildren within reach and all of them eager to visit, monotony and boredom hold no threat. During rounds of informal luncheons, teas, dinners, and bridge parties, they share with their foreign-service friends memories of years and decades of joint struggles to make a go of life in some of the remotest corners of the world. A small stream of visitors from External Affairs in Ottawa brings them up to date on the comings and goings in the Lester B. Pearson Building.

Terence and Evelyn point out that their retirement is such a success not only because they have been lucky, but because they planned it. For years beforehand, they had discussed how they wanted to spend that part of their life. All of their children had participated in the planning, and at some point a number of options had been put to a vote. Once the basic plan was made, everyone set to work on the details. The children living in Canada and New Jersey were responsible for selling the property in Ottawa, the daughter in Britain was assigned the job of finding a house near her own home, and the parents oversaw the Portugal operation. It took years, but eventually it worked out well because they had approached the project as they would have a particularly complicated hardship posting.

Bert is quietly convinced that his retirement is bound to turn into the worst hardship assignment he has ever had. Nothing had prepared him for the feeling of having been dropped, something he is experiencing daily as he sits out his last months at headquarters. With an expression of anger in his face and voice, he explained to me that his official position is that of 'special adviser,' but that he is practically unemployed. He was called back from his last posting earlier than he had wanted. Admittedly, he adds, his time was up, but he had asked to stay in the overseas post for his last year in the service. For some reason, his request was not granted. To add to his troubles, he had not got along well with his boss, an unfortunate situation that was reflected in his annual rating. He had, however, made friends outside the mission and would have greatly enjoyed their company when the inevitable end of his career came around.

He cannot conceal his disappointment about having remained below the goal he had set for himself in the hierarchy of his occupational group. For the past fifteen years, the day on which the promotion lists were published was a black day for him. He feels like a failure, he says.

His recent divorce has contributed to that feeling. 'If you start a posting on the wrong foot, you are in trouble,' he explains. His family's first overseas assignment was, according to his own account, a disaster from the first day to the last. After that episode, his marriage went slowly and steadily downhill. The one good posting to London, during which life began to look more promising, had to be terminated after only six months. One of their children had come down with a severe case of asthma, and the Health and Welfare physician recommended immediate evacuation of patient and family to the healthier climate of Ottawa. Ten more years of marital struggle on three continents followed before his wife left him. His two teenaged girls opted to stay with their mother. 'Twenty years down the drain,' Bert mutters, and shrugs his shoulders.

He now lives in a house that he had never seen as anything more than an investment and a shelter to be used for 'a few years of purgatory in Ottawa' between postings to where he felt real life was – Asia, Australia, and Latin America. Such overseas assignments offered a most welcome distraction from his wife's steady complaints and from other family problems. He wonders now whether he should not have spent more time trying to deal with unresolved family conflicts rather than simply deflecting his attention to the problem with too many superficial friendships. His friends are scattered all over the world, but he has not a soul in Ottawa to whom he feels close. 'Sure, I have nice neighbours,' he replies to my question. Most of them have never left Canada, though, and he does not have much in common with them, other than the street they live on.

Although it seems to him that he has already been taken off the list of foreign-service personnel, he still has to report for duty each morning. He dreads the moment when he must leave headquarters for the last time as he has no idea where to go. 'Nothing will bring me back into this building,' he blurts out angrily. But the tone of his voice softens quickly, and a grin appears on his face. He has already made up his mind to convert the three hundred days of leave he has accumulated over the last few years into cash and use the money to visit some of his oldest overseas friends. Since his diplomatic passport will no longer be valid then, he will have to re-enter the building to apply for an ordinary Canadian passport. Asked what he plans to do after his return from abroad, he replies: 'I don't know!'

Dan and Isabel had foreseen that they would be susceptible to the retirement syndrome they had watched afflict some of their colleagues unless they carefully planned a course of action. Pastimes such as reading, golf, and travelling would not suffice to make their retirement a satisfactory period of life. Their only daughter was living in Europe with her husband and one child, and they could not count, as many of their colleagues could, on regular visits from a growing crowd of grandchildren to brighten their days. But, even if that had not been the case, turning into full-time grandparents was not their idea of the perfect retirement. Dan knew that his lifelong interest in international affairs would not come to an end on his last day in External Affairs, just as Isabel's lifelong passion for drawing and painting would not vanish suddenly. Both of them decided to go back to school. Dan had been asked to give lectures and to lead a seminar on international relations at one of the universities in Montreal and Isabel had signed up for advanced art courses.

To celebrate the beginning of this new stage of their life, their friends organized a dinner in their honour, an evening of reminiscing about more than thirty years in the foreign service that they had shared in twelve postings around the world, with intermittent periods in Ottawa. Looking back on his career through the eyes of so many of his active and retired colleagues, who promised to remain friends beyond the threshold of retirement, convinced Dan and Isabel that they had more reason to celebrate than to mourn.

Released from a life of incessant moves and seemingly endless duties as hostess for thousands of official visitors, Isabel feels reborn. Her studio is filled with sketches, drawings, watercolours, and paintings, testimony to her immersion in the world of creative art. In his study next door, Dan prepares the reading list for his students, which is almost as much work as the course itself, he tells me. He has just accepted a part-time job as a consultant for an international corporation and will soon be travelling again.

Their nineteenth-century house beside the Rideau River remains a centre of conviviality. Although Isabel had sworn upon returning from their last assignment abroad never again to entertain, both of them are eager to remain in touch with their former colleagues, old and young alike. They do send out invitations for small concerts or dinners, and at times their house is filled with the light of a hundred candles and the sound of harpsichord and chamber orchestra, followed by the lively conversation of an audience largely consisting of international transients.

Happily occupied in their own world, Dan and Isabel watch with a mixture of relief and nostalgia as the younger generation gets ready for exotic places, returns from far-away countries, and continues to be caught up in a posting cycle that is mercifully no longer of any consequence to them.

Sam and Abby opted for a less dynamic golden age. Their last posting had taken them to an usually difficult country in the Near East. Sam felt he had never received the recognition he deserved for his work. Promotions had eluded him even after he had mastered the most challenging tasks in the worst possible postings. But he had always seen the attractions of foreign-service life as rich compensation for his rather disappointing career. Both he and Abby began to miss the challenge and excitement of rotational life one year after they had settled down in their home in Lindenlea.

The Lester B. Pearson Building lies within walking distance of their house. Several times a week Sam strolls to 125 Sussex Drive, deposits and cashes cheques in the same bank he has been using ever since it was opened in External Affairs almost twenty years ago, takes a glance at newspapers and magazines in the library, and then looks around in the cafeteria for the familiar faces of former colleagues who also like to combine banking, socializing, and keeping an eye on developments in the department.

Lately Sam has been dropping in more frequently. One of his and Abby's sons, discontent with the vacuum left in his life by his parents' retirement, cleared all hurdles in the foreign-service exam and is now an officer on probation. The position Sam had always dreamt of for himself without ever attaining it is now within reach of his son. Sam likes to think of his son's decision in favour of the foreign service and his access to the Officer category as a belated form of recognition of his own career choice and of the way he and Abby have steered their children through the storms of rotational life.

The family is back in the department, Sam tells me with undisguised paternal pride. Father and son have changed roles. Sam wonders whether addiction to foreign-service life is passed on through the genes or acquired. Whatever the case may be, he says, he and Abby are now waiting for their son's first assignment abroad. In a way the posting cycle has started all over again for them.

Each retirement story is unique, but types are discernible. Other than the large number of individual components, certain key variables can unite to turn retirement into a satisfying or dissatisfying experience: the degree of general contentment with job and career, the nature of the last posting prior to retirement, the amount of recognition received from superiors and the way the end of professional life has been marked by the organization and by colleagues have as much power to shape retirement as some of the main elements determining private life, such as the quality of relationships with family and friends, the sense of familiarity attached to the home and community chosen for retirement, the state of personal or family finances, and the degree of contentment derived from retirement activities.

In many ways, ideal lives in retirement from the foreign service are no different from those of other occupations. They resemble architectural structures whose stability rests on two rows of equally strong pillars. One set of pillars represents time devoted to private goals, to loving relationships with family and friends, to a home within a community, to financial security, and to the development of hobbies and other personal interests. The second set of pillars stands for energy invested in pursuit of professional goals, job satisfaction, official recognition measured by promotions and other forms of rewards, and finally cooperation and fellowship with colleagues.

What distinguishes retired foreign-service personnel from other pensioners is the extreme adversity foreign-service staff encounter under the impact of rotationality in their attempt to erect throughout their lives the equivalent of such a structure. Satisfying the demands of a career that amounts to a new job in a different country every two to four years and fulfilling, in constantly changing surroundings, the needs of a marriage and family require almost superhuman dedication and effort.

Foreign-service members who radiate contentment during retirement have usually made a conscious attempt to counter the disruptive and destabilizing effects of rotationality by carefully nurturing warm relations with family and friends and by creating and maintaining close bonds with the community in Canada, thus finding a vital sense of continuity and stability for themselves and their family.

Troubled retirements, in contrast, await employees who are unwilling or unable to recognize the dangers inherent in fragmentation of work and personal life and who fail to balance the all-embracing demands placed on them from two separate sources. Too many employees focus on their career at the expense of private life. They deprive themselves and their families of the sense of security that close human relationships would bring to their otherwise frayed and frazzled lives. Living one posting at a time, as all too many foreign-service members do, blissfully blind to long-term plans or goals in their private world, ultimately leads to being tossed about anchorless during inevitable storms. Such individuals and families are the first ones to complain bitterly about a sense of homelessness and an emotional void when the dreaded retirement is upon them.

Most foreign-service members, however, manage – some better than others – to bring to their own lives and to those of their families the much-needed sense of stability and continuity that makes up for the unsettling disruptions rotational life imposes on them. They discover long before they have to face golden age that their life structure is best supported by more than one set of pillars, and that a strong private life is as essential to shore up the crushing weight of a rotational career as a challenging occupation within the foreign service.

Retirement is usually the time during which former foreign-service members find out how well they have understood the possibilities, and the limitations, of their unique type of life and how wisely they have acted on their insight.

PART III

Lessons in Foreign-Service Living

12

Fellow Transients

Anyone who has watched, in train stations of European capitals, a band of backpackers come across another detachment of the same brotherhood will confirm that such encounters are bound to lead to an eager exchange of adventure stories and travel wisdom. I have observed small and large congregations of transients surrounded by the tools of their trade – rucksacks, sleeping-bags, and maps – stretched out on stone floors, munching salami sandwiches and asking each other the kinds of questions that any member of the international foreign-service fraternity will recall from slightly more staid social gatherings: 'Where are you from? How long have you been here? Where are you going next? How are you enjoying this place? On how much have you been able to get along? What made you decide to come to this part of the world? Does gypsy life appeal to you, now that you have tried it out?'

In the case of foreign-service personnel conversations with fellow migrants often amount to lively comparisons between general living and working conditions in their own and other countries' diplomatic services. They discuss age and size; recruitment practices; family policy in the areas of health, education, and spousal employment; allowances; home leaves; and a large number of other issues that determine the quality of life within the service.

To some extent the history of foreign services can be likened to the story of human beings: their birth is accompanied by labour pains, and their progenitors tend to have high hopes for them; the offspring suffer from childhood diseases, grow, may blossom for shorter or longer periods, mature, and eventually begin to decline. Each one of them will require critical self-assessment, flexibility, and constant adjustment to the larger reality in order to avoid untimely deterioration. Each foreign service has a unique personality, mirroring its country's social, political, and economic conditions, and shaped by a residue of forces that have shaped the country's history and current perceptions of how the foreign service should meet the needs of tomorrow. They can be young and vigorous or middle-aged and heavy-set, or they may suffer from the saddest symptoms of old age, such as memory loss, deafness and blindness, paralysis, and general decay. Most of them look and act their age, but some try to mask their decline with the organizational equivalent of cosmetic surgery. Others cherish their original vitality, carefully preserve their creative energy, and maintain a youthful appearance through continuous renewal and adaptation, even at advanced stages in their existence.

Foreign services cannot be held responsible for the extreme demands they place on their personnel. Such demands are dictated by the rules of international mobility. They are the same in every service. What differs dramatically, however, are the rules each service has designed to help employees cope with inevitable hardships.

Through frequent conversations with fellow transients, members of Canada's Department of External Affairs stay up to date with the regulations that govern living conditions in other countries' foreign ministries. They look to other services for ways to improve their own situation, and members of other services continue to point out to their authorities that the Canadian foreign-service directives possess considerable merits, too.

A look at the foreign services of nineteen countries will reveal solutions to common problems. Any foreign ministry ambitious enough to aim at long-term organizational health might find the catalogue of the finest features of some of the world's most distinguished diplomatic service stimulating reading on the road to effectiveness and excellence.

Australia is a leading example of a country that believes that systematic professional training for foreign-service personnel is neither unnecessary nor an unaffordable luxury. During the late 1980s, the Ministry of Foreign Affairs in Canberra decided that the previous policy of learning on the job had to be replaced, and introduced, in 1990, in a joint effort with the Australian National University, a two-year, graduate diploma course in foreign affairs and trade for officer candidates. This academic approach to the education of future diplomats follows the French and German tradition. But the Australian model, unlike the European versions, was primarily intended to be a university program, although the courses were designed in close cooperation with Australian practitioners and experts in the field of diplomacy.

The new emphasis on thorough instruction is not limited to those entering the Officer category or to those who are about to join the foreign service. Ministry and university have opened the doors to this diploma course to other staff members as well, while personnel in each one of the occupational groups and at all levels of the hierarchy are encouraged to take professional-development courses throughout their careers.

Thus the Australian foreign service has got one step ahead of other training-conscious services by promoting the concept of continued education and extends it to members of all occupational groups.

Somewhat like the kangaroo, the Australian foreign service's spousal-employment policy moves in leaps and bounds. Occasionally such a jump turns out to be a dramatic event. Australians manning their embassies around the world rubbed their eyes in disbelief when, in 1989, after long and laborious deliberations on the issue, out of their diplomatic pouch jumped the news that not only were foreign-service spouses allowed to be gainfully employed in the same mission as their marriage partner, but even an ambassador's spouse was henceforth entitled to be hired in the embassy over which that ambassador presided, provided, of course, a regular position was vacant. The Australian service seems to be the first to have taken spousal-employment policy quite that far. The policy was formulated in response to employees' complaints that the overseas-allowance structure did not permit families to maintain their home standard of living when only one spouse had an income, a major problem encountered by marriage partners in many other foreign services as well.

The diplomatic service of the *People's Republic of China,* struggling with a problem that is perceived by its members, as well as by foreign colleagues, as the most heart-rending by-product of their particular lifestyle, has managed to turn a hardship into a virtue. Without exception, a foreign assignment means separation of parents and children. No Chinese foreign-service child is allowed to accompany parents abroad or even to visit them in a foreign country. Children of all ages are put in the care of the large Chinese extended family, and the separation from parents usually lasts for years. Foreign-service employees are told by their government that health care abroad for children is an unaffordable luxury and that it is impossible to set up Chinese schools in foreign countries. Chinese diplomats admit openly that their homesickness and pain of separation are surpassed only by their children's, at least during the first year. After a while the children begin to forget their parents, especially if they were very young when the parents left. The worst moment for foreign-service mothers and fathers arrives when a child does not recognize his or her parents after years have gone by. A young Chinese father told me sadly that his little boy did not know what to do with the stranger and simply ignored him.

Faced with years of separation and the prospect of losing the children altogether, Chinese parents frequently give up their career, salary, and privilege of living and travelling abroad. Those who remain 'are prepared to suffer,' a veteran Chinese diplomat confessed. Since the miserable situation is universal among personnel with children, each is expected to ease the other's pain. Feeling the same kind of heartache creates a powerful bond. Embassy colleagues treat each other like family members, regardless of position in the hierarchy. 'We have dances together, we watch films, we play cards and table tennis and have many activities. We live together,' an experienced member of the service told me, and added that an affectionate family atmosphere within the chancery and the residence does, indeed, help the healing process.

Spousal employment is administered primarily as a painkiller. 'A job takes a woman's mind off the missing children,' employer and employee repeat to each other. It almost sounds like a quotation from Chairman Mao's *Little Red Book* that seems more convincing every time it has been recited. Wives are encouraged to devote their time and energy to the mission, and positions are always made available for them. Each embassy has several working couples. Sharing an office also seems to promote the quality of marriages, a Chinese husband remarked, after having spent most of his professional life in the company of his wife.

'Marriages don't break up, at least not in the older generation. I don't know of any in our service,' he said, but then laughed and qualified his earlier statement, pointing out that working together all day long creates tension between partners, and marriages do break up between younger couples. 'The younger generation is different,' he muttered.

While the forced separation of parents and children seems to represent the most exacting of the requirements put forward by any foreign service, the development of a sense of compassion, the mutual support within the community, and the promotion of spouses' careers are characteristics that should be nurtured in other countries' foreign services, independently of the cruel circumstances that brought about such qualities in the Chinese case. Quietly suffering Chinese parents hope that the situation will eventually improve for them and their offspring and wonder whether a little push from fellow transients might not speed developments up a bit. 'We are all human beings; we must try to find solutions for our common problems,' a Chinese diplomat suggested, and expressed interest in obtaining a copy of the Canadian foreign-service directives to pass on to the powers that be at headquarters in Beijing.

The foreign service of *Egypt* believes in introducing its budding diplomats to foreign countries and cultures at the earliest possible moment. The Diplomatic Institute of Foreign Affairs, on the shores of the Nile, brings together for one year of formal training not only Egyptian officer candidates who have passed the first round of a four-day entrance examination at the foreign ministry, but also a large number of future diplomats from other African countries. The young people who will make up the African diplomatic corps of the future share with their Egyptian hosts seminar rooms, lecture halls and libraries, and tables in the cafeteria. At that stage in their training, their hearts and minds are open to different cultures and countries, and a solid foundation is laid for close cooperation with neighbours in the African world.

'Good psychology,' an Egyptian friend called such a policy, and added that his foreign ministry does not limit the exposure of its young diplomats to African and Arabic peoples and their issues. For the last month of the year of formal training in Cairo, the crew is divided into two groups. One group is sent to France, the other group to Germany.

The Ministère des Affaires Etrangères in Paris and the Auswärtiges Amt in Bonn are expected to put the final touches on the apprenticeships. According to veteran foreign-service officers, this last portion is the highlight of their year as candidates for the Egyptian foreign service. Those who have served at the Quai d'Orsay and at the Adenauer Allee can't emphasize enough how much the program promotes friendships with future colleagues and prepares the ground for teamwork on the international stage.

In pursuit of renewal and excellence, some foreign ministries do pioneer work that sets new standards by which their counterparts in other countries are eventually going to be measured. The diplomatic service of *Germany* fits into this category. Continuous attempts to improve the quality of its operations have resulted not only in a meticulously chosen and superbly trained team of professionals who command the respect of their foreign colleagues around the world, but also a wholly new approach towards enhancing living conditions for personnel and their dependents, a concept which deserves to be studied and emulated.

Over the years, the German foreign ministry, the Auswärtiges Amt, has gradually introduced principles and guidelines of personnel management that experts consider partially responsible for the rebuilding of Germany's postwar economy. Prominent among them is utmost thoroughness in the selection and training of the occupational group that will eventually produce senior executives. The entrance examination for future diplomats consists of written tests in which candidates have to demonstrate fluency in reading and writing English and French and extensive knowledge in the areas of economics, history, politics, and international law. Only those candidates who do well are invited to present themelves to a selection committee for two and a half days of extensive oral examination in language skills and in knowledge and understanding of international relations, international law, economics, history, and politics.

No foreign service I have studied ascribes as much importance to the next phase of the selection process as the Auswärtiges Amt does. A number of organizational psychologists, hired for the occasion from German industry, subject the contestants to an uninterrupted three- to four-hour session in which character, intelligence, aptitudes, and the ability to withstand stress are carefully scrutinized. This test also consists of a written and an oral part. To those candidates who wonder whether this kind of investigation does not carry thoroughness a bit too far, psychologists point out that future foreign-service officers are being exposed to nothing more merciless than the standard tests given to applicants for senior positions in German industry.

Two years of professional training at the Foreign Service Academy follow. Graduates of law schools who have completed their articling enrol for only one year. During that period all of them are trained in international law and international relations, history, politics, economics, consular affairs, and languages. They are also put through their paces in public speaking, in the all-important field of personnel management – an area of training that does not seem to be part of any other foreign service's curriculum – and in group work. Candidates whose command of English and French does not need improvement are launched on a third-language program and sent abroad for a three-month immersion course. Those who should polish their English or French go to Britain or France for three months, where they combine language studies with courses in economics. This training period closes with elaborate written and oral exams.

Besides its rigorous training regimen, what distinguishes the German service from those of other countries are three institutions, which have been gradually introduced during recent decades and seem to have contributed to the growing confidence of its members.

The concept of 'organizational democracy' was institutionalized in the Council of Personnel (Personalrat), a body of democratically elected representatives of all occupational groups within the service. Every three years, at headquarters and in embassies around the world, foreign-service members from all occupational groups elect by secret ballot the person whom they want to see as their representative on the council. The number of council members allotted to each occupational group depends on the number of employees in the group. In order to allow council members to devote themselves completely to their duties, they are released from their ordinary responsibilities in the ministry for a three-year term and are supplied with a special office and staff. Each embassy abroad maintains its own miniature council to discuss minor administrative issues and make decisions on local matters. The central

Council of Personnel at headquarters, however, holds an influential position in the internal management of the ministry.

In 1986, the position of Commissioner for Women and Family Issues was created under the pressure of alarming problems affecting single women, spouses, and families in the service. The position was immediately filled by a female career foreign-service officer. During an interview in the Auswärtiges Amt in Bonn, the commissioner explained to me that her division pursues two main goals: first, to assist all foreign-service women, employees and wives, in furthering their careers and finding employment during home postings and on assignment abroad; and, second, to provide practical help to women and families throughout the posting cycle with information about various aspects of a posting, such as climate, health conditions, housing, schooling, and a host of other issues that are potentially problematic.

A list of major accomplishments during the commissioner's first three years in office includes the regulation that women foreign-service employees married to fellow employees are sent out on a posting as part of a husband-and-wife team, not as an unemployed dependent, or 'trailing spouse,' the telling term previously used, which realistically described their situation. A spouses' skill bank has been started; unemployed wives have filled out questionnaires indicating more than one area in which they would like to work. The labour office in Bonn has been approached and has promised assistance in finding employment for wives returning from abroad. A children's nursery and a daycare centre have been opened. Emergency accommodation for up to five families has been established near the ministry to offer shelter to individuals and families after evacuation for medical and other reasons, to house women and children after marriages have broken up abroad, and to provide a modest home for relatives of foreign-service patients who are under medical care in hospitals in Bonn. Children whose education abroad has put them behind in German schools are granted full financial coverage for tutoring for up to one year.

In January 1991 a new foreign-service act became law. The Gesetz Auswärtiger Dienst constitutes a landmark in the history of the German diplomatic service. The same group of enthusiastic and determined foreign-service members who had led the successful campaign for the creation of the position of commissioner was also responsible for drafting this important document and guiding it through the legislative obstacle course.

The German government's arguments in support of the legislation apply equally to other countries' foreign services and could be used by them to improve the quality of their services as well. According to the German reasoning, an efficient administration of the foreign service requires its own legal foundation, since existing regulations, tailored to the domestic situation, do not do justice to the special conditions foreign-service members encounter abroad. Demands placed on the foreign service have grown. Contrary to economic and social developments in Germany, working and living conditions have deteriorated in many other countries. A majority of foreign postings expose foreign-service employees to risks and dangers to their well-being, health, and security. Since the foreign service insists that it has to hold its position in an ever-increasing competition for qualified personnel to send abroad, while the number of personnel prepared to go abroad is noticeably decreasing, the foreign service has to offer to its members appropriate personal and professional possibilities.

The new law has translated these general considerations into specific regulations. It seems to be the only document of its kind in which the employer, the Minister of Foreign Affairs, 'assumes responsibility for care and protection of personnel' and sees to it 'that a foreign assignment will not result in disadvantages to the employee and his [sic] family.' What this abstract principle means in practical terms is explained at greater length throughout the text:

- In cases of birth, sickness, or death abroad, appropriate financial support is granted to the employee and family.
- According to paragraph 17, the foreign service maintains its own health service in an attempt to prevent medical problems. Social-care institutions can be maintained by the foreign service, or maintained jointly with members of the European communities and other international organizations.
- Paragraph 19 asserts that, in order to protect marriages and families, the foreign service promotes spouses and children accompanying the employee abroad. Practical support in relocating families is guaranteed.
- Paragraph 20 calls for support of the spouse in her or his role as a partner in performing official duties.

- According to paragraph 24, the employer takes care that the spouse of an employee resumes an independent occupation while abroad and upon returning home.
- Paragraph 55 represents a mile-stone decision. It rules that married employees will receive a special allowance of up to 5 per cent of their income abroad as compensation for the particular hardship foreign-service life imposes on their spouses.

Some members of the German foreign service take a cautious attitude and say it remains to be seen whether the Gesetz Auswärtiger Dienst will make the necessary reforms possible. It has set the stage for major improvements; now, it is up to the main actors in the foreign ministry to bring the spirit of the law to life.

Whatever the results will be for the German service, the legislation has created a new standard for foreign-service living conditions that other countries' services will eventually be expected to meet.

Anyone in search of suitable pieces for the ideal foreign-service mosaic would be wise to evaluate a piece's desirability separately from that of its provenance. A long talk I had with the ambassador of the former *German Democratic Republic* took place in March 1990 when his state's rigor mortis had already set in. Four days after our conversation, the citizens of his country would vote overwhelmingly in favour of the state's dissolution and amalgamation with West Germany. Never before had a large public service – including a foreign service – simply ceased to exist because of the decision of the population the bureaucracy had previously claimed to be serving. It was a poignant moment for the ambassador and his wife. Before their state, and its institutions, were laid to rest in one of the darker corners of history, a few highlights emerged.

The East German foreign ministry, whose members were noted for their excellent language training, had always maintained close links with universities, and selection committees made up of professors and a ministry representative were used to choose candidates for a career in the foreign service. Students who wished to pursue a foreign-service career could begin to specialize as early as the first semester. Long-term planning and thorough training were mainly responsible for the reputation East German diplomats enjoyed as accomplished linguists and specialists. Not all members of Western foreign services were able to compete with them in that important field of expertise.

As was the case with other members of the former Communist empire, the most promising East German future diplomats were invited to take their university education at the Institute for International Relations in Moscow. Graduates of that academy, even if they had turned into cynics during six years in the Soviet Union or had buried their faith in Communism by the Kremlin Walls, came away with a high regard for the international atmosphere in classrooms, seminars, and dormitories and could not recommend strongly enough that such a forum be established to train an international network of future colleagues. North and South American, Asian, and European diplomats might give some thought to the project of a common training-ground for their diplomatic apprentices.

Unlike their counterparts in a regrettably large number of foreign services on all five continents, members of the foreign service of *Great Britain* seem to be looking at the future of their career with a certain amount of optimism. 'We are recognized by,' many of them say, 'and on good terms with Parliament.' Like their German colleagues, they made a conscious effort to gain the trust and confidence of Parliament and won not only recognition, but also the promise that foreign-service working and living conditions would be reviewed by a parliamentary committee at least every ten years. New and old problems and conflicts are bound to be brought to light and have a good chance of being dealt with in a creative way.

Although the Foreign Office maintains strict entry requirements, democratic principles are practised conscientiously in the venerable buildings of Whitehall. The selection board responsible for the final decision on which candidates for the Officer category succeed in passing the three-day entrance examination is not made up exclusively of diplomats, as is the case in most other foreign services, but includes a civil-service mandarin, an academic, a trade-unionist, a diplomat, an industrialist, and a writer.

Not all is lost for those who falter at the officer's hurdles. Admission requirements for commercial or administrative officers and all support-staff groups are less stringent. Once inside the gates, a member of any occupational group, including clerical staff, can reach the diplomatic wing. Her Britannic Majesty's foreign service prides itself on having established a classless hierarchy that maintains open avenues to all senior positions. 'We have a formal structure that allows clerks to become ambassadors,' a British ambassador told me. 'Plenty of our people have started in the humbler jobs and got to the top.'

In all job categories up to half of the successful candidates are women. A particular effort is made to reflect in its membership the wide social, ethnic, and racial range of British society.

Most recently the Foreign Office has addressed the critical issues of spousal employment in an innovative way that satisfies some spouses, but by no means all of them. Payment for spouses of diplomats who often work full-time in support of a wife's or husband's career had been demanded by many spouses. The proposal was evaluated and rejected, but a new rule was introduced, a unique British arrangement. Spouses can claim a fixed rate for every hour of work put in for official entertaining and for time spent preparing meals and arranging formal receptions. Ambassador's spouses, however, are not eligible.

Although a large number of British foreign-service spouses seem to regard the offer as token, members of other foreign services see it as a mile-stone. It appears to them as the first firm step in the direction of concrete recognition of spouses as partners in a husband-and-wife team. The new provision has given rise to the hope among European and other countries' foreign-service members that the British service, so obviously recognized, valued, and supported by Parliament, and by the public, might lead the way towards urgently needed improvements of living conditions in other foreign services as well.

The dramatic changes that swept Eastern Europe in 1989 left their mark on social, political, and economic institutions in the former Communist world. *Hungary* ranked among the pioneers of peaceful transition. In the capital city, Budapest, at every street corner a grey, crumbling structure was gutted and rebuilt or torn down altogether and replaced with a bright apartment or office building, and political institutions and government agencies underwent drastic changes as well. The Hungarian Ministry of Foreign Affairs led the charge against outdated organizational structures and management practices. Openness to new faces and new ideas became the hallmark of the Kulugyminiszterium. When I volunteered my services as management consultant, I was received with open arms by all members of the organization, from the minister to support staff. Never before had the ministry been assessed in an attempt to improve operations and to enhance working and living conditions. I was granted unlimited access to foreign-service personnel and to relevant documents. Six months of extensive interviews and discussions with senior managers culminated in my giving a seminar attended by the foreign minister and his advisers. My detailed analysis of the strengths and weaknesses of the ministry and several recommendations for a reorientation and reorganization of structure and management process were accepted and are now gradually being implemented.

An eagerness for critical evaluation of principles and practices had been apparent in Hungary before the drastic changes of 1989. In 1988, the Foreign Affairs Committee of Parliament reserved for itself the right to examine every candidate for the position of ambassador in any of the ninety-four (December 1992) missions Hungary maintains around the world. During a hearing, the twenty-three-member committee attempts to establish a candidate's suitability for the proposed assignment. Following the presentation, a vote among committee members confirms or rejects the applicant. In the short history of this new institution, one nominee was unceremoniously turned down on the grounds of incompetence.

Reform-mindedness is apparent in other important areas as well. The foreign ministry discarded its old directives and asked Western foreign services for suggestions on the drafting of new ones.

All doors at the Kulugyminiszterium have been flung open to admit Western ideas and experience. Scholarships for young Hungarian diplomats are pouring into the ministry. 'We get offers from foreign governments, universities, international organizations, and endowment funds,' a veteran diplomat told me. They are invited to spend periods of time abroad, anywhere from three months to two years. 'Who should do the work in our ministry while the entire new generation is studying in Western Europe and North America?' he wondered aloud. His sigh turned into laughter, and he offered what sounded like a Western pragmatic compromise: 'We will work out a solution! It is too important!'

The Department of External Affairs of *India* believes in thorough professional training for its foreign-service officers. Of the 100,000 applicants who write the public-service examination each year, approximately 10 candidates with the highest overall marks qualify to become foreign-service officers. As soon as they have passed all entry tests, they start four months of intensive courses in public administration at the Lal Bahadur Shastri Academy of Administration and are sent for six months into the province to get a feel for the country's administration at the grass-roots level, before returning to New Delhi for a six-month follow-up at the Foreign Service Institute.

Language training is usually part of a first foreign assignment. Depending on the degree of difficulty a language presents, the young probationary officers devote one or two years to their studies while attached to the local Indian embassy. Only after they have passed language exams and yet another exam in Indian administration are they formally appointed public servants and officers of the Department of External Affairs. Altogether the training period takes two and a half to three and a half years.

Such an approach to learning and professional training compares favourably with the attitude taken by a large number of foreign services, where a few months or a year of 'learning on the job' can often amount to picking up all the mistakes that have been passed on from one generation of foreign-service employees to the next.

Some foreign ministries offer many well-shaped and colourful tiles to the mosaic of an ideal foreign service. The occasion to sift through a few gems presented itself during a long conversation I had with one of the most senior members of the Ministry of Foreign Affairs of *Israel* during a warm night under the star-lit skies of Jerusalem. It could have been an even more pleasurable treasure hunt if it had not been for the black shadow of the Gulf War moving closer every day and the Scud missiles looming everywhere on the horizon. The distribution of gas masks to the population had begun on that day. It struck me that, for an embattled country, a superbly trained, professional foreign service is almost as essential as are superior armed forces.

For the foreign service of Israel, excellence begins at the gates to the ministry, which appear to be the best guarded in the world. Applicants are subjected to more extensive and thorough scrutiny than in any other service. After a candidate completes two days of written tests, two separate selection boards, composed of distinguished university professors, senior members of the foreign ministry, other public servants, a respected representative from public life, and two psychologists, cross-examine him or her for two more days. Unsuitable candidates have no chance. During the next two years of formal training, apprentices serve a three-month period in each of the major departments of the ministry. It is a time of concentrated and focused learning. 'We trained the trainers,' a member of the personnel department told me. The young diplomats are watched carefully and assessed every three months. Parallel to this training run language courses. All reports about a candidate's performance are critically evaluated before he or she is accepted as full member into the service.

Unlike many foreign ministries that send their employees to different posts every two to three years, the Foreign Ministry of Israel believes in fewer and longer assignments. Five years in a country allow families to learn the local language, to get to know its people, to make friends, and to become familiar with the culture. Foreign postings alternate with a few years of rest and recovery at home. Families cherish this regular rhythm. They see their life as more predictable than those of members of most other services. In fact, a regulation stipulates that employees must be told at least six months in advance where they will be sent next.

Throughout the history of the Israeli foreign service, economic necessity has forced foreign-service spouses to earn a living outside the home, and Israel's spousal-employment program is unequalled in the international foreign-service community. If the foreign ministry has no vacancy for a spouse in a mission abroad, one of the other ministries represented in the embassy – Trade, Agriculture, Science, Defence, and Finance – will help out. Spouses for whom employment cannot be found within the mission can count on the ministry's support while they search the local market. On their behalf, the foreign ministry will approach friendly organizations, shipping lines, or any Israeli company, and international organizations may be contacted. Cases of spouses who are unemployed although eager to work are rare.

Spouses of foreign-service employees who are public servants themselves are now legally entitled to be reinstated to the position they held prior to departure for a foreign assignment, provided they agree to 'leave without pay' in the meantime. Spouses with jobs in the private sector who decide to give up the job for good in order to depart for a posting abroad must be paid a lump sum by their employer. The compensation amounts to one month's salary for each year worked in the company. The foreign ministry established its own rule about spousal employment. It is simple and has turned out to be satisfying to a large majority of spouses: each case is examined conscientiously by the personnel department so that a suitable solution can be arranged.

The foreign service of Israel has done pioneer work in the area of personnel management altogether. During the late 1980s, the introduction of the concept of a personnel officer's personal responsibility for the physical and psychological well-being of the entire family of his charges 'started a new era,' as a veteran diplomat put it. Spousal employment, and children's health and education, began to receive official attention. 'We wanted more emphasis on the human side,' a former member of the personnel team who promoted the new approach told me. 'We did not want complaints. We wanted the right decisions,' he added.

The introduction of the principle of personal responsibility has worked wonders. Complaints have diminished to an absolute minimum. I could not find another foreign service where personnel managers received such high ratings from staff and their families, and above all, from the unions. The price personnel managers pay for such good marks, however, is steep. They have to commit themselves to a period of four uninterrupted years at headquarters in Jerusalem during which they 'parent' dozens of families scattered around the globe. They are on twenty-four-hour call, and pre-dawn cries for help from Asia or Africa where a marriage may be in danger of breaking up or a child has come down with a life-threatening illness are not unusual.

The new rule demanded another innovation: complete openness about all personnel decisions. 'We put everything on the table,' a personnel officer stated. 'We don't have any secrets. If someone complains that he did not get a job, he gets the exact answer, with all the unpleasant reasons. What we have achieved is much less tension.'

In order to support the work of personnel managers, preventive psychological care for employees and their families was brought in. The foreign ministry engaged a psychologist to prepare personnel for a peaceful and harmonious transition to unfamiliar surroundings. Another psychologist set out to visit all missions abroad where individuals and families might be struggling with unresolved conflicts. For those foreign-service members who prefer anonymity during emotional crises, the ministry pays for up to five visits to a foreign psychologist for every family member, no questions asked. The ministry also hired a full-time social worker and enlisted the services of a physician who is known for his experience with medical conditions abroad and enjoys the highest regard of the entire foreign-service community.

Does a country have to be under severe threat from neighbouring countries before it feels the need to develop and maintain a close-knit, personal, warm, and yet highly professional and effective foreign service? This unorthodox question is likely to occur to an outsider who is struck by the most attractive features of the foreign service of Israel. Each foreign service will have to find its own answer to the question.

In the finest tradition of Roman law and order the foreign service of *Italy* enjoys the Pax Romana of a foreign-service act. The Foreign Service Act of 1967 sets out the ground rules, rights, and duties of foreign-service personnel. In 1972, the Civil Service Law reaffirmed the Foreign Service Act by specifically excluding all diplomatic personnel from civil-service regulations. Determined to maintain their special position within the civil service, Italian diplomats fought bitterly against the general trade unions who, since 1980, had been trying to push through a unified civil service. In December 1988 the foreign service emerged from the struggle with a draft bill revised in their favour. A decision is pending, and Italian diplomats are confident that the new law will reflect the special conditions under which they and their families live and work at home and abroad.

The case of the Italian foreign service highlights the contentious issue that affects every foreign service: should diplomatic personnel be subject to a general public-service law or should they be granted special status? Many foreign services have decided in favour of or against special status for such personnel once and for all. Some have never debated the case, and others have been through elaborate discussions without finding a satisfactory solution. A sufficient number of points in favour of both solutions have been tabled, in theory and in practice, that each service facing the problem can do so from a position of knowledge.

Each country's foreign service is as distinctive as the country and culture it represents. Most foreign services mirror not only a country's contemporary social, political, and economic conditions, but also its size and history and such intangibles as national values and vision of the future. The ideal of excellence seems to act as a guiding principle not only to the average Japanese businessman, but to members of the Foreign Ministry of *Japan* as well. The selection process for the officer group ranks among the longest and most thorough of all such exams. Candidates who have passed the initial written tests live under one roof for a few days in the company of all members of their selection committee. They are watched constantly. The same attention is given to their training. Successful candidates spend one year at the Foreign Service Institute, studying mainly the language of their choice, before being sent to a university abroad for two years to engage in further studies, for example, law and economics at Harvard or Cambridge, or international relations at the Sorbonne. These first two years overseas and the subsequent assignment at the local Japanese embassy for two to three years are generally seen as the most difficult period in the life of a young foreign-service officer. Whether married or not, the future diplomat is expected to immerse himself totally in the local language and culture during the first year. Under such a rule, there is no time for a wife and children. They must stay behind in Japan.

Such complete immersion in a foreign country produces astonishing results. Anyone who has had the privilege of talking to a Japanese graduate of Harvard or Cambridge can testify to the degree of language mastery and cultural assimilation that has been achieved.

Such professional excellence is usually hard earned. A veteran member of the Japanese service told me that new arrivals in the diplomatic field are often psychologically not prepared for life in foreign countries, least of all if it means separation from family. The culture shock they are bound to experience can be overwhelming and leads, in some cases, to depression and illness. To avoid or at least to ease such problems, a distinctive Japanese institution specifically created to minister to the lonely and the miserable comes into play; namely, the mentor. 'Paternalism,' the interpersonal relationship for which employees of Japanese companies are noted, has been reigning in the foreign service for generations. Stories of warm and lasting friendships established between a young officer and an older diplomat and his family abound, and are lovingly recalled and retold.

Some Western services have tried to introduce this concept. The results have not been promising. Nevertheless, the idea must be appealing to anyone who has listened compassionately to the tales of suffering of dislocated and disoriented young members of any foreign service.

The foreign ministry of the *Republic of Korea* has swiftly moved to the forefront among the more dynamic foreign services. Korean embassies have been springing up in a lot of countries. Enthusiastic and competent personnel are needed. The Foreign Service Act of 1981 enables the ministry in Seoul to promote the young and vigorous. The act was the result of a long debate about the positive and negative sides of such a regulation. Eventually the arguments that rotationality and international mobility required special legal status, that slow promotions and a sense of stagnation prevailing in the domestic public service could discourage the most desirable candidates from joining the foreign service, and that special arrangements for personnel on the international stage would be needed won out over the arguments that special legal status would set the foreign service apart from the general public service and that too much competition in a young and fast-moving service would exclude experienced older personnel.

The well-known competition in the foreign ministry does not deter candidates. An average of 2,000 candidates write the entrance exam each year. Entry requirements are as high as those of the most demanding Western services. 'Our emphasis is on training,' a Korean ambassador told me. Future diplomats study at the Institute for Foreign Affairs for six months before they are sent to universities in other parts of the world to devote themselves to foreign cultures and languages. Competence through constant learning is the key concept for the progress-minded service. Promotion rules set out in the Foreign Service Act reflect this attitude. Employees who do not reach certain ranks in the hierarchy within a specified time have to leave the service.

Like their British colleagues, Korean foreign-service members enjoy the attention and trust of their Foreign Affairs Committee. The 1989 parliamentary review of foreign-service policy, budget, and general living and working conditions made committee members aware of the fact that an increasing number of foreign-service employees are reluctant to go out on postings because of the often deleterious effects international mobility has on marriages and families. A well-informed parliamentary committee represents the first step towards reform of a troubled political institution.

Review and renewal are also the main themes of the foreign service of *Mexico* in the 1990s. What exactly the outcome of the changes will be is difficult to predict. But the intentions are clear. A young Mexican diplomat seems to voice the opinion of reformers in the capital: 'People belonging to another era should leave the service. We need productive people!'

The ministry has had its eyes on reform for some time. In 1981 a new foreign-service act was brought in; entry requirements were tightened, and the right to select new officers went to a jury of four distinguished university professors, all of them experts in the field of international relations. Included in the exam is also a psychological check-up. Young probationary officers receive ten months of training at the School of Diplomacy. Only those who pass final exams are eligible for membership in the foreign service and postings abroad.

The service has become exam-happy. As part of its striving for rejuvenation and professionalism, it has set up a new system of promotions. A candidate for promotion must be exposed to the independent judgment of a jury of outsiders. This, the reformers say, is the only way to eliminate poor performers and to promote those who can respond to the challenges of the future. Members of various foreign services are wondering whether the Mexican model might not contribute to the reform of rating and promotion practices, particularly in those services where members have lost confidence in the fairness of their own promotion system.

The foreign service of *The Netherlands* recently took an unusual step that runs contrary to changes introduced to other countries' foreign ministries. The special legal status that members of the service had been enjoying ever since the Royal Decree of 1848 had established the ministry was converted to ordinary public-service status. Whether such a decision constitutes progress or regression is considered a contentious issue. Any foreign service interested in changing the legal status of its membership may want to study the extraordinary case of the Dutch service.

In another development unique to the foreign service of The Netherlands, an officer in training, who attends the Institute for International Relations in The Hague, has been granted the right to bring his or her spouse along for all lectures and language lessons.

Senior members of the service point out a problem many foreign services around the world have to contend with: competing with aggressive recruitment by international giant corporations, such as Shell and Unilever in The Netherlands. Each year the foreign ministry competes with them for the best university graduates. Such companies are able to offer to employees and their families substantial benefits. Whether the generous financial support the Dutch Ministry of Education grants for up to six years to foreign-service children who are attending university is part of an attempt to remain competitive with private international organizations is not entirely clear. It is, however, certain that foreign services, if they want to attract the best candidates, will eventually have to adjust their family benefits, such as education allowances, home leaves, family reunions, and spousal employment, to the level that is being established by powerful representatives of the private sector.

Asked about the finest tile he would like to contribute from his own collection to the mosaic of the ideal foreign service, a veteran Dutch diplomat emphasized the importance of a personnel department that is independent of outside influence. Political appointments are difficult to reconcile with the concept of a professional and competent diplomatic service.

A growing number of foreign services have to face the new challenge of two-career couples. The foreign service of *Norway,* confronted in the late 1980s with six such 'tandem couples,' experimented with a solution that insiders attribute to an 'uphill battle' won by the husband-and-wife teams concerned. In 1988, the Ministry of Foreign Affairs in Oslo, for the first time in its history, agreed to a working arrangement that entered the foreign-service vocabulary under the terms 'job splitting.' A young couple, unable to find two jobs at the same embassy and unwilling to separate in order to work in two different Norwegian missions abroad, were granted the right to share one position in the same mission. Each of them worked half time. The husband took the morning shift in the office, while the wife attended to domestic duties. In the afternoon, the roles were reversed.

Splitting a position between husband and wife, the intiated say, is, in the final analysis, more beneficial to the foreign ministry than to the couple. The ministry 'gets the work of two for the price of one,' since both partners tend to do a lot more than half a day's work. Their meals at home often double as staff meetings. The family income is cut in half. For this reason, most young couples who do opt in favour of such a solution try to limit the time they devote to the shared job. Job splitting does, however, serve the interests of marriage and the family, especially when the children are young. Luckily, as one tandem couple remarked with a smile of contentment, later experience has shown 'that this is not necessarily something that hampers career development in the longer run.'

A carefully designed job-sharing program can meet the needs of husband-and-wife teams during an important phase in their family life and could at the same time fulfil the organizational requirements of any foreign service.

The foreign service of *Sweden* has carried the democratic principle of equal rights and equal opportunities for all citizens to its logical conclusion. The front doors to the diplomatic service have been opened wide. Preconditions are no longer attached to writing the officer exam, or any other entry test for that matter. Whether a university graduate or not, any Swede can walk in and try his or her luck. Membership in the selection committee is not the privilege of public servants, or foreign-service officers either. Representatives of trade unions, universities, banks, large export companies, and multinational corporations are invited to decide who should be their envoys abroad.

Women in the foreign service enjoy equal opportunities. Two-career couples are generously accommodated. Collective bargaining was introduced as early as the 1950s. Members of the Swedish service can take for granted what members of many other services can only dream of.

In spite of its modern democratic practices, the foreign ministry seems beset by the same weaknesses that have befallen a strikingly large number of their counterparts in other countries. 'The foreign service has lost its monopoly on life abroad,' a Swedish diplomat stated. 'Private companies offer better possibilities.' Young Swedes looking for an international career seem to have got the message. The number of applicants is steadily declining. In the private sector, companies are not forced 'to set up shop,' as a veteran member of the service called it, in every country with whom Sweden has established diplomatic relations. As a result, the number of hardship posts that a private company can impose on an employee is much smaller than in the foreign service, where more than half of all posts are hardship assignments. Benefits, too, are known to be much more generous in international corporations. They are granted and perceived as a form of recognition and reward, and constitute a strong incentive for recipients and their families to try to master a difficult life. In the public service, however, benefits are no longer considered worth the hardships.

The majority of members of the Swedish foreign ministry are concerned about the direction their service is taking and wonder whether Sweden could not use its dwindling numbers of applicants to convince public and parliament that the government service has to offer tangible forms of recognition to its employees if it wants to become competitive with the private sector and enjoy the first choice of qualified candidates. In this aim, Swedish diplomats find themselves united with their colleagues in many foreign services.

Although the foreign service of *Switzerland* attracts by far the smallest group of university graduates among all the services I have examined – in 1988 only forty-two young men and women wrote the entrance test for the officer category, of whom seventeen were eventually accepted – standards don't seem to have been compromised. Candidates must have graduated from university and speak at least three of Switzerland's four official languages: German, French, Italian, and Romansch. In addition, applicants have to demonstrate their fluency in at least one other world language, such as English, Russian, or Mandarin.

Every bit as rigorous as the entry requirements is the probationary officers' training. Only after two years of studies at the Institut des Hautes Etudes Internationales in Geneva and one year of practical work at a mission abroad is the budding diplomat considered ready to take a final exam. A high-powered commission, composed of members of the foreign ministry, parliamentarians, university professors, and representatives of industry and of the National Bank, decides whether the candidate is fit to represent all aspects of Swiss interests in foreign countries. Most recently, a psychologist has joined the board.

The foreign service of the Confoederatio Helvetica has made a uniquely Swiss contribution to the solution of the spousal-employment problem. In the absence of a clear statement about the rights and duties of foreign-service spouses such as that enshrined in the German Foreign Service Act of 1991, the role assigned to spouses is of an ambiguous nature. Duties are no longer defined, and rights have yet to be guaranteed. The interim arrangements are splendid. According to the Official Report of the Swiss Parliament for the year 1988, a group of thirteen foreign-service wives attended a two-week training course at the Hotel Academy in Lausanne. A partial abandonment of the traditional concept of Swiss neutrality? It could be argued that an alliance with a host of masters in the realm of gastronomy, combined with the exchange of professional secrets, constitutes a weapon system in support of the stragetic goals of the Auswärtiges Departemente, and thus contravenes neutrality. Do fellow diplomats of other countries' services regard such a development with grave concern? On the contrary, members of the international brotherhood of foreign-service employees are bound to regret that their Swiss colleagues will most likely not be persuaded to make marriage to a graduate of a Swiss Restaurant and Hotel Academy a prerequisite for membership in Switzerland's diplomatic service. Under such a rule, invitations to Swiss National Day receptions and official luncheons and dinners would have become one of the most coveted prizes for membership in any country's foreign service.

The issue the Swiss foreign service has unintentionally brought up in this context is relevant for other services. Since foreign ministries are bound to remain dependent on the support of experienced gastronomists, it might be beneficial to all sides involved if foreign services encouraged spouses to take professional training in this field. The service could eventually draw on such expertise – offering remuneration, of course, as well as the traditional thank-you note.

An exceptionally large number of members of the foreign service of the

United States have no doubt that u.s. public opinion recognizes their work and achievements. They like to present the Foreign Service Act of 1980 as proof. Conceived at the emotional height of the hostage crisis, after most members of the u.s. embassy in Tehran had been seized as hostages on 4 November 1979, the act was meant to recognize and honour the service diplomats and support staff were rendering, to the point of self-sacrifice, to renew the mandate the u.s. people had given to the foreign service in earlier legislation and, as the preamble states, to strengthen and improve the foreign service.

The act is a comprehensive document, containing 2,202 sections in 12 chapters; its language, unlike that of several other foreign-service documents, is transparent and comprehensible, even to the uninitiated reader. Other foreign services intent on attracting and retaining highly qualified and motivated personnel will find inspiration, particularly in the chapters devoted to training and benefits. In pursuit of professional excellence, the service insists on 'impartial and rigorous examination ... in accordance with merit principles'; introduces a five-year probationary period for candidates for the Officer category; and puts forward the concept of 'time in class,' which is a mechanism for weeding out those whose work does 'not meet the standards of performance for his or her class.' In practical terms, 'time in class' means that foreign-service members who fail to receive promotions within a designated time frame are discharged after twenty years of service, or are 'selected out,' as a more merciful term describes the process. It is a highly competitive system designed to encourage excellence.

For those who clear all obstacles on the admissions course, recognition is generous. Benefits are intended 'to encourage and reward outstanding performance.' Spousal employment ranks high on the list of family benefits. A complex system has been put in place to accommodate all conceivable career wishes. The law states that 'the Secretary [of State] ... shall give equal consideration to employing available qualified family members of members of the Service ... assigned abroad.' Most u.s. missions around the world have a reputation of doing their utmost to comply with this regulation, and a large number of spouses have found a job in their husband's or wife's embassy. On the basis of this act and its implementation record, the u.s. foreign service – together with the foreign service of Israel – enjoys the reputation of having the most open-minded, flexible, and accommodating spousal-employment policy of all foreign services in the world. The act also includes provisions for the employment of foreign-service children.

At the same time, Americans can claim for themselves the most generous health-care system of any foreign service. At headquarters a health clinic and an elaborate medical office look after physical examinations for all foreign-service members and their families who are on their way to an assignment abroad. A team of forty nurse practitioners – young women with a master's degree – run health clinics around the world, and forty physicians are placed in the largest capitals on all five continents. From this base they travel extensively to visit the clinics operated by nurse practitioners in surrounding smaller posts. The regional physician in Kinshasa, Zaire, for example, travels constantly, visiting the fifteen African countries in which u.s. missions are located that come under his responsibility.

Seven psychiatrists serve as resident physicians and specialists in some of the major urban centres in the world. They must also call regularly on their charges in the region, which in some cases encompasses half a continent. Once a year, the entire medical team gathers for a conference to listen to lectures given by physicians, psychologists, psychiatrists, and other experts on subjects relevant to their work. Insiders call the annual event a most important refresher course, a program of continuing education, and an excellent training session towards improvement of their service.

The Association of American Foreign Service Women (AAFSW) is an important and powerful institution, determined to influence the quality of living conditions in the service. Members of other countries' foreign services might want to study closely for their own purposes the beneficial role this organization has been playing over the last decades. Under pressure from this group, the Department of State, in 1972, issued the by now almost fabled directive 'Policy on Wives of Foreign Service Employees.' It stated that the marriage partner of a foreign-service employee 'is a private individual,' not a government employee; that the service has 'no right to levy any duties upon her,' and that she is 'free to follow her own interests.' A large number of foreign-service wives hailed the document as the foreign-service equivalent of the Declaration of Independence. When it became clear in the following years that too many women felt their contribution to their husbands' careers had been retroactively devalued, that they had been deprived of a rather cherished set of activities, and that the directives had torn apart a valuable social network, the AAFSW came up, in 1977, with another landmark paper, 'Report on the Concerns of Foreign Service Spouses and Families.' It suggested a complete reorientation of the State Department in the area of spousal employment. This intervention resulted in the establishment, in 1978, of two important institutions: the Family Liaison Office (FLO) at headquarters in Washington, and a community liaison office (CLO) in U.S. missions throughout the world. The Family Liaison Office was designed to provide foreign-service members with information on foreign-service living, to communicate individual and collective concerns to the management of various foreign-affairs agencies, and to participate in the development of legislation and regulations affecting the quality of foreign-service life. The 135 community liaison offices in all mission abroad provide, on a smaller scale, the same services for the local foreign-service community. Both institutions have become an unqualified success. In 1992, they still draw high praise from foreign-service members.

The AAFSW remains in close touch with senior management of the State Department and with legislators and institutions. Some of its eloquent members have testified at parliamentary hearings in preparation for the Foreign Service Act and have made important contributions also to laws that were to follow, including the establishment of retirement benefits for divorced foreign-service spouses in 1987 and other far-reaching benefits for foreign-service members in the Omnibus Anti-Terrorism Bill of 1989.

The U.S. foreign service is the only service with a permanent institution to monitor, assess, and improve its quality on a regular basis. According to the Foreign Service Act, the inspector general must submit to the president a report about conditions in the service once a year, which 'shall include a description of significant problems, abuses and deficiencies ... and a description of the recommendations for corrective action.'

Members of other foreign services are convinced that such a regular, independent evaluation would serve not only the foreign-service community, but the public, whose interests foreign-service members represent abroad under sometimes extremely difficult circumstances.

The diplomatic service of the *Vatican* (the Holy See) in some ways is a category unto itself: its 230 members come from every corner of the world and constitute the only international foreign service in the world. All of them are ordained priests. At the same time they qualify as regular diplomats, since the rules apply equally to them. Every few years they have to change continents and countries and must come to terms with a new culture. Among their foreign colleagues, Vatican diplomats enjoy the highest reputation for their professional training and outstanding linguistic achievements. Preparations for the job are extensive. Each member of the service has completed studies in theology and has served as a parish priest in his home diocese before being handpicked by his bishop and sent to Rome to devote himself to years of studies in canon law at the Lateran University and attend simultaneously the Holy See's School of Diplomacy. Members also have to learn English and French, and usually a third language, in addition to Italian, the language of instruction at the Lateran University. Among Vatican diplomats, fluency in five or six languages is more the rule than the exception.

What can foreign services representing secular national governments and their social, political, and economic interests learn from a diplomatic service representing the spiritual values of a world church? My discussions with members of the Holy See's service revealed that personnel management at headquarters has much to offer to other foreign services. Apostolic nuncios, the Vatican's ambassadors, and their younger colleagues enjoy belonging to a small and close-knit service, where attention to individual needs, continuity, and stability are considered values. Unlike personnel officers in other foreign services who change positions every few years, the team in Vatican City remains in place for ten to fifteen uninterrupted years. Head of the personnel department is the Pope. Insiders know that he takes a warm and lively interest in the small community over which he presides. His frequent travels abroad allow him to stay in close personal touch with every member of his diplomatic family. Each new assignment abroad carries his signature.

Vatican personnel policy sees to it that members of the service return to their roots at least every three years. Although they carry a Vatican state passport, their home is the diocese in which they were ordained as priests, which can be anywhere on five continents. Vatican diplomats point out that, as priests, they draw their inner strength from a particular vocation and from dedication to a spiritual life, but as international nomads, they consider reunions with parents, sisters, brothers, and other relatives to be of great importance. Personnel officers in the Vatican know that the cold restlessness of a rotational existence makes a haven of warmth and stability and a deep sense of belonging necessities, regardless of the level at which transients are seeking a home.

What are the main features of those foreign services that enjoy the highest possible degree of their employees' satisfaction and loyalty? Anyone who has talked extensively to internationally rotational migrants will confirm that key characteristics are easily itemized. Their staff has been chosen with careful attention to professional as well as psychological suitability and has been thoroughly trained in a wide range of skills. Continued education is considered an essential part of daily life and is promoted by their ministry. Living and working conditions on home postings and abroad reflect their government's conviction that both partners – employees and employer – benefit when employees' needs and organizational requirements are reconciled. Within their community foreign-service members experience a sense of belonging to a coherent group with common interests and values, which they often describe as a 'family feeling.' Beyond their immediate community, they can count on recognition from the political institution on whom they have to rely for support, their country's public opinion, parliament, government, and the media. Foreign services that rest on such a foundation provide their members with an extraordinary sense of confidence and security. Many transients told me that such circumstances offered them a much-cherished portable home they could use to balance the uncertainties of a life permanently in transition. A positive impact on motivation and professional performance could be expected as well.

13

In Quest of the
Ideal Foreign Service

'Whatever its origin, I know that in men's minds, especially in superior minds, resides an innate longing to see new places, to keep changing one's home. I don't deny that this longing should be tempered and held in bounds by reason. Your own experience will lead you to agree with me that this taste for wandering about the world mingles pleasure with its pains, while those who sit forever on one spot experience a strange boredom in their repose' (Catherine Moriarty, ed., *The Voice of the Middle Ages in Personal Letters, 1100–1500*). In this letter, written to a friend in 1352, the Italian humanist and poet Petrarch seems to have defined some of the main characteristics of foreign-service personnel and to have described the impact transitory life has on impassioned migrants. 'Which is the better course, in this as in man's other problems?' Petrarch mused. As it happens, the mind of a Renaissance scholar pondered the same problem that many international nomads of the twentieth century, according to their own admission, put to themselves almost every day: to wander or not to wander?

Modern times have made itinerant business people and diplomats key players on the international stage. Under such circumstances, any humanist would recognize the need to ask, what lessons can be learned from the personal stories told by rotational staff about their living conditions, and how can they be applied to the organization of an ideal foreign service in which individuals and families can serve their country or private company in foreign countries with a minimum of pain and a maximum of pleasure? I have been asked that question ever since I began to work on this book. For more than three years, I have been trying to find the answer and the search has been arduous. Innumerable forces shape life within every foreign service. They are hard to identify and even more difficult to measure, but their interaction and ultimate effect on personnel can be understood only if they are examined separately. At times I felt I was looking not for one needle in a haystack, but dozens, all invisibly connected with each other and yet treacherously elusive.

'What are people like who enjoy such a life?' This question has been following me throughout my life as foreign-service spouse. Usually the query is put in a friendly way by outsiders, out of genuine curiosity; but occasionally, it takes a condescending if not contemptuous form, as if foreign-service members were a strange and rather disagreeable lot. Ever since I had decided to become part of the group, the issue has intrigued me, too.

Interviews with hundreds of members of the Canadian and other national foreign services and of private companies' teams reveal that some people thrive on international rotationality, while others only survive in some form or another, and still others wilt and fade. Employees, spouses, and children who thrive under such conditions and who are generally aware of their contentment come in countless variations, but some characteristics predominate and are common among members of foreign services around the world.

When asked what serves as their centre of stability while being tossed about abroad, single employees speak eloquently about a close and warm relationship with mother, father, sisters, brothers, and other relatives, or friends. In the course of conversations, such bonds turn up time and again, and reveal themselves as the most significant component in the life of transients who express satisfaction with their living conditions and their work. Family and friends fulfil many of the transient's needs. They act as lifeline to the home country and culture, as admirers and cheerleaders for the brave globe-trotter who returns their attention and affection from any remote part of the world where fate, in the person of a personnel manager at headquarters, has deposited him or her for a while. Phone calls, letters, parcels, and even visits back and forth form an uninterrupted chain of communication, a visible sign of a sustaining human bond. The family's house serves as point of departure to foreign lands, as refuge during vacations from hardship posts, and as a home port to which to return safely at the end of a turbulent voyage. There, international nomads tell their stories, distribute exotic gifts, and recharge their batteries among loved ones.

Where family ties are less pronounced, where parents are dead and no other relatives exist, close friends assume the role of family.

Employees who are married and those with children name their spouse and the nuclear family as a focal point and stable centre of their life, and make it clear that the well-being and happiness of every member of that unit constitute their *raison d'être* at every stage of even the most chaotic posting cycle.

But such attachments are generally not limited to humans. Most of the persons who display signs of deep satisfaction with their life and work express also strong emotions for their country, not in the form of gratuitous national pride, but rather as fond approval of their people, the land, the country's history, and its cultural achievements. Often self-deprecating humour and a healthy perception of their own culture's weaknesses are mixed into such sentiments. Those who emigrated during childhood or youth retain affectionate feelings for their country of birth while nurturing a warm kinship with their chosen country, which has been unconsciously modelled after the ties with their country of origin. In all such cases a calm sense of rootedness is clearly linked to cordial human relationships as well as to an awareness of belonging to a culture they cherish. I found loyalty towards their home culture as evident among them as hearts and minds open to other parts of the world where they had served on postings. Many of them appear to be in possession of a formula for establishing and maintaining close ties with people and their cultures, affiliations that seem to give them an equal amount of inner security and pleasure.

Most of the people who prosper in foreign-service life speak about a happy childhood. Although the majority of them spent their first fifteen to twenty years of life in a stable setting, an amazingly large number recall early exposure to changing environments, the results perhaps of a parent in the military, in a university structure, or in an international corporation. Many of them mention childhood experiences with representatives of foreign cultures. They encountered foreigners who came to their home as private or business visitors, or through family travels and temporary postings abroad during sabbaticals or transfers to military bases overseas. Their parents held positive views about other cultures and introduced their children to stories about foreign countries, thus initiating in the young mind a strong curiosity about and eagerness to explore the world beyond home.

A number of employees who had been prompted to join the service by such childhood fascination described to me how their initial curiosity had turned – in some cases rapidly and intensely – to a passion for everything foreign, different, and exciting, so much so that eventually they were willing to face risks, dangers, threats, and hardships of almost any sort in order to satisfy their longing. Some foreign-service members told me their infatuation with parts of the world unknown to them became quite overwhelming at times. One ambassador who would enthusiastically place himself in this category likened his own attitude to that of an anthropologist who eagerly takes notes as he watches his research assistant being boiled by natives in some remote part of the world, knowing full well that he will be the next course on the local menu and maintaining only one ardent wish – that someone will rescue his manuscript and pass it on to the scholars waiting at home for written eyewitness accounts of native cooking and eating habits 'in ... wherever,' as the ambassador suggested with a laugh.

An open mind, free of crippling prejudices, and a passionate desire to see and understand the world are essential elements in a foreign-service explorer's mindset, but they are not sufficient. Skills to cope with the complexities of that unknown world they crave are indispensable. Only extensive training in languages; intercultural sensitivity; insight into the origin and significance of local beliefs, values, traditions, customs, expectations, and fears will provide dedicated anthropologists, linguists, and cosmopolitans with the tools necessary for life outside their own familiar realm. Such a survival kit has the added advantage of furnishing its owners with an invaluable sense of competence and strengthens their confidence in their ability to come to terms even with the strangest surroundings. In spite of such expertise, enough will remain incomprehensible and difficult to handle. Anyone who wants to thrive in foreign countries must match his or her fervour for a local culture and the rotational life with cross-cultural qualifications. At more than one point, adversity is bound to creep up on the newcomer. It can be overcome only with the appropriate weapons.

Experience on the international stage is a necessity that follows at close range. Some transients relished telling me hair-raising stories about their own abysmal ignorance and cross-cultural incompetence in some foreign setting early in their career. Such slip-ups became permanent reminders to take cultural differences seriously and to be better prepared in the future.

Personality traits of foreign-service members who flourish in this particular type of life are subject to cultural and individual differences and for that reason are more difficult to identify than some of the other characteristics they share. Classification will vary according to the typology model used. If the Jungian distinction between extrovert and introvert, thinking and feeling type, sensation and intuitive type is applied, it may be fair to say that all type combinations are represented among international migrants. Extroverts seem present in great numbers. They like action and variety, act quickly, dislike slow and complicted jobs, are interested in results of their work, enjoy having people around, and communicate freely and easily. But introverts are equally well represented. Their strength consists in their penchant for quiet and solitary work. As linguists among them who are fluent in five, six, and more languages will confirm, foreign languages can be mastered only through patient and painstaking study, and insight into the psychology of a culture requires extensive reading. But diplomats must also collect a wealth of information, ponder an issue in all its complexities, and examine the implications of any decision they have to take. Much of their work demands solitude. The eternal joke about diplomats 'who think twice before they do nothing' must have been originally directed at the so-called introverts among them.

Whether a matter of natural disposition or not, foreign-service employees who thrive on their many duties have to be people oriented, a feature typical of feeling types. But they are also expected to be analytically gifted, attuned to other people's thoughts, a characteristic of the opposite, thinking types. They like to solve new problems and dislike doing the same thing repeatedly, a trait of intuitive types, but must do things in the old, established way, as sensation types prefer. On close examination, it appears that efficient and contented international nomads have to unite in themselves all conceivable characteristics, even if such features happen to be contradictory or mutually exclusive.

Foreign-service spouses do well if they possess similar personality traits. Those who thrive on such a life have a daily opportunity to make use of a large variety of characteristics. Spouses list bonds with partner, children, extended family, and friends as their primary source of security and emotional stability. They express love for their country and culture and joy in home postings and home leaves. They feel intensely curious about the world and are prepared to face serious hardships in order to satisfy that curiosity. They take pleasure in learning languages and acquiring intercultural competence by living abroad. They seek contact with the local population rather than isolate themselves within the foreign community. If they have no career of their own or if they don't practise their profession while living abroad, they often throw themselves into the numerous duties international mobility imposes on them with the same vigour they would employ in learning a trade or pursuing a career. Many spouses who do have jobs are prepared to drop everything at home for another round as explorer, although their numbers seem to be declining. Summing up the disposition of contented foreign-service spouses, a friend of mine stated with conviction: 'I am a gypsy! I clean out and start new!' After a moment of reflection, she added: 'Every new posting gives me new energy.'

Such spouses often regard life and travels abroad as a privilege and see the inner rewards they gain from exposure to other cultures as invaluable compensation for the chaos they have to put up with or the loss of a job at home. Many among them somehow manage to turn the most dismal posting into a pleasant environment by virtue of their positive and humorous approach to any of the hundreds of problems that come their way. I have met dozens of such spouses and recall with admiration a typical representative of this group, the wife of a Canadian colleague. She had graduated from an Ikebana school in Tokyo and continued during her husband's subsequent assignment in Moscow to make the most beautiful flower arrangements out of the local raw material. Since the Soviet capital remained devoid of flowers for about eight months a year, she had to rely on weeds much of the time, which were available in great profusion. She accomplished miracles with them. The activity of surveying vacant lots, sidewalks, and children's playgrounds for hidden floral treasures and the results of her forays into the neighbourhood brought joy to her, her husband, and everyone within range of her refreshing and invigorating personality. She remains a model for me not only for her beautiful grass, nettle, and dandelion creations, but for the positive attitude her Ikebana arrangements represented. Women like that are bound to take a constructive stand in any situation and will bring light to even the gloomiest surroundings.

On the whole, such women represent a force that has made inestimable contributions directly to the psychological well-being of their husbands and indirectly to the efficient and harmonious running of missions and company offices abroad. The value of their emotional sanity is never more apparent than on occasions when they are juxtaposed with ill-suited or deeply unhappy wives.

A lot more complicated is the situation of foreign-born spouses, who make up 30 to 40 per cent of all spouses in Western government services. Although a fair number count themselves among spouses who derive pleasure from this life, they often had to overcome formidable obstacles on their way to satisfaction and joy. They have mastered the art of maintaining close ties with their home culture while simultaneously forging an emotional bond with their new country and culture. Every foreign-born spouse who has succeeded in striking a balance between feelings for his or her home culture and adopted culture will confirm that the road to a harmonious bicultural personality and to a peaceful and affectionate bicultural marriage and family in the turmoil of international rotationality is covered with thorns and thistles. Beds of roses are few and far between.

Foreign-born spouses have a particular problem to overcome. They spend only a few years on home postings, rarely enough to feel at home in the new environment and to put down roots. Abroad they have to sail under their partner's flag and – if they are part of the diplomatic group – are expected to entertain on behalf of a country, its people, and its government, to whom they feel little or no loyalty. Spouses who flourish under such conditions have usually brought a well-balanced personality, a positive outlook on life, an ability to adapt and to learn, an enormous amount of goodwill, and a great deal of humour to their marriage.

Their off-stage work for embassies and private corporations has always been taken for granted. Women who derived personal satisfaction from their role as spouse did not feel the need for formal recognition for a long time. This situation has been changing dramatically. Ever since the late 1960s, their numbers have been declining. By the year 2000, few will be content with their status as 'trailing spouse' or their official position as 'dependent wife.' The Women's Movement and economic necessity have joined forces in convincing most young women to learn a trade and pursue a career. More and more of these women refuse to drop job, income, social benefits, and status in order to follow a husband around the world and to act as unpaid support staff for his employer.

For the time being, however, many wives in foreign services around the world are content with their lot and would go so far as to admit to deriving pleasure from their role. They act as a reminder of the invaluable contribution women have made to foreign-service operations without ever receiving more official recognition than a friendly word from their husband's superiors.

According to the Hormuth Study, a comprehensive scientific study on the impact of foreign-service life on children, commissioned by the German foreign ministry and carried out by the Institute of Psychology at the University of Heidelberg in 1986/7, a mother's attitude towards the organization for which her husband works and towards her own role in the tasks assigned to him shapes children's attitudes towards the life of international mobility they are forced to lead. My own findings confirm this conclusion. Mothers who appreciate the opportunities and who see more positives than negatives in their situation will most likely pass their own contentment on to their children. In its own special area, the German study corroborates what Anna Freud, the daughter of Sigmund Freud and herself a trained psychoanalyst, discovered during the Battle of Britain. In *Homeless Children,* she describes how children, on the basis of a strong mother-child bond, identify with the mother and adopt as their own her attitude towards threatening circumstances. The extent of fear a mother showed during critical hours in the air-raid shelters resurfaced later and for long periods with the same intensity in her child, while a more relaxed maternal approach to the terrors of war produced a more casual reaction in the child. The German study also confirms what has been common knowledge among perceptive observers of foreign-service families all along: spouses and mothers qualify as key players on the foreign-service stage.

Whenever I find myself with rotational families who strike me as wholesome and happy, I notice that family members are open to talking about themselves and equally eager to listen to others. They appear to be well-balanced, secure, easy-going with each other, and humorous in their attitude towards themselves and their turbulent life. All of them seem engaged in a number of absorbing occupations, in which they invest much energy and love. Many of them mention their foreign-service life as a particular asset for their family. They are constantly working on the same project, they say, such as making a go of a move or turning an assignment abroad or at home into a success for each one of them. Their rotationality presents them with a challenge to which the united family rises cheerfully and efficiently. A husband and father could have been speaking on behalf of all his contented colleagues and their families when he told me on the eve of his retirement, after having spent decades in the foreign service: 'It has been for the entire family stretching, enriching, stimulating and amusing, a career enjoyed and savoured!'

In the course of formal interviews and informal conversations, it became clear to me that individuals, marriages, and families that were flourishing had not been blessed with cloudless skies throughout their foreign-service lives. Many of them had struggled hard to achieve a state of equilibrium. A developmental dimension obviously had to be taken into account when evaluating their circumstances. Both female and male employees spoke about their initial difficulties in coming to terms with constant changes of jobs, with working hard to acquire competence in a position in one country and having that hard-earned expertise become valueless in the next. It takes a strong disposition, they told me, to be recognized as a specialist in a field while speaking the local language and understanding the local cultural psychology, and to accept graciously every few years the fate of being reduced to the status of an ignorant newcomer who cannot utter a sound in the local tongue, does not understand a word of what is said around him or her, does not know a soul in the city, feels like a helpless, exposed child, and yet has to function efficiently on behalf of his or her government or company. One senior executive's story is a case in point: on his first day on a new overseas job, he was lectured to in front of a whole streetcar full of local residents. Since his car was still in transit from one continent to another, he had decided to take public transportation to the office in order to establish immediate contact with the local population. He had got on the tram without realizing that tickets had to be purchased in advance. His money in hand, he had waited for the conductor, who seemed to be slow in coming. Finally a man in uniform appeared on the scene. He was not a conductor, but a controller, and he began to yell at the foreigner, accusing him of having cheated and demanding he pay a massive fine. When the new arrival explained the circumstances as best he could, he failed to convince the official. The shouting continued. At some point the fellow travellers began to rally around the newcomer and argue in his favour. Eventually the controller gave up, but not without issuing a stiff warning to foreigner and locals alike. The Canadian ended his account of the incident with the remark that contact with the local population had definitely been established, but not of a type he would have wished for. 'The fellow made me look like a criminal,' he said.

All foreign-service members must learn to accept as inevitable the loss of proficiency every three years and be prepared to start from scratch. Wives who dropped their jobs, incomes, colleagues, and friends in order to follow their husbands abroad reported temporary dissolution of self-confidence. Their sense of identity seemed threatened, they told me. Their inner support structure appeared to have collapsed under them. They were suffering from the symptoms of bereavement, they confessed. Their children found themselves in a similar state, having lost their home, friends, school, neighbourhood, country, and culture all at once.

To overcome such serious difficulties, to regain one's bearing, to recognize the many opportunities international mobility offers, and eventually to come out of a sense of bereavement requires a robust emotional constitution, well-grounded self-confidence, cordial human relations that nourish a single employee across oceans and continents, a loving and supportive family, a passionate interest in the assignment at hand, a sense of purpose, social and cultural skills in establishing new sustaining human bonds on location, and a huge reserve of humour. Altogether, a tall order for any foreign-service member!

Families in which every member thrives under the impact of such a life are unfortunately a minority. A large number of individuals, married couples, and families whom I interviewed more appropriately could be described as survivors. If foreign-service members were asked to place themselves on a scale ranging from ten to one, where ten represents 'Thriving,' five 'Surviving,' and one 'Failing,' approximately 70 per cent could be expected to gather somewhere between seven and three, with the heaviest concentration around five, the survival point.

A host of obstacles prevent them from ever getting beyond the survival stage, let alone coming close to or reaching the point where they feel they flourish. All foreign-service personnel to whom I talked, whether they were single, married, divorced, young, middle-aged, or retirement age, employees, marriage partners, or children, spoke openly about the darker sides of international mobility, about some of their most personal experiences and their deepest feelings. They complained that they had lost control over their lives and were at the mercy of a huge impersonal bureaucracy, that their personnel managers at headquarters were primarily interested in their own careers and insensitive to human issues, that under the strain of life abroad small personal problems suddenly become enormous and unmanageable, that each move constituted a trauma and promoted feelings of rootlessness and homelessness. They also pointed out that counselling abroad was inadequate, that half of all emergency evacuations from abroad were necessary for emotional reasons, that the potential for serious problems abroad was generally underestimated, and that headquarters had failed to prepare its personnel adequately for the minefield that lay ahead of them.

All these statements, however varied and telling, reveal only part of the truth. They do not include difficulties of which personnel are not aware or conflicts they find too embarrassing or painful to discuss. But whether international transients are aware or unaware of the danger zone in which they are moving, trouble can encroach on them from three major sources: individual, marital, and family conflicts; poor personnel management at headquarters; and unfortunate circumstances in a foreign country, which may be beyond anyone's control, such as a serious threat to health, violence, natural disasters, or wars.

Personal predicaments range from using rotationality as a means of escaping conflicts in the hope that a change of scene will make the problems vanish, weak marriages, and difficulties with children, to a lack of life skills or blinding ambition to which family is sacrificed.

Employers sin against personnel and their families through untrained, incompetent, and sometimes irresponsible personnel managers, a lack of understanding of basic psychology, an inability or unwilling-ness to coordinate family needs and organizational requirements, and generally through poor human-resources management.

Unfortunate circumstances or 'bad luck,' as particularly difficult hardship posts are often called, constitute a powerful force that can be expected to descend on every foreign-service member at some point in his or her career. Some employees and their families are hit harder and more frequently than others. Some such assignments can deal a crush-ing blow from which it may be impossible to recover.

If destructive forces from two of these three sources combine, employees and/or their families are bound to be in trouble. If an ill-suited and poorly prepared individual or family is hit by one or more hardship posts, considerable emotional damage may result. Most of the time, personnel are able to scramble out of the rubble when they feel the world has collapsed above their heads, or recover their bearing in some form or another after they have temporarily lost their equilibrium because of extreme and prolonged strain. Often they lose their taste for foreign-service life. The trauma may prevent them from ever reconciling themselves to the positive aspects of international mobility. They will spend much of their time in the service trying to forestall similar disas-ters, unable to see beyond the circumstances that shaped their attitude about this lifestyle once and for all. Members of this group congregate at the survival point on the 'Thriving' / 'Failing' scale.

Their opinion about the impact rotationality has on their own lives may change from one posting to the next. I have watched employees, marriages, and whole families who seemed to be managing foreign-ser-vice life well in the 1960s disintegrate in the 1970s and others who appeared comfortable with their foreign-service lot dissolve into misery in the 1980s. A colleague who radiated pride in his work and life twenty years ago retired a bitter man, disillusioned with his choice of a career. He confessed that he would never choose this profession again. And I observed others who seemed to be staggering along for years until they gradually found their stride.

A danger point is reached when fires begin to smoulder or flare up on all three fronts at the same time. When an inconsiderate personnel deci-sion and an especially difficult posting meet unresolved personal, mari-tal, or other family conflicts, individuals or families are trapped.

Sometimes the persons involved don't notice the danger. Others try to ignore the flames in the hope that the fire will extinguish itself. Members of another group try to reduce their problem to a case of local arson and demand a transfer to another country. Still others feel too ashamed to admit that they are in difficulties and need to be rescued. Unless some local authority – a physician, psychologist, or social worker – puts out the fire immediately and other help arrives, damage may be irreparable. Unfortunately such cases are not uncommon. However, since a stigma is attached to so-called failures, many such problems remain hidden. But social workers, psychologists, and physicians who have had experience with crises among personnel told me that even the known cases are all too numerous. The sheer magnitude of some of the human catastrophes some employees described to me in detail places each one of them into a special category.

Personal tragedies labelled 'failures' come in many forms. I have listened to single employees who, towards the end of their careers, dubbed themselves a failure in both the personal and the professional part of their life. They were convinced that their aimless wandering around the world was responsible for their unresolved problems. Others claimed that rotationality had forced them to choose between career and marriage. They had either never married, or had sacrificed wife and children (sometimes more than one wife) to professional ambitions and were now certain that they had done everything wrong. Not even the coveted professional success, one of them confessed, had materialized. One day, the all-embracing occupation had come to an end with retirement, and they were left with no one and nothing.

I talked to middle-aged male employees who sadly volunteered the information that they had been driven by mindless ambition to succeed in the organization. Their careers were flourishing, but they were divorced, with ex-spouses under psychiatric care or children with serious and lasting emotional scars.

I sat with employees who praised their wives as highly supportive partners in their career aspirations. As a couple they had enjoyed themselves greatly and would have benefited even more if it had not been for their child or children somehow not adapting to the life. Some of these children had dropped out of school, tried their hands at various trades, experimented with marriage, and seemed to drift. Others fared worse.

'We have psychologically damaged kids,' one mother admitted. In doing so, she stated openly what other parents did not have the courage to put quite as bluntly, but conceded indirectly. Some parents blamed themselves for their children's difficulties and seemed to feel the need to accuse themselves of ignorance, insensitivity, selfishness, irresponsibility, and blindness to their children's plight. Others insisted that the family had become a collective victim of a series of arbitrary personnel decisions made somewhere in the unfathomable depths of the organization.

Wives lamented that they had sacrificed their physical and emotional health to their husbands' jobs in return for little from them and nothing from the organization. All too many of them looked back at a history of depressive episodes.

Many wives complained bitterly about a fate that had prevented them from ever establishing themselves professionally. With their decision to marry an international transient, they had in fact surrendered themselves to a bureaucracy that controlled the entire family's life. They felt shoved around by personnel managers who did not know their charges and did not care about them. Ignored as individuals by their husbands' employers, often emotionally abandoned by career-oriented marriage partners, with no careers of their own, few possibilities to set themselves up in a trade, and economically completely dependent, they experienced as the deepest pain their failures as mothers.

The saddest stories I came across involved children. Their school phobias, behaviour problems, eating disorders, drug and alcohol dependence, or desire to take their own life had not erupted over night. All such tragedies had been growing slowly in an environment where family fires had been allowed to smoulder quietly: where parents' individual or marital battles were aimlessly fought; and where mother and father, instead of devoting energy to identifying and taking care of the obvious problems in the course of a peaceful assignment at home, had sought one foreign posting after another in the hope that somewhere in the heart of Africa or on the beaches of Latin America their unresolved family conflicts would disappear without a trace. Under the strain of numerous moves and their attendant culture shock, such problems only grew. Parents failed to recognize the early warning signals sent out by their children. Too many children have thus ended up as helpless victims of a deep-seated family problem that was treated with the emotional equivalent of poison: accelerated international mobility. In some particularly severe cases, parents reacted to signs of distress from their offspring with a strong dose of the poison: a cross-posting. A new country, climate, house, school, and neighbourhood somewhere in a totally different part of the world would surely do the trick. Personnel managers at headquarters, not knowing the family circumstances and often not even knowing the employee or his or her family, would deliver the requested potion. In one extreme case, a child of fourteen years had attended eleven different schools on four continents. A succession of personnel managers had contributed to such a record. But if parental ignorance born of a lack of foreign-service life-skill training joins forces with personnel managers' blindness, children have no advocate. They are doomed to carry parental conflicts and an organization's mismanagement of human resources to a bitter and inevitable end.

As I was in the middle of writing this book I received the news that one of my oldest and closest friends had committed suicide. She had been in her mid-thirties and was the daughter of a distinguished ambassador. Her sister, an equally dear friend of mine, sent me a photocopy of C.'s farewell letter. It was, of course, one of the most heart-rending documents I have ever read. Throughout my research for this book, I had my friend's story in my mind. I had always seen her as the victim of devoted and well-meaning parents who had nevertheless been completely unprepared for the minefield that lies in wait for all foreign-service members, and of an erratic personnel policy of her father's ministry. Her parents, who had also been among my closest friends before their sudden death, had agreed with my assessment of the reasons for C.'s thoroughly likeable, but unbalanced personality. They had always been delighted and grateful when I had occupied myself with their daughter and had said to me, time and again, how much they wished they had known about the danger zones for foreign-service families before they had thrown themselves into that life. With the permission of C.'s sister, I am giving a brief account of C.'s story because both her sister and I are certain that C. herself, as much as her parents, would approve wholeheartedly of my decision to use the case of one of my dearest friends in an attempt to assist parents and personnel managers in their work with families and to draw attention to avoidable mistakes.

In some ways, C.'s is an ordinary foreign-service tale. It could have happened to any foreign-service child around the world. In fact, I can think of dozens of children who will recognize their own childhood and youth in hers.

C. had been six weeks old when the family was posted to a country in Asia, where she spent the next five years, largely in the care of servants, while the parents fulfilled their diplomatic duties – her father in the mission; her mother, as was the custom in the 1950s, at luncheons, teas, cocktail parties, dinners, and charity bazaars. Such activities were considered an important contribution to the husband's work and were taken seriously by superiors and by the wives who engaged in them. Not all wives were thrilled about such tasks, but there was constant pressure to raise money for the poor and wretched at their doorsteps, which acted as a powerful incentive for those women who did not care much for the social whirlwind. If gatherings with members of the foreign community could serve a charitable purpose, then such events made sense for a lot of wives. C.'s mother belonged to this latter group. Servants and nannies were regarded as the appropriate company for small children, freeing parents for their time-consuming engagements with adults. After all, they convinced themselves, whole generations of children had grown up under similar circumstances in colonial times.

When C. was five years old, the family returned home to an ordinary existence. But neither parent could find his or her way back into life in a country and environment that felt bland and tedious after the colourful and intensive life in exotic surroundings. The next six years were fraught with enormous adaptation problems for the entire family. C. quickly began to resent that strange and boring place called 'home' as much as the unpleasant institution of 'school.' She never made her peace with either of them. Everyone in the family saw life in the home posting as an unfortunate interlude between foreign assignments, a period during which real life had to be suspended for a regrettably long time.

Finally, when C. was eleven years old, her parents were thrilled to learn that real life would once again return to them: they had been posted to Asia, to a smaller capital than the last time, where appropriate schooling for C. and her sister was not available. Boarding-school was a familiar solution. Many of their friends and colleagues sent their children away to give them a suitable eduction. C.'s mother had also been raised away from home. She had been miserable, but that was considered a matter of the past and, besides, foreign-service life left no choice. Both parents went to great pains to choose the best possible girls' school in Europe, delivered their two daughters to the matron, looked around, found everything to their liking, and went off to Asia. A family reunion was scheduled to take place within four months, at Christmas.

C. suffered greatly from homesickness, much more than her sister. She lived from one grey and lonely day to the next, waiting for letters and for the two occasions each year when all her suffering would come to an end – at least temporarily – and she could climb on a plane that would take her to Asia to see her mother and father for a few weeks. The holidays were never quite free from tensions between parents and daughter, although everyone had the best intentions and wanted their brief time together to be a success. There were many happy occasions together. Photos full of smiling and laughing faces show C. on horseback and family and friends in luscious gardens and on white beaches. But, deep down, C. felt, her parents disapproved of her poor marks at school and her erratic behaviour both at school and at home, and occasionally her parents admitted that such was the case.

C. was twenty-one when both parents died suddenly. She moved from Europe to North America and embarked on a successful artistic career. During long vacations, she travelled around the world and returned for a visit to the country in Asia that she remembered as her childhood home. She got married, enjoyed a few years with a much older husband and stepchildren, divorced, resumed her artistic endeavours and her travels, and sank deeper and deeper into a depression that ended with her jump from a bridge.

An excerpt from a four-page letter addressed to her sister, written a few hours before C.'s death, will allow a glance at C.'s side of the story:

I no longer want to do anything. My life the way it was has been terrible: I have probably already shortly after my birth locked myself up and lived in my own phantasy world. I was never an active part of a community. Have always felt weak among others and was so often a victim. Through the years I have withdrawn more and more into my own world: eating, alcohol, shopping, giving presents, travels ... Everything nothing but flight ... I believe in reincarnation ... My problems seemed to me so large that I was prepared to accept the uncertainty of the future rather than remain here ... I have realised what a separate life I have lived from other people ... My old I wants to die and the New will come back some day. I realise that I will then have just as many 'problems.' Only different ones! ... And I also know that I may be reborn with an illness ... But I will probably no longer remember my present life and it will therefore be not quite as bad for me to tolerate the next life. I hope that in the hereafter I will get closer to the question of being. I am dearly longing to find my task ...

In many foreign-service stories, children are torn out of their environment and transplanted into another soil; fathers are deeply and often exclusively committed to their careers; and mothers struggle to be supportive marriage partners to the point where they unintentionally neglect their children. In some, servants take over the role of parent and are all too often a child's only source of human warmth and tenderness. Such a universe collapses when children are removed to another part of the world, on a home posting, where parents, who had always maintained a rather detached and cool relationship with their offspring, are now the sole providers of emotional security in an environment from which they themselves feel alienated.

The truth is that many internationally rotational families do experience life at home as inconsequential at best, unreal at worst, compared to life abroad. One employee summed up the feelings of many of her colleagues: 'At home the level of life intensity is low ... Life is good abroad, bad at home.' Children pick up such convictions through a hundred small signals each day and assume that life in a home posting is indeed unreal and therefore not worth living.

Life abroad, as they find out in the course of their first posting, has its own overpowering conflicts. Even the few postings in the world that may appear to have paradisical qualities are only temporary abodes for the international migrant. At the end of a tour of duty, the employee and his or her family are not only tossed out of that Garden of Eden, but cut off from human bonds as well. After such an experience, children may, and often do, come to the conclusion that more grief than happiness has to be expected from personal ties with people and their cultures since they are bound to end sooner or later, and that any form of emotional commitment is dangerous and must therefore be avoided at all costs. Left with an insufferably cold and turbulent world, children withdraw into an inner realm and gradually lose the ability to establish and maintain affectionate attachments within the family or in the wider community. This situation is reminiscent of classical Greek tragedy: in order to avoid looming disaster the hero heads straight into catastrophe.

For such a child, boarding-school can be the next stop on the road to tragedy. Whereas older children, who are well rooted and secure with family and community, and within their culture, may more easily develop healthy independence in such a social environment, children whose potential for building a network of human relationships, for shaping their own personality after role models, and for putting down roots in a country or culture has been destroyed will find that boarding-school only throws a glaring light on their troubles, confirms and hardens their status as outsiders, and pushes them faster and farther into a self-created world that bears little resemblance to reality.

Such children often feel weak and as victims of circumstances beyond their own and their parents' comprehension and control. Every few years, out of some huge and mysterious office buildings, come marching orders for the entire family. Children can't help but wonder where they originate and what they mean. Parents who perceive their organization and its personnel managers as untrustworthy – according to their own explicit statements, an overwhelmingly large number of foreign-service members fit into this category – pass on their resentment of superiors and their fear of powerful bosses to their children. For many such children, the world is a cold and frightening place where they are pummelled by dark and devious forces.

C. represents dozens of children I have met, and probably hundreds, if not thousands, in other foreign services all over the world. They are helpless victims of the combined destructive forces of parents ill-suited and unprepared to cope with the many pitfalls of international mobility, of human-resources managers who are not aware of the special needs of each family, and of unfortunate circumstances. Her story sheds light on one of the key problems foreign-service personnel face, whether they serve private corporations or go abroad on behalf of their government. With the exception of only the best private companies and not more than a few national foreign services, organizations generally lack a deep-seated sense of responsibility for the well-being of employees and their families. Personnel managers' vision is limited to company goals. The interests and needs of employees and families are subordinated to organizational requirements.

A list of employers' sins against foreign-service members makes unsettling and, at times, painful reading. The register I have obtained through my conversations and interviews with long-suffering insiders corresponds to collections compiled by other members of foreign services in both the public and the private sector. Many of the people who tell their own story in publications such as Enid Gordon and Morwenna Jones's *Portable Roots* feel like victims of systems in which human needs are not considered to be significant. There is general consensus among internationally rotational staff that women and children carry the heaviest burden.

What can be done to prevent human catastrophes in the future? Does an ideal foreign service, where employees and their families can flourish, lie within the range of possibilities? According to Dostoevsky, 'all the Utopias will come to pass only when we grow wings and all people are converted into angels.' Government services and private companies bracing themselves for the challenges of the future and intent on acquiring wings – not so much those of angels as of effectiveness – might find the following thoughts useful. They are the result of reflections on the life stories of hundreds of migratory individuals and families.

Twelve Ideas for Improving Personnel Management of Internationally Rotational Employees and Their Families

1 / Employees who commit themselves to international mobility merge their professional and private lives. They surrender to their organization authority over their own lives and those of their spouses and children. Senior managers should become aware of the responsibility they are assuming and respond with a personnel policy that coordinates human needs with organizational requirements.

2 / Human-resources managers implement top executives' attitudes towards staff and families. Organizations ought to employ, on a long-term basis, trained and experienced professional personnel managers

who devote themselves conscientiously to each employee and his or her dependents and who are held personally accountable for their decisions by their superiors. In national foreign services, where members of the internationally rotational team take turns as human-resources managers, a group of non-rotational professionals must add the expertise, continuity, and strong sense of responsibility that are believed to be lacking among most rotational personnel managers.

3 / An international career is widely seen as the quickest and safest road to an entertaining, comfortable, and somewhat glamorous life. For this reason, crowds of applicants knock at the doors of organizations that maintain international teams. Only a small minority of those who are eager to join can be deemed eligible. Candidates should be examined not only for their professional qualifications, but for their psychological suitability. Statistics reveal that too many ill-suited employees slip through the nets of selection teams, creating enormous emotional problems for themselves and their families, and imposing huge financial burdens on their employers in the private and public sector.

4 / Competence in international living should be seen as an essential part of each employee's professional qualifications. Rotational staff must receive extensive formal training in foreign-service life skills. Such education should, however, not be limited to learning languages, acquiring cross-cultural proficiency, or practising stress management. Employees have to be systematically endowed with vital skills, such as mastering life as a single person in constantly changing cultures, making the best of marriage, and raising children. Workshops should be established where case-studies are presented. During simulation exercises, newcomers to the international team could role-play conflicts they are likely to encounter in order to open their eyes to the potential for problems in such a lifestyle. They should also be encouraged to work out solutions themselves. Such training can act as a survival kit. No internationally rotational employee or a member of his or her family should ever be allowed to go abroad without such training.

5 / Spouses require special attention. Unlike their marriage partner, who has opted for this career and who has been chosen by the organization

for his or her qualifications, spouses usually drift into a life of international mobility and are largely ignored in most organizations. They hold, however, the key to the family's health and happiness, and indirectly to an employee's effectiveness in his or her job. Organizations would be well advised to recognize the leading role spouses play in the family team. They should be interviewed before their marriage partner is hired, thoroughly informed about the life that lies ahead of them, take part in life-skills training, be consulted by personnel managers at every stage of the posting cycle, and receive the organization's full support if they want to pursue a career of their own.

6 / Foreign-born spouses, who represent 30 to 40 per cent of partners in Western foreign services, experience exceptional demands as a result of international mobility on their bicultural marriage and family. Not all foreign-born spouses are capable of meeting such demands. Experience shows that they are at high risk for being disoriented or depressed for shorter or longer periods in their chosen culture as well as in foreign countries to which they are sent. In many cases, their well-being depends on personnel managers' conscious efforts to draw them into the foreign-service community. Almost all of them need and want recognition as individuals; as all-important spousal support staff for the employee; and, not least of all, as parents of internationally rotational children who have to cope with two domestic cultures in addition to the succession of foreign cultures in the course of their posting history.

7 / Children are the most vulnerable members of the rotational family unit. In spite of the popular belief that young minds and hearts adjust easily to any situation, too many children suffer severely from the fall-out of their parents' nomadic life. Research has established that international mobility is not exclusively responsible for such problems. Damage is often caused by a combination of frequent moves and unresolved family conflicts. Personnel managers must not only see to it that parents are trained in child-rearing skills, but get to know the families in their care, including the children. Occasionally they may have to assume the role of a child's advocate if parents act irresponsibly.

8 / Despite their eagerness to leave their country of origin and to

change their residences frequently, international transients cherish roots and yearn for a home. Home and roots come in many forms, they say, and cite family, friends, houses, cities, countries, and cultures as sources of a sense of belonging. A large number of international nomads, however, mention a sense of homelessness and rootlessness as their greatest problem. It is in the best interests of an organization to train personnel in the complex art of creating an atmosphere of home wherever they live. Those employees who lament that they feel at home nowhere can learn much from their colleagues who have shown that they are at home in many worlds. Regular and prolonged postings to headquarters should be treated as an important phase in the rooting process, especially for families with children.

9 / A number of international transients confessed to me that they wander around headquarters upon return from a foreign posting in search of familiar faces. They told me that anyone who remembers them gives them a sense of being back in place. They feel upset when they find not a soul who acknowledges their arrival home. Their need for a stable centre in a life of constant flux could be satisfied with a community centre, where experienced veterans of the rotational team, social workers, and psychologists introduce individuals and families to skills in international living, where human bonds are established in the process that will encourage the migrants to drop in during home leaves or to sit down over a long conversation with their life-skill teachers after return from a hardship assignment. In such a community centre, young children might lose their fear of the big and mysterious organization if management would set up for them a haven of toys and books, in which they could amuse themselves with other children while their parents receive guidance, encouragement, and reassurance. The growing number of single, separated, and divorced employees and spouses could be expected to cherish such an institution as a home within the organization and as source of a sense of security.

10 / 'If I had only known earlier what I know now' is a remark made to me by many rotational employees who were themselves suffering from emotional injuries or who felt guilty for having inflicted psychological

damage on spouses or children out of ignorance. Much of their trouble could have been eased or avoided altogether. Organizations might want to devote more of their resources to preventive care. In practical terms, a switch from reactive to preventive care would amount to establishing the special needs of every employee and his or her family before they are exposed to hardships, and trying to accommodate them, rather than waiting for problems to occur before giving them attention. A comprehensive body of knowledge about reasons for success and failure in such a life is available and so are experienced and thoughtful veterans of rotational services, social workers, and psychologists familiar with foreign-service life. They are capable of pointing out to employees and families where the danger zones are and what to do in order to avoid them.

11 / 'Tie your cart to a star!' This title of one of my favourite collections of poems suggests that human life resembles a slow and arduous ride in a humble wooden cart. Tied to a guiding, enlightening, and inspiring higher entity, however, the cart acquires mysterious powers that will allow the rider to overcome all obstacles on the road. I met a good many individuals and families who seemed to have attached their cart to a star, and to flourish in this life. Not only their affectionate human relations appeared to give wings to a heavy vehicle that had to overcome seemingly insurmountable obstacles. Also their interests, hobbies, and creative passions carried them along as if the law of gravity somehow did not apply to them. They managed to defeat the inevitable adversities that international mobility threw in their path with the overpowering joy they found in seeing mountains and oceans they loved, in experiencing tropical landscapes and climates they had been dreaming of, in admiring flora and fauna in a particular region of the world, or in gazing at the artistic achievements of a culture that had captured their imagination. Others felt transported because of their passion for learning languages or getting to know a country and trying to understand local history, politics, and a people's psychology. Yet others did not notice bumpy roads in hardship postings because they were absorbed in learning how to play a musical instrument; engaged in drawing or painting, ballet, or skating lessons; or busy capturing with their cameras magnificent landscapes and the colourful life of other cultures. The art of some poets and writers has blossomed in foreign environments. No

impediment was high enough to affect their delight in the ride or to stop the cart from following its star. But I came across a much larger number of people whose cart was obviously not tied to any celestial body. They seemed to be dragging it around themselves. Some of them used their international careers in the hope of escaping boredom or personal problems. Others were searching for adventure. Without the invigorating energy of a private passion they often appeared to be heavily and aimlessly running in circles or blindly staggering in the dark, upset and stalled by every minor obstruction. Organizational counsellors would be wise to convince personnel that carefully nurtured interests and hobbies possess the power to overcome hardships and can grant a redeeming sense of purpose, direction, and light in a world of darkness and uncertainty.

12 / The atmosphere in a private company is mainly determined by senior management. Members of many national foreign services pointed out to me that emotional climate and mood in their service are largely dictated by outside forces; namely, the attitude towards the service held by the general public, parliament, government, and the media. In all cases these outsiders have a well-deserved reputation for being poorly informed – if not misinformed – about the subject, being more interested in gossip than in hard facts. In some of the worst cases, the media use their country's foreign service for target practice. The less some journalists know about the foreign service or the people who have committed themselves to it, I was told time and again, the more they tend to lash out at it. Public, parliament, government, and media in every country might want to re-examine thoroughly their prejudices against their foreign service and consider replacing adversarial attitudes with a spirit of cooperative partnership.

Some private companies that are recognized as the best in their field and a few national foreign services have already implemented several of these ideas. Management of Johnson and Johnson is carefully coordinating organizational requirements with the personal needs of employees and their families. The company's stated human-resources mission for the next decade is to 'provide an atmosphere that enables employees to work to their full potential.' It has listed among its specific objectives for the 1990s 'helping families to meet their family responsibilities while pursuing careers with J&J' (Kevin Barham and Marion Devine, *The Quest for the International Manager*, pp. 42–3).

The foreign service of Israel is holding its personnel managers personally accountable for their decisions. The best-run private companies and some of the most efficient national foreign services – those of the United States, Britain, Germany, and Japan, for example – consider psychological testing a most important part of their extremely thorough entrance examinations and do not hesitate to tell those who did not pass why they have failed. They owe such a policy to their international team, they point out and insist that they do applicants who are obviously not qualified a favour by turning them down. 'We spare them a lot of trouble,' I was told.

The best private companies have been training their managers in cross-cultural skills for years and will be improving their courses over the next few years. Some national foreign services, among them Canada's, offer to employees and their spouses a variety of workshops on such subjects as 'your first posting,' 'stress management and transcultural adaptation,' and 'going abroad with young children.' Such courses are a promising beginning to life-skill training, but much remains to be done, especially in the area of individual and family posting preparations.

Spouses have captured the attention of outstanding private companies. Among them is Rhône-Poulenc, the eighth-largest chemical company in the world. Before being sent abroad, an employee and his or her spouse are interviewed. Managers insist on the importance of 'checking that there are no mixed feelings about going abroad' (Barham and Devine, p. 53). Johnson and Johnson has committed itself to 'genuine placements and services to the spouse' (ibid., p. 45). Among national foreign services, those of the United States and Israel maintain the most elaborate and efficient spousal-employment policy. The new German Foreign Service Act goes as far as to state that 'the employer takes care that the spouse of an employee resumes an independent occupation while abroad and upon return home.'

Foreign-born spouses are nowhere accorded the special attention and care they deserve. Not even private companies noted for their excellent personnel management seem to have focused on this rapidly growing group. It remains to be seen which international corporations or national services will be proud to do the pioneer work and set up a model program.

Children are given more care, in both the private and the public sector. One of the world's largest airlines, which is noted for its superb personnel management, systematically guides the children of its foreign representatives through the critical phase leading from school to the choice of a career. The foreign service of Israel has introduced all-embracing care for children. The psychological, educational, and physical needs of every child are examined with the utmost care and attention to detail. Solutions are painstakingly worked out for each case. The Canadian foreign service invites teenagers to take part in workshops prior to an assignment abroad and upon returning from a posting to disuss issues of common interest and to help them adjust to their new circumstances.

The foreign service of Israel deserves to be watched for its policy of helping personnel establish roots in the foreign-service community abroad and during regular and long postings at home. The u.s. foreign service, with its Family Liaison Office at headquarters and the Community Liaison Office at every mission abroad, has in fact set up a type of community centre where personnel can feel at home within the organization at every stage of the posting cycle.

Preventive psychological care was introduced in some of the best private companies a long time ago. National foreign services have been slow to catch on. The services of Israel and the United States seem once again to be leading the way, with their teams of psychologists and psychiatrists and an elaborate system of communications between them and personnel.

Promoting the development of hobbies and artistic talents among its members does not appear to be an important issue in any of the organizations I examined. Only the Canadian foreign service encourages creative endeavours, with an annual art show at headquarters. It is always considered a great success, in terms of both the quality of the exhibition pieces and the number of enthusiastic visitors.

The issue of the relationship between a national foreign service and the public whose interests it represents has been addressed in the most convincing fashion in Britain. The Foreign Office prides itself on its close cooperation with Parliament. Members of the service feel recognized by the public and know that they can count on a parliamentary enquiry into living and working conditions in their service at least every ten years. They highly recommend such a partnership.

Much has been accomplished to improve the lot of international migrants. Even more remains to be done. In preparation for the challenges of the next decades, the best private companies and a few national foreign services have set new standards for human-resources management by which other organizations will inevitably be measured in the future.

Providing 'an atmosphere that enables employees to work to their full potential' (Johnson and Johnson) amounts, in the case of rotational personnel, to nothing less than an attempt to ensure that employees and their families flourish in their work and their life wherever in the world they are settling down for a while. 'Helping families to meet their family responsibilities while pursuing careers with J&J' constitutes a decisive step on the road to reconciling human needs and organizational requirements. It is altogether an awesome task. But much knowledge on how to go about the business has been accumulated, and a wealth of experience on the rules to follow and the mistakes to avoid is readily available.

Nature sometimes serves as the most convincing teacher. In the spring of 1991 a close friend, Andrew, surprised me upon his arrival in Budapest with a wonderful gift. He had brought me four trilliums, wild lilies that grow in eastern Canada in great profusion and are known under the Latin name 'Trillium canadensis.' We had often talked about transplanting this uniquely Canadian treasure from its natural habitat to Hungary. He had taken the initiative and had carried in his hand-luggage all the way across the Atlantic four young plants with their bulbs and root system firmly embedded in mother soil. One of them showed the first sign of two blossoms. With the help of our gardener we transferred the Canadian soil and its precious contents into Hungarian ground.

A few days later, an enormous snowstorm raged over Budapest. It was bitterly cold. I felt as if I had exposed newborn quadruplets to the fury of the elements. Fearing for their life, I covered each plant with a plastic bag. Would they survive such a merciless onslaught so soon after their arrival in a foreign environment? I kept them in the makeshift incubator until the cold spell had passed, and checked them constantly. At no point did they show the slightest sign of distress or damage. They stood tall and strong, as if they had never been removed from their original home. In a way they had remained in familiar territory. The roots, in their dark, rich soil, had not been affected by a change of continents.

Two weeks after we had put them in our garden, one of the trilliums opened two snow-white blossoms. A healthy and sturdy plant, nourished through deep roots in familiar soil, carefully taken out of the nursery, lovingly transferred with the home environment intact, watched and protected during a first critical phase, had burst into flower. It was a day for celebration. I could not help but see similarities between transplanting flowers and people.

To wander or not to wander? Petrarch's question remains relevant for individuals and families who are driven by a desire to explore the world and can't predict which one will outweigh the other, pain or pleasure. For private companies and for national foreign services and their partners in government and parliament who know that the successful representation of their interests abroad depends on dedicated people willing and able to subject themselves and their families to risks and hardships, the issue presents itself in a different form: how to create suitable living and working conditions in which wanderers can best serve their employer's cause while living lives of permanent transition – at home and abroad.

Bibliography

Barham, Kevin, and Marion Devine. *The Quest for the International Manager: A Survey of Global Human Resources Strategies*, Special report no. 2098. London: Ashridge Management Research Group 1991

Becker, Ernest. *The Denial of Death*. New York: The Free Press 1975

Bridges, William. *Transitions: Making Sense of Life's Changes*. New York: Addison-Wesley 1980

Canada, Royal Commission on Conditions of Foreign Service. *Report*. Ottawa: Government Publishing Centre 1981

Eberwein, Wilhelm, and Jochen Tholen. *Managermentalität*. Frankfurt am Main: Frankfurter Allgemeine Zeitung 1990

Foreign Service Community Assocation. *Mobility Study: Selected Papers on Mobility and the Family in the Canadian Foreign Service*. Ottawa, 1980

Gordon, Enid, and Morwenna Jones. *Portable Roots: Voices of Expatriate Wives*. Maastricht: Presses Interuniversitaires Européennes, n.d.

Herz, Martin F., ed. *Diplomacy: The Roles of the Wife: A Symposium*. Washington, DC: Institute for the Study of Diplomacy, Georgetown University 1981

Hilliker, John. *Canada's Department of External Affairs*. Vol. 1: *The Early Years, 1909–1946*. Ottawa: Institute of Public Administration of Canada 1990

Hormuth, Stefan E. *Auswirkungen häufigen internationalen Wohnortwechsels auf die Sozialisation von Kindern und Jugendlichen im Auswärtigen Dienst der Bundesrepublik Deutschland*. Heidelberg: Psychologisches Institut der Universität Heidelberg, January 1988

Ignatieff, Michael. *The Needs of Strangers*. New York: Viking Penguin 1985

Jung, Carl Gustav. *Psychological Types*. Vol. 6 of the Collected Works. Princeton, NJ: Princeton University Press 1974

Moriarty, Catherine, ed. *The Voice of the Middle Ages in Personal Letters, 1100–1500*. New York: Paul Bedrick Books 1991

Sagan, Leonard A. *The Health of Nations.* New York: Basic Books 1987
Schein, Edgar H. *Organizational Psychology,* 3rd ed. Englewood Cliffs, NJ: Prentice-Hall 1980